Sports Law

Sports Law

The Hon. Michael J. Beloff QC, Barrister

Tim Kerr, BA (Oxon) Barrister

and

Marie Demetriou, BA, BCL (Oxon) Barrister

·HART·
PUBLISHING

OXFORD – PORTLAND OREGON
1999

Hart Publishing
Oxford and Portland, Oregon

Published in North America (US and Canada) by
Hart Publishing c/o
International Specialized Book Services
5804 NE Hassalo Street
Portland, Oregon
97213-3644
USA

Distributed in the Netherlands, Belgium and Luxembourg by
Intersentia, Churchillaan 108
B2900 Schoten
Antwerpen
Belgium

Distributed in Australia and New Zealand by
Federation Press
John St
Leichhardt
NSW 2000

Hart Publishing Ltd is a specialist legal publisher based in Oxford, England.
To order further copies of this book or to request a list of other
publications please write to:

Hart Publishing Ltd, Salter's Boatyard, Oxford OX1 4LB
Telephone: +44 (0)1865 245533 or Fax: +44 (0)1865 794882
e-mail: mail@hartpub.co.uk

British Library Cataloguing in Publication Data
Data Available
ISBN 1 84113–073–7 (hardback)

Typeset by Hope Services (Abingdon) Ltd.
Printed in Great Britain on acid-free paper
by Biddles Ltd, Guildford and Kings Lynn.

Foreword

by Sir Roger Bannister

Though I am not legally qualified in any way, I feel sure that there is a great need for this book. Since my own sporting days there has been an astonishing and alarming escalation of legal cases. Sport, essentially simple in nature, is increasingly threatened by issues of professionalism, sponsorship, serious injury, illegal drug use, and much more. These problems affect the essential fairness of sport, and without fairness sport is nothing. Anyone interested in sport must welcome the clarification provided by this comprehensive legal analysis. It is my fervent wish that all the legal problems of sport should be speedily settled with a maximum of good sense and justice.

Oxford
August 1999

Contents

1   Introduction – The Nature of Sports Law   1
    An introduction to the subject   1
    The development of sports law   6
        Freedom of contract   9
        Pacta sunt servanda   9
        Force majeure   9
        Clausula rebus sic stantibus   10
        Good faith   10
        Protection of legitimate expectations   10
        Necessity of seeking the parties' intent   11
        In dubio contra proferentem   11
        Doubt benefits the party assuming a contractual obligation   11
        Nullum crimen, mulla poena sine lege   11
        Equal treatment   12
        Proportionality   12
        Good faith   12
    The aim of this book   12

2   Overview: The Framework of the Law Relating to Sport   17
    The legal nature of sporting associations   17
    Rights and obligations created by contract   22
    Interpretation of the rules of sporting bodies   30
    Sport and the criminal law   33
    The law of tort   34
    Public law   35
    Statute law   36
    European Community law   36
    The European Convention on Human Rights   37

3   Access to Sporting Competitions   39
    Introduction: entry criteria in sport   39
    The duty of fairness owed by sporting bodies to outsiders   41
    Contractual and contract related claims concerning access to
    sporting competitions   47
    The restraint of trade doctrine   52
    Non-contractual claims relating to access to sporting
    competitions: free standing challenges   57
    Competition law and access to sporting competitions   63

Contents

4	Players' Rights	67
	Introduction	67
	The formation of the player/club relationship	67
	Transfer fees	68
	EC law in sport: an introduction	68
	EC law: Article 48 (now Article 39) and the other free movement provisions	
	Introduction	71
	Application to transfer fee systems	75
	EC law: Articles 85 and 86	80
	Restraint of trade	83
	Nationality restrictions	85
	Nationality restrictions imposed by leagues	86
	Immigration rules	90
	The content of the player/club relationship	92
	Terms and conditions of work	93
	Discrimination	96
	Common law	96
	The anti-discrimination statutes	97
	Areas of discrimination	98
	Justification	99
	Exemptions	100
5	The Regulation of Play	103
	Introduction	103
	Prohibited sports	106
	Organisation and competition	107
	Introduction	107
	Statute	108
	Tort and Sport	111
	Generally	111
	Negligence	112
	Duty of participants to each other	113
	Duty of participants towards spectators	116
	Duty of referees	117
	Duty of coaches	118
	Duty of schools	119
	Organisers/promoters	120
	Defences	122
	Contributory negligence	122
	Volenti non fit injuria	122
	Nuisance	125
	Assault	126

	Damages	126
	Practical issues arising in sporting injury claims	128
	The criminal law	129
	Litigation determining the outcome of a game	131
6	Broadcasting, Marketing and Competition Law	133
	Introduction	133
	Broadcasting	133
	Introduction	133
	What are broadcasting rights?	134
	Copyright over broadcasts	136
	How are broadcasting rights regulated?	138
	Statutory regulation	138
	Competition law	140
	An introduction	140
	Article 85 (81)	141
	Undertakings, associations of undertakings	142
	Agreements, decisions, concerted practices	143
	Prevention, restriction or distortion of competition	144
	Effect of inter-state trade	145
	Article 85(3) (now Article 81(3))	146
	Enforcement	146
	Article 86 (now Article 82)	147
	Market definition	148
	Dominance	149
	Abuse	149
	Broadcasting and competition law	150
	The relevant market in sports broadcasting cases	150
	(i) Type of television	150
	(ii) Type of sport	151
	(iii) Live and recorded sport	152
	(iv) Geographic market	152
	Collective selling	153
	Collective purchasing	156
	Exclusivity	159
	Other anti-competition practices	162
	Marketing	163
	Ticket sales	163
	Merchandise sales	165
	Note on the judgment of the restrictive practices court in the FA Premier League case	167
7	Disciplinary Proceedings in Sport	171
	Introduction: disciplinary proceedings in sport generally	171

The validity and meaning of disciplinary rules: jurisdiction of
disciplinary panels   175
Evidence and proof in disciplinary proceedings   184
Disciplinary procedures – the content of procedural fairness   191
Penalties in disciplinary proceedings   206
Costs in disciplinary proceedings   210
Appeals in disciplinary proceedings   211
The practical management of disciplinary issues   211
Postscript: general principles of CAS case law especially in
doping cases   217
   General principles   217
    Judicial self-restrict in sporting matters 217
    The right to be heard   217
    Unbiased tribunal   218
    Good faith   218
    The benefit of the doubt   219
    Rules and guidelines   219
    Legitimate expectation   219
   Principles specifically related to doping   219
    Strict liability   219
    Anti-technicality   219
    Sanctions   219

8   Remedies: The Resolution of Legal Disputes in Sport   221
Introduction   221
Court proceedings – remedies in public law   224
Remedies under the European Convention on Human Rights   232
Court proceedings – remedies in private law   234
   Declarations   235
   Injunctions   237
Multiplicity of proceedings   248
Damages   250
Unfair prejudice petitions in company law   252
Arbitration in sport   253
Jurisdiction, choice of law and conflict of laws   264
The way forward: towards a unitary system of sports dispute
resolution   268

Table of Cases and Statutes   271

Index   293

For Judith, Nicola and
Aidan with love

1

Introduction: The Nature of Sports Law

An introduction to the subject

We have chosen the title for this book to give expression to our view that the **1.1**
time has come for the term "sports law" to become accepted as a valid description of a system of law governing the practice of sports. We are conscious that
the term is not yet universally accepted among lawyers. Nor is it in common use
among practitioners or administrators of sport. The existence of sports law as a
discipline with sufficient homogeneity to justify distinct treatment is now recognised by, *inter alia*, the existence of sports law degrees at Manchester
Metropolitan University and the Anglia Polytechnic University, the postgradu-
ate Certificate in Sports Law at King's College, London, and the formation in
March 1997 of the Bar Sports Law Group. The British Association for Sport and
Law publishes the *Sport and the Law Journal*, and lists of experts in sports law
appear in lawyers' directories such as *Chambers and Partners Directory*, and *the
Legal 500*. There is a National Sports Law Institute at the Marquette University
in Milwaukee. As the title to this book implies, our contention is that the subject is now sufficiently developed to merit recognition as a discrete field of law,
and that in consequence it is legitimate to use the term "sports law".[1]

It must be accepted at once that to make good that thesis it is insufficient **1.2**
merely to show that there is a phenomenon, sport, which exists in our society,
and that legal rules impact on its practice. The law intrudes into many aspects
of public and private life: yet not every human activity has a body of legal rules
to go with it. Some do and some do not. We travel by ship and by air, and we
have shipping law and aviation law. We also do cooking and gardening, and
there are laws which apply to both activities but one could not usefully speak of

---

[1] For an invaluable compendium of sports laws of various nations in three volumes, see
Wise and Meyer, *International Sports Law and Business* (Kluwer, 1998). The other main
books on sport and the law are: Gardiner, Felix, O'Leary, James and Welch, *Sports Law*
(Cavendish, 1997) ("GFOJW"); Grayson, *Sport and the Law*, 2nd ed. (Butterworths,
1994) ("Grayson"); Griffith-Jones with Adrian Barr-Smith (consulting editor), *Law and
the Business of Sport* (Butterworths, 1997) ("GJBS"); and Moore, *Sports Law Litigation*
(Birmingham CLT Professional Publishing, 1997) "Moore" and, in the USA, Weiler and
Roberts, *Sports and the Law*, 2nd ed. (1998). The major journals are *Sport and the Law
Journal*, published by the British Association for Sport and Law ("SLJ"), and *Sports Law
Bulletin* ("SLB") published by the Anglia Polytechnic University. [Wise and Meyer is
reviewed by Michael Beloff QC. SLT vol. 7, issue 1].

culinary law or horticultural law – or not yet anyway. To justify the use of the term "sports law", then, something more must be shown than the existence of laws which affect sport. Some insight into the question how a distinct field of law is identified can be gained by observing a distinction between branches of the law defined by reference to a particular human activity, for example, aviation law, and those which are identified by reference to the nature of legal rules themselves, for example the law of tort and the law of trusts.

1.3   Both the latter branches of the law describe categories of legal rules embodying rights and obligations which apply irrespective of the subject matter of a particular case in which they are relevant. They could therefore be termed, so to speak, horizontal law; whereas the former categories of law defined by reference to a human activity, could be termed vertical law. If, as we maintain, sports law exists, it exists principally as a vertically defined, or activity-led branch of the law which must take its content from rule-led branches of the law: tort, contract, restitution, crime and so on.

1.4   The claim of sport to have a system of law of its own arises from its importance in ancient and modern social life. Sport is one of society's most important leisure activities. It is a primary and atavistic form of self-expression. Bill Shankly, the legendary manager of Liverpool Football Club, once said memorably that football is not just a matter of life and death; it is more important than that. (He also said somewhat unkindly on another occasion that there were two teams in Liverpool: Liverpool and Liverpool reserves.) Examples of the potency of sport as a force in civil society are legion. In South Africa the effort to end apartheid was driven forward, with considerable success, by the sporting boycott. Rights of full citizenship for all aroused high passions in South Africa, but so did rugby, cricket, athletics and soccer, for access to which white South Africans were prepared to pay a high political price.[2] When Georgia became an independent state after the dissolution of the Soviet Union, one of the first acts of its inaugural government was to apply to join FIFA, the world governing body of association football. To the Georgian people, this was probably as much a badge of sovereign independence as formal recognition by other states, membership of the United Nations and other conventional indicia of statehood.

1.5   It cannot, then, seriously be disputed that sport is a vitally important social force. The thesis that sport influences politics (and association football more than any other sport) has been convincingly demonstrated[3] and is widely accepted. It is therefore no great surprise to discover that the claims of sport to

---

[2] In a case which never came to trial, the South African Athletics Federation argued that it had been invalidly expelled from the International Amateur Athletics Federation, alleging failure to follow the correct procedures and invocation of inappropriate grounds; see Beloff, "Pitch, Pool, Rink . . . Court ? Judicial Review in the Sporting World", [1989] *PL* 95, at p. 98 n.14.

[3] See Simon Kuper, *Football Against the Enemy* (Orion Books 1994).

the attention of lawyers vie with those of health, education and the other great activity-led branches of our public and semi-public law. Yet, as already conceded, in order to show that a system of law governing sport exists, it is not enough to show that sport is influential and that laws affect it. One must go further and propound a definition of sports law, however qualified and approximate such a definition may be. To define sports law one must delineate its scope, however blurred its edges and however indistinct its outline.

Lawyers who may be sceptical of the utility of the term "sports law" as a term **1.6** of art, may argue that this merely amounts to a series of examples of cases in which the parties happen to be concerned in sport. Thus a sporting dispute may in truth be one arising in the law of tort, contract or other "true fields of law". The traditionally minded, purist lawyer, may indeed distrust any activity-led, "vertical" field of law, preferring the surer, traditional ground of rule-led "horizontal" law. We have much sympathy with that position, and we ourselves firmly reject the primacy of "vertical" legal classifications over "horizontal" ones. It is true that, traditionally, the bodies which regulate sporting activity have been treated by English lawyers as a species of domestic tribunal, governed by the same principles as apply to clubs (if unincorporated) or private companies (if incorporated). Likewise, sporting activity has, according to the traditions of English law, been treated as a private activity subject to the rules of private law.

We do not, however, agree with the view that "there is no such thing as sports **1.7** law".[4] The answer to the argument that sports law is merely law in which the parties happen to be involved in sport, is that the law is now beginning to treat sporting activity, sporting bodies and the resolution of disputes in sport, differently from other activities or bodies. Discrete doctrines are gradually taking shape in the sporting field, which are not found elsewhere, not even necessarily in the case of non-sporting domestic tribunals. There are now clear signs that the English courts are beginning to treat decisions of sporting bodies as subject to particular principles better known in the field of public than private law, but

---

[4] Charles Woodhouse, an eminent sports lawyer, quoted in *SLJ* Vol. 5 issue 2 (1997) at p. 12, in "Birth of a Legal Area: Sport and the Law or Sports Law?", *ibid.* at pp. 10 ff. Simon Gardiner, the author of the article, also quotes the views of Professor Grayson, author of *Sport and the Law* ("No subject exists which jurisprudentially can be called sports law. . . . it has no juridical foundation"); of John Barnes, author of *Sports and the Law in Canada* ("Sports law deals with state interests and the resolution of conflicts according to general legal norms"); and of Hayden Opie, author of *Sports Associations and their Legal Environment* ("'Sports law' is . . . applied law as opposed to pure or theoretical law; . . . [it] is concerned with how law in general interacts with the activity known as sport"). Gardiner concludes that a legal theory of sports law is now needed, and suggests that either "the law is providing a functional role in the context of the modern commercial complexity of sport . . . This fits in with a functionalist perspective on sport and society"; or that "the law is a form of regulatory power, a form of control. This fits in with a critical perspective on sport and society. . .".

most accurately described as principles which are *sui generis.*[5] The cornerstone of what could be called the founding principles of sports law is the definition of the respective territories of the courts and the bodies which govern sport. The courts in England and elsewhere have firmly established a region of autonomy for decision making bodies in sport, a region within which – unless the reasons for doing so are compelling – the courts decline to intervene. Equally firmly they have charted the outer limits of that region and insisted that those limits be observed by the decision makers in sport, on pain of judicial intervention. We regard that relationship of constitutional equilibrium between courts of law and sports decision makers as the foundation of a developing law of sport.

1.8   We do not, in consequence, accept the view of some lawyers that the law relating to sport can be regarded simply as part of ordinary private law, that is to say, as part of the corpus of law governing private transactions between citizens in which the state's only interest is to provide a forum of last resort, i.e. the courts which enable disputes to be resolved. The public's limitless enthusiasm for sport and its importance to our cultural heritage makes sports law more than mere private law. That view has recently received direct support from no less a figure than Lord Woolf MR in *Modahl v British Athletic Federation Limited.*[6] Counsel for Ms Modahl invited the court to treat the relation between her and the Federation as one of simple contract, to reject the Federation's "administrative law approach", and to draw a sharp distinction between an action for breach of contract and proceedings for judicial review, treating Ms Modahl's claim for damages as falling into the former not the latter category. Lord Woolf MR's response was that counsel was:

> "wrong in suggesting that the approach of the courts in public law on applications for judicial review have no relevance in domestic disciplinary proceedings of this sort . . . the complaint in both cases would be based on an allegation of unfairness . . . I can see no reason why there should be any difference as to what constitutes unfairness or why the standard of unfairness required an implied term should differ from that required of the same tribunal under public law."[7]

1.9   There is another feature of sports law which makes it unique. Most fields of law, defined by reference to the specific human activity or subject, are firmly grounded in legislative intervention by governments. Obvious examples are health, education, social security, consumer credit, compulsory purchase, and

---

[5] See, for example, *McInnes v. Onslow-Fane* [1978] 1 WLR 1520, per Megarry J at 1535 F-H; *Cowley v. Heatley, The Times* 24 July 1986, per Sir Nicholas Browne-Wilkinson V-C; *Gasser v. Stinson*, transcript 15 June 1988, per Scott J at pp. 37–40; and *Stevenage Borough FC Limited v. The Football League Limited*, transcript 23 July 1996, per Carnwath J at pp. 35–40 of the transcript.

[6] Transcript, 28 July 1997, CA; appealed on a narrower point: HL, transcript, 22.7.99.

[7] *Ibid.*, at pp. 20 F–21 C.

so forth. They exist as discrete fields of law in England because the legislature has consciously decided to create them by legislative intervention in society. These are the fields of law best suited to the modern form of loose leaf encyclopaedia, well known to English lawyers, based on the core of the governing statutes and regulations, regularly updated, and commented on in textual annotations. Such books are immensely useful to the specialist practioner but, without any disrespect to the eminent lawyers involved in their compilation, they are sometimes necessarily light on discussions of principle.

Sports law, however, differs markedly from such other activity defined or ver-   **1.10**
tical fields of law in that it is developing under its own impetus, without any legislative underpinning to speak of – at any rate in the United Kingdom.[8] Legislation is, after all, still mainly a national phenomenon, even in the era of the European Union, the European Convention on Human Rights and many other international legal instruments. Sports law, by contrast with other fields of law, is developing under its own steam. A powerful mixture of international competition, commercial interest and public demand is fuelling the development of legal doctrines particular to sport in a manner which marks sports law as inherently international in character. Its normative underpinning derives not from any treaty entered into between sovereign states, but from international agreements between bodies, many of which are constitutionally independent of their national governments – particularly the Olympic Charter and the rules of the various international governing bodies in sport. Thus sports law is not just international; it is non-governmental as well, and this differentiates it from all other forms of law.

We subscribe to the view that   **1.11**

> "international sports law provides a dynamic, although still incomplete process to avoid, manage and resolve disputes among athletes, national sports bodies, international sports organisations and governments."[9]

Such observations serve to confirm the obvious point that sports law is certainly not a hermetically sealed, self contained body of law. It is still somewhat amorphous. It crosses boundaries. It demands of its students as well as its practitioners familiarity with traditional areas of horizontal law. What do they know of sports law, who only sports law know ? But we have embarked upon this book because we believe it does now merit treatment as a branch of law in its own right.

---

[8] Contrast, e.g. Malaysia, where sport is heavily regulated by statute.

[9] Polvino, "Arbitration as Preventative Medicine for Olympic Ailments; The Olympic Committee Court of Arbitration for Sport and the future for the settlement of International Sporting Disputes" [1994] 8 *Emory Int L.Rev* 349–352, cited in Nafziger, "International Sports Law as a Process for Resolving Disputes", [1996] Vol. 45 *ICLQ* 130 at 131. Dean Kino of Magdalen College, Oxford, has submitted a Doctoral thesis in 1999 on "The incursion of the law into the Rules of Governing Sports Bodies: a Commonwealth and EC Comparison". See S. Weatherill "Do Sporting Associations make 'law' or are they merely subject to it". *European Business Law Review* July/August 1998, 217.

1.12   With that preamble, we offer the following tentative definition of sports law: it is a loose but increasingly cohesive body of rules governing the practice of sport and the resolution of disputes in sport. That body of rules straddles the boundaries between many well known branches of our law, but has at its centre an unusual form of international constitutional principle prescribing the limited autonomy of non-governmental decision making bodies in sport.

The development of sports law

1.13   The stakes in the world of sport have never been higher and they seem to go on and on rising. The psychological pressures on sportsmen and women in the competitive arena grow ever greater, as the gulf between success and failure tends to widen. At the same time, technological and financial sophistication is increasing the complexity of the regulatory machinery in sport. These developments have increased the potential for conflict between those who participate in sport and those who run it. Judges confronted with the task of adjudicating upon such conflicts in national courts have to strike a balance between avoiding, where possible, the courts becoming embroiled in sporting disputes, and the need to do justice where the facts demonstrate that the regulatory or disciplinary machinery in sport is operating unfairly.

1.14   There has undoubtedly been a rise of legalism in the world of sport. It is often deprecated by sports administrators, as it is customary to deprecate the entrée of lawyers into new fields of law. Lawyers are not always popular with the public, but are often very popular with their clients when they win cases (and correspondingly less popular when they lose them). The rise of legalism in sport has been encouraged by lawyers, without doubt, but lawyers did not invent it. Their clients did. It is a natural function of raised financial stakes produced by increased sophistication, particularly of a technological nature, and by a ready market fuelled by the demands of a public whose craving for sport appears insatiable.

1.15   More lawyers and more law in sport does not necessarily mean more justice in sport, but it may do, and it should do. The growth of legalism in sport is borne of a desire for higher standards of justice, demanded by the sporting community as a consequence of the rise of professionalism and the increase in earnings potential within sport. If one wishes to make a cogent case against increased involvement of lawyers in sport, one must make a corresponding case against the increase in the power of sports administrators to affect the lives and livelihoods of sportsmen and women, and, conversely, the increased power of sportsmen and women to dictate terms to sports administrators. For it is this increase in power within sport, less often criticised within the sporting community than legal intrusion into its sphere of influence, that leads the sporting community more frequently than in the past to seek advice and representation from lawyers. In short, the more there is at stake, the more astute must be the law to prevent injustice.

As a consequence of increased legalism in sport, there is now a body of sport- **1.16**
ing case law from the Commonwealth and other jurisdictions on which English
(and Welsh) lawyers can readily draw. Cross-fertilisation from other common
law jurisdictions is a feature of our legal system. But more than in other
branches of law, international sporting competition has helped to break down
the barriers between civil law and common law countries. As we have remarked
elsewhere,[10] the Commonwealth authorities disclose a litany of complaints, successful and unsuccessful, including bias or a risk of bias on the part of the tribunal; charges laid or convictions brought in under the wrong rule; charges
disclosing no disciplinary offence; procedural unfairness; unreasonable restraint
of trade; infringement of statutory competition law; unfair prejudice in the running of a company; and even infringement of the "right to work". The courts
have had to rule on issues as diverse as the validity of a decision to ban a cricketer who played in South Africa; the proper construction of rules against horse
doping; the *locus standi* of individuals to challenge decisions of bodies of which
they are not members; and whether a sporting association qualified for a tax
exemption given to public but not private bodies. The expanding Commonwealth sporting jurisprudence now includes authorities arising out of horse racing in South Africa, athletics in Singapore, cricket in Barbados, rugby league in
New Zealand and trotting in Australia.

There is a further wealth of authority, less familiar to English lawyers. The **1.17**
establishment of the Court of Arbitration in Sport, based at Lausanne in
Switzerland (and referred to in this book as the "CAS"), has led to the phenomenon of a tribunal with an English lawyer president applying Swiss law,[11] and,
at the 1996 Olympics in Atlanta, applying "general principles of law and the
rules of law"[12] – a broader concept than which would be difficult to formulate.
In *Volkers v. FINA*,[13] the CAS presided over by a distinguished Nairobi attor-
ney, with a common law background like ours, "found it possible and appropriate to resolve the dispute in accordance with the rules of FINA, and in
accordance with general principles of law".[14] This is law which is truly international.[15]

The influence of civil law domestic legal systems is not a mere curiosity for the **1.18**
English sports lawyer. Cases such as *Lehtinen v FINA*[16] may affect future decisions before English, foreign or international sports law tribunals or national

[10] See Beloff and Kerr, "Judicial Control of Sporting Bodies: the Commonwealth
Jurisprudence", SLJ, Vol. 3 issue 1, Spring 1995 at p. 5.
[11] See *Cullwick v. FINA*, CAS 96/149, February 1997.
[12] See Article 17 of the Ad Hoc Rules and *Andrade v. Cape Verde NOC*, CAS – Ad
Hoc Division, No. 002, July 1996.
[13] CAS 95/150, September 1996.
[14] *Ibid.*, para. 20.
[15] For the CAS jurisprudence, see Recueil de Sentences du TAS; *Digest of CAS Awards
1986–1998*, ed. M. Reeb (Stämpfle Editions SA, Berne, 1998).
[16] CAS 95/142, February 1996.

courts, whichever law they may be applying. In that case the CAS entertained, but dismissed, a claim for damages against an international sporting association by applying Articles 41 and 49 of the Swiss Code of Obligations.[17] While the CAS rules[18] provide for Swiss law to be applied in the absence of an alternative choice of law by the disputant parties,[19] it is notable that the decisions of the CAS reflect and promote the distinctive sporting principles of fair play and good sportsmanship[20] in applying technical rules;[21] the equality of athletes before the law; [22] the construction of sporting rules so as not to distort their purpose;[23] a respect for sporting decisions; and a flexible and pragmatic approach to entry deadlines.[24] These same principles are also enunciated in the rules of many international sporting bodies.[25]

1.19   Article 17 of the ad hoc rules for the CAS Ad Hoc Panel at the Commonwealth Games in Kuala Lumpur in 1998 provided that a panel shall resolve the dispute

> "pursuant to the Constitution of the Commonwealth Games Federation ['CGF'], the applicable regulations, general principles of law and the rules of law, the application of which it deems appropriate."

The same formula was used in Article 17 of the Rules for the Ad Hoc Panel of the CAS at the Atlanta Olympics in 1996, save that there was a reference to the Olympic Charter instead of to the constitution of the CGF. The "applicable regulations" included primarily the rules of the relevant international federations and, possibly, the regulations of the domestic Commonwealth Games or Olympic bodies. The "rules of law, the application of which [the panel] deems appropriate" gave the panel wide freedom in determining applicable rules.

1.20   Since in each instance, the juridical seat of the arbitration (in defiance of geographical reality) was said to be Lausanne, Switzerland, the panels were able to look to Article 187 of the Swiss Private International Law Act, which provides

---

[17] CAS 95/142, February 1996, para. 63 et seq.

[18] The Code of Sports-related Arbitration or *code de l'arbitrage en matière de sport*, in which the French and English texts are equally authentic (Rule R.67), entered into force on 22 November 1994.

[19] *Ibid.*, Rule R.45. The parties may authorise the arbitrators to decide *ex aequo et bono* ("statuer en équité").

[20] Notably in *Cooke v. Fédération Equestre Internationale*, CAS 98/184, September 1998.

[21] For example, what is a low blow in boxing; see *Mendy*, OG Atlanta (1996), 004.

[22] *R. v. IOC*, OG Nagano (1998), 002 para. 5.

[23] *Czech Olympic Committee and Swedish Olympic Committee v. IAAF*, OG Nagano (1998), 004–005.

[24] *US Swimming v. FINA*, OG Atlanta 001.

[25] See, for example, Article 168 of the General Regulations of the Fédération Equestre Internationale, 19th ed. ("the common principles of behaviour, fairness and accepted standards of sportsmanship"), which was in play in *Cooke v. FEI supra.*, n. 20.

"The arbitral tribunal shall decide the dispute according to the rules of law chosen by the parties or, in the absence of such a choice, according to the rules of law with which the case has the closest connection."[26]

The term "rules of law" did not necessarily mean national law only and, within a national law, allows *dépéçage*. "General principles of law" were properly interpreted to comprise rules commonly observed in legal systems worldwide, but not those particular to a discrete area, in terms of either subject matter or country (such as, e.g., Japanese unfair competition law).[27] As a concept, "general principles of law" were adapted to the context: different principles are accordingly engaged when the context is arbitration from those in play when it is the law of nations.

In the context of sport, general principles of international contract law may **1.21** be material.[28] The most commonly applied principles are the following:

Freedom of contract

The parties to a contract may reach agreement on any matter they wish within the boundaries of mandatory provisions of domestic or (if applicable) international law. Such freedom of contract extends to choice-of-law clauses, by which the parties select the legal framework, again within the boundaries of mandatory provisions.[29] The principle of freedom of contract means by corollary that agreements which are not freely entered into are invalid.

Pacta sunt servanda

A party which freely enters into an agreement and assumes obligations under it must perform as agreed unless excused by reasons beyond its control.[30]

Force majeure

If reasons beyond a party's control prevent it from performing in accordance with the contractual terms, that party may be excused from performance. The

---

[26] Cf. also Article 13.3 of the Arbitration Rules of the International Chamber of Commerce.

[27] See *Staatsfabriek Viking BV v. German Speed Skating Association*, CAS, NAG 3.

[28] For a general and authoritative presentation, see Goldmann, "La lex mercatoria dans les contrats et l'arbitrage internationaux: réalité et perspectives", in *Journal de Droit International* 106 (1979) p. 475 et seq.

[29] Lalive, "Transnational (or Truly International) Public Policy in: Comparative Arbitration Practice and Public Policy in Arbitration", ICCA Congress Series No. 3, Deventer 1987, pp. 257–318, 301–4.

[30] See Dasser, *Internationale Schiedsgerichte und Lex Mercatoria*, Zurich 1989, pp. 109–110 and references therein.

party is discharged from liability for non-performance only if it has made its best and reasonable efforts to overcome the outside event and to perform.[31]

Clausula rebus sic stantibus

This doctrine[32] proceeds from the premise that parties enter into a contract with a certain set of circumstances in mind. If the circumstances change in an unforeseeable manner and to a material extent, then the basis of the contract lapses. The principle is not universally accepted in national laws; for example, French law does not recognise it in private law, only in administrative law. However it is widely recognised in international arbitration whenever the arbitrators apply general principles of law and *lex mercatoria*.

Good faith

This is a universal principle according to which all persons are bound by a duty to act in a loyal, frank and open manner.[33] For example, when one party acts or makes statements knowing that another party will act in reliance on these statements or acts, the former is precluded from reversing its position at the latter's expense (*venire contra factum proprium*)[34]. In common law systems this would be characterised as estoppel.

Protection of legitimate expectations

Arbitrators and tribunals should not depart from the clear intent of the parties unless there is paramount reason for so doing.[35] It must be assumed that parties to an agreement intended it to be valid and enforceable. Furthermore, arbitrators must be careful not to apply rules of a law which the parties obviously did not have in mind.

1.22   International arbitration practice has developed or adopted the following principles of interpretation of contracts:

---

[31] See Dasser, *Internationale Schiedsgerichte und Lex Mercatoria*, Zurich 1989, pp. 110–2 and references therein.

[32] Equivalent to frustration of contracts under Anglo-American law, commercial impracticability under US law, Wegfall der Geschäftsgrundlage under German law, and imprévision under French law.

[33] Dasser, *supra.*, n. 30, pp. 108–9 and references therein; Lalive, *supra.*, n. 29, p. 306; Mayer, "Le Principe de Bonne Foi Devant les Arbitres Internationaux", in: *Etudes en l'Honneur de Pierre Lalive*, (Basle/Frankfurt am Main, 1993), pp. 543–556 and extensive references.

[34] Applied by the CAS in *AEK Athens and Slavia Prague v. UEFA*, CAS 98/200, Procedural Order of 17 July 1998, p. 14, para. 56.

[35] Bucher, "L'attente légitime de parties", in: *Rechtskollisionen, Festschrift für Anton Heini*, (Zurich, 1995), pp. 95–102; Lalive, *supra.*, n. 29, pp. 305–6.

Necessity of seeking the parties' intent

The interpretation of contracts must attempt to reach a result which is in accordance with the real or presumed intent of the parties. The starting point for interpretation must be the contract itself.

In dubio contra proferentem

When one party has drafted a contract and the other party has merely adhered to its terms, e.g. the athletes' agreement to an arbitration, any doubt arising from the contract's wording benefits the adhering party, and is adverse to the proponent. The same principle also applies to the rules and regulations of sports bodies. The *contra proferentem* principle is, of course, well established in English law.[36]

Doubt benefits the party assuming a contractual obligation

When a contract (or rule or regulation) is unclear, then any doubt benefits the party which would assume an obligation. In other words, no contractual duties can be held to exist unless clearly set forth in the contract.

The last two principles are to be applied only in cases of ambiguity.

The main type of dispute submitted to international arbitral bodies in sport **1.23** is disciplinary. The context is therefore closer to administrative or even criminal law than to contract law. International sports dispute resolution engages the following general principles of public and criminal law:

Nullum crimen, mulla poena sine lege

Sanction cannot be imposed unless there is a violation of a rule and unless sanctions are provided for in the rule. This rule has been enshrined in Article 7 of the 1950 European Convention on Human Rights.[37] Although this basic principle has its origins in criminal law, it also applies in administrative law; any infringement of personal freedom by an administrative body must have a statutory basis.[38]

---

[36] Chitty on Contracts, 27th ed., Vol. 1 para 14–009. It was applied eg: by the (BAF) Drug Advisory Committee in the case of Douglas Walker (1999); para 4.4.

[37] See for example, Ashworth, *Principles of Criminal Law*, 2nd ed., (Oxford Clarendon Press, 1995), pp. 67–71; Pradel, *Droit Pénal, Tome 1, Introduction Générale, Droit pénal général*, 10th ed., (Paris 1995), pp. 169–171.

[38] See Erichsen, *Allgemeines Verwaltungsrecht*, 10th ed., (Berlin, 1995), pp. 106–7; Moor, *Droit Administratif, Vol. I, Les fondements généraux*, (Berne, 1988), pp. 45–7.

Equal treatment

Equal (or at least very similar) situations must receive equal treatment; conversely, unequal situations must receive different treatment.[39] The general principle requires the tribunal carefully to examine the facts of the relevant cases to detect material similarities or differences and to explain the same.

Proportionality

Although the imposition of a particular sanction is a matter, within the range provided by the rules, for the discretion of the relevant authority, the principle of proportionality means that a sanction must be proportionate to the offence and that the sanction must be necessary to achieve the result sought by the body imposing it.[40]

Good faith

In administrative law in civil law jurisdictions, the good faith principle applies when an administrative body gives assurances to an individual that certain future actions by that individual are legal when in truth they may not be. If such assurances are given (and provided that the body in question was empowered to decide such matters), no sanctions can be taken against the individual acting illegally in reliance on these assurances.[41] Another application of the good faith principle (which flows from the doctrine *venire contra factum proprium*) is that a party may not create an ambiguous situation, for example by conflicting or unclear statements, and then take advantage of the ambiguity which it has itself brought about. Finally, the good faith principle precludes a party from availing itself of a rule in a manner which is contrary to the rationale of the rule (*abus de droit*).

The aim of this book

1.24 The fact that sports law is in its infancy and lacks hard edges serving to distinguish it from other areas of law, leads to a difficulty of presentation in structuring a book such as this. One cannot be a sports lawyer in isolation from other fields of law. To be a good sports lawyer one must also be a good non-sports

---

[39] Moor, *supra.*, n. 38, Vol. I, pp. 376–9.

[40] Erichsen, *supra.*, n. 38, pp. 109–10; Moor, *supra.*, n. 38, pp. 305–53; de Smith, Woolf and Jowell, *Judicial Review of Administrative Action*, 5th ed. (Sweet and Maxwell, 1995), p. 850.

[41] Erichsen, *supra.*, n. 38, p. 110; Moor, *supra.*, n. 38, pp. 358–65.

lawyer, though, mercifully, not a good lawyer sportsman or woman.[42] Our own legal background in commercial law, constitutional and administrative law, European Community law, tort and employment law, is as good a grounding as any for a sports law practice. In this book, we attempt to identify where the interface occurs in sports law between those fields, and others such as personal injury in which we are considerably less well versed.

To the non-lawyer involved in sport as a player, coach or administrator, it **1.25** may be unnecessary to think of sports law as anything more than simply the law which he or she encounters at work within the sports industries – irrespective of what label a lawyer would use to describe that law. This book is intended to assist in answering the questions that may confront practitioners of sport and administrators in the course of their work, and we hope it will be useful to non-lawyers as well as to lawyers. Our hope is fortified by the fact that administrators in sport are, not infrequently, qualified lawyers; and indeed a few lawyers are even notable sportsmen themselves. Some members of the CAS panel of arbitrators are Olympians.

But we do not intend this book to serve as a reference manual for the sports **1.26** administrator. Rather, it constitutes our attempt to provide a theoretical foundation for sports law. A *lex specialis* is taking shape from a line of decisions, especially of the CAS, some of which we mention in this book. Publication of reports of those cases is underway, hampered only by obligations of confidentiality owed to participants in the relevant proceedings. A hallmark of a developed system of law is that its content can be easily ascertained by lawyers and by the public. This is not yet the case with sports law, even though publications are beginning to proliferate. We refer to some of them in the footnotes of the pages which follow. As for our own professional experience, we have had to restrict ourselves as to the degree of detail that we can condescend to in some cases, because of confidentiality obligations which we owe to our clients and to arbitral tribunals under their rules. We hope this book will contribute to the development of sports law, *inter alia*, by lending impetus to systematic reporting of sporting cases. In particular we would like to see *regular* reports of decisions of the CAS and other international sports tribunals, and we have reason to believe that this will happen before long.

We have already stated that in our view, sports law is by nature international **1.27** in character. The term "English sports law" is of only limited utility and usually best avoided, since an account of the law relating to sport confined to English statute and case law would necessarily be fragmentary, incomplete and inadequate. One must think of sports law as a body of law which transcends international boundaries, like European Community law and public international law. The Olympic Charter as a *fons et origo* of international jurisdiction is a

[42] Examples of lawyer-sportsmen include Lord Alverston CJ (judge), an athletics blue; Douglas Lowe (barrister), double Olympic gold medallist at 800 metres, Johnny Searle (solicitor), Olympic gold medallist oarsman, and Brian Moore, Litigation solicitor and British Lion.

phenomenon unique to sports law. But every lawyer is conditioned by the jurisdiction in which he or she primarily practises. As English lawyers, albeit ones
with a Community law and international dimension to our work, our account
of the subject is necessarily Anglocentric. Accordingly, where we refer below to
domestic law, we are referring to the domestic law of England and Wales except
where we state otherwise.

1.28   This book is not intended to deal, except in passing, with non-contentious
aspects of sports law, such as the practical considerations involved in negotiating a sponsorship or broadcasting contract, or a contract with a player.
Specialist lawyers offer expertise in contract negotiation. Our primary focus is
the law regulating sporting activity and in particular the law governing disputes
in the sporting world, and the various means devised by and under the law for
resolving them. We aim to give a coherent account of that body of law.

1.29   There are other topics which we could have included in this book but have
chosen not to, partly because they are not central to our expertise and experience, and partly because they seem to us to occupy territory at or near the edges,
or even beyond the outer limits of, the subject. Topics not covered here include
taxation of sporting activity;[43] planning and property law relating to sports
premises including stadia; and sport in the law of education. Nor do we attempt
to give an account of the political, administrative and commercial structures
which govern sport in this country and internationally. These are changing
swiftly and may already be familiar to many of our readers. In any case their
nature is not a matter of law, but of commerce and politics.

1.30   We pay tribute to pioneers in the field, in particular Professor Edward
Grayson, the "onlie begetter" of the subject, David Griffith-Jones and Adrian
Barr-Smith.[44] We have directed the reader at various junctures to these works
where we believe it would be advantageous to pursue a particular topic further.
But our approach to the subject is different from theirs, and we do not consider
that there are as yet too many players on this particular field.

1.31   Our approach is to marry theory with practice. We believe that the best way
of moving towards a coherent account of sports law as a discrete body of rules
is to proceed inductively, deriving principle from practical professional experience. In any case, as busy practising barristers, we lack the leisure to view the
subject through the medium of profound academic scholarship and thorough
research, although it may be that this short book will inspire others to do so.

1.32   As to the structure of the chapters which follow, we reject conventional horizontal legal classifications, which would divide the subject by considering traditional fields of law (tort, contract, etc.) and explaining their application to
sport. This is because sports law straddles so many of them. Nor would it meet
our objective to present the material by reference to specific sports (rugby, boxing, etc.) since our law generally does not treat as *ipso facto* relevant which sport

---

[43] For an account see Grayson at pp. 366–89.
[44] The author and consulting editor of GJBS.

is being practised; legal principles applied to tennis normally also apply to squash. To deal with different sports individually would take the concept of vertically defined law to an absurd extreme.[45]

Any book on sports law carries with it the danger that it will contain little **1.33** more than information. We have tried to avoid that, even at the risk of not providing enough information. As a field which has yet to be subjected to thorough treatment from a theoretical perspective, sports law lends itself well, in our view, to broad general chapter headings and discussion of principles under those headings untrammelled by detailed and narrow sub-headings, which could lead to the account becoming bogged down in detail, putting information above exposition. In a complex regulated society which often wearies the practising lawyer with its vast amount of regulatory detail and information overload, we have found this a refreshing experience, and we hope our readers will share in it.

---

[45] We have assumed throughout that sport is itself a recognisable concept, although lacking precise definition in English law. It has been accepted that a trust for the mere promotion of a particular sport is not charitable as being for the promotion of education: (In *Re Nottage* (1895) 2 Ch. 649; whereas a trust to provide sports facilities for students will be: *IRC* v. *McMullen*, 1981, ACI. See also *R.* v. *Oxfordshire CC ex p Sunningwell Parish Council* [1999] 3 All ER 385 at p. 396–7.

2

Overview: the Framework of the Law Relating to Sport

In this second chapter our aim is to provide an overview of the manner in which **2.1** the law impacts on sporting activity. We seek to give an account here of the ways in which the law creates rights and obligations which impact on participants in the sports industries. Our primary purpose here is not to state the detailed content of those rights and obligations, but to identify and explain in brief the legal nature of the bodies which govern sports, and the sources of rights and obligations to which sportsmen and women, and their governing organs, are subject.

The legal nature of sporting associations

All who follow sport in the media are familiar with various acronyms or sets of **2.2** initials denoting the bodies which administer particular sports. We take for granted that "the FA" means the Football Association, "the RFU" means the Rugby Football Union, and "the WRU" the Welsh Rugby Union. Devotees of squash may be aware that the "SRA" means the Squash Rackets Association. On the international plane, most sports aficionados probably know that "the WBC" means the World Boxing Council but, unless they speak French, are unlikely to know what "UEFA" stands for (Union des Associations Européennes de Football). Many people who work in sport may never need to concern themselves with the differences in the legal nature of these bodies.

To lawyers and some sports administrators, however, the differences can be **2.3** critical. If a dispute arises, it may be of legal importance that the Football Association is in fact a limited company, the Football Association Limited, incorporated in England; that the World Boxing Council is a limited liability company incorporated in Puerto Rico; that UEFA is a limited liability company incorporated in Switzerland; that the RFU is a special kind of body corporate registered under the Industrial and Provident Societies Act 1965; and that the WRU and the SRA are unincorporated associations of members.

It is not just the bodies which administer sport that may differ in their legal **2.4** nature. The clubs and individuals which win or lose the games may play to the same rules on the field, but off the field they may differ from each other in their legal characteristics. The FA Premier League includes Middlesbrough Football and Athletic Company (1986) Limited, trading as Middlesbrough Football Club; Tottenham Hotspur Football & Athletic Company Limited, a wholly owned subsidiary of Tottenham Hotspur plc; and Chelsea Football Club Limited (to name some of the clubs we have had the privilege of representing). Individual sportsmen and women naturally have the same status in law as any other individual person.

2.5   Most, but by no means all, national sporting bodies in this country, particularly in professional sports in England, are incorporated as companies with limited liability. But there is no requirement in English law that sports clubs or associations take any particular legal form. They may be limited liability companies, companies limited by guarantee, or unincorporated associations. They enjoy the benefits and are subordinate to the obligations of the particular form that they have selected in the same way as other non-sports bodies. They are not statutory bodies and do not require to be licensed or registered as in some countries, for example, Malaysia.

2.6   International sports bodies are also usually limited liability companies registered in whichever jurisdiction they find most convenient; Switzerland being popular with the European bodies and some worldwide bodies such as FIFA and the international Olympic bodies. Governing bodies are treated in most legal systems as private authorities but exercising quasi-public functions, particularly where they exercise monopoly power over a particular sport. They are strongly autonomous and independent, and therefore can perhaps be expected to act in less predictable ways than if they were statutory bodies created by legislation.[1]

2.7   In the world of sport the main distinction is between bodies which are incorporated and those which are not. A corporation has a legal existence independent of the individuals who are members of the corporation, and is therefore said to have legal personality. The shareholders are not liable for the company's debts. An important consequence of corporate identity is that the company can bring and defend legal proceedings in its own name. Where the company is limited by shares, the shareholders are liable to the company only up to the amount unpaid on their shares; where limited by guarantee, the guarantors are liable only up to the amount of their guarantee.[2] Particular laws in the fields of taxation, insolvency and others apply to them.[3] It would go far beyond our purpose to attempt any exposition here of the different types of body corporate encountered in the sporting world. Reference should be made to standard works on company law, the most comprehensive of which is Palmer's *Company Law*.

2.8   For the purposes of our bird's eye view of the framework of sports law, it is sufficient here to mention only some of the principal attributes of a limited

---

[1] See for example, Charles Woodhouse, "Sport and Law in Conflict: Role of Sports Governing Bodies", conference paper at Stamford Bridge, 25 November 1996: "There is little or no standardisation in their constitutions".

[2] Gower, *Company Law*, 8th ed., (London, Sweet and Maxwell) p. 97.

[3] It has been suggested that "having a distinct stand alone entity, separate from committee and members alike, can make for clearer management and decision making structures"; Woodhouse in Sport and Law in Conflict: Role of Sports Governing Bodies; Euroforum's First Annual Sports Forum '96 (25 November 1996).

liability company. Its legal existence and the limited liability of its members are well known. Other important features of a company are its governing constitutional documents, the memorandum and articles of association; the fiduciary duties owed to it by its directors; its susceptibility to an administration order or to liquidation (compulsorily, in winding up proceedings, or voluntarily, by resolution); and the particular statutory remedy available to minority shareholders who may wish, and in certain circumstances are permitted, to complain about the manner in which the company's affairs are being conducted.[4]

These and other aspects of company law too numerous and complex to mention here, are the subject of a vast tapestry of interlocking regulatory provisions enacted by statute and statutory instrument, all admirably expounded in Palmer's *Company Law* and other specialist works. Expert legal and accounting advice is given to administrators in sport to help them to determine which legal animal to select as the most appropriate form for the governing body in question. The choice of form has implications for accounting methods, tax liability régimes and other practical matters. It is not part of the exercise undertaken in this chapter to provide an explanation of those factors, or of the advantages and disadvantages of particular legal forms. The decision how best to create a body to administer a sport should be informed by the detailed circumstances of the case including specialist advice. **2.9**

If a sporting body is not incorporated as a company, then, in English law, it will be classified as an unincorporated association. English law regards such associations as no more than a group of individuals comprising the members of the association, who have collectively agreed between themselves by contract to abide by the contents of the rules of the association as amended from time to time. We will look further at this organisational model when considering the impact of contractual terms in sport, below. Unincorporated associations are common inhabitants of the English law landscape. They are not confined to the sporting world; on the contrary they are very common outside it as well as within it. For example, most barristers' chambers operate as unincorporated associations of their members. **2.10**

Sports clubs often take the form of unincorporated associations as well. A common example is that of a village cricket club, an association with a simple written constitution providing for government by a committee, an annual general meeting and for certain major decisions to be taken only at such an annual general meeting or at an extraordinary general meeting. Such is the paradigm case in sport. Bodies concerned with the government of professional sport are more likely to be incorporated as limited companies, though some still are not. The essence of an unincorporated association is that its legal identity is no more than that of the sum of the individuals who are its members. Its constitution **2.11**

---

[4] See for example, section 459 of the Companies Act 1985, enabling a minority shareholder to petition the court for relief on the ground that the company's affairs are being managed in a manner prejudicial to the interests of the minority.

records its objects and method of decision making, and derives from the contract between them.

2.12   The common law supplements the normal express provisions commonly found in the constitutional documents of such associations by implying into the rules certain fundamental principles: in particular, (subject to any contrary provision) the principle of decision by simple majority, and the right to resign from membership. Subjection to the court's jurisdiction in matters of law is also fundamental and cannot be negated by any contrary provision in the rules. A fuller account of the law relating to unincorporated associations and members' clubs would stray beyond the territory of sports law. The sports lawyer may be confronted – and not only in a disciplinary context of the type considered in chapter seven – with issues of construction and interpretation arising in this field of law. A useful account of that law can be found in Halsbury's *Laws of England*.[5]

2.13   As an example of a dispute in the context of sport over the meaning and effect of the rules of an unincorporated association, it is instructive to mention *Baker v. Jones*.[6] A judge held that the British Amateur Weightlifters' Association did not, on the true construction of its rules, have the power by its central council to authorise the use of the Association's funds to pay the personal legal costs of some of its members in defending proceedings brought against them in their personal capacity. The officers had been sued in actions alleging the torts of conspiracy and defamation. The reasoning of the judge was that a particular provision authorising the central council to act on behalf of the Association regarding any matters not dealt with by the rules, had to be read in conjunction with the object of the Association which was to promote weightlifting as a sport and weight training as a means of physical improvement.

2.14   Other disputes which have from time to time exercised us professionally have involved questions as to whether a dissentient member, unpopular with the leadership of the association in question, had satisfied the conditions for establishing an automatic right to membership of a successor body to the association involved; whether a particular procedure proposed by the chairman of an international sporting body for the election of his or her successor was valid or invalid under the rules of the body in question; and other similar legal issues arising from clashes of personalities or politics within the internal administration of a sport. Such disputes can and do also arise in connection with incorporated sporting bodies operating as companies. In such cases, the dispute falls to be resolved by reference to the distinct, but to some extent related, body of prin-

---

[5] See 4th edn. (reissue), Volume 6, paras 201–75. See also Shackleton, *The Law and Practice of Meetings*, 9th edn. (London, Sweet and Maxwell, 1997); Shaw, *The Law of Meetings*, 2nd ed. (Macdonald & Evans, 1990); Josling and Alexander, *The Law of Clubs*, 5th ed.

[6] [1954] 2 All ER 553, Lynksey J; but cf. *Hill v. Archbold* [1968] 1 QB 668, CA (trade union entitled to support libel action by officers; the decision casts some doubt on *Baker v. Jones*).

ciples which has grown up through case law dealing with the interpretation of successive company law statutes over the past few centuries.

One important procedural point arises from the nature of a sporting (or **2.15** other) association. If the body is incorporated, and can therefore sue and be sued in its own name, ordinary legal procedures can be followed, in the same way as where the party suing or being sued is an individual person and not a corporate person. If, however, the association is unincorporated, it cannot bring or defend legal proceedings in its own name, i.e. in the name of the association. Instead, any action must be brought against, or defended by, individual representative defendants, being the officers of the association acting in their official capacity for and on behalf of all other relevant members for the time being of the association. Rules of court make specific provision for such representative proceedings. By Order 15 rule 12 of the Rules of the Supreme Court[7] proceedings may be begun by or against any person or persons as representing other persons, where "numerous persons have the same interest in any proceedings . . .".[8]

In sporting cases it is consequently common for proceedings by a dissident **2.16** member or members of an association to bring an action whose title describes the plaintiffs in terms such as

"X Y Z, suing on his own behalf and on behalf of all other members of the A B C Sports Association who voted in favour of a motion numbered 1 2 3 at the Annual General Meeting held on 18 January 1997"

and the defendants are described as, for example

"E F G and H J K, sued as, respectively, the Chairman and Secretary of the A B C Sports Association, on their own behalf and on behalf of all other members for the time being of that Association except the plaintiffs."

This form of proceeding is not confined to litigation in sport but extends to any litigation in which representative proceedings are appropriate by reason of identity of interests of numerous persons in the same subject matter. It gets over the difficulty of absence of legal personality where an association is unincorporated. However, it can create complications in relation to legal costs, where an organisation is split and the powers to incur legal costs may themselves be in dispute – as shown by the decision in *Baker v. Jones*[9]. Such complications do not so frequently arise in the case of corporate bodies, where the power to litigate and incur legal costs is normally provided for uncontroversially in the company's memorandum and/or articles of association, and can be exercised by the board of directors acting in the name of the company.

We have included in our overview brief mention of the consequences of legal **2.17** personality, or the lack of it, in order to draw attention to the way in which legal

---

[7] See Supreme Court Practice ("the White Book") 1999 ed. Volume 1 pp. 248–57.
[8] RSC Order 15 rule 12(1), Civil Procedure Rules Part 50 and Shedule 1.
[9] *Supra*, n. 6.

forms may have practical effects on disputes arising in sport. The trend in professional sport is away from unincorporated associations, which still have something of the flavour of a private club, towards a modern corporate model conducive to sport being run on business lines. The Middlesex Cricket Club (MCC), a private club, was formerly the governing body for cricket in England. That would be difficult to contemplate now. The incidence of unincorporated associations is likely to diminish further in professional sport but will remain important in the amateur sports and in particular in the administration of sport at local level, exemplified by a village football team, perhaps sponsored by a local building firm, playing in a local league within the county.

Rights and obligations created by contract

2.18 We now move away from the legal nature of the bodies which administer sport to consider the nature of the rules determining the content of rights and obligations in sport. Here we take a brief look at sports law from the perspective of a traditional "horizontally minded" lawyer, dividing up the subject by reference to the well known legal classifications of contract, tort and other renowned sources of law. We begin with the law of contract because it is the most important determinant of the content of variable legal relationships in sport. It is the legal tool with which the stage designers of sport create the scene; and it contains the script used by the sporting actors to play to the public.

2.19   Contract often, but not always, delineates the scope of rights of access to sporting competitions, which we consider in chapter three. It governs many aspects of the rights and obligations of players, coaches and officials vis-à-vis their club, as we shall discover in chapter four which is concerned with players' rights. Contract is usually the ultimate source of the regulatory jurisdiction of referees and governing bodies in sport, enabling the latter to determine the laws according to which sport is played (examined in chapter five), and the former to implement those laws on the field of play. The law of contract plays a pivotal role in determining the scope of rights to market and broadcast sporting competitions and associated merchandise. That aspect of the law is considered in chapter six. The law of contract is also of crucial importance in shaping and delimiting the punitive jurisdiction exercised by disciplinary bodies in sport, which we consider in some detail in chapter seven.

2.20   It is worth looking a little more closely at the nature of legal rules created by contract in the world of sport. Contractual relationships abound in sport. Firstly, contracts of membership exist between individuals and the sports club or association of which they are members. If the body in question is unincorporated, then each of its members, by joining, will have entered into a contractual relationship – whether expressly, by signing a form, or perhaps impliedly, by conduct i.e. having notice of the rules and behaving as a member – on the terms of the rules of the club. Those rules may be amended from time to time in accordance with the proper constitutional procedures forming part of them. Provided those procedures are properly followed, amendments to the rules will be binding in contract on the members without the need for express notice to each of them of any change.

In the case of an unincorporated members' club or association, the contractual relation of each member is with every other member of the club. Thus there is a "horizontal" matrix of contracts binding each member to all the other members. There cannot in such a case be a "vertical" contract binding each member to the club itself, for the club itself has no legal existence, being unincorporated, as explained above. A simple example of such a body would be a local amateur golf club. There are probably thousands of such clubs active in local sport throughout this country. Indeed, until quite recently at least one of the top rugby union clubs, playing in the highest echelons of the game in England, was still an unincorporated club run on a traditional committee basis, underpinned in law by a horizontal matrix of contracts between the members.   **2.21**

We should note here the difference between an unincorporated sports club of the type just mentioned, and a proprietary club formed as a commercial venture to enable its members to take exercise at their leisure, for a price. In recent years many such commercial gymnasia have sprung up in the private sector. Our readers will have noticed them and may have joined one. Obviously, such an entity differs from a traditional sports club in that it exists not to promote competitive sport for its own sake, but to offer a service to its members in return for a subscription. A ten pin bowling club to which members resort for recreation and perhaps friendly competition, is another example of such a body. The difference between a members' club and a proprietary club is that a body of the latter type, such as a commercial sports club, is likely to be incorporated as a limited company and the members will enter into a contract of membership with that company "vertically" and pay their subscriptions to it. They will not have any contractual obligations to fellow members unless and except to the extent that the rules so provide. Commercial sports clubs make an important contribution to social and leisure activity, but are not central to our account of sports law because they do not exist directly to promote any particular sporting competition.[10]   **2.22**

The notion of a "web" or "horizontal matrix" or contracts between persons with an interest in sport, is not confined to the context of membership of a sporting association or club. The same contractual position may pertain in the case of participants in a particular sporting enterprise, or an individual competition. In *The Satanita*[11] the House of Lords ruled on a maritime collision claim   **2.23**

---

[10] Proprietary clubs are not required by law to be incorporated as companies, but frequently are. They are sometimes, under their rules, managed by a committee but the proprietor usually reserves to itself ultimate control; see *Halsbury's Laws*, 4th ed., (Butterworths) Volume 6 (reissue) para. 208–9.

[11] Also sub. nom. *Clarke v. Dunraven* [1897] AC 59, HL.

between competitors in the Mudhook Yacht Club regatta. The Satanita ran into and sank the Valkyrie in breach of the eighteenth rule of the competition. Their Lordships decided that the competitors were under a contractual liability, *inter se*, to observe the rules of the competition and, it followed, to make good all damage caused by a breach of those rules. This had the consequence that the crew of the Satanita could not avail itself of a limitation of liability provision in section 54 of the Merchant Shipping (Amendment) Act 1862. The case is commonly cited as authority for the proposition that generally, in the case of a competition, "competitors enter into contracts with each other to observe the rules of the competition"[12] – despite the difficulty of analysing the process of entering into those contracts by reference to the traditional contract theory of offer and acceptance familiar to first year law students.

2.24 So groups of people involved in sport may bind themselves to each other contractually either in relation to the rules of a particular body, or in relation to an individual competition administered by such a body. Yet in *Earl of Ellesmere v. Wallace*,[13] the Court of Appeal entertained a representative action in which representatives of the Jockey Club, then an unincorporated body,[14] successfully sought a declaration that contracts between entrants to horse races and the Club were not void as gaming and wagering contracts. The importance of that issue was that gaming and wagering contracts cannot be enforced, but if the contracts were valid, the Club would be able to recover the entry fee if an entrant did not pay it. By agreement the relevant contracts were treated as contracts between the race entrants and the Club, not between those entrants and other entrants, nor between all the members of the club, *inter se*.[15] *The Satanita* was not cited to the Court of Appeal. However "on the pleadings questions were raised as to the party entitled to sue . . . but these possible questions were not argued . . ."[16] The case should not be regarded as authority for the mistaken proposition that an unincorporated club can sue in its own name; it cannot. The contracts under consideration were merely treated as having been made with the Jockey Club as a convenient shorthand to describe what, in strict legal analysis, should be described as a contract between the horse race entrant and each of the members of the Club.[17]

---

[12] Chitty on Contracts 27th ed., Volume 1, para. 2–079.

[13] [1929] 2 Ch 1, CA.

[14] The Jockey Club was incorporated by Royal Charter in 1970 following a merger with the National Hunt Committee.

[15] See at pp. 4–5: "It was not disputed that the contracts made by nominating a horse were, so far as the plaintiffs or any of them were parties to them, contracts with the Jockey Club, and that the other plaintiffs between them could properly be treated as the Jockey Club for that purpose."

[16] *Ibid.* at p. 7, in the judgment of Clauson J *infra*.

[17] See also Chitty on Contracts, *supra*., n. 12, Volume 1 para. 18–006 ("multilateral contracts"); and Phillips 90 LQR 499.

In the case of sporting bodies which are incorporated as companies, lack of **2.25** contractual capacity does not arise. Consequently directly enforceable horizontal contractual rights as between members to compel observance of the rules of the body do not assume the same analytical importance as in the case of unincorporated bodies. Mutual obligations between members may exist in relation to the rules of a particular competition or otherwise, depending upon the terms on which the body's rules are framed. In England, many of the most powerful governing bodies in sport are limited companies, including the Football Association (whose full title is the Football Association Limited) and the Premier League (the Football Association Premier League Limited). Under the corporate model, the incorporated sporting association can sue and be sued in its own name so that the representatives action procedure described above is not necessary or permissible.

Each member of the body, by joining it, will enter into a "vertical" contract **2.26** with the limited company, agreeing by virtue of that contract to abide by the rules established from time to time pursuant to the constitutional documents establishing the company, namely its memorandum and articles of association. Each member may also be a shareholder, often taking a nominal £1 share as a badge of membership, making him, her or it a member of the company in the company law sense of being a shareholder in the company. All shareholders in a company are bound by contract to observe the company's rules, since its articles of association take effect as a contract between its members.[18] But the extent of the members' mutual obligations may be limited by the rules themselves. Thus where one club complains about another club in the league, there will normally be a contractual right to complain to the association about another member on specified grounds. The association may then have its own powers of adjudication; or it may have been given the power under its constitution to respond by taking disciplinary action against the member complained against; or both members may be bound by a rule of the association to submit the dispute to arbitration.

So much then, for contracts binding sports bodies and their members. We **2.27** move on to look briefly at contracts of employment between players and their club, and between other employees and their club. In individual sports such as tennis and boxing it would be highly unusual to encounter a contract under which the individual competitor is employed to practise his or her sport. Individual sportsmen and women are normally self-employed, i.e., like barristers, they work on a case by case, or tournament by tournament, basis. In team sports, however, the norm is that the players, the coach, the administrative and ground staff, and others such as catering staff, are all employed under contracts of employment requiring them to render service to their employer, the club, which will normally be a limited company. At the highest level in professional team sports, particularly football, the terms of such contracts of employment

---

[18] Companies Act 1985 Section 14.

dealing with remuneration have become highly favourable to players whose negotiating position has become very strong of late. Negotiation of the terms of these contracts of employment is becoming something of a specialist legal discipline in its own right, ably offered by certain firms of solicitors in this country and elsewhere.[19] Such contracts may be negotiated by players' agents, who themselves, if fortunate, will receive a lucrative cut often expressed as a percentage of the player's remuneration or of the fee for obtaining his services.[20]

2.28 A contract of employment between a sports club and its playing and other staff brings into play the ordinary common law obligations of the parties to such a contract to observe its terms. The employer's right to receive service, the employee's right to remuneration, the right of both parties in certain circumstances to treat the contract as terminated, on notice or by reason of a repudiatory breach of contract by the other party, are all normal incidents of the employment relationships found in the world of sport as elsewhere. These common law rights can be extremely valuable in the highest echelons of sport, where claims for very large sums may turn (as in a current dispute between a major Premiership football club and its ex-manager) on whether the employee left of his own free will or was compelled to leave by the club; a point that may depend on the interpretation of conversations conducted in highly colloquial (and not necessarily intelligible) language.

2.29 Contracts of employment also act as the trigger for various statutory rights enjoyed by employees – i.e. by those employed under a contract of service – under English employment legislation, particularly the Employment Rights Act 1996. The scope of those statutory rights is a vast topic which it is not our task to explain in detail in this book.[21] Those statutory rights are, in the main, intended to benefit lower paid employees in more humble occupations in life than playing for Manchester United FC or managing Chelsea FC. The financial limits on compensation – with the important exception of cases involving discrimination on the ground of sex, race or disability – are too low to be of more than passing interest to our most highly paid celebrated sporting figures. They are however of considerable interest to the lower ranking members of staff employed by a club or league. Employment rights are touched on briefly in our discussion of the rights of players in sport (in the widest sense) in chapter four.

---

[19] See for example, Mel Goldberg, "Securing the Best Deal for Your Client: Players' Contracts, Salary Structures and Other Crucial Matters"; and Richard Moon, "Rugby and its Players; Where are We Now?", conference papers presented at Chelsea FC, 25 November 1996.

[20] As to agents' contracts, see *SLJ*, Vol. 4 issue 1, Miller, at p. 36 ("Not every agent is a bad guy"); *ibid*. Vol. 4 issue 3, Goldberg: "Football Contracts; Seeking the Best Deal for your Client", p. 101.

[21] For a good detailed exposition including the annotated text of the relevant statutes, see the loose leaf encyclopaedia, *Harvey on Industrial Relations and Employment Law* (Butterworths).

In professional sport, contracts of employment between players and their **2.30** club, and between officials and their club, often incorporate as part of their terms the rules under which the club operates within the sporting body of which it is a member. Thus, for example, football players, coaching staff and other club officials must abide by the rules of the FA and the league to which the club belongs. They must do so because the club which employs them is required by the rules of those bodies, to which it in turn belongs, to extract a contractual obligation on the part of its staff that they too undertake – though not themselves members of the FA or any league – to observe their rules. This is achieved by the promulgation of standard form contracts in a number of professional sports in this country. Regulation of this type by the sporting body limiting the freedom of the employing club and the player or official to negotiate their own terms, is common. However the legal validity of such restrictions can sometimes be questioned, as we explain in chapter four.

We have now mentioned two links in a chain of contracts – that between **2.31** player and club, and that between club and league or association. We next move one link further up the chain and observe that the league or association may itself be connected by contract with other bodies, either within one country or operating internationally, which are leagues of leagues or associations of associations. The structure of the Olympic movement is a case in point. The National Olympic Committees are affiliated to the International Olympic Committee (IOC). Various national athletic federations are likewise members of the International Amateur Athletic Federation (IAAF). A similar arrangement is found in football, in which the national associations in Europe are members of UEFA (which is a limited company incorporated in Switzerland); those associations are bound to observe UEFA's rules and require observance of them by their own members; UEFA in turn is bound by its membership of FIFA, football's world governing body, to observe the latter's rules and to require observance of them by its constituent members.

Such a chain of contractual obligations to observe rules emanating from a **2.32** higher level within the sport concerned ensures the supremacy of the world governing bodies within their sphere of influence, and also marks out the territory of autonomy for national and local or club level decision making in sport. Contract is the legal mechanism whereby local and national bodies in sport are obliged to comply with rules and rulings of their international sporting counterparts. In sports which are tightly structured, a matrix of interlocking contracts may need to be consulted by the sports lawyer in order to ascertain the extent of rights and obligations of a particular participant in the sport concerned. It follows that a player or coach may be subject to the disciplinary jurisdiction of a sporting body with which he or she is not in a contractual relationship. The body may exercise jurisdiction by virtue of its contact with the player's club, and the player may owe a contractual obligation to the club to submit to the disciplinary jurisdiction of the sporting body. Or, alternatively, a direct contractual nexus between the two may, depending on the circumstances, be implied or inferred by treating the club as agent for the individual in constituting an ad hoc contract, *inter alia*, to submit to the body's disciplinary jurisdiction.

2.33   This phenomenon can lead to proceedings, of a type further discussed in chapters three and seven, in which the player and his or her national association are on the same side of a dispute, pitted against the international association. The interests of the former may coincide with those of the player in a case where, for example, the national body has already acquitted the player of wrongdoing, and that acquittal is challenged on appeal by the international federation. This has occurred in cases before the CAS in which national bodies have decided that players should not be banned in alleged doping cases, in circumstances where the player is shortly to compete in an international competition for his or her country; while the international federation concerned has sought to have the verdict overturned and secure a ban which will weaken the national side in a forthcoming competition.[22]

2.34   Lawyers and others involved in sport also need to be aware that contract law is of prime importance in the promotion of one-off or individual sporting events. This is particularly common in boxing where attention is focussed so closely on individual bouts between boxers that the sport lends itself to contracts which govern particular fights rather than seasonally recurring competitions. An example of litigation arising out of such a contract can be found in *Lennox Lewis v. World Boxing Council and Frank Bruno*.[23] A contract to stage an exhibition match by the Harlem Globetrotters would be another example.

2.35   Still on the subject of contract in the law of sport, we now move away from contracts regulating the game itself, or employment within sport, and identify certain species of contract regulating commercial interests associated with sport. The first is the contract of sponsorship. Such a contract is found in two main forms. The first is a contract between a sportsman or woman, or a club, and a commercial body concerned to promote its products, whereby the sporting party undertakes certain obligations intended to assist in promoting the business of the commercial party, in return for financial support. The product of the sponsor may or may not be connected with sport. Examples of this type of contract are well known: a celebrated player or club agrees to use exclusively the product of a particular manufacturer. Thus, the 1998 World Cup Final between France and Brazil was also, in a sense, between Adidas and Nike, with the victory going to France and Adidas at the expense of Brazil and Nike. The second type of sponsorship contract is one between two commercial bodies, of which at least one has some connection with sport, and each of which is con-

---

[22] See eg. *Quigley v. Union Internationale de Tir*, CAS 94/129 and *Lehtinen v. FINA*, CAS 95/142. In *Quigley* the outcome directly affected the number of places open to the United States in an international shooting competition.

[23] CH Div., unreported, transcript 3 November 1995, Rattee J. Mr Lewis attempted unsuccessfully to obtain and injunction preventing Frank Bruno and the World Boxing Council (WBC) from accepting a challenge to Mr Bruno by Mike Tyson. Lennox Lewis subsequently became WBC world heavyweight champion.

cerned to promote its product. By the terms of the contract they agree to join forces in their promotion. An example of this type of contract is found in the recent collaboration between Capital Gold Sport, the London radio station, and Holsten Pils, a middle European lager brewed to taste a little bit different. During football matches the radio commentator was required to make this point, duly naming the product, at defined intervals.[24]

Another species of commercial contract ancillary to sporting activity, but **2.36** increasingly of critical importance to the financing of sport, is the contract regulating broadcasting rights. So important have these contracts become in relation to satellite television that they are now widely regarded as capable of determining the entire future, or lack of it, for particular sporting competitions, at least in highly paid professional team sports. A contract to allow broadcasting of a sporting event is, in its simplest form, no more than a licence to enter property coupled with the right to set up broadcasting equipment, and use it, on the property. However allocation of broadcasting contracts is frequently channelled through leagues and associations rather than individual clubs, in sophisticated modern commercial conditions. The impact of this type of contract, and the subjection of such contracts to English and European Community law rules regulating competition – in the economic, not the sporting sense – are examined in detail in chapter six of this book.

Finally we must mention in passing the effect of contract on the rights of spec- **2.37** tators at sporting events. The first important aspect of such contracts is that they determine whether, and on what terms, the spectator may have a right of admission, or a preferential right to purchase tickets for admission, to a sporting event. They may also determine the circumstances in which a club is entitled to refuse admission to a spectator who may believe he has a right of admission although he may arrive at the ground in possession of, say, numerous cans of lager or a wooden club. Secondly, the terms of a contract conferring a right of admission may have an effect on any claim the spectator may have in tort in the event that he or she is injured.[25] We will look further in chapter five at the effect such terms may have on claims in which personal injury is the cause of action.

---

[24] See Steele, "Sponsorship Contracts; 'the Full Monty' ", *SLJ*, Vol. 5 issue 3, p. 25; IAAF International Symposium on Sport and Law, Monte Carlo, 1991; Session 5 ("Sponsorship, etc."), p. 81; Session 6 ("Economic Interests of Athletes and their Agents: Trust Funds and Individual Sponsorship Contracts"), p. 113; "Commercial Exploitation of Sport", *SLJ*, Vol. 6 issue 2, p. 59; Abramson, *Whose Rights Are They Anyway?*, *ibid.* Vol. 4 issue 3, p. 100; IAAF; Sport and Law; Supplement; chapter 3 (Cooper: *Drafting of Sponsorship Contracts*); chapter 5 (Barr-Smith: *Television*); Steele, "Personality Merchandising, Licensing Rights and the March of the Turtles", *SLJ*, Vol. 5 issue 2, p. 14; Ebsworth, *ibid.* p. 34: "Reputations for Rent"; "Product Endorsement". *Conchita Martinez v. ElSpa* 30.3.99 (CA) (unreported) involved the interpretation of a promotional contract for a sportswoman where payments were dependent upon world ratings.
[25] See for example, *White v. Blackmore* [1972] 2 QB 651, CA (effect of exemption clause (accident at jalopy race meeting)).

Interpretation of the rules of sporting bodies

2.38 Thus far we have concentrated, in our description of the framework of law regulating sport, on the legal nature of sporting bodies, and the importance of contracts of various types in determining rights and obligations. We now consider briefly the way in which the rules of sporting bodies are and should be interpreted. Their interpretation is a matter of considerable importance. A court may have to determine the meaning and effect of contract terms found in the rules of such bodies. They are not necessarily interpreted in the same way as other kinds of contract terms found in other types of contract. The rules of sporting bodies are often drafted by lay people, not lawyers. This is changing, but many sports bodies, particularly smaller locally based ones, have not had their rules looked over by lawyers. Those which have are not guaranteed to have clearer rules – they may do. The CAS has recently criticised a lack of clarity in the rules of a body appearing before it, referring to "drafting that engenders controversy".[26] The task of construing the meaning of such rules is undoubtedly one for the court.[27] That task is not made any easier where additions and amendments have been made without reference to the structure as a whole.[28]

2.39 One thing at least is clear: that the rules may not take away from the court its function of determining their meaning. Older rules of sporting and other associations derived from times when they were less familiar with the risk of their rules being scrutinised in a court of law, frequently refer to the Chairman's decision on any matter of interpretation being "final and binding" or some similar expression. Such provisions necessarily mean that the "finality" of the association's own interpretation is subject to correct application of English law subordinate to a ruling of the court.[29] The jurisdiction of the courts cannot be ousted save by statute. This does not prevent a body from providing in its rules that a dispute of a particular type must be submitted to arbitration. Such clauses have long been recognised as valid[30] and enjoyed statutory recognition, most recently in the Arbitration Act 1996, as further explained in chapter eight.

[26] See *National Wheelchair Basketball Association v. International Paralympic Committee*, CAS 95/122 at paras. 34–5. See also *Cullwick v. FINA*, CAS 96/149, para 13; *Hall v. FINA*, CAS 98/218 paras 19–20.

[27] See *Williams v. Reason* [1988] 1 WLR 96, per Stephenson LJ at 104 (Welsh rugby union full-back's action in respect of an allegation that he had infringed the regulations of the International Rugby Football Board by writing a book for reward); cited also in Beloff, "Pitch Pool Rink . . . Court? Judicial Review in the Sporting World", [1989] PL 95, at 96–7.

[28] See also *Reel v. Holder* [1981] 3 All ER 321, per Lord Denning MR at p. 325 ("one can argue to and fro on the interpretation of these rules . . . the Courts have to reconcile all the various differences as best they can").

[29] See Chitty on Contracts, *supra.*, n. 12, Volume 1 paras. 16–038 and 039; Forbes, *The Law of Domestic Tribunals*, pp. 211–2; *Lee v. The Showmen's Guild of Great Britain* [1952] 2 QB 329, CA. Nor may CAS jurisdiction be ousted, *ITF v. Korda*, CAS 99/223, applying an earlier decision of the English Court of Appeal June 1999 (unreported).

[30] *Scott v. Avery* (1856) 5 HLC 811.

The rules of a sporting body should not be construed in an over technical **2.40** manner as though they were the words of a statute. They should be interpreted sensibly and in accordance with the spirit of the activity to which the rules apply. In the parallel field of trade union government, Lord Wilberforce has commented that such rulebooks:

> "are not drafted by parliamentary draftsmen. Courts of law must resist the temptation to construe them as if they were; for that is not how they would be understood by the members who are the parties to the agreement of which the terms, or some of them, are set out in the rule book, nor how they would be, and in fact were, understood by the experienced members of the court. Furthermore, it is not to be assumed, as in the case of a commercial contract which has been reduced into writing, that all the terms of the agreement are to be found in the rule book alone . . ."[31]

However, one should not take that proposition too far, for in another case Viscount Dilhorne took a more restricted view:-

> "I do not think that, because they are the rules of a union, different canons of construction should be applied to them than are applied to any other written documents. Our task is to construe them so as to give them a reasonable interpretation which accords with what in our opinion must have been intended."[32]

Although those two judicial statements of approach did not concern sporting bodies, the approach is similar in the sporting field. Thus in *Cowley v. Heatley*[33] Sir Nicholas Browne-Wilkinson V-C declined to interpret the French word "domicil" in the sense of a legal term of art derived from the rules of private international law, preferring to treat it instead, in the context of its use in the rules of an international sporting body determining eligibility to compete in international competitions, as an ordinary word.[34] Likewise in the international sporting arena the CAS, interpreting anti-doping provisions contained in the rules of an international federation, adopted a "purposive construction" of the relevant rules, stating that they were seeking to "discern the intention of the rule-makers, and not to frustrate it".[35]

From time to time the difficult question may arise, what effect, if any, the legal **2.41** form of a sporting association may have on the approach of the court required

---

[31] *Heatons Transport v. TGWU* [1973] AC 15, at 100–1.

[32] *British Actors' Equity Association v. Goring* [1978] ICR 791, at 794–5.

[33] *The Times*, 24 July 1986.

[34] A similar approach was applied to the rules of the Rugby Football League in *Widnes RFC v. Rugby Football League*, unreported, Ch Div, Parker J, 26 May 1995.

[35] *Cullwick v. FINA*, CAS 96/149, paras. 5.8–5.10, holding that prior notification of inhalation of a potentially permitted substance used to treat asthma was a pre-condition of its permitted status, and not merely a free standing duty.

to interpret its rules. In principle, words used in the rules of such a body ought to mean the same thing irrespective of whether the body is a limited company or an unincorporated association; but allowance must be made for the tighter drafting often encountered in the case of the former than the latter. In one particular context the scope of the general duty to act fairly, implied into the rules of sporting and other bodies exercising regulatory or disciplinary functions, has had to be considered with reference to the type of body exercising them. In *Gaiman v. National Association for Mental Health*[36] Megarry J had to consider this issue in the context of a claim by scientologists that a resolution requiring them to resign, passed without complying with the principles of natural justice, was invalid, as was the provision in the Association's articles of association under which the resolution had been adopted. The Association was a company limited not by shares but by guarantee.

2.42   The judge rejected the submission that every member had a right to be heard before being expelled. His analysis proceeded mainly from consideration of the different types of body to which the tenets of natural justice have been held to apply or not to apply. He did not fully accept the scientologists' proposition that:

> ". . . it would be odd if a club to which the principles of natural justice apply could be stripped of those principles merely because the club had been turned into a company limited by guarantee."[37]

He concluded that the position is different in the case of a corporation, from that of a club, for in the former but not the latter case, the governing council or directors of the corporation must exercise their powers bona fide in what they believe to be the interests of the corporation. However he added, importantly, that his conclusion might have been different if the case had been one in which the expelled members' livelihood or reputation had been in question. That was not the position, since the Association's principal object was to work for the preservation and development of mental health, i.e. it operated in what would now be called the voluntary sector.

2.43   In so far as Megarry J's conclusion turns on the proposition that the duty of fairness is the more onerous, the more is at stake for the person to whom the duty is owed, it is unobjectionable and consistent with a mass of other authority in fields as diverse as trade union law, the law relating to private clubs, and indeed sporting cases.[38] However the decision was only one on motion for interlocutory injunctions, not at full trial. In so far as the judge's conclusion might turn on the proposition that a body could absolve itself from the obligation to observe natural justice by changing its legal form from that of a club to that of

---

[36] [1971] Ch 317.
[37] *Gaiman, supra.*, n. 36 at p. 335D-E.
[38] The celebrated decision in *Russell v. Duke of Norfolk* [1948] 1 All ER 488 was among the authorities cited, at p. 336F in the decision.

a company (whether limited by shares or by guarantee), the decision appears questionable. The committee of a club should be required as a matter of contract to act in the best interests of the club, as the directors of a limited company must act in support of the company's interests. We take the view that the content of the duty of fairness ought not to be influenced, particularly in sport, by the legal form of the body owing the duty, but rather its content should depend on the subject matter under consideration and, especially, on whether a person's reputation or livelihood is at stake – as it clearly is in, for example, a case where doping or ball tampering is alleged.

Sport and the criminal law

Such cases also serve to remind us that those involved in sport may be accused **2.44** in disciplinary proceedings, or in criminal proceedings, or both, of conduct amounting to a criminal offence. Where crime and sport meet, the disciplinary function of the governing bodies overlaps with the state's role as enforcer of the criminal law. A recent example occurred when prosecutions were unsuccessfully brought in England against two goalkeepers and a businessman arising from an alleged plan to rig matches in return for money. We now move, at last, away from the law of contract and mention next, briefly, the function of the criminal law in sport. Needless to say, the criminal law is imposed and enforced by the state irrespective of any question of agreement between the parties. It is part of the general law of the land.

The impact of the criminal law in sport is examined more fully in chapter five. **2.45** In all countries, the criminal law affects the practice of sport. However, even under a penal régime, what sporting participants have agreed is not wholly irrelevant. Perhaps the most important function of the criminal law in sport is to lay down distinctions between conduct which is tolerated in the context of sports involving physical contact – and would not necessarily be tolerated outside that context – and conduct sufficiently extreme as to transgress the criminal law irrespective of its sporting context and, sometimes, irrespective of the consent of the victim. The law has a role to play in visiting with penal sanctions some very serious instances of violence on the field of play. Deliberate assault, as well as being a tort, is a criminal offence of varying gravity according to the seriousness of the injury inflicted.

The criminal law also serves to outlaw corruption in sport, making punish- **2.46** able the fraudulent manipulation of sporting competition, including match fixing and other forms of corruption such as the payment of illegal "backhanders" (in football parlance known as "bungs", particularly if paid in cash). Criminal sanctions against offences involving corruption in sport are becoming increasingly important in an era of high financial rewards and correspondingly increased temptation to err. Where the conduct complained of infringes the criminal law as well as any disciplinary rules to which the perpetrator is subject, the criminal courts have jurisdiction in the case additional to the jurisdiction of the relevant disciplinary bodies, and their powers of sanction are invariably greater.

2.47 The criminal law even prohibits some sporting activity altogether. We refer briefly in chapter five to some controversial forms of sport. This leads naturally into a discussion *en passant* of the question what a "sport" actually is, a question which has not yet seriously taxed the intellectual powers of sports lawyers but may do so in the future when legal systems include fully developed doctrines of sports law.

The law of tort

2.48 Without the need for any contract, the law of tort imposes negative obligations on certain classes of persons for the protection of other classes of persons, creating a right in the victim to damages or, sometimes, an injunction in circumstances where the victim suffers injury or damage through the wrongful act of the other person, called the tortfeasor or wrongdoer. The law of tort is not particularly concerned with sport over and above other forms of human activity, but an explanation of how tort law impacts on sporting activity is essential to a full account of the law relating to sport.

2.49 Torts occasioning personal injury require proof of deliberate assault or negligent infliction of injury. These are considered in chapter five. The courts remain the final judges of conduct on and around the field of play, though where the conduct complained of occurs in the actual course of a match, judges have generally been reluctant to interfere, preferring to leave such matters in the hands of referees and disciplinary bodies. However the English courts have in recent years shifted the focus away from their traditional pro-defendant approach, founded on the concept of acceptance of risk in the sporting arena, towards an approach which evinces a greater willingness than hitherto to hold participants in sport liable under the law of tort for physical injuries inflicted on the field of play.

2.50 Economic torts are also relevant in sport. There the wrongdoing consists of a deliberate act, not involving a breach of contract towards the victim, causing economic loss. Claims of this type usually arise in the course of disputes over access to competitions and in that context are touched on in chapter three, or over transfers of players between clubs, dealt with in chapter four. The essence of such a claim is usually the assertion that contractual relations are being interfered with. The relevant contract may be between a club and a player; between a league and a player; between a club and a league; or between any of the above and a commercial entity such as a sponsor or broadcasting company.

2.51 There are other torts which arise incidentally in the course of sport rather than as an intrinsic feature inherently likely to arise from the practice of sport. The best example is the tort of defamation, which is not specific to sport or different in the sporting field than in any other field, but which periodically gives rise to well publicised cases involving celebrated and notorious sporting figures. We do not consider that defamation merits separate treatment in its application to sport in a book such as this, and we therefore touch on it only in passing.

Public law

We consider in chapter eight the difficult and controversial question to what **2.52** extent sports law is public in character, and thus deserving of inclusion within the framework of administrative law. In England, the development of legal doctrine in the sporting field has, in some of the most important cases, occurred at the very frontier between public and private law.[39] Throughout the process whereby the law of England and Wales came to include a developed system of administrative law, uncertainty has dogged lawyers and the courts as to whether, and if so to what extent, rights of participation in sport and the right to fairness in sport, should form part of that body of administrative law, or should be treated as separate from it and concerned only with private rights.

It is no coincidence that sporting cases have made such a major contribution **2.53** to the debate over the nature of public rights during the formative period of English administrative law in the last thirty years or so. The vitality and importance of sport as a force in modern society corresponds to the place occupied by celebrated sporting cases in the development of our conception of public and private rights – or what can now even be called human rights. We set out more fully in chapter eight (and we touch on also in chapters three and seven) our reasons for rejecting the view that rights in sport are merely private in character. If they were, they would principally arise merely as a matter of contract; yet in *Nagle v. Fielden*[40] there was no contract but the court was prepared to countenance the grant of relief against an unfairly discriminatory practice in sport affecting a woman's ability to ply her trade as a trainer of horses.

The question whether sports law overlaps at all with public law is of great **2.54** importance from the standpoint of a theoretical foundation for sports law. But it is not just an academic question. We go on to consider in chapter eight the practical effects in sport of the present state of the law which normally denies judicial review as a remedy in sports law, with consequential ramifications for the form of proceedings, time limits and the types of remedy available.

---

[39] Examples are *Nagle v. Feilden* [1966] 2 QB 633, CA; *McInnes v. Onslow- Fane* [1978] 1 WLR 1520; *R v. Disciplinary Committee of the Jockey Club ex parte Aga Khan* [1993] 1 WLR 909, CA; and *Stevenage FC Limited v. The Football League Limited*, transcript 23 July 1996 and CA (1997) 9 Admin LR 109.

[40] *Supra*, n. 39.

Statute law

2.55 This is a short topic, for the role of legislation in sport is, in the United Kingdom, relatively slight. Indeed, we have already pointed out in chapter one that absence of frequent legislative intervention in sport is one of the features that differentiate sports law from activity based branches of the law. In England, domestic statute impacts little on sporting activity. This reflects the traditional laissez-faire attitude of the state, which usually proceeds from the premise that politicians should not run sport and that self-regulation should prevail where possible.

2.56 It is elementary that rules created by statute are superior to all other sources of law in this country; but our legislators are not disposed to use their powers to impose a code of sports law from the top downwards. There is little sign that Parliament is willing to take the lead in legislating widely in the sporting field. The only area of importance in which the state has, in this country, been moved to intervene in recent years, has been that of public safety and public order. We consider briefly in chapter five such legislation as has been enacted in England in support of those policy objectives. We are certainly no advocates of wholesale statutory regulation in sport. *Non sequitur* that the lack of it leads to the conclusion that sport is a purely private matter.

European Community law

2.57 The European Community (EC) has not adopted any legislative measures directly regulating the practice of sport itself within the European Union. It is possible that it may do so in the future, although the position is made more complicated by the fact that various European wide sporting bodies are active in promoting and administering particular sports, and the membership of many of them is wider than that of the European Union, as presently constituted. For example, Community law does not apply directly in Switzerland, a country whose law governs many sporting disputes, not least because of the presence there of the CAS, the International Olympic Committee, FIFA and UEFA among other organisations.

2.58 Community law is nonetheless of considerable importance in international sports law. Article 48 (now Article 39)[41] of the Treaty of Rome enacts the principle of the free movement of workers within the Community. It applies to sport in so far as sport is an economic activity within Article 2 of the Treaty. The same

---

[41] The Treaty of Amsterdam has resulted in the renumbering of the Articles of the Treaty of Rome. Throughout the book we have referred to the old number first, followed by the new number in brackets.

is true of the competition law provisions of Articles 85 (now Article 81) and 86 (now Article 82), now mirrored in domestic legislation in the form of the Competition Act 1998. Community law is applied by the CAS, even though it sits in Switzerland, in cases where the dispute falls within the scope of relevant EC law provisions.[42] A dispute still pending before the CAS raises questions under Article 52 (now Article 43) of the EC Treaty, requiring member states to abolish and not to introduce restrictions on the freedom of establishment of nationals in the territory of another member state; and Article 73b, guaranteeing freedom of movement of capital within the Community.

Community law forms part of our account in chapter three of the law gov- **2.59** erning access to sporting competitions, which can be affected by questions of competition law, using the term "competition" in its economic sense. Community law assumes considerable importance in our narrative in chapter four of the law relating to players' rights, and of the law relating to broadcasting and marketing in chapter six, in which competition law plays a central role.

Like English law, Community law insists on recognising a region of auton- **2.60** omy for the organisers of sport, within which the law will not interfere. This autonomy is afforded to rules which are characterised as being "of sporting interest only"; by way of an exception to the applicability of Community law. The dimensions of the exception are uncertain.[43] The frontier dividing purely sporting rules from other rules affecting sport as an economic activity, has not yet been precisely charted, and is under review by the CAS. The jurisprudence of the Court of Justice at Luxembourg has clearly identified the distinction but has not yet worked out its application in particular cases. The distinction is fundamental to our conception of sports law as explained in the previous chapter. European Community law has played a major part in sculpting that conception.

The European Convention on Human Rights

At the time of writing, the Human Rights Act 1998 has received the Royal **2.61** Assent[44] but, apart from certain administrative provisions, has not yet entered into force. Accordingly it is premature to speak of directly applicable rights under the European Convention in this country. Nevertheless, in our exposition of remedies in sports law in chapter eight, we make certain observations on the likely impact of the Act in the field of sport.

In summary the Act, when in force, will provide that most of the rights guar- **2.62** anteed by the European Convention shall have effect in domestic law. It will

[42] *AEK Athens FC and Slavia Prague FC v. UEFA*, Procedural Order of 17 July 1998, CAS 98/200, para. 29; *Beeuwsaert v. Fédération Internationale de Basketball* CAS 92/80, pp. 7–8.

[43] M. J. Beloff QC "The Sporting Exception in EU Competition Law", *European Current Law* (forthcoming) analyses the extent to which restraints of sporting interest only are outwith the reach of the Treaty provisions.

[44] The Royal Assent was bestowed on 9 November 1998.

place an obligation on public authorities, broadly defined, not to act in a manner incompatible with incorporated Convention rights. It will require domestic courts and tribunals to interpret legislation, where possible, in a manner consistent with those rights, and to take account of decisions emanating from the Court of Human Rights at Strasbourg, and from the (former) Commission on Human Rights there. It will empower the higher courts in England to declare domestic legislation incompatible with the incorporated Convention rights, and will enable courts and tribunals here to award damages and other remedies in respect of breaches of Convention rights, where a duty to observe them is owed.[45]

2.63 The potential of this momentous reforming measure to spur further development of the law relating to sport is substantial, but as yet an unknown quantity. The Human Rights Act 1998 is a constitutional reform comparable in its importance with the European Communities Act 1972. An assessment of its impact in sports law will have to await a future edition of this book. For the present, we confine ourselves to certain observations in chapters seven and eight about possible future developments in the application of human rights law to sport.

[45] See generally J. Wadham and H. Mountfield, *Blackstone's Guide to the Human Rights Act* (1999).

3

Access to Sporting Competitions

Introduction: entry criteria in sport

3.1 In this chapter we seek to explain the content of the law which determines **3.1** directly whether or not a particular individual, or a particular club in the case of team sports, may or may not take part in a particular competition, or generally in competitions administered by a particular sporting body. We are not concerned in this chapter to give an account of rules governing entitlement to participate in sport arising indirectly, through the medium of an employment or similar relationship between a player and a club. In those cases it is the club which is the primary competitor; the player's right to compete arises only indirectly, if he is selected to play by the club which employs his services and which itself is eligible to take part in particular competitions. Rights in sport arising indirectly in this way are examined next, in chapter four, under the heading of players' rights.

We are concerned here to consider the existence or otherwise of direct rights **3.2** to compete (and in some cases, obligations to compete) which the law, in certain circumstances, gives to individual players or, in the case of team sports, to clubs. The question whether and when such rights exist is a matter of profound importance to competitors and sports administrators alike. It is often taken for granted that, for example, the winner of the First Division football championship is entitled to compete in the Premier League the following season, or that the winner of the Grand National was eligible to enter it. But such commonplace propositions are derived from a set of rules establishing entry criteria for particular competitions, or for tournaments played under the auspices of a particular sporting association.

It is self-evident that such rules must exist, for access to sporting competitions **3.3** must be controlled if organised sport is to be conducted in an orderly fashion. The public's enjoyment of sport would be negated if competitions were a shambolic free-for-all. The Olympics would not command the attention of millions across the globe if entry were not restricted to those with proven ability to perform to a high standard through rigorous selection processes at national level. And it would be absurd to suppose that the Oxford versus Cambridge boat race could take place if the dark blues and the light blues had to contend with other motley crews aboard semi-afloat craft of differing shapes and sizes. Sport must be well organised if it is to be entertaining, as the public demands it must be. An important aspect of good organisation is that competitions should pitch against each other participants of potentially similar ability in comfortable and safe conditions, and on (figuratively and sometimes literally) a level playing field. A major contribution to the achievement of that objective is made by the application of entry criteria.

3.4 It falls, then, to the administrators of sport to devise, promulgate and apply the sets of rules which must govern rights of entry to sporting competition, if the public demand for entertainment from sport is to be satisfied. Such rules must separate those eligible to participate from those excluded from competing, a process which by its nature is likely, on occasion, to generate disputes over the application of entry criteria and even legal challenges brought by disappointed aspiring entrants to a particular competition or a particular type of sporting activity regulated by an association. These challenges may call into question either the validity of the relevant entry criteria themselves, or the manner in which they are applied to the aspiring participant in a particular case, or both.

3.5 Sometimes, as in the case of professional boxing in this country, a licence issued by the organiser of the sport is a precondition of entitlement to compete in all competitions organised or recognised by that body. If the body has quasi-monopolistic powers, failure to obtain such a licence may in practice prevent participation in the sport concerned at all. Where professional men and women earn their living from sport, either by direct competitive participation or through sport-related employment regulated by a sporting association, difficult questions may arise as to the extent to which the law is prepared to protect their livelihood.

3.6 Access to sporting competitions may be sought not only by aspiring entrants who are not yet members of the organising body. Those already eligible to compete, by virtue of membership of the body, possession of a licence, or performance on the field of play, may have to fulfil further criteria set by the organising body in order not to lose their eligibility. Once a person or club has attained entry, rules generally regulate continuing eligibility to participate in the following season or tournament. Simple examples are rules providing for the bottom clubs in a division of a league to be relegated or, if already in the bottom division, excluded from the league. Failure to win sufficient points to stay off the bottom of the table means failure to meet one of the criteria for entry to the same division in the following season.

3.7 A sportsman or woman, or a club, may wish to assert a legal right to participate in a particular competition or sport. The legal form of such a claim depends on the circumstances. One of several causes of action may be open to such a claimant, all founded on the assertion that the claimant fulfils the necessary entry criteria. The most likely types of proceeding are:

(1) a claim by an existing member of the organising body to enforce an existing contractual right to participate;
(2) a claim by a non-member of the organising body for a declaration to enforce a free standing non-contractual right to participate, or expectation of being permitted to participate; or

(3) a claim in tort by or against a third party – i.e. not the body which runs the competition – seeking to prevent inducement of a breach by the players or by the body which runs the competition of contractual rights to participate or to require participation.

Recently, attempts have also been made to establish rights of participation founded on the competition law provisions of the Treaty of Rome or under English domestic competition law previously enacted in the Restrictive Trade Practices Act 1976, now replaced by the Competition Act 1998. However no such attempt has yet, so far as we are aware, succeeded.

We consider these various causes of action below. In doing so, we begin by **3.8** considering the content of the duty of fairness owed by sporting bodies to aspiring entrants who are not, but seek to become, members of the body. Next, we consider the position where there is, or is alleged to be, a pre-existing contractual relationship establishing continuing eligibility rules, between the aspiring entrant and the sporting body. We will then look at non-contract based claims in which an outsider attempts to surmount a more difficult hurdle by asserting a right to join a competition or take part in a competition or sport without prior membership of the organising body. Finally, we will consider in brief certain related topics including the potential for asserting rights of access to sporting competition in reliance on domestic and European competition law.

Necessarily, there is a degree of overlap between this chapter and chapter **3.9** seven which deals with the exercise of disciplinary jurisdiction in the sporting field. Disciplinary sanctions can include match bans or loss of the right to enter or apply to enter particular competitions. However, in this chapter we are concerned with the law regulating entry to a competition other than as a disciplinary measure. The body of law governing sporting discipline may shade into the topic under consideration here in that the distinction between exclusion from a competition as a punishment and exclusion from a competition through noncompliance with entry criteria, may be a fine one to draw on the facts of a particular case. But the two phenomena are conceptually distinct, for the former presupposes that the person excluded possessed a right (or at any rate a contingent right) to compete which he has lost as a punishment; while the latter entails that he never possessed such a right in the first place.

The duty of fairness owed by sporting bodies to outsiders

The right to take part in particular competitions may hinge on membership of **3.10** the body organising them, as in the case of the Football League and the Premier League in association football. Or it may depend on possession of a licence issued by a controlling authority. This is the case in professional boxing in Britain, in which challengers for the various titles, as well as promoters and managers, must possess a licence issued by the British Boxing Board of Control, which administers those competitions under its auspices. Applications for such a licence, or for membership of a sporting body, are usually dependent on the fulfilment of entry criteria. If a dispute arises as to whether those criteria have been met, the applicant may wish to obtain a finding to that effect in legal proceedings and, relying on that finding, seek an order compelling the body to admit the applicant as a member.

3.11   But such a claim may invite the retort that the applicant for membership has no pre-existing relationship with the body which he (or it) seeks to join, and therefore no right – not even a contingent right – to join, even on the footing that the relevant entry criteria are met. The question is an important one, since an applicant for membership of a sporting body, or an applicant for a licence issued by such a body, will be able to achieve little through litigation if even a successful claim to have fulfilled the necessary criteria does not generate the legal remedy necessary to confer entitlement to participate. We therefore consider the question here.

3.12   Historically, the courts have declined to compel an association by injunction to admit a member which it is unwilling to admit. The law's reluctance to enforce admission against the will of the association's existing members is firmly grounded in the notion of freedom of contract. Given that, as we saw in chapter two, a club is regarded as a combination of individuals who voluntarily associate together in a common activity (whether by contract only, or as an incorporated body), traditional freedom of contract would point to the conclusion that it is for the existing members, and not the court, to decide whether to accept a new applicant. However the possibility of a court being prepared to depart from that position and, in an extreme case, compel a sporting body to accept a new member against its will, cannot be excluded.

3.13   In *Stevenage Borough FC Limited v. The Football League Limited*.[1] the issue was whether Stevenage was entitled to membership of the Football League, having won the Vauxhall Conference and thus fulfilled the playing requirement for promotion to the League, but having failed to meet the League's criteria relating to its ground and finances by the date set by the League. As we shall see shortly, Stevenage challenged the validity of the criteria which it had failed to meet, but the League argued that, on authority,[2] the court ought not to order it to admit Stevenage as a new member against the will of the League even if the allegedly offending criteria were struck down as invalid. Carnwath J noted that:

---

[1] Unreported, 23 July 1996, Carnwath J; Stevenage's appeal was dismissed but on the ground of delay (1997) 9 Admin LR 109, CA.

[2] *R. v. Master and Warden of the Company of Surgeons in London* (1759) 2 Burr. 893; *R. v. Dr. Askew et al.* (1768) 4 Burr. 2185 (both decisions of courts presided over by Lord Mansfield); *R. v. Benchers of Lincoln's Inn* (1825) 4 B. and C. 854; *Faramus v. Film Artistes Association* [1964] AC 925, at 941–942 (Lord Evershed); and at 944–948 (Lords Hodson and Pearce); *Lee v. The Showmen's Guild of Great Britain* [1952] 2 QB 329, CA, per Denning LJ at 342–4, citing *Baird v. Wells* (1890) 44 Ch Div 661, per Stirling J at 676.

"no case has been cited in which the court has forced a private organisation to admit a member against its will, even where the organisation controls the member's right to work"[3]

but concluded that it was unnecessary to decide the point. If, as we believe, sporting bodies should be viewed as bodies which sometimes exercise public or quasi-public functions,[4] the objection to enforced admission based on freedom of contract is less than compelling.

The related question whether a body which issues licences to participate in **3.14** professional sporting activity could be compelled by injunction to issue such a licence, would probably yield the same answer. We do not, in principle, agree with the view that a body which controls the right to work in a particular profession and can therefore make or break people's livelihoods, can – as a matter going to the court's jurisdiction – never be compelled to admit as a member or issue a licence to a person who fulfills the criteria announced in advance by the body as qualifying that person for membership or a licence. In an appropriately strong case there seems no objection in principle to the court asserting jurisdiction to require the existing members of the association to stand by their word; though we recognise that such cases would be rare.

The cases in which it has been said that an injunction will not be granted to **3.15** compel membership of a club are best viewed as authority only for the proposition that the discretion to grant such an injunction will be exercised sparingly and with extreme caution, in view of the lack of a pre-existing legal relationship between the parties. Indeed in *Nagle v. Feilden*[5] a Court of Appeal presided over by Lord Denning MR pointedly refused to strike out a claim which included a claim for an injunction ordering the stewards of the Jockey Club to grant the plaintiff a licence to train horses, which she said had repeatedly been refused affecting her livelihood, for no other reason than that she was a woman. *Nagle*'s case therefore establishes that our view is arguable.[6]

Nevertheless, given that it is at least extremely difficult to gain access **3.16** to sporting competitions as an outsider without prior membership of the body controlling access, and against its will, the question next arises to what extent the outsider can achieve the lesser objective of requiring the sporting body to conduct itself in a fair manner when considering applications for participation rights and compelling the body by court order to reconsider a failed application for participation rights. Here we encounter the now well-known duty of domestic tribunals to act fairly. That duty has evolved through a series

---

[3] Transcript at pp. 34–6.

[4] A view we discuss further in chapter eight, which draws strong support from, *inter alia*, Carnwath J's judgment in *Stevenage*, transcript pp. 35–40.

[5] [1966] 2 QB 633, CA.

[6] See Lord Denning's judgment at p. 647F ("she may have a good case to ask for a declaration and injunction").

of cases,[7] mainly (in the case of sporting bodies) concerning disciplinary decisions. These are discussed more fully in chapter seven. But there have also been non-disciplinary cases raising the question of the scope of the duty to act fairly, in which access to sporting competitions or professional activities in the sporting field, has been at stake. In the United States of America, the courts have regarded failure to observe fair procedures in adopting and enforcing the rules of sporting associations as a ground for holding them invalid. Failure to entertain comments on a proposed change of rule by those affected, prior to adopting it, can lead to invalidation of the rule.[8] Even a rule which is reasonable in itself and adopted after fair consideration can be invalidated if it fails to set forth guidelines for its application or fails to allow the affected party a hearing.[9]

3.17   In England, the content of the duty to act fairly includes at least an obligation not to refuse an application for membership or a licence on grounds which can be characterised as arbitrary and capricious. The best known authority for this proposition is *McInnes v. Onslow-Fane*,[10] a case brought in private law which has profoundly influenced English public law both within and outside the sporting field. Within that field, Megarry J's decision can fairly be regarded as the first English judicial development in the shaping of a corpus of law particular to sport; a process now, arguably, sufficiently advanced to warrant use of the term "sports law". Mr McInnes was a former amateur boxer who had become a professional promoter and had held a promoter's licence issued by the British Boxing Board of Control which had expired. He had also held a Master of Ceremonies' licence which had been withdrawn after a disagreement. After applying and reapplying for a manager's licence several times, he brought an action asserting the right to be informed of the "case against him", and an oral

---

[7] See for example, *Russell v. Duke of Norfolk* [1949] 1 All ER 109, CA; *Breen v. Amalgamated Engineering Union* [1971] 2 QB 175 (especially the celebrated passage from Lord Denning MR's dissenting judgment at pp. 189–191).

[8] *Linseman v. World Hockey Association* 439 F. Supp. 1315, 1322 (D. Conn. 1977) (rejection of league rule prohibiting persons under 20 years old from playing hockey); *Gunter Harz Sports, Inc.*, 511 F. Supp. at 1122 (". . . in order to avoid liability under Section 1 of the Sherman Act . . . [a league's] notice and comment procedure concerning the proposed rule [must be] sufficient to inform those potentially affected by the rule . . . as well as to allow interested parties to be heard regarding the proposed rule.")

[9] *Los Angeles Memorial Coliseum Commission v. National Football League*, 726 F. 2d. 1381, 1397 (9th Circuit 1984), US Court of Appeals (rule against team relocation held contrary to Sherman Act, *inter alia*, because it lacked an "objective set of guidelines" as well as any "procedural mechanism" for applying such guidelines); similarly, *Denver Rockets v. All-Pro Management*, 325 F. Supp. 1049 (C.D. Ca. 1971) NBA rule prohibiting teams from signing players until at least four years after their high school graduation struck down as there was "no provision for even the most rudimentary hearing before the four-year college rule is applied to exlude an individual player".

[10] [1978] 1 WLR 1520, Megarry J.

hearing of his application, while the Board maintained that it had considered his application and rejected it, and that he was not entitled to a hearing.

The judgment of Megarry J broke new ground by drawing attention to three **3.18** categories of cases, which he termed application cases, forfeiture cases and expectation cases. In straightforward application cases, where "nothing is being taken away",[11] an applicant for membership of a body had no right to observance of the tenets of natural justice or fairness; the body was free to admit him or deny him membership on whatever grounds it wished. In forfeiture cases, where there is a threat to take something away, as in the case of an existing member subject to disciplinary sanctions, the member has the right to be treated fairly by being given notice of the allegations, an opportunity to speak in defence against them, and an unbiased tribunal to consider them.[12] In an intermediate category of cases, which the judge termed the "expectation" cases, the applicant is seeking membership or a licence but in circumstances giving him the right to expect that it will be granted unless there is reason to the contrary, as where he has previously been considered suitable to hold a licence. The judge held that Mr McInnes' case was not an expectation case, since he had never before held a manager's licence, only a promoter's licence and a Master of Ceremonies' licence, which were insufficient to establish the expectation.

He went on to consider the extent of the duty owed to an applicant in a pure **3.19** application case. The Board accepted a limited duty to reach a conclusion honestly and without caprice or bias,[13] but denied any more extensive duty to give the applicant notice of the reasons why it was minded to refuse his application, and an opportunity to make representations in support of his application and in rebuttal of those reasons. The judge agreed, noting that the courts had recently brought about "a marked expansion of the ambit of the requirements of natural justice and fairness, reaching beyond statute and contract",[14] but pointing out that refusal of the licence did not entail any finding of dishonesty or reprehensi-

---

[11] *Ibid.*, at 1529D-G

[12] *Ibid.*; the content of the duty of fairness in disciplinary cases is more fully considered in chapter seven.

[13] In the US, a court has refused to uphold summarily a hockey league's decision to bar a team from competition, on the ground that the league was "motivated by financial considerations to eliminate [the team] as a competing amateur hockey team", an allegation that had to be balanced against the league's assertion that the decision was made "in order to develop American amateur hockey and improve the quality of young American hockey players." (*Tondas v. Amateur Hockey Association of the US*, 438 F. Supp. 310 (W.D.N.Y. 1977), at 314). Similarly in *Heldman v. US Lawn Tennis Association*, 354 F. Supp. 1241, 1252 (S.D.N.Y. 1973) the court held that a rule barring players who had participated in tournaments sanctioned by other leagues would "cross the line of legality" if the rule were "intended to or [had] the natural effect of defeating competition", such as an intent to prohibit the plaintiff, a tennis promoter, from establishing a competing tennis circuit.

[14] *Ibid.* at 1528A-B, citing *Nagle v. Feilden, supra.*, n. 5.

ble conduct; and doubting that the notion of a "right to work" could be said to include the right to begin a new career of the worker's choice, as distinct from continuing an existing career. However, it may be doubted whether the judge's limitation of the duty owed to an applicant represents the modern law: in particular where refusal impacts upon a person's reputation, he may have an entitlement to make representations.[15]

3.20   In *Wayde v. New South Wales Rugby League Ltd.*[16] the High Court of Australia had to consider a claim by representatives of the Western Suburbs District Rugby League Football Club to set aside the decision of the League to reduce from thirteen to twelve the number of clubs allowed to participate in the following season's premiership competition, and for an injunction restraining the League from implementing the decision. The Board of the League, which was a limited company operating under New South Wales company law statutes, had made the decision in what it considered to be the interests of the company, i.e. of the League. The excluded club, represented by the plaintiffs, was aggrieved at the decision, being the unfortunate recipient of notification that its entry for the 1985 competition had been refused. The plaintiffs had initially obtained an order from Hodgson J restraining the League from implementing the decisions on the ground that they were oppressive[17] to the plaintiffs, but the League had obtained the reversal of that decision by the Court of Appeal.

3.21   On a further appeal to the High Court of Australia, five judges rejected the claim, accepting the League's reasons for reducing the size of the premiership competition – in essence, too many matches in a too long season – observing that the League was expressly constituted to promote the best interests of the sport and empowered to determine which clubs should be entitled to participate in competitions conducted by it, and distinguishing sharply between adverse impact on the complainant club, and oppressive or unfairly prejudicial conduct which was not made out.[18] Thus, recourse to company law procedures did not enable the disappointed aspiring entrant to narrow the width of the discretion allowed to sporting bodies by the courts in administering sporting competitions. The decision was an important vindication of the power of sporting bodies to control access to their own competitions.

---

[15] See de Smith, Woolf and Jowell, *Judicial Review of Administrative Action*, 5th ed. (Sweet and Maxwell, 1995) at paras. 8–008 to 8–010, 8–023, 8–027; *R. v. Gaming Board for Great Britain ex p Benaim* [1970] 2 QB 417.

[16] (1985) 61 ALR 225.

[17] Under Section 320 of the New South Wales Companies Code, a statutory variant, with common ancestry, of our own Section 459 of the Companies Act 1985 (as amended by the Companies Act 1989).

[18] Noted in Beloff and Kerr, "Judical Control of Sporting Bodies: The Commonwealth Jurisprudence", *SLJ* (1995) Vol. 3 issue 1, at p. 8.

In *Ray v. Professional Golfers Association Limited*[19] a golfer excluded from   **3.22**
certain competitions through failure in golf related examinations set by the
Association of which he was a provisional, or trainee, member, rather opti-
mistically sought access to golfing competitions relying, *inter alia*, on denial of
an opportunity to be heard by the Association. The claim failed. The right to
continued participation in golfing competitions under the Association's auspices was subject, under its rules, to success in the examinations. The duty of
fairness was satisfied by giving the plaintiff the opportunity to show his suit-
ability by sitting the examinations. Fairness did not require any right to make
further representations.

3.23 We can conclude this part of our survey by observing that the content of   **3.23**
the duty to act fairly depends on the context in which it arises. Where access to
a sporting competition or a livelihood derived from sport is in issue, the English
courts are sympathetic to claims where arbitrary or capricious conduct is genuinely shown, or where a willingness to listen to representations is absent in circumstances where it should be present. But the sympathy of the court will
always be tempered with proper respect for autonomy in decision making by
sporting bodies best placed to regulate access to competitions, and also to the
various ways of earning a living which such competitions generate.

Contractual and contract related claims concerning access to sporting competitions

Having considered the procedural duty on sporting bodies not to treat outsiders   **3.24**
arbitrarily, we turn next to consider the substantive law determining whether or
not, in a particular case, the aspiring entrant can establish his right to enter the
fray. We deal with this aspect of the law by looking first at claims to participation rights which depend in some way on assertion of a contractual right,
whether directly against the administering body, or in a tort claim against a
third party charged with procuring a breach by the administering body of the
aspiring entrant's contractual right to participate. Secondly, we consider non-
contract-based claims founded on fulfilment of valid eligibility criteria, conferring an expectation or alleged "right" to compete.

In a simple case, there may be a contractual right to compete in a certain com-   **3.25**
petition by virtue of a pre-existing contract of membership between an individual or club and a sporting body, on terms which confer a right to compete on
fulfilment of entry criteria. An example would be the right of a football club to
compete in the second division of a football league after winning the third division championship the previous season. In that example, the club has a contract
of membership of the league on terms set out in the league's rules, as properly
amended from time to time. Those rules include the normal rule that the winner

[19] Unreported, 15 April 1997.

of the third division championship shall be promoted to the second division. Winning the third division championship thus converts the club's contingent right to compete the second division into an accrued right to do so.

3.26   The winning club's right of access to the second division could be enforced in the normal way, by obtaining an injunction to restrain breach of contract. If the league attempted to block the promotion of the winning club, it would be in breach of the club's contractual right to promotion unless some other rule entitled the league to stop the promotion taking effect. In that example, the respective rights of the parties are clear. Precisely because they are clear, the practitioner of sports law is not confronted with numerous authorities to support the existence of enforceable contractual rights to promotion. Such rights are deduced from established principles of ordinary contract law.

3.27   But in other cases contractual rights to compete are less clear. In *Lennox Lewis v. World Boxing Council and Frank Bruno*,[20] the well-known boxer Lennox Lewis claimed against the promoters of the WBC world heavyweight title a contractual right to challenge the holder, Frank Bruno, for that title, and sought an injunction restraining Bruno from accepting a challenge instead from the notorious boxer Mike Tyson, which Lewis claimed would be a breach of his contractual right to challenge for the title. Lewis relied on his status as "designated official mandatory challenger" under the WBC's rules, which defined the challenger as:

> "the number one rated contender, or the next higher rated if the number one cannot or will not participate in the bout, or if he is the winner of an official tournament to determine an official challenger."

3.28   Lewis had defeated Lionel Butler in an official WBC "elimination bout" shortly before the hearing, only to find that the WBC proposed to pit Tyson and not Lewis against Bruno for the title. The parties agreed that Lewis was in a contractual relationship with the WBC arising out of the arrangements for the final eliminator bout, even though he was not a member of the WBC, whose members were associations, not individuals, but the scope of the WBC's obligation to Lewis was in issue. The WBC and Bruno denied that Lewis had a contractual right to challenge for the title by virtue of having won the eliminator bout, claiming that the only obligation was to "officially sanction" the eliminator bout, without any right in the winner to challenge for the world title. In the event the court did not determine what Lewis' rights were because it decided that England was not the appropriate forum for the dispute, the claim against Frank Bruno in England being merely ancillary to the main claim against the WBC. But the case throws up an interesting example of direct contractual relations arising between a competitor and a federation in relation to rights to compete.

---

[20] Unreported, Rattee J, 3 November 1995. Lewis lost the application for an urgent injunction, but later became the WBC world heavyweight champion.

Another case in which disputed rights of participation were ventilated in an   **3.29**
English court was *Widnes v. Rugby Football League*.[21] The RFL had decided to
start a new league competition, with the benefit of monies helpfully provided by
a company controlled by Mr Rupert Murdoch, in return for broadcasting rights.
Widnes, a traditionally great club which had suffered from poor form, was not
offered a place in the new league having finished poorly at the end of the previous season. Widnes argued, *inter alia*, that it had a contractual right by virtue of
its membership of the RFL to a place in the new league, and went so far as to
seek an injunction, in a representative action against officers of the RFL,
restraining the RFL from proceeding with the new league at all unless Widnes
were accommodated within it. The claim failed on the facts, as Widnes could
not show that the RFL had acted outside its rules in adopting a structure for the
new league which excluded Widnes from it. The *Widnes* case was an instance of
administrative realignment in sport prompted by commercial sponsorship in
pursuit of profit from broadcasting, causing a disappointed club, left out in the
cold, to attempt a forced entry via the court to the newly constituted league.

Litigation over rights of access to sporting competition may take the form of   **3.30**
a battle between sporting bodies seeking to preserve their role in administering
competitions, and commercial interests determined to supplant them, using
financial muscle to attract the players and legal proceedings, or the threat of
them, to induce the sporting body to come to terms. In *News Limited v.
Australian Rugby Football League Limited*,[22] the League responded to rumours
that *News Limited* was preparing to establish a new superleague, to replace the
national competition, by offering twenty clubs admission to the national competition for five seasons on condition that each agreed to participate for those
seasons, and not in any other competition unless conducted or approved by the
League. The twenty clubs signed a contractual commitment to that effect. *News
Limited* sought to bring the League on board, but the League rejected overtures
that would have given it control over the proposed new superleague. *News
Limited* then signed up large numbers of players and coaches for new clubs
intended to form a competing superleague of twelve clubs. It also sued the
League, seeking to set aside the latter's agreements on competition law grounds.
The League, and clubs aligned with it and not with *News Limited*, counter-
claimed against the clubs aligned with *News Limited* for breach of those latter
clubs' contractual duties. Coaches and players who promised services to new
clubs aligned with *News Limited*, would plainly be acting in breach of their duty
of fidelity to the clubs which employed them if they fulfilled those promises. The
League and its allied clubs also claimed against *News Limited* for inducing
breach of those contractual duties by enticing away coaches, players and rebel
clubs.

[21] Unreported, Parker J, High Court (Manchester), 26 May 1995.
[22] (1996) 135 ALR 33; and on appeal to the Full Court of the Federal Court of
Australia, see (1997) 139 ALR 193.

3.31   The trial judge, partly applying Australian competition law and partly on common law contractual principles, held that the League's contracts were valid, were not vitiated by economic duress and were consequently enforceable. It followed that *News Limited* was liable for inducing breach of those contracts. The judge made orders the effect of which was to prevent the *News Limited* interests from setting up a superleague until the year 2000. However the full Federal Court allowed an appeal brought by the *News Limited* interests (except as to the economic duress argument which was not pursued on appeal), set aside the judge's orders, declared some of the relevant contracts void on competition law grounds and restrained the League from enforcing them, but held that certain other limited contractual rights were valid and enforceable, had been breached, and that *News Limited* had induced breaches of them. The Court commented that the orders made at trial had had the practical effect of reducing substantially, if not removing altogether, whatever competitive advantage and head start the *News Limited* interests might have gained from its tortious conduct.[23]

3.32   For present purposes, the case illustrates no more significant legal principle than that a club may not gain access to a competition if to do so would be inconsistent with its prior contractual commitment owed to the organiser of another competition, to participate in that other competition. The organiser of the first competition can prevent this by injunction. This is merely an example of the principle that prior contractual obligations (if valid) take precedence over subsequent ones – a simple point but one worth restating in an epoch in which substantial financial rewards may tempt clubs away from their allegiance to their governing bodies.

3.33   Similar upheavals have recently threatened rugby union in England.[24] A well publicised dispute in 1996 between the Rugby Football Union in England and the unions of France and the Celtic nations over the future of the Five Nations Championship,[25] was eventually settled, but not before France and the Celtic nations had publicly threatened to exclude England from the tournament, again over a dispute involving broadcasting rights. A club threatened with exclusion from a competition in breach of its contractual right to participate, could in principle obtain an injunction preventing its exclusion, though this would be subject to the discretion of the court which could be reluctant to interfere in the face of clear evidence that the club was not wanted by the other competitors; especially if the plaintiff club had been guilty of any delay.[26]

---

[23] *News Limited v. Australian Rugby Football League Limited* (1997) 139 ALR 193, judgment of the court at 293.

[24] The advent of professional rugby union also gave rise to the celebrated "EPRUC" dispute in which players threatened to break away from the Rugby Football Union. That dispute has not lead to litigation either.

[25] The dispute briefly flaired up again in early 1999; see for example, *The Sunday Times*, 17 January 1999 ("England threatened with Five Nations Axe").

[26] See *Newport AFC v. The Football Association of Wales Limited*, unreported, 12 April 1995, Blackburne J, further discussed in chapter eight.

International tournaments such as the Five Nations Championship usually take place by virtue of a contractual arrangement between the promoters of each country's team. The same type of contract may establish the rights of sporting clubs within one country to participate in competitions run by different sporting bodies, as in the case of the English league football clubs which take part in league and cup competitions established under a complex interlocking set of contractual rules regulating relations between the clubs, their players (and other staff) and the governing organs, the Football Association, the Football League, the Premier League and other less prominent bodies such as the Vauxhall Conference.

Litigation over access to competitions can take place in an international set- **3.34** ting as well as in the domestic courts. The dispute before the CAS involving football clubs controlled by the English National Investment Company plc (ENIC) is an example.[27] In May 1998 UEFA adopted a rule which prevented two or more clubs in common ownership from participating in the same UEFA administered competition. At the time UEFA organised the Champions' League, the European Cup Winners' Cup and the UEFA Cup. One of the three clubs controlled by ENIC, AEK Athens FC, had already qualified for the UEFA Cup before the rule was adopted; another, SK Slavia Prague, qualified shortly after the rule had been announced. UEFA purported to exclude AEK Athens from the UEFA Cup, adopting a "points coefficient" system to determine which of the two clubs should be excluded. But the clubs successfully obtained an interim ruling by the CAS, applying Swiss and EC law, preventing UEFA from excluding AEK Athens, mainly on the ground that AEK had already qualified and UEFA could not lawfully deprive it retroactively of its place in the competition.[28]

The President of the Ordinary Arbitration Division of the CAS did not found **3.35** her decision on conventional contractual principles as a court in a common law jurisdiction might have done. The clubs were not direct members of UEFA but were "indirect members", in that they were members of their respective national associations which in turn were members of UEFA. The Swiss law of associations protects the rights of indirect members in certain circumstances, in particular, by imposing a duty of good faith on the association's governing organs. But the same result could have been reached on a common law analysis by inferring the existence of limited direct contractual relations between the clubs and

---

[27] *AEK Athens FC and Slavia Prague FC v. UEFA*, CAS 98/200, interim order of 17 July 1998.

[28] The foundation in Swiss law for this proposition was Article 2 of the Swiss Civil Code, as applied in the decision of the Swiss Supreme Court in *Grossen* (ATF 121 III 350) where the Swiss Wrestling Federation was ordered to pay damages to a wrestler whom it had excluded from a competition after he had qualified, by imposing a late change to the admission requirements designed to favour another wrestler. The Association was held to have breached its duty of good faith. (After winning one round, AEK Athens was knocked out by Vitesse Arnhem of the Netherlands.)

UEFA, from the clubs' membership of their national associations, the obligations of the clubs and those national associations to comply with UEFA's competition rules, and from subjection of the clubs to UEFA's disciplinary régime.

3.36   The existence of contractual rights in the examples given above, of a type which would ground a possible injunction to restrain exclusion of a club from a competition, is usually evidenced by documents, such as the rulebooks of the relevant sporting bodies and minutes of meetings of those bodies or of "umbrella" bodies linking national associations at international level – as in the case of International Rugby Football Board, an unincorporated association whose members are the national unions of the countries taking part in the Five Nations Championship. The willingness or otherwise of the court to grant an injunction in a case of threatened wrongful exclusion from a tournament, is another matter. The court would have a discretion, and, depending on the facts, might well decide to leave the wrongfully excluded club to its remedy in damages, by analogy with cases in which the courts have refused to grant injunctions whose effect is to compel close cooperation between parties at loggerheads with each other.[29]

The restraint of trade doctrine

3.37 In most of the cases we have been considering so far, the aspiring entrant to a competition alleges a contractual right to compete relying simply on the terms of the relevant contract. The case law, however, frequently arises from disputes in which the plaintiff seeks to avoid a term of the relevant contract which would negate his (or its) right to compete, or would subject it to the judgment of an unfavourably disposed sporting body. Unless the terms of an existing contract entitle the would-be participant to argue that he qualifies to compete under them, it is necessary for him first to get rid of other terms which, on their face, constitute a bar to entry.[30] Most commonly, the plaintiff club or player seeks to achieve this by arguing that terms which block entry constitute an unreasonable restraint of trade and as such are unlawful and void, or more accurately voidable at the plaintiff's option.

3.38   The restraint of trade doctrine is a well known inhabitant of the common law world of contract. It is not our purpose here to give a detailed exposition of its nature and scope.[31] The doctrine evolved as an aspect of a broader public

[29] The scope of injunctive relief to secure participation rights in sport is further discussed in the context of remedies in chapter eight.

[30] In the litigation against UEFA involving clubs controlled by ENIC, already mentioned, the clubs sought to achieve this but, the claims proceeding under Swiss not English law, without using the common law restraint of trade doctrine considered here.

[31] See Chitty on Contracts 27th ed., chapter sixteen for a comprehensive account of the doctrine.

policy bar to the enforcement of certain contract terms considered offensive; such as contracts to commit crime, to promote immoral purposes, and so forth. Contracts in unreasonable restraint of trade developed as a category of contract terms looked upon with disfavour by the common law courts on the ground that they inhibit freedom of trade and prevent the party restrained from exercising his talents and earning a living from them. Modern legal systems now have more sophisticated means of eliminating anti-competitive behaviour, and these are considered elsewhere in this book; but the restraint of trade doctrine is mentioned here because it has a particular relevance to regulation of access to sporting competitions.

It is sufficient for our purposes to set out the salient features of the doctrine **3.39** which figure where it is relied upon in sports law cases. First, the leading authority of *Nordenfelt v. Maxim Nordenfelt Guns and Ammunition Co Limited*[32] established that a contractual term embodying a restraint prohibiting the exercise of a trade was prima facie void as an interference with individual liberty of action, but might be valid and justified if shown to be reasonable by reference to the interests of the parties concerned and the interests of the public. This requirement has since, in ordinary commercial restraint of trade cases, sometimes been expressed by the proposition that the restraint must go no further than is reasonably necessary to protect a legitimate interest of the party in whose favour it operates.[33]

Second, the courts are more inclined to strike down as unreasonable some **3.40** forms of restraint than others. A contract term restraining an employee after the end of his contract of employment will be more jealously scrutinised and less readily allowed to stand than a similar contract term exacted by the purchaser from the vendor on a sale of the goodwill of a business.[34] This is important in the context of sport, for it is inherent in arrangements regulating sporting competition that governing bodies must have powers to determine criteria for entry to competitions. If such criteria were subjected to the degree of scrutiny practised in relation to restraining clauses in employment contracts preventing ex-employees from working for competitors or soliciting customers, few sporting restraints would survive and orderly regulation of sport would be severely hampered. Consequently, as we shall see, eligibility criteria are viewed with relative tolerance by the English courts.

Thirdly, the onus of proving the reasonableness of a contractual restraint as **3.41** between the parties to it, is on the party seeking to justify and benefit from the restraining term in the contract; whereas the onus of proving that a contractual restraint operates in a manner contrary to the public interest is on the party seeking to strike down the provision. The latter question is one of public policy,

---

[32] [1894] AC 535, HL.

[33] See for example, *Esso Petroleum Co Limited v. Harper's Garage (Stourport) Limited* [1968] AC 269, HL.

[34] See *Herbert Morris Limited v. Saxelby* [1916] AC 688, HL.

not merely one of fact, and the onus is "no light one".[35] In sporting cases it had been thought, until recently, by practitioners in the field that the onus of proving unreasonableness lay with the sporting body seeking to rely on a restraint. This view proceeds from the perceived applicability of orthodox commercial law principles to sporting contracts (and, as we shall see below, also to non-contractual arrangements).[36]

3.42   However, in *Stevenage Borough FC Limited v. The Football League Limited*[37] Carnwath J accepted the League's submission that the doctrine as applied in the sporting context brought into play the public interest aspect of the test as expounded in the *Nordenfelt* case, despite the controversial case law (considered below in chapter eight) normally ruling out the availability of judicial review of decisions of sporting bodies. Carnwath J drew on that case law, coupled with other authorities in which the Court of Appeal, presided over by Lord Denning MR, had developed the duty of fairness owed by domestic tribunals,[38] and concluded from his scholarly analysis that the orthodox view "gives insufficient weight to the distinction between the private and the public aspect" and that:

> "where the restraint is part of a system of control imposed by a body exercising regulatory powers in the public interest. . . [and] the system of control itself can be seen as in the public interest then. . . the onus lies on those seeking to challenge it to show that the particular rules under attack are unreasonable in the narrow sense."[39]

3.43 Importantly, Carnwath J's reference to the "narrow sense" of unreasonableness reflected his view that the standard to be applied was probably that applicable in judicial review of public law decisions; thus requiring a plaintiff to show that the rule under challenge was arbitrary or capricious (the standard apparently considered correct by the Court of Appeal in *Nagle's* case), or that it operated so harshly that its adoption was wholly outside the scope of the discretion of any reasonable sporting body. This conclusion tallied with the comment made by Megarry J in *McInnes v. Onslow-Fane*[40] cited in several judgments since:

> "I think that the courts must be slow to allow any implied obligation to be fair to be used as a means of bringing before the courts for review honest decisions

---

[35] Per Lord Parker in *Attorney-General of Australia v. Adelaide Steamship Company* [1913] AC 781, 796–7.

[36] See *Eastham v. Newcastle United FC Limited* [1964] 1 Ch 413, Wilberforce J; *Greig v. Insole* [1978] 1 WLR 302, Slade J; *Newport AFC Limited v. The Football Association of Wales Limited*, unreported, 12 April 1995, Blackburne J.

[37] Unreported, transcript, 23 July 1996.

[38] *Nagle v. Feilden* [1966] 2 QB 633; *Enderby Town FC v. The Football Association* [1971] Ch 591; *Breen v. Amalgamated Engineering Union* [1971] 2 QB 175.

[39] Transcript, 23 July 1996, at pp. 38–8.

[40] *Supra*, n. 10.

of bodies exercising jurisdiction over sporting and other activities which those bodies are far better fitted to judge than the courts. This is so even where those bodies are concerned with the means of livelihood of those who take part in those activities. Concepts of natural justice and the duty to be fair must not be allowed to discredit themselves by making unreasonable requirements and imposing undue burdens. Bodies . . . which promote a public interest by seeking to maintain high standards in a field of activity which otherwise might easily become degraded and corrupt ought not to be hampered in their work without good cause. Such bodies should not be tempted or coerced into granting licences that otherwise they would refuse by reason of the courts having imposed on them a procedure for refusal which facilitates litigation against them . . . The individual must indeed be protected against improprieties; but any claim of this or anything more must be balanced against what the public interest requires."[41]

The contribution of Megarry J in the late 1970s, and that of Carnwath J in the late 1990s, lend support to our view that sports law leans more heavily toward the public than the private law end of the legal spectrum.[42]

The upshot of the preceding discussion is that it is not always clear (1) where **3.44** the onus of proof lies in a restraint of trade case involving a sporting body, nor (2) precisely how the applicable standard of reasonableness should be formulated. We favour the view of Carnwath J which equates decisions and rules of sporting bodies with those of other bodies which exercise public functions. However we recognise that the contrary view founded on orthodox contract principles has enjoyed some judicial support[43] and cannot be dismissed. A practical consequence of such uncertainty in this area of sports law is that, in preparing a restraint of trade challenge, or in preparing to resist such a challenge, a party would be well advised to plead and prove his or her case by identifying the specific factors which go to establish, or as the case may be, to undermine, the reasonableness of the rule for decision under attack.[44]

It is striking that cases concerning access to sporting competitions, as distinct **3.45** from those involving employment related players' rights against their clubs, have for the most part failed insofar as founded on avoidance of rules alleged to

---

[41] *Ibid.* at p. 1535 F-H.

[42] See per contra, Hoffmann LJ in the *Aga Khan* case [1993] 1 WLR 909, CA; and see the discussion of judicial review in chapter eight and in Beloff and Kerr, *Why Aga Khan is Wrong* [1996] JR 30.

[43] For example, from Blackburne J in *Newport AFC Limited v. The Football Association of Wales Limited*, unreported, transcript 12 April 1995 (full trial, Blackburne J; Jacob J's decision granting an interlocutory injunction is reported at [1995] 2 All ER 87).

[44] Cf *Pharmaceutical Society of Great Britain v. Dickson* [1970] AC 403, HL, where the claim succeeded on the basis that justification for the Society's strictures on new entrants to the pharmacists profession had not been pleaded or proved. Cf. *Conteh v. Onslow Fane* and others (1) TLR. 5 June 1975 (2) TLR. 26 June 1975.

operate in unreasonable restraint of trade. Thus in *Gasser v. Stinson*[45] it was held that an automatic disqualification rule of the International Amateur Athletic Federation (IAAF) applicable to any athlete, regardless of guilty intent, whose urine should contain a banned substance, was justified by the need for certainty and avoidance of evidential difficulties even though "the morally innocent may have to suffer in order to ensure that the guilty do not escape".[46]

3.46 Again, in *Ray v. Professional Golfers Association Limited*,[47] a challenge to golfing related examination requirements as a precondition of eligibility to compete in certain tournaments, was rejected. Although the learned judge appeared to hold (in our respectful view wrongly) that the restraint of trade doctrine did not apply at all because Mr Ray's contract was a training contract and not a trading contract, the judge clearly felt that any restraint in the contract was justified and referred to very full evidence from the Association showing why it was justified: namely, in order to protect the Association's legitimate interest in maintaining high standards by encouraging the concept of the well-rounded professional, versed not only in playing golf but in knowledge of other golf-related matters.

3.47 Subsequently in *Williams v. Pugh*,[48] the Cardiff and Ebbw Vale rugby football clubs alleged against the Welsh Rugby Union that the latter's insistence that clubs wishing to be part of the union must commit themselves to membership of it for at least ten years, was in unreasonable restraint of trade. Refusal to enter the ten year commitment meant not being allowed to play in a European competition the following season. Popplewell J considered the Union's evidence supporting its submission that the ten year requirement was incontestably reasonable and that the decision to adopt it was neither arbitrary nor capricious. He did not have to decide whether the submission would succeed at a full trial, since the application was for an interim injunction, which the clubs obtained on the basis that their restraint of trade argument was not doomed to fail, and that the injunction should be granted to allow the clubs the chance of competing in Europe, and in the Premier League, the following season, applying classical principles governing interlocutory injunctions.[49]

3.48 Challenges to contractual or other provisions operating in restraint of trade, including those setting criteria for entry to sporting competitions, sometimes bring into play the question whether an offending term can be severed from other valid parts of the document. The law relating to severance of unlawful terms is well established from case law in the commercial field, and we do not

---

[45] Unreported, 15 June 1988, Scott J.
[46] Transcript, 15 June 1988, at p. 39G.
[47] Unreported, 15 April 1997, Judge Dyer QC.
[48] Unreported, transcript, 23 July 1997.
[49] See *American Cyanamid v. Ethicon Limited* [1975] AC 397, HL.

propose to treat it in detail here.[50] The guiding principles are (1) that the court will not rewrite a contract (or other document) by altering its nature; (2) the court will not sever unenforceable parts of the document unless it accords with public policy to do so; and (3) it must be possible to excise the offending parts of the document without affecting the sense of the remaining valid parts – a process usually explained by referring to use of a "blue pencil" which can be used to delete portions of the document but not to write in corrections on it. The question of severance arose in the *Stevenage* case, already mentioned above, but did not have to be decided because both the judge and Court of Appeal decided to refuse any relief in the exercise of discretion despite criticisms of the Football League's entry criteria.

Non-contractual claims relating to access to sporting competitions: free standing challenges

We look next at cases in which aspiring entrants to sporting competitions have **3.49** attempted, sometimes in reliance on the restraint of trade doctrine and some-times independently of it, to achieve access to a sporting competition through litigation in the absence of any contractual right, contingent or otherwise, to participate. We have already mentioned the difficulty faced by a non-member of an organisation seeking to compel membership of it. However, a plaintiff whose private rights are affected by the operation of a restraint may seek a declaration from the court that the restraint is invalid, and possibly, an injunction prevent-ing it from being acted upon. It used to be supposed that a declaration could not be obtained for want of any underlying cause of action. But it is now established that, where private rights are affected, the free standing right to a declaration is itself a cause of action sufficient to found declaratory relief.[51]

The restraint of trade doctrine has taken tentative migratory steps into the **3.50** quasi-regulatory field, having begun life as quintessentially a creature of nine-teenth century contract law. This expansion of the doctrine occurred, no doubt, with the advent of an increasingly regulated society leading to a developed system of administrative law. A feature of this development was the extension of the doctrine to non-contractual cases, sporting cases among them. Carnwath J has rejected the argument that the doctrine is too blunt an instrument with which to judge the conduct of a sporting body in setting and

---

[50] For a useful exposition in the leading standard work on contract law, see Chitty on Contracts *supra.*, n. 31, Volume 1 chapter 16 at paras. 16–164 et seq.

[51] See *Eastham v. Newcastle United FC Limited* [1964] Ch 413 at 443, Wilberforce J; Zamir and Woolf, The Declaratory Judgment, 2nd ed. at pp. 203–11, esp. 210 (paras. 5.24); *Greig v. Insole* [1978] 1 WLR 302 (Slade J); cf. *Pharmaceutical Society v. Dickson* [1970] AC 403, 440 C, per Lord Wilberforce ("The 'doctrine' of restraint of trade has never been limited to contractual arrangements . . .").

enforcing standards governing entry to sporting competitions; preferring instead to adapt the doctrine, putting the onus of proof on the plaintiff and affording a considerable margin of appreciation to the sporting body.[52] Scott J rejected a similar argument in *Gasser v. Stinson*, pointing out that authority favoured applicability of the doctrine to the rules of the International Amateur Athletic Federation of which the plaintiff athlete was not a member.[53]

3.51 The court's jurisdiction to grant a declaration at the suit of an employee not only against his employer but also against "the association of employers whose rules or regulations place an unjustifiable restraint on his liberty of employment" was established by the judgment of Wilberforce J in *Eastham v. Newcastle United FC Limited*.[54] George Eastham was able to obtain a declaration not merely against his employer, Newcastle United Football Club, but against the Football League, of which Newcastle, but not he, was a member. That approach was followed in *Greig v. Insole*[55] by Slade J,[56] in which the plaintiff cricketers succeeded in obtaining declarations against the International Cricket Council (ICC) and the Test and County Cricket Board (TCCB) (in each case through their representatives), though the plaintiffs were members of neither body. In *Eastham*, the restrictive retention and transfer system embodied in rules of the Football Association and of the Football League were declared invalid as an unreasonable restraint of trade. In *Greig*, rule changes intended to prevent English county cricketers from signing contracts to play in test matches organised outside the auspices of the ICC and TCCB, and promoted by Mr Kerry Packer, were held to constitute a tortious inducement to players to break their contracts with Mr Packer's company (which also sued) and an unlawful interference with those contracts, which were not themselves an unreasonable restraint of trade. The cricketers obtained declarations of invalidity in relation to the ICC and TCCB's rule changes similar to that obtained by George Eastham. Thus he secured access to league football (his club in fact consenting to his transfer to Arsenal before the trial) after refusing to contract with Newcastle on expiry of his previous contract. And the cricketers in *Greig* vindicated their right of access to Mr Packer's competition which the established cricketing powers had sought to deny them.

3.52 However a swimmer named Cowley was less felicitous in litigation she undertook against officers of the Commonwealth Games Federation which had sought to declare her ineligible to compete in the Commonwealth Games representing England. She challenged the decision of the officers of the Federation

---

[52] *Stevenage Borough FC v. Football League Limited*, *supra.*, n. 37.

[53] See likewise Scott J's subsequent decision in *Watson v. Prager* [1991] 1 WLR 726, at 745 D-F.

[54] [1964] 1 Ch 413, at 440–6. The passage cited from p. 446 follows a useful review of prior non-sporting authority.

[55] [1978] 1 WLR 302.

[56] See at p. 345 E-H.

that she was not "domiciled" in England, within the meaning of that word in the relevant rule requiring that the competitor must be domiciled in the country she represents. The decision turned on the meaning of the French word "domicil" in its context. Sir Nicholas Browne-Wilkinson V-C said that it was not necessary for the court to decide the further question whether Miss Cowley had the necessary standing to bring an action for a declaration against a body with which she had no contractual relationship. He held that, if he had jurisdiction to grant the declaration in question, he would not do so in any event, citing the abstentionist approach embodied in the dictum of Megarry J already quoted above.[57] He is also famously reported in *The Times* as having said in his judgment:

> "Sport would be better served if there was not running litigation at repeated intervals by people seeking to challenge the decisions of the regulating bodies."

But the jurisdiction to entertain such proceedings and grant relief is not seriously in doubt, whether the challenge is founded on restraint of trade or, as in *Cowley v. Heatley*, on alleged misconstruction by the sporting body of its own rules.

Indeed in one New Zealand case the right to bring proceedings for a declara- **3.53** tion was stretched to its very limits, the plaintiffs having remarkably tenuous links to the defendant body, the New Zealand Rugby Football Union Inc. In this celebrated litigation two members of local rugby football clubs in Auckland sought an injunction to stop the defendant Union from accepting an invitation for the All Blacks to tour South Africa. Initially they failed on the ground of lack of standing to bring the action, but, on appeal the Court of Appeal in Wellington decided that they had sufficient standing as they were linked through a chain of contracts to the defendant Union. An interim injunction was granted and the tour of South Africa became administratively impossible as a result, though an appeal was pending. The plaintiffs therefore achieved their objective of stopping the tour, although their private rights were affected only to the extent that their local clubs had the right to appoint delegates to be members of the Auckland Union which in turn was affiliated to the defendant New Zealand Union which had accepted the invitation. Thus the plaintiffs were members of clubs whose delegates were members of a member of the defendant.[58]

Mention should be made of the successful action by Newport Football Club **3.54** and two other clubs against the Football Association of Wales in which the clubs succeeded both in obtaining an interim injunction and, at the full trial in 1995, a declaration that the Welsh FA's resolution preventing Welsh football clubs

---

[57] *Cowley v. Heatley, The Times*, 24 July 1986.
[58] *Finnigan v. New Zealand Rugby Football Union Inc.* [1985] 2 NZLR 159; noted in Beloff and Kerr, "Judicial Control of Sporting Bodies : The Commonwealth Jurisprudence", *SLJ* Vol. 3 issue 1 (1995), at p. 8. For an example of an Antipodean case similar to *Eastham, supra.*, n. 54, see *Kemp v. New Zealand Rugby Football League Inc.* [1989] 3 NZLR 463, HC.

from playing in the English Football League, and to prevent them playing home matches in Wales other than within the Welsh FA, was invalid as an unreasonable restraint of trade. The interim injunction allowed them, pending the full trial, to play home matches in Wales during the 1994–95 football season. At the full trial Blackburne J held, adopting orthodox restraint of trade principles, that the decisions under attack went further than was reasonably necessary for the protection of the Welsh FA's legitimate interest in promoting and administering football in Wales.[59]

3.55 The *Newport* challenge predictably succeeded because the Welsh FA had overestimated the scope of its power to allow or prohibit its member clubs (and indeed ex-member clubs, for the three clubs resigned from the FA of Wales before commencing proceedings) to play football in Wales, on grounds unrelated either to performance on the field of play or the quality of facilities available. By contrast Stevenage Borough Football Club, and before it, Enfield Town Football Club, failed to gain access to higher level competitions administered by bodies of which they were not members, but whose entry criteria relating to performance on the field of play they had satisfied by winning the lower level competition.[60]

3.56 Finally under this heading we return to cases brought before the CAS, but by individuals, in which access to sporting competition has had to be adjudicated upon. We have already mentioned the (ongoing) ENIC litigation in the context of rights of access to top level European football competitions. On the other side of the Atlantic, in a case heard in Montreal in March 1996,[61] the issue was whether José Cruz, a baseball player born in Puerto Rico and a Puerto Rican national but with USA citizenship, was entitled to choose to play baseball for the USA national team, or whether the Puerto Rican federation was entitled to insist that he should play exclusively for Puerto Rico. The International Baseball Federation had been unable to resolve the dispute and had initiated a reference to arbitration before the CAS.

3.57 The Puerto Rican Federation argued that nationality and citizenship are not synonymous; that Cruz had US citizenship only, not US nationality; and that he should not be allowed to play against his own country. The respondent federation contended that the Olympic Charter recognised the right of an athlete to choose between playing for his country of birth and his country of citizenship,

---

[59] *Newport AFC Limited v. The Football Association of Wales Limited* [1995] 2 All ER 87, Jacob J (interim injunction); *ibid.*, unreported, transcript 12 April 1995 (full trial, Blackburne J).

[60] See *Stevenage Borough FC Limited v. The Football League Limited*, at first instance, Carnwath J, unreported, 23 July 1996; cf. *Enfield Town FC*, arbitration (1995), Sir Michael Kerr and two senior QCs, referred to at pp. 39–40 of Carnwath J's judgment. Enfield Town's restraint of trade based challenge to the Conference's financial criteria, which it had failed to meet, was unsuccessful on the facts.

[61] *Puerto Rico Amateur Baseball Federation v. USA Baseball*, CAS 95/132, 15 March 1996.

and that Cruz having chosen the USA, his choice must be respected. The panel decided that the source of applicable law was the Olympic Charter to which express reference was made in the rules of the International Baseball Association. Applying the relevant provisions of the Olympic Charter,[62] it decided that Cruz possessed two nationalities; that the Olympic Charter recognised dual nationality; that an athlete could choose which country he wished to represent in such cases, but could not elect more than one country; that Cruz had elected to play for the USA and had not played for Puerto Rico; and that his choice to play for the USA was valid.

In two further decisions of the CAS sitting in Sydney and Melbourne in July **3.58** 1996, decided within ten days of each other with opposite outcomes,[63] cyclists challenged their exclusion from selection for the Australian Olympic team due to compete in Atlanta in the 1996 Olympics. In the first case, Lynette Nixon argued that the selectors had not followed the criteria for selection set out in the Federation's document issued in January 1996, by failing to take into account performance in certain races in Europe in which she had taken part, and by failing to take account of psychological and physiological test results. She sought an order that the selectors should be required to reconsider the selection of the Australian Olympic team taking account of those factors. The jurisdiction of the CAS was established by an appeal agreement and was accepted by the parties. The applicable law was not dealt with in the brief written decision. The claim failed on the facts and on the construction of the selection criteria.

In the other case, Kathryn Watt sought to quash a decision of the same **3.59** Federation to select another cyclist in preference to her to represent Australia in the women's 3,000 metres track cycling event, and further requested an order that the Federation honour a written guarantee that Watt would be selected. The parties agreed in a live telephone link up to submit the dispute to arbitration at very short notice. Four days later Winneke J, President of the Court of Appeal of Victoria, gave his decision in favour of Kathryn Watt. The case was extremely unusual in that the Federation had actually announced to the media that it had "guaranteed Kathy Watt's nomination as the rider in the Women's 3000m individual pursuit at the Atlanta Olympic Games in July", though the "guarantee" was qualified in the event of illness or a "unique ride" by another competitor "equal or near to the new world record".[64] The judge noted the caution which courts traditionally exercise in interfering with decisions of domestic bodies (citing *McInnes v. Onslow-Fane*) but held that the CAS was not a court of law but an arbitral body whose very purpose was to entertain disputes referred to it, *inter alia*, by agreement. He regarded the agreement to submit the

---

[62] Rules 45 and 46 and their respective bye-laws, concerning eligibility and nationality of competitors.

[63] *Nixon v. Australian Cycling Federation Inc.*, CAS 96/152, and *Watt v. Australian Cycling Federation Inc.*, CAS 96/153.

[64] CAS 96/153, transcript at pp. 8–9.

matter to arbitration by way of an appeal as requiring him to determine whether the decision was arrived at fairly and with due and proper regard to the interests of the appellant.[65]

3.60   He found in favour of the appellant cyclist, on the basis that her legitimate expectation of selection had been unfairly denied by the Federation in that the guarantee had been reneged upon without cause, and that Watt had relied on the guarantee by spending time, effort and money in preparing herself in accordance with a training schedule set by the Federation's coach and agreed to by the Federation. In a strong decision worthy of Lord Denning's most celebrated contributions to this field of law, yet not one apparently founded on any contract, Winneke J held that the Federation was "duty bound to honour its commitment to the Appellant unless circumstances of the type which qualified that commitment came to pass".[66] He declined to remit the matter back to the Federation for further consideration and directed it to nominate Watt instead of the other cyclist. For good measure, he stated as a general proposition that:

> "Where a sporting organization, in circumstances deemed by it to be appropriate, chooses to depart from its established rules of selection procedure and to nominate, in advance, a particular athlete as its selected choice for a particular event and, in doing so, creates expectations in and obligations upon that individual, then in my view it should be bound by its choice unless proper justification can be demonstrated for revoking it."[67]

Winneke J's decision could be regarded as the high water mark of judicial interventionism in the affairs of sporting bodies exercising discretion in the selection of competitors. He noted that the decision should be regarded as confined to its own facts, and it should not be assumed that the general proposition cited above can necessarily be applied to other factual situations in other jurisdictions.

3.61   In the first case to be heard before the Ad Hoc Division of the CAS at the 1996 Olympic Games in Atlanta,[68] the US Swimming Federation, supported by the German and Netherlands swimming teams, challenged a decision of the International Swimming Federation (FINA) to allow the Irish gold medallist Michelle Smith to compete in the 400 metres freestyle. Had the challenge succeeded, a formidable rival to the celebrated US swimmer Janet Evans would have been eliminated while still on dry land. The basis of the complaint was that Ms Smith's entry had been submitted too late. In a swift decision given the night before the race, the panel of arbitrators decided that as late entries for specific

---

[65]   CAS 96/153, transcript at pp. 12–13.

[66]   *Ibid*. at p. 18.

[67]   *Ibid*. at p. 27.

[68]   *US Swimming v. FINA*, CAS Ad Hoc Division, 21 July 1996, reported in Mealey's International Arbitration Report, February 1997 at pp. 25–6, by Gabrielle Kaufmann-Kohler, President of the Ordinary Arbitration Division of CAS, and President of the Ad Hoc Division in Atlanta.

events were frequent in many sports, and as FINA's rules did not impose a stricter régime than in other sports, it would be unfair to single out one late entrant and penalise her with disqualification. Ms Smith won the gold medal the following day.

Competition law and access to sporting competitions

We have already touched in chapter two on certain rules derived from **3.62** Community law, and their domestic law equivalent, intended to penalise and render void certain practices constituting unfair competition. We will have more to say about competition law rules in chapters four and six, when dealing with players' rights and broadcasting rights. The impact of such rules on rights of access to sporting competitions is more limited, and it is necessary to mention them only briefly in the present context. The rules which fall to be considered are, principally, those contained in Articles 85 and 86 (now 81 and 82) of the Treaty of Rome. They are mirrored by the domestic provisions of the Competition Act 1998, which will be interpreted in the light of, and so as to give effect to, their European origin. A fuller introduction to the general scope of those provisions will be found in chapter six, since their application to the marketing of sport is more important than their role in regulating the actual practice of sport.

Competition law seeks to ensure a state of free and fair competition between **3.63** participants in a particular market by targeting trade practices which have the effect of restricting or distorting competition. Anti-competitive behaviour may eliminate competitors from the market place altogether; or it may prevent or deter competitors from entering it. However, competitors and potential competitors may also be eliminated and excluded from the market precisely because the market in question is a competitive one. Thus, undertakings which are inefficient and unable to compete with more successful competitors will eventually fail. Competition law theory holds that this is of benefit to consumers; indeed, the main object of a competition régime is to achieve free, competitive markets with efficient participants. The task of competition law is to distinguish between the use of legitimate and illegitimate means of eliminating competitors from the market.

Thus far, we are speaking in general of "competition" in its economic sense, **3.64** not specifically of competition in the sporting arena. It is self-evident that rules regulating access to sporting competitions by definition have the effect of preventing some players from playing in the competition. An aspiring entrant may be disentitled from taking part, perhaps because club facilities are inadequate, or because the player has not paid his subscription, or simply because he has been knocked out by another competitor in the previous round. Decisions or rules regulating access to sporting competitions do not *per se* infringe competition law. They do so only if they result in a distortion or restriction of competition. As in other fields, competition law must distinguish in the sporting field between legitimate and illegitimate rules and decisions regulating access to sporting competitions.

3.65   A rule regulating access to a sporting competition may have to be assessed under Article 85 (now Article 81) of the Treaty of Rome to determine whether it constitutes a decision by an association of undertakings; and under Article 86 (now Article 82) to determine whether, properly analysed, it is a decision taken by an undertaking which occupies a dominant position within the market.[69] The applicable principles are, in the main, common to both provisions. In order to escape condemnation as anti-competitive, the rules under scrutiny must be reasonable, objective in nature and capable of application in a non-discriminatory manner. As yet there is no direct European authority in the sporting field for that proposition,[70] but it logically follows from authorities dealing with the similar issues that arise in the context of rules regulating membership of trade associations.[71]

3.66   In the *Stevenage FC* case,[72] it was argued by the plaintiff club that the requirement that clubs that win the Vauxhall Conference must fulfil certain criteria relating to the quality of the ground facilities and their financial soundness,

---

[69] See the more detailed discussion in chapter six, for a fuller account of this body of law.

[70] See Cases T–528/93, etc. *Metropole Television v. Commission* [1996] 5 *CMLR* 386, [1996] ECR II–649m at paragraph 102; (entry criteria must be precise); see also *Cauliflowers*, OJ 1978 L21/23, [1978] 1 *CMLR* D66, where access to the auctions selling 90% of Brittany's cauliflowers, artichokes and early potatoes were restricted to dealers who, *inter alia*, established a local packing centre, even though most of the vegetables were auctioned pre-packed. The Commission held that Article 85(1) was infringed. The agreement did not qualify for exemption under Article 85(3) since the conditions of admission were neither reasonable nor objective. See also *Sarabex*, VIIIth Report on Competition Policy (1978), at points 35–37 (market entry cartels should be under strict governmental supervision, criteria must be precise, there must be procedural safeguards); *Spa Monopole/GDB*, XXIIIrd Report on Competition Policy (1993) at point 240.

[71] Cf. the position in the United States of America, where the federal appeals courts have declined to follow the reasoning in a case in which a federal trial court judge had upheld the National Basketball Association's refusal to allow a plaintiff to acquire control of a basketball team, on the basis of a league rule against multiple ownership. The trial judge had reasoned that the plaintiff was seeking to join the NBA in a partnership for profit, not to compete with it. The US Court of Appeals rejected the judge's premise that "there could never be any competition among league members", concluding instead that "it is well established that [sports] clubs also compete with each other . . . for things like fan support, players, coaches, ticket sales, local broadcast revenues, and sale of team paraphernalia": see *Sullivan v. NFL*, 34 F. 3d 1091 (1st Circuit 1994), disapproving the reasoning in *Levin v. NBA*, 385 F. Supp. 149 (S.D.N.Y. 1974); see too *Mid-South v. NFL*, 720 F. 2d 772, 787 n.9 (3rd Circuit 1983), cert. denied, 467 U.S. 1215 (1984) in which the Court of Appeals also refused to embrace the reasoning in *Levin*; see also *Piazza v. Major League Baseball*, 831 F. Supp. 420, 430 (E.D. Pa. 1993) (disapproval of potential buyer restricted competition in market for baseball clubs).

[72] *Supra*, n. 60, at first instance, Carnwath J, unreported, 23 July 1996.

before being admitted to the League, was contrary to Article 85 of the Treaty of Rome in that the criteria were more onerous than those imposed upon clubs which were already members of the Football League. This argument would have had considerable attraction in that the disparity between the standard applied to existing members and that applied to new applicants for membership could be said to show a lack of objectivity. However the court did need to decide that point since the club failed to surmount the hurdle of demonstrating that the measure under attack had an appreciable effect, actual or potential, on trade between member states of the European Community.

More recently, returning to the *AEK Athens* litigation before the CAS,[73]   **3.67** UEFA's rule preventing commonly owned clubs from taking part in the same competition has been under challenge by the clubs affected on the ground that it infringes, *inter alia*, Articles 85 and 86 (now Articles 81 and 82) of the Treaty of Rome. The clubs argued that the Regulation fell within the scope of Article 85(1) (81(1)) in that it was not necessary to protect the integrity of European football competitions and was disproportionate in its impact to the attainment of that objective, in particular because it applied in blanket fashion and did not allow for exceptions in cases where, for instance, the common owner would pass a "fit and proper person" test.[74] As it had not been notified to the Commission it should, therefore, be declared void pursuant to Article 85(2) (81(2)). The clubs further argued that UEFA enjoys a position of dominance in the market for European football competitions, and that the decision to adopt the rule under challenge constituted an abuse of that dominant position.

An interim order in July 1998 preventing UEFA from excluding AEK Athens   **3.68** from the 1998/99 UEFA Cup, was made on other grounds,[75] not on the basis of applying EC competition law. The President of the Ordinary Arbitration Division held that the outcome of the competition law arguments could not be judged at the preliminary stage; a final determination would have to await additional factual and legal investigation not feasible within the time constraints of the preliminary proceedings. The President went on to observe that, with respect to competition law, the integrity of sporting competition "certainly appears a major concern likely to justify *some* restriction to competition". On the other hand, "European case law . . . consistently requires that any exception to competition rules relate to sports exclusively and be limited to its 'proper objective' or original purpose . . ."[76] The President considered further that determination of that issue would require an analysis of whether the rule under

---

[73] CAS 98/200, *supra.*, n. 27.

[74] As, for example, in the case of the rules of the English Premier League and the Scottish Football Association, both of whose rules restrict multiple shareholdings in clubs except with the prior consent of the association or league.

[75] Viz., a prima facie violation of the principle of good faith through retroactive effect on AEK Athens after that club had fulfilled pre-existing qualification criteria.

[76] CAS 98/200, Procedural Order of 17 July 1998, para. 66 (emphasis in original).

challenge related to sport exclusively, or whether it sought to achieve a purpose beyond the protection of UEFA competitions from contamination through conflicts of interest in the event of commonly owned clubs playing against each other. That is because Community law treats rules which are of sporting interest only as falling outside the scope of the Treaty of Rome altogether, as we shall see in our discussion of players' rights in the next chapter.[77]

[77] In the United States of America, some lawyers and scholars advocate giving professional sports leagues virtually complete exemption from antitrust laws, but the decisions of the US courts do not support that position; see, for example, Professor Gary Roberts, "The Antitrust Status of Sports Leagues Revisited", 64 *Tul. L. Rev.* 117, 118 (1989) ("I argue that league governance rules and decisions should be beyond the scope of section 1 [of the Sherman Act].")

4

Players' Rights

Introduction

This chapter concerns the rights and obligations of players vis-à-vis their **4.1**
employers. We are concerned not only with players in the narrow sense of
sportsmen and women but with participants in the sporting world, more
broadly. Thus, most of the principles discussed here are applicable to persons
employed by sports bodies in other capacities, such as coaches, managers and
physiotherapists. For convenience, this chapter refers to employers of players as
"clubs". Unless otherwise stated, that term should be taken to include any other
type of sporting body which may employ players.

This chapter examines players' rights in two stages. We deal, first, with the **4.2**
formation of the relationship between player and club and, second, with the
content of that relationship. The latter includes the circumstances in which the
relationship can be terminated; but it is not central to our purpose to dwell on
the law governing dismissals in sport, which do not occupy a position of promi-
nence in sporting jurisprudence.

In respect of the majority of sports, a player must be employed by a club in **4.3**
order to participate professionally. Thus, a player's freedom to join a club is
closely connected with his ability to play in sporting competition and, therefore,
to work. The first section of this chapter focuses on the nature of that freedom
and the legality of restrictions placed upon it. The other side of the same coin is
the freedom of a player to leave a club by which he or she is employed and join
another. The related issue of access to competitions, outside the employment
context, in respect of those sports where employment by a club is not a prereq-
uisite to competition has already been covered in chapter three.

If the main theme of the first section of this chapter is freedom of movement, **4.4**
that of the second is employment rights. We do not attempt to summarise the
law of employment; where appropriate the reader is directed to specialist works
on the subject. Our aim is to illustrate how that area of law applies to the particular features of employment in the context of sport.

The formation of the player/club relationship

In most professional sports there is not a perfectly free market in players. In **4.5**
other words the ability of a club to purchase and sell players and the corresponding ability of players to join and move clubs is not unconstrained. There

are a number of potential obstacles. Some of these are imposed by the rules of leagues and/or governing bodies to which the clubs belong. Thus, a league may prescribe that its member clubs have to pay a transfer fee when buying a player from another member club. Others stem from the contractual nature of the player/club relationship. For example, it may be difficult for a player to leave a club before the contract between them has expired. Obstacles may also be imposed by legislation. An example of this is the requirement imposed by the immigration legislation on most foreign players to obtain a work permit before they can play for a British club.[1]

Transfer fees

4.6 Transfer fee systems are extremely common. They are generally administered through the rules of a particular sport's league or governing body. Transfer rules are, thus, contractually enforceable as between clubs either directly or indirectly through their common membership obligations, as direct or indirect members of the organising body. Transfer fee systems are peculiar to the context of sport. It is difficult to think of another context in which prospective employers are subject to financial disincentives to recruitment. The rationale is said to be that they provide compensation for the training and development of players.[2]

4.7 Transfer systems may differ in their detail from one sport to another but they all share common features. Essentially, they impose a scheme of player registration such that a player becomes registered with a particular club upon joining it. Registration confers the right to play and must relate to a single club at any one time. Any other club wishing to employ that player must pay the first club a transfer fee in order to purchase the player's registration.

4.8 Although transfer rules govern the business relationships between clubs rather than the employment relationships between clubs and players, they clearly affect players' opportunities for finding employment and the terms under which such employment is offered.[3] The transfer system may impede the ability of a player to join the club of his or her choice if a transfer fee cannot be agreed. Thus, players may be prevented from simply selling their labour freely to the employer willing to pay the most once their employment has come to an end. Further, it has been said that high transfer fees have a deflationary effect on players' wages.

4.9 Leagues and governing bodies are not, however, unrestricted in the transfer rules they impose. The law is astute to ensure that transfer systems do not unduly curtail three important freedoms. First, the freedom of movement of

[1] See *R v. Secretary of State for Education and Employment ex parte Portsmouth Football Club Ltd.* [1998] COD 142 and paras. 4.66–4.71 *infra*.

[2] See for example, FIFA Transfer Rules 14 and 16.

[3] See, ECJ judgment in Case C–415/93 *Union Royale Belge de Societes de Football v. Jean-Marc Bosman* [1995] ECR I–4921, para. 5.

players within the European Union, a right which is protected by Articles 48 (now Article 39),[4] 52 (now Article 43) and 59 (now Article 49) of the EC Treaty. Second, the right of clubs freely to compete in the labour market. This right is protected by competition law, notably Articles 85 and 86 (now Articles 81 and 82) of the EC Treaty as well as analogous provisions of UK law. Thirdly, it is important that the operation of transfer systems does not unduly restrict the right of players to work. This right is protected by the common law doctrine of restraint of trade. These three areas of law and their impact on the operation of transfer systems are discussed in turn below.

EC law in sport: an introduction

Sport is subject to Community law in so far as its constitutes an "economic **4.10** activity" within the meaning of Article 2 of the EC Treaty.[5] That term is construed broadly. There is no doubt that professional and semi-professional sports fall within its ambit. As a general proposition then, rules and decisions affecting the way in which sport is organised fall to be assessed under the provisions of the Treaty. However, there is undoubtedly a need to distinguish between rules which are purely of a sporting nature (such as the offside rule) and those which are economic in nature. The former will not be within the scope of the Treaty and so do not fall to be assessed according to its provisions. This distinction is a difficult one to draw and is not helped by conflicting messages from the European Court (ECJ) as to whether one looks at the *purpose* of the rule or at its *effect* in determining whether it is of a sporting or economic nature.

The ECJ has held that rules restricting participation in football matches to the **4.11** nationals of a particular state is incompatible with the provisions of the Treaty:

"unless such rules . . . exclude foreign players from participation in certain matches *for reasons which are not of an economic nature, which relate to the particular nature and context of such matches and are thus of sporting interest only.*[6]

This test was repeated by the ECJ in *Bosman* in the context of its consideration of rules limiting the number of foreign players that clubs could field in any one match. It is clear, however, from the manner in which it applied the test in that case that the Court will not be satisfied by mere assertion that the purpose behind a rule is sporting in nature but will scrutinise it carefully in order to assess whether it really is a necessary and inherent feature of the particular sport.

[4] Case 36/74 *Walrave and Koch v. Union Cycliste Internationale* [1974] ECR 1405 at para. 4. Case 13/76

[5] *Donà v. Mantero* [1976] ECR 1333 at para. 12. S. Weatherill "Do Sporting associations make 'law' or are they merely subject to it?" *European Business Law Review*, July/August 1998, 217.

[6] *Donà v. Mantero, supra.,* n. 5, para. 19.

4.12   In a challenge by two football clubs, AEK Athens and Slavia Prague, to the common ownership regulations adopted by UEFA,[7] the defendant governing body argued that a regulation preventing more than one club with a common owner competing in the same UEFA-organised competition is a rule of sporting interest only and does not fall to be assessed against Articles 85 and 86 (81 and 82) of the Treaty. UEFA asserted that the regulation is of sporting interest in that it is necessary in order to preserve the integrity of competition. The plaintiffs, on the other hand, argued that the regulation affects the economic interests of the clubs and of their owner and, in those circumstances, cannot be said to be "of sporting interest only". On 20 August 1999 the court of Arbitration for Sport held in its final award that the rule was not within the so-called sporting exception, but upheld its legality on the basis that it did not violate EC or Swiss competition law, or Swiss association law, as it was not a disproportionate response to the legitimate aim of guaranteeing uncertainty of results.

4.13   The nature of the sporting exception was also considered by the Court of Appeal in *Wilander v. Tobin*.[8] The defendant officials of the International Tennis Federation argued that a rule providing for the suspension of tennis players where they had failed anti-doping tests did not come within the scope of application of Community law on the ground that it was "confined to the manner in which a sport is conducted";[9] the plaintiffs' argument based upon Article 59 (49) of the Treaty should, therefore, be struck out. Lord Woolf MR for the Court of Appeal saw "considerable force" in this argument but was not prepared to determine that there was no arguable case to the contrary.

4.14   Subsequently, in *Edwards v. BAF and IAAF*,[10] Lightman J considered a rule of the International Amateur Athletic Federation ("IAAF") permitting the IAAF to reduce bans imposed on athletes suspended by their national federations because of positive drugs tests. The plaintiff's application to the IAAF for reinstatement pursuant to this rule was rejected on the ground that he had failed to show "exceptional circumstances". The IAAF regarded this condition as satisfied only where it was shown that the ban was unlawful according to the domestic law of the athlete's federation. In this case, the plaintiff's four year ban was not unlawful under English law. It was common ground that a four year ban would be unlawful in some of the other member states of the European Union. The plaintiff argued that the rule was, therefore, discriminatory contrary to Article 59 (49) of the Treaty. Mr Justice Lightman rejected this claim holding

---

[7] *AEK Athens FC and Slavia Prague FC v UEFA*, CAS 98/200 and see M. J. Beloff QC "The Sporting Exception in EU Competition Law *European Current Law* (forthcoming 1999) which analyses the extent to which restraints of sporting interest only are outwith the reach of the Treaty provisions. See Further Preliminary Guidelines on the Application of Competition Rules to the Sports Sector. EU Commission 15.2.99 ("EU guidelines") paras. 51–54.

[8] *Wilander v. Tobin* [1997] EuLR 265, CA.

[9] At 274B.

[10] *Edwards v. BAF and IAAF* [1997] EuLR 721, Lightman J.

that Article 59 (49) had no application at all. The rule in question merely regulated the conduct of participants in athletics. The four year ban was reasonable, justified and proportionate.

> "Necessarily the imposition of the sanction may have serious economic consequences for those who breach the rules, and the IAAF and all concerned must obviously at all times have appreciated this. But this is a mere incidental and inevitable by-product of having the rule against cheating. A rule designed to regulate the sporting conduct of participants does not cease to be such a rule because it does not allow those who break it to earn remuneration by participating in the sport for what is (by common consent) an appropriate period."[11]

Although the ECJ has talked in terms of the "purpose" of a rule, it is artificial **4.15** to look at its purpose alone. A rule or practice may have aims which are sporting in nature and at the same time have wide ranging economic effects contrary to the aims of the EC Treaty. It is an inherent part of the interpretation of Community rules that the Court looks to substance rather than merely form. Thus, Article 85 (81) expressly applies to practices which have the *effect* of restricting competition even where their object is benign. Our own view is that there is a clear difference between a rule which affects the conduct of a sport and a rule which affects the economics of a sport. We consider that a rule should be considered as a purely sporting one only if it is a reasonably necessary condition for the creation or the organisation of a given competition.

Although the language of the ECJ has been somewhat ambiguous, it is inter- **4.16** esting to note that in each of the leading cases where the "sporting exception" has been in issue, the exception has been held not to apply. The ECJ has recognised the need to construe the exception strictly by carefully weighing up the need for rules in the course of assessing whether they are of sporting interest only.[12]

There are a number of Community law provisions which are potentially **4.17** applicable to sport. Of significance in the context of transfer systems are Article 48 (39) of the Treaty providing for freedom of movement for workers and Articles 85 (81) and 86 (82) which prohibit anti-competitive conduct.

EC law: Article 48 (now Article 39) and the other free movement provisions

Introduction **4.18**

Article 48 (39) of the Treaty provides as follows:

> "(1) Freedom of movement for workers shall be secured within the Community.
> (2) Such freedom of movement shall entail the abolition of any discrimination based on nationality between workers of the Member States as regards employment, remuneration and other conditions of work and employment.

[11] At 726G-H.
[12] *Walrave, Donà v. Mantero, Bosman, supra.*, n. 3 and n. 5.

(3) It shall entail the right, subject to limitations justified on grounds of public policy, public security or public health:

    (a) to accept offers of employment actually made;

    (b) to move freely within the territory of Member States for this purpose;

    (c) to stay in a Member State for the purpose of employment in accordance with the provisions governing the employment of nationals of that State laid down by law, regulation or administrative action;

    (d) to remain in the territory of a Member State after having been employed in that State, subject to conditions which shall be embodied in implementing regulations to be drawn up by the Commission.

(4) The provisions of this Article shall not apply to employment in the public service."

4.19   The provision represents an application in the specific field of employment of the fundamental Community rule contained in Article 6 (Article 12) of the Treaty prohibiting any discrimination on the ground of nationality within the scope of application of the Treaty. Article 48 (39), in turn, has been amplified by secondary legislation which clarifies the scope and nature of the prohibition against discrimination based on nationality.[13] Article 48 (39) prohibits indirect as well as direct discrimination. The prohibition against indirect discrimination strikes at apparently nationality-neutral criteria which nonetheless impose burdens which are such that fewer non-nationals than nationals can comply with them. Thus, the prohibition extends to measures which have discriminatory effects even though their objects may not be discriminatory. For example, an increase made by the German Post Office in the separation allowance paid to workers employed away from their place of residence within Germany was held by the Court of Justice to be discriminatory.[14] The increase was not paid to workers whose place of residence at the time of initial employment by the Post Office was abroad. Thus, the increase was not directly discriminatory as it was given to foreign nationals who were resident in Germany at the time of their initial employment and, conversely, not granted to German nationals who were resident abroad at that time. However, it was indirectly discriminatory as it was less likely to be given to foreign nationals than German nationals.[15] Article 48

---

[13] Thus, Directive 64/221 governs the main derogations from the right to free movement of workers; Directive 68/360 ensures entry and residence for Community workers; Regulation 1612/68 elaborates on the equal treatment principle setting out many of the substantive rights or workers and their families; Regulation 1251/70 protects the rights of workers and their families to remain in the territory of the member state after employment.

[14] Case 152/73 *Sotgiu v. Deutsche Bundespost* [1974] ECR 153.

[15] For a fuller analysis and further examples of the application of Article 39 (ex Article 48), see Barnard, *EC Employment Law* (London, Chancery Wiley Law, 1996), Craig and de Búrca, *EC Law, Text Cases and Materials* (Oxford, Clarendon Press, 1995), Wyatt and Dashwood, *European Community Law* (London, Sweet and Maxwell, 1993).

(39) not only prohibits discrimination by the receiving member state but also prevents the member state of origin from hindering the departure of a worker.[16]

The prohibition on discrimination on grounds of nationality imposed by **4.20** Article 48 (39)[17] is not absolute. Derogations are permissible under section 48(3) but they must be for the purpose of achieving aims of public policy, public security or public health and they must be proportionate to those aims. The courts will rigorously scrutinise action purporting to derogate from the free movement provisions of the Treaty in order to assess whether they are necessary to meet their stated aims.

Article 48 (39) applies to sportsmen and women if they fall within the mean- **4.21** ing of "worker". The concept of a "worker" is a Community law concept which has been given a broad definition by the Court of Justice. In particular, the touchstone of the employment relationship is that "for a certain period of time a person performs services for and under the direction of another person in return for which he receives remuneration".[18] The work must constitute an economic activity within the meaning of Article 2 of the Treaty[19] and, in particular, must be "effective and genuine" and not on such a small scale as to be regarded as "marginal and ancillary".[20] The Court of Justice has taken a broad view of what constitutes effective and genuine activity. Thus, the fact that a worker's earnings are low and that he may have to supplement his income from other sources, or that he works part-time, will not in themselves prevent a finding of genuine and effective employment.[21]

It follows that Article 48 (39) applies not only in respect of sportsmen and **4.22** women who are fully professional but also in respect of those who have a semi-professional status. Indeed, the Court of Justice expressly held in *Donà v. Mantero*[22] that semi-professional football players are "workers" for the purposes of the provision. Thus, a footballer playing for a small club in one of the lower divisions who receives a low salary which he has to supplement by other means is a "worker" within the meaning of Article 48 (39). So is a player who provides services in return for remuneration for a club in a sport which still has an "amateur" status, such as – until recently – rugby union. Conversely, a sportsman or woman who is not remunerated by the club or entity for which he plays but receives money as an indirect result of the sport, for example through sponsorship, would not constitute a worker. Nor would sportsmen and women competing in individual events, such as tennis, athletics or golf. However, such solo

---

[16] Case 81/87 *R v. HM Treasury and Commissioners of Inland Revenue ex parte Daily Mail* [1988] ECR 5483.

[17] And by the other provisions on free movement: Articles 52 (43) and 59 (49).

[18] Case 66/85 *Lawrie-Blum* [1986] ECR 2121, paras. 16–17.

[19] Case 36/74 *Walrave and Koch v. Union Cycliste Internationale* [1974] ECR 1405, paras. 4–5.

[20] See for example, Case 53/81 *Levin* [1982] ECR 1035.

[21] Case 139/85 *Kempf* [1986] ECR 1741.

[22] Case 13/76 *Donà v. Mantero* [1976] ECR 1333.

players might well be able to benefit from the principles of non-discrimination set out in Articles 52 and 59 of the Treaty (43 and 49) which provide the freedom to establish oneself as a self-employed worker and the freedom to provide services without discrimination on grounds of nationality. The application of these provisions is discussed further below.

4.23 It is trite law that Article 48 (39) is directly effective and thus may be relied upon directly by litigants in the English courts.[23] What is less obvious is the category of person to whom it applies. It clearly has vertical direct effect; in other words, it can be relied upon by an individual against the state. The precise extent to which the provision has horizontal direct effect, and can therefore be invoked against private persons, is a matter of some conjecture.[24] However, it was established in *Walrave and Koch*[25] that the provision not only applies to the actions of public authorities "but extends likewise to rules of any other nature aimed at regulating in a collective manner gainful employment and the provision of services". In that case, the Court of Justice held that the rules on free movement were applicable to the Union Cycliste Internationale, an association of national bodies concerned with cycling as a sport. The Court has further found the rules to be applicable to national football associations[26] and to UEFA and FIFA, the European and world football associations.[27] In common with the other provisions of the Treaty ensuring free movement, Article 48 (39) does not apply to situations which are wholly internal to one member state. Thus, on the whole, nationals cannot invoke Article 48 against their own member state. Nor does it apply to movement outside the European Economic Area.

4.24 It is convenient as this point to make mention of the other provisions of the Treaty ensuring free movement. Article 52 (43) and Article 59 (49) provide for the freedom of establishment and the freedom to provide services without discrimination on the ground of nationality. As adumbrated above, it is these provisions which will give equivalent protection to that supplied by Article 48 (39) to solo sportsmen and women who are not employed by any club. As with Article 48 (39), it must first be established that the discriminatory rule or practice under challenge is an "economic activity" rather than of "sporting interest only" and therefore subject to Community law in the first place. Once that hurdle has been surmounted, there is then the question of whether the rule is nonetheless compatible with Community law on the basis that it is justified by "compelling reasons of the general interest"[28] and complies with the principle of proportionality.

[23] Case 41/74 *Van Duyn v. Home Office* [1975] ECR 1337.

[24] This issue is discussed in more detail at paras. 4.27 et seq. below.

[25] See *supra.*, n. 7, at paras. 17–22. See, also Case C–415/93 *Union Royale Belge de Sociétés de Football v. Jean-Marc Bosman* [1995] ECR I–4921, para. 82.

[26] *Donà v. Mantero, supra.*, n. 23.

[27] Case C–415/93 *Union Royale Belge de Sociétés de Football v. Jean-Marc Bosman* [1995] ECR I–4921, paras. 82–87.

[28] *Bosman, supra.*, n. 27 at para. 190.

At issue in *Wilander v. Tobin*[29] was the validity of an International Tennis **4.25**
Federation ("ITF") rule providing for the suspension of players in the event of
positive drugs testing. The plaintiff tennis players argued, *inter alia*, that their
suspension, pursuant to the rule in question, constituted an infringement of
Article 59 (49) of the Treaty as it prevented them from competing and, therefore,
providing services in other member states of the European Union. The Court of
Appeal held that this part of the plaintiffs' claim should be struck out as disclosing no reasonable cause of action. In particular, it considered that the ITF
rule was justified by compelling reasons of general interest and that it fulfilled
the requirement of proportionality. This conclusion was contrary to that
reached by Lightman J at first instance who considered it arguable that the rule
was not proportionate because it did not provide for any right to appeal against
a positive anti-doping test. The Court of Appeal was satisfied that the rule was
proportionate on the basis that there were other avenues of redress for players,
including the courts, and that these provided sufficient protection.[30]

Subsequently, in *Edwards v. BAF and IAAF*,[31] Lightman J held *obiter* that **4.26**
there was no unlawful discrimination on the ground of nationality contrary to
Article 59 (49) when the IAAF upheld a four year ban for a UK athlete but remitted the last two years of such a ban for a comparable German athlete where
German domestic law had held that a four year ban was in unlawful restraint of
trade.[32]

Application to transfer fee systems

In the celebrated *Bosman* case,[33] the Court of Justice held that Article 48 (39) of **4.27**
the Treaty precludes the application of rules whereby a professional footballer
who is a national of one member state may not, on the expiry of his contract
with a club, be employed by a club of another member state unless a transfer,
training or development fee is paid.[34]

Jean-Marc Bosman was a Belgian footballer who had been employed by FC **4.28**
Liège, a Belgian first division club. His contract expired at the end of June 1990.
In April 1990 the club offered him a new one year contract at a very unattractive
salary. Bosman refused this offer and was transfer listed at a "compensation" fee
of BFR 11,743,000. Interest in Bosman was shown by US Dunkerque, a French

---

[29] *Wilander v. Tobin* [1997] EuLR 265, CA.

[30] At 274–275B.

[31] *Edwards v. British Athletics Federation and International Amateur Athletics Federation* [1997] EuLR 721.

[32] The primary basis for Lightman J's decision was that the complaint did not raise a
question under Article 59 (49) at all as it fell within the sporting exception: at 725D–726H.

[33] See *supra.*, n. 27. Much has now been written on the meaning and implications of
the *Bosman* case. For an admirably clear analysis, see the article by Professor Weatherill
in (1996) CMLRev 991. See also Ulhom, "The Bosman Case: Freedom of Movement and
its Implication" *European Current Law*, October 1998.

[34] Para. 114 of the Court's judgment.

second division club. In July 1990 the two clubs agreed a contract for the transfer of the player for one year only at a price of BFR 1,200,000, including an option allowing Dunkerque subsequently to buy the player at an additional cost of BFR 4,800,000. Both the contract between the two clubs and that between Dunkerque and the player were subject to the receipt by the French Football Federation of the transfer certificate issued by the analogous Belgian federation. FC Liège entertained doubts as to US Dunkerque's solvency and did not ask the Belgian federation to forward the certificate in question. As a result, neither contract took effect. On 31 July 1990, FC Liège suspended Mr Bosman thereby preventing him from playing for the entire season.

4.29 Transfer rules vary from state to state though UEFA and FIFA regulations provide a transnational underpinning. There was a dispute in *Bosman* over which were the applicable transfer rules.[35] Further, it was argued that the football industry had recently been liberalised with the result that the business relationship between clubs would not exert an influence on a player at the end of his contract who would be free to play for his new club, with any disagreement as to transfer fee to be resolved by an independent panel.[36] However, it is clear from the broad approach of the Court's judgment, that its ruling is based on the general requirement that a transfer fee be paid post-termination of a player's contract. It should not, therefore, be thought that the application of the Court's ruling is dependent upon the particular details of the various transfer systems operating within the European Union.

4.30 The Court held that the transfer rules in question constituted an obstacle to freedom of movement for workers prohibited in principle by Article 48 (39) of the Treaty. It reasoned that Article 48 (39) precludes measures which might place Community citizens at a disadvantage when they wish to pursue an economic activity in the territory of another member state. That includes measures which preclude or make it more difficult for a Community national to leave one member state and enter another in order to work. The transfer rules clearly fell within that category.[37] The fact that the transfer rules applied also to transfers of players between clubs within the same member state, and therefore did not discriminate on nationality grounds, did not mean that they were consistent with Article 48 (39). This is because Article 48 (39) prohibits not only measures which are directly or indirectly discriminatory, but also measures which hinder movement between member states of the European Union.[38]

[35] *Ibid.*, paras. 12 and 15.
[36] Para. 114 of the Court's judgment, paras. 18–21.
[37] *Ibid.*, paras. 94–97.
[38] This aspect of the Court's ruling emphasises a difference between Article 48 (39) and Article 30 as interpreted in Joined Cases C–267/91 and C–268/91 *Keck and Mithouard* [1993] ECR I–6097. In *Keck* the Court held that Article 30 does not apply to measures which restrict or prohibit certain selling arrangements so long as they apply to all relevant traders operating within the national territory and so long as they affect in

Having found that the transfer rules were prima facie contrary to Article 48 **4.31**
(39), the Court went on to consider whether they were capable of justification
on any of the public interest grounds contained in Article 48(3). The parties
resisting Mr Bosman's claim argued that the transfer rules were justified by the
need to maintain a financial and competitive balance between clubs, and to support the search for talent and the training of young players. These arguments
were rejected by the Court. The Court held that the application of transfer rules
does not achieve the first of those aims since they do not prevent the availability
of financial resources from being a decisive factor in competitive sport. As
regards the second aim, the Court accepted that the prospect of receiving transfer fees is likely to encourage clubs to seek new talent and train young players.
However, bearing in mind that it is impossible to predict the sporting future of
young players with any certainty, and that transfer fees do not reflect the actual
cost of training players, the Court found that the prospect of receiving such fees
was not a decisive factor in encouraging recruitment and training and the
infringement of Article 48 (39) was therefore not objectively justified.[39]

Several observations may be made as to the scope of the *Bosman* judgment. **4.32**
First, it goes without saying that the Court's ruling is not limited to football but
applies equally to similar rules in the context of other professional and semi-
professional sports. Second, the EC Treaty confers rights only on nationals of
EU member states. Thus, national sports associations could, without infringing
Article 48 (39), apply transfer rules to players who are not European Union
nationals moving between clubs in the EU or between a club inside and a club
outside the EU. However, it should be noted that analogous rights to those contained in Article 48 (39) are to be found in the European Economic Area
Agreement and would avail players from Norway, Liechtenstein and Iceland
(Norwegian nationals being, in practice, most likely to benefit). Third, the purpose of Article 48 (39) is to facilitate movement between member states of the
European Union. Therefore, it does not bite upon the application of transfer
rules to players who are EU nationals moving between a club within and a club
outside the European Union. Hence Monaco FC's recent refusal to pay a transfer fee to Celtic FC for John Collins.[40] It should be noted in the context of football that FIFA, after ratifying the *Bosman* judgment in 1996, implemented a
regulation of its own in March 1997 extending the *Bosman* principle to players
of all nationalities moving between clubs in two different EU member states. A
transfer fee may therefore still be demanded and is payable when a UK club

the same manner, in law and in fact, the marketing of domestic products and of those
from other member states. A case currently pending before CAS, *Celtic plc v. UEFA* (CAS
98/201) will determine whether *Bosman* applies when the transfer is to a club (Monaco
FC) which is in a territory outside the Community, but plays in a League within the
Community.

[39] Paras. 105–114 of the Court's judgment.
[40] Currently under challenge before CAS.

buys, for example, a Brazilian from a club in Brazil, but this cannot be recouped if the player is transferred to a Spanish club after the expiry of his contract.

4.33 Further, Article 48 (39) does not prohibit the application of transfer rules within the purely domestic sphere as discrimination within a member state against a national of that state, known as "reverse discrimination", does not come within the scope of the EC Treaty.[41] This does not, however, mean that domestic transfer rules are necessarily compatible with Community law as there remains the question of the impact of the competition rules discussed below.

4.34 *Bosman* was concerned with the impact of Article 48 (39) on the requirement for transfer fees once a player's contract with the selling club has ended. There remain, however, other aspects of transfer fee systems which are potentially susceptible to challenge under Article 48 (39). Perhaps the most important question is the validity of rules requiring a transfer fee to be paid when a player is sold *before* his contract with a club has come to an end. This was not discussed by the Court in *Bosman*. It seems to have been widely assumed that such rules do not contravene Article 48 (39). Thus, clubs have responded to the threats posed by players leaving for nothing when their contracts come to an end by putting them on longer term contracts. It has even been suggested that clubs might opt for indefinite contracts which are subject to a notice period of, say, three years.

4.35 Two comments may be made about this. First, long term and, *a fortiori*, indefinite contracts may be susceptible to challenge under the restraint of trade doctrine and competition law, discussed below.[42] Second, the blanket assumption that the application of transfer rules to players still under contract is compatible with Article 48 (39) is, in our view, flawed. It is highly arguable that the reasoning in the *Bosman* judgment may successfully be applied by extension to challenge a transfer system applicable to in-contract players too. Naturally, a player leaving a club whilst still under contract would be in breach of that contract and liable to the club in damages. Similarly, there may be liability on the part of the acquiring club for inducing breach of contract. The player's original club would, therefore, be entitled to compensation in private law. However, it is arguable that transfer rules enabling fees to be exacted which are higher than the level of compensation obtainable under private law contravene Article 48 (39). The additional sanctions imposed by such rules would impede movement between member states.[43]

---

[41] See para. 89 of the Court's judgment. It should be noted that the for the purposes of EC law (though not for football administration) movement between England and Scotland is viewed as purely internal. Therefore, Article 48 (39) of the Treaty does not prohibit the application of transfer rules to British players moving between England and Scotland though *quaere* whether it would prohibit the application of transfer rules to nationals of other EU member states moving between English and Scottish clubs.

[42] On this analysis it is still advantageous to clubs to enter into longer-term contracts with good players (subject to restraint of trade and competition law) because this may yield higher damages in the event of breach.

[43] See *Chitty on Contracts*, 27th ed., at para. 26–061.

We should interject here that, depending how they are framed, such transfer **4.36** rules could also be void in that they offend against the rule prohibiting penalties in contracts governed by English law. The rule renders void any clause in a contract which prescribes a fixed sum by way of damages exceeding the amount of a genuine pre-estimate of the actual damage flowing from a breach of the obligation triggering the alleged penalty clause.[44]

There are other common features of transfer systems which are susceptible to **4.37** challenge under Article 48 (39). It appears that transfer systems frequently treat transfers to clubs abroad less favourably than a transfer within the national association. In his opinion in *Bosman*, Advocate General Lenz referred to the system in Denmark where the rules governing the calculation of the transfer fee lead to a higher fee where a player is moving to a club abroad than where he is moving between clubs in Denmark.[45] Such rules would infringe Article 48 (39) as their effect is to hinder the free movement of players between Denmark and other member states of the EU. Similar are systems where the rules of the national association in conjunction with the rules of UEFA or FIFA, lead to unequal treatment.

Advocate General Lenz pointed to a feature of the system then operating in **4.38** France where under the rules of the French association a transfer fee is payable only if it is a professional player's first change of club. Further transfers within France may therefore take place without payment of a fee. However, if a player wishes to move to a club abroad, the UEFA and FIFA rules, which assume the payment of a transfer fee, apply. This too constitutes a breach of Article 48 (39).[46] A similar rule in Spain was recently disapplied to the benefit of the Brazilian forward, Ronaldo. He was under contract with Barcelona and wanted to join Inter Milan. Under the Spanish league rules he could buy himself out of his contract with Barcelona, provided he went to another club in Spain. As it seemed clear that the rule in question in principle breached Article 48 (39), Ronaldo was eventually able, even though not himself a national of any EU state, to buy himself out of his contract in the same way as he would have done had he gone to another Spanish club. The Advocate General also considered the requirement in some systems that in all transfers to clubs belonging to a different association, a clearance certificate be obtained from the player's previous association.[47] That requirement too, being capable of preventing or hindering free movement between member states, is contrary to Article 48 (39).

Currently pending before the Court of Justice is a preliminary reference seeking to determine whether rules of sports organisations which establish fixed **4.39** periods for the transfer of players are compatible with Articles 48 (39), 85 (81)

---

[44] Para. 155.
[45] Para. 156.
[46] Para. 160.
[47] Case C–176/96 *Lehtonen v. ASBL.*

and 86 (82) of the Treaty.[48] In its observations to the Court, the Commission has submitted that rules establishing fixed periods for transfers do not contravene the Treaty. They may well be essential for the survival of clubs, particularly small ones, and for maintaining a certain balance between large and small clubs given that the possibility of signing players, particularly in the final stages of the season, has the potential for significantly altering the balance between clubs by artificially impacting upon their chances of success.

4.40   Given its conclusion that the transfer rules contravened Article 48 (39), the Court found it unnecessary to rule on the argument advanced by M. Bosman that the rules also breached Articles 85 (81) and 86 (82) of the Treaty.[49] This is a significant question as the scope of the competition rules is quite different from that of the rules on free movement and it may be, for example, that Articles 85 (81) and 86 (82) could be used to challenge elements of a transfer system that would be viewed as purely internal for the purposes of Article 48 (39).

EC law: Articles 85 and 86 (81 and 82)

4.41 The meaning and effect of these provisions are discussed in chapter six. This section focuses on their application to transfer rules. Although this question was argued in *Bosman*, the Court did not perceive the need to decide it given that the case could be determined on the basis of Article 48 (39). However, it was considered in some detail by Advocate-General Lenz. Taking Article 85 (81), the first issue to consider is whether a set of transfer rules constitutes either an agreement between undertakings or a decision by an association of undertakings. As explained in chapter six, there is little difficulty in classifying clubs as undertakings and governing bodies as either undertakings or associations of undertakings.[50] The European Commission and Courts have adopted a broad approach to the meaning of "undertaking" such that the word includes any entity carrying on activities of an economic nature. In *Distribution of Package Tours During the 1990 World Cup*[51] the Commission explained that an activity of an economic nature is one that involves economic trade whether or not profit-making. This broad definition means that Article 85 (81) is applicable not only to large and profitable sports clubs, but also to smaller clubs which carry on only minor commercial activities.[52] It follows that national and international sports governing bodies are themselves undertakings to the extent that they

---

[48] Para. 138 of the judgment.

[49] See paras. 254–256 of AG Lenz's opinion.

[50] OJ [1992] L326/31.

[51] See para. 255 of AG Lenz's opinion.

[52] See also Case T–46/92 *Scottish Football Association v. Commission* [1994] ECR II-1039 in which the Scottish FA did not dispute before the CFI the power of the Commission to rely against it on Regulation 17/62 implementing Articles 85 (81) and 86 (82).

carry on economic activities. Indeed, in its decision on *Distribution of Package Tours During the 1990 World Cup*, the Commission held that FIFA, the Italian Football Association, and the local organising committee were each undertakings for the purpose of Article 85 (81).[53]

Further, there would seem to be little difficulty in establishing that a system **4.42** of transfer rules constitutes either an agreement between clubs or a decision taken by a governing body which is itself an association of undertakings. The precise analysis may depend on the structure of a particular league. For example, if the governing body is monolithic and independent in structure, then any transfer system is more likely to be deemed a decision taken by an association of undertakings. However, if a governing body provides in effect no more than a talking shop for its members, then the analysis is likely to be that of an agreement between the clubs themselves. Which of these two characterisations is adopted matters little, as it does not affect the substantive issue of whether the transfer system is caught by Article 85 (81). However, the issue is important as far as enforcement is concerned, as it will dictate whether it is the clubs or the governing body which is liable for any infringement of the competition rules.

The next and important question is whether transfer rules can have the effect **4.43** of restricting or distorting competition. The view of both the Commission and Advocate-General Lenz is that rules requiring the payment of a fee after the expiry of a player's contract, such as those at issue in *Bosman*, clearly can. In particular, they deprive clubs of the possibility of competing freely with respect to the signing of players. If there was no obligation to pay transfer fees, then a player would be free at the end of his contract to choose the club which offered him the best terms.[54] A Belgian court has now, in the case of *Balog v. Royal Charleroi Sporting Club*,[55] referred to the ECJ the question whether it was compatible with Article 85 (81) for a club located within the EU to demand a transfer fee for an out-of-contract non-EU national player to be transferred within the same EU member state, or to a third country either inside or outside the European Economic Area.

Thus, it is likely that the obligation to pay a transfer fee in respect of an out- **4.44** of-contract player is caught by Article 85(1). Would such a restriction benefit from exemption under Article 85(3)? Advocate General Lenz thought not. He acknowledged that professional football is substantially different from other markets in that clubs are mutually dependent on each other. Football cannot be

---

[53] An undertaking or association which acts in breach of Article 85 (81) or 86 (82) is liable to be fined by the European Commission or may face an action for damages from an injured third party. This is explained in greater detail in chapter six.

[54] See para. 262 of AG Lenz's opinion.

[55] The Tribunal de Première Instance de Charleroi in its decision of 2 July 1998. We are indebted to M Jean-Louis Dupont, the lawyer for M Balog and M Bosman for this decision.

played if there are no other teams to play against. Therefore each club has an interest in the health of other clubs and generally does not aim to exclude its competitors from the market. Likewise, the economic success of a league depends on the existence of a certain balance between its clubs.[56] Advocate-General Lenz could envisage the possibility of certain restrictions on competition being necessary in order to maintain that balance. However, the transfer rules at issue could not benefit from exemption under Article 85(3) (81(3)) as they were not indispensable for attaining such objectives. Less restrictive alternatives existed, such as the redistribution of a proportion of income.[57]

4.45   Article 85 (81) can potentially be used to challenge elements of a transfer system that would be viewed as purely internal for the purposes of Article 48 (39). Indeed, it is known that the prospect of a legal challenge relying on Articles 85 (81) and 86 (82) in the context of an intra-UK transfer from Scotland to England, enabled Chelsea FC to avoid paying the six million pounds initially demanded by Glasgow Rangers FC for the transfer of Brian Laudrup after the end of his contract with Rangers. The demand was consistent with the relevant rules but, despite that, was not supported by the Scottish or English leagues, nor by the European Commission. Moreover, a Belgian court has actually granted interim relief restraining a Belgian club from pursuing its claim to a transfer fee as a precondition of allowing a Hungarian national to be transferred to another club in France, Norway or within Belgium itself. The player could not rely on Article 48 (39), being a non-EU national, but relied instead on Article 85 (81).[58]

4.46   A more difficult question is the extent to which other aspects of transfer fee systems might fall within Article 85 (81). It appears that the Commission does not exclude the possibility that transfer rules permitting clubs to demand disproportionately large transfer fees in respect of players still under contract might be caught by Article 85(1) (81(1)).[59]

4.47   Might the imposition of transfer rules also amount to an abuse of a dominant position contrary to Article 86 (82) of the Treaty? Advocate General Lenz thought not.[60] The relevant market must be the market in players. That is a market in which clubs participate and not governing bodies. Therefore, no issue as to the dominance of a governing body or association arises. At the same time, no single club is likely to be dominant in that market. In any event, transfer rules are not generally imposed by any single club but amount to agreements between clubs. Nor does the concept of joint dominance add much to this analysis. It is entirely possible that clubs be united by such economic links that they hold a collectively dominant position. However, it is difficult to see how transfer rules

---

[56] Para. 227.

[57] Para. 270.

[58] *Balog v. Royal Charleroi Sporting Club, supra.,* n. 55.

[59] Speech given by Karel van Miert, then Competition Commissioner, in Brussels on 5 May 1995.

[60] Paras. 279–282 of his opinion.

to which all such clubs are party could amount to an abuse. Transfer rules only produce anti-competitive effects as between the clubs themselves. They do not produce such effects as between the clubs on the one hand and any competitors, customers or consumers on the other.

Finally, in order for the EC competition rules to apply at all there has to be an **4.48** appreciable effect on inter-state trade. This effect may be actual or potential and is generally easy to satisfy, though it should be noted that the European institutions have taken a much broader approach to the requirement than have the English courts. In *Bosman*, the Advocate-General considered that there was the requisite impact on inter-state trade. This was illustrated by statistics showing that in the 1995–96 season, the eighteen clubs in the Italian first division, spent more than ECU 51,000,000 on foreign players. The requirement may not be satisfied in respect of lower leagues or sports which are less fully commercialised where there is no real exchange of players with other member states of the EU. It should be borne in mind, however, that this jurisdictional matter will become much less important once the Competition Act 1998 comes fully into force allowing equivalent legislation to Articles 85 (81) and 86 (82) to be enforced in a purely domestic context.

Restraint of trade

The application of the restraint of trade doctrine to sport is discussed in chap- **4.49** ter three in the context of access to sporting competitions . Here, we deal with the application of the doctrine to transfer rules.[61]

The restraint of trade doctrine has always been applied to covenants con- **4.50** tained in contracts of employment which limit the freedom of the employee to work after the termination of the employment.[62] A feature of transfer systems is that they almost always have this restrictive effect, and so the main question is whether the restraints inherent in the transfer system are reasonable with reference to the interests of the parties concerned and of the public.

This question was addressed in respect of the then transfer rules of the FA in **4.51** *Eastham v. Newcastle United FC*.[63] The transfer rules were, at that time, coupled with powers of retention whereby a club could debar a player joining another club at the end of his contract simply by continuing to pay him a reasonable wage. Wilberforce J held that the transfer and retention systems, when combined, operated in restraint of trade, that the defendants had not discharged the onus on them of showing that the restraints were no more than was

[61] See, generally, McCutcheon, "Negative Enforcement of Employment Contracts in the Sports Industries", *SPTL* Vol. 17 No.l (March 1997) 65; Darren Bailey, "The Tie That Binds; Restraint of Trade in Sports", conference paper presented at Chelsea FC, 25 November 1996.
[62] See *Chitty on Contracts*, *supra.*, n. 43, para. 16–082.
[63] *Eastham v. Newcastle United FC Limited* [1964] Ch 413.

reasonable to protect their interests and that, as such, they were unenforceable.[64] In assessing whether the restraints were capable of justification, the judge held that it was unnecessary to consider whether the justifications put forward by the defendants corresponded to categories of interests, such as goodwill and trade secrets, which the law recognised as constituting interests which employers were entitled to protect. Rather, he acknowledged that the context of sport in which the restraints operated, was different from that of industrial employment, and found that those concerned with the organisation of professional sport had legitimate interests worthy of protection.[65] The judge went on to consider the various justifications put forward, including that they enabled clubs to be maintained in smaller towns and that, in the absence of transfer rules, clubs would be dissuaded from spending money on training players. He held, however, that in so far as these concerns were made out as legitimate on the evidence, they could be met by less restrictive means.

4.52   Similar issues were at stake in *Greig v. Insole*,[66] a case which concerned not transfer rules but rules of the International Cricket Council (TCCB) and the Test and County Cricket Board which, in effect, prevented cricket players taking part in competitions organised by another body to which they had already signed up.[67] After finding that the rules were such as to "substantially restrict the area in which it will be open to professional cricketers to earn their livings",[68] Slade J went on to consider whether they were nevertheless justifiable. Applying what was essentially a proportionality test,[69] Slade J found that though the defendant had legitimate interests worthy of protection, the restraints went further than was necessary to protect them. Both of these cases also establish that an action for restraint of trade may be brought by a third party. The plaintiffs in *Eastham* and *Greig* were not themselves in a contractual relationship with the organising body whose rules they sought to challenge. This was not, however, a bar to relief.[70]

4.53   That the necessity for transfer rules must be carefully assessed if they are to pass muster under the restraint of trade doctrine is also well established in Commonwealth jurisprudence. In one Australian case,[71] one hundred and fifty

---

[64] At 446–7.

[65] See the judgment at 433–437. It is notable that the justifications put forward bear a striking similarity to those invoked in *Bosman*, over twenty years later.

[66] *Greig v. Insole* [1978] 1 WLR 302.

[67] This case arose from Kerry Packer's attempts to set up a rival series of test matches.

[68] At 345B-C.

[69] See 347H.

[70] A significant case in this context is *Faramus v. Film Artistes Association* [1964] AC 925 in which it was held that an organisation with effective monopolistic power over a particular field of activity, such that compliance with membership rules is a pre-requisite to earning a living in that field, is subject to the restraint of trade doctrine at the suit of individuals whom it prevents from earning a living.

[71] *Adamson v. New South Wales Rugby League Ltd* (1991) 103 ALR 319.

four rugby league players challenged the validity of rules of the New South Wales Rugby League providing that players wishing to be transferred at the end of the 1990 season had to nominate terms and conditions on which they were prepared to play. Thereafter the clubs had the right to select any particular player, provided it was willing to meet the terms asked, in an order of precedence which was the reverse of that in which the teams were ranked at the end of the preceding competition. There were to be several such "drafts" during the season, so that if a player was not selected in the first draft, he could submit himself at the next draft, and so on. The last such draft was in June, the relevant competition having already begun in March. The Federal Court declared these rules void as an unreasonable restraint of trade, commenting that the "draft" system did little to protect the interests of the League but much to infringe the freedoms and interests of players.[72]

It can be seen from the above discussion that transfer fees and other rules of **4.54** sports federations which restrict freedom of employment will generally fall to be considered both under competition law rules and under the restraint of trade doctrine. Usually, the focus of competition law is different to that of restraint of trade, being more concerned with the public interest question of competitiveness in the marketplace generally, as opposed to the private law question of the effect of a particular contract on one person's ability to trade. However, transfer systems – by their nature – are implemented via rules affecting a large number of participants in a sport. For this reason, whilst they impact upon each individual's freedom to trade, they are also liable to have a much wider impact on the competitiveness of the market.

Nationality restrictions

This section concerns bars to a player joining a club which are based on nation- **4.55** ality. Such bars commonly take one of two forms. First, there may be quotas laid down by leagues or governing bodies limiting the number of foreign players or non-local players that are eligible to appear in a team. Second, national immigration rules restrict clubs from freely engaging any foreign player they choose. In considering these two obstacles a line can broadly be drawn between those players who are nationals of other member states of the European Union and those who are not. As discussed below, European Community law largely prevents any restrictions on the flow of EU workers between member states and this includes restrictions on players joining clubs.

---

[72] See also, *Buckley v. Tutty* (1971) 125 CLR 353.

Nationality restrictions imposed by leagues

4.56 Following *Bosman*, it is clear that leagues may not restrict the number of EU nationals that may be employed by a club or may be fielded by the club in any one team. At issue in that case was the legality of the "3+2 rule" adopted by UEFA whereby clubs could field three foreign players and two "assimilated" players.[73] The Court held that the rule did restrict the free movement of workers within the meaning of Article 48 (39) of the Treaty. The fact that it concerned not so much the employment of other EU nationals, but the extent to which their clubs could field them in official matches was irrelevant, given that participation in matches is the essential purpose of a professional player's activity. A rule which restricts participation also restricts the chances of employment of the player concerned.[74]

4.57 There are clearly, however, some forms of nationality rule which do not fall foul of Article 48 (39). In *Donà v. Mantero*[75] the Court held that Article 48 (39) did not:

> prevent the adoption of rules or of a practice excluding foreign players from participation in certain matches for reasons which are not of an economic nature, which relate to the particular nature and context of such matches and are thus of sporting interest only, such as, for example, matches between national teams from different countries.

However, in order not to infringe Article 48 (39), such restrictions must go no further than their proper objectives require.[76] In its judgment in *Bosman*, the Court considered whether the "3+2" rule was justified on non-economic grounds but held it was not. The arguments put forward by the football federations were that such rules serve to maintain the traditional link between each club and its country, are necessary to create a sufficient pool of national players to provide the national team with top players, and help to maintain a competitive balance between clubs by preventing the richest clubs from appropriating the services of the best players.

4.58 The Court doubted the legitimacy of the first of these arguments. It reasoned that a club's links with the member state in which it is established cannot be regarded as any more inherent in its sporting activity than its links with its locality, town or region and, even though national championships are played between clubs of different regions, there is no rule restricting the right of clubs from fielding players from other regions. As to the second argument, the Court

---

[73] The rule was the result of a compromise between UEFA and the Commission in 1991. "Assimilated" players are those who have played in the country of the relevant association for an uninterrupted period of five years, including three years as a junior.

[74] See para. 120 of the Court's judgment in *Bosman*.

[75] [1976] ECR 1333.

[76] Paragraphs 14–15 of ECJ 's judgment in *Donà v. Mantero*.

made the point that whilst national teams must be made up of players with the nationality of that country, those players need not necessarily play for clubs in that country. Thirdly, it stated that the nationality rule did not maintain a competitive balance between clubs as there was nothing to prevent the richest clubs recruiting the best national players.

In what circumstances will nationality restrictions be compatible with the EC **4.59** Treaty? It was established in *Walrave v. Union Cycliste Internationale*[77] that rules preventing foreign players playing for a national team do not infringe Article 48 (39). Beyond that, however, the question is quite difficult to answer not least because of the rather confusing way in which it has hitherto been approached by the Court. It appears that in some circumstances nationality rules will not infringe Article 48 (39) because they are of "sporting interest" only and therefore fall outside the scope of the Treaty. This was the approach of the Court in *Walrave* and *Donà v. Mantero* and was its stated approach in *Bosman*. The Court speaks in terms of assessing the "purpose" of the rule with a view to determining whether it is of "sporting interest" only. In reality, however, it applies a far more rigorous scrutiny than that. In *Bosman*, the Court first looked at the *effect* of the nationality rule. It found that it applied "to all official matches between clubs and thus to the essence of the activity of professional players". In those circumstances, the rule clearly infringed Article 48 (39).[78] The Court then worked backwards from this to conclude that the rule was not inherent in the sporting activity of football clubs.

In practice, then, the approach of the Court in *Bosman* was to look at the **4.60** effect of the rule and not merely assess whether or not it was economically motivated. Thus, we do not consider it possible to conclude that all nationality rules which are not economically motivated fall outside the scope of Article 48 (39). In our view, the Court will look beyond motivation to effect and – in practice – will only conclude that a rule is "of sporting interest only" and so "falls outside the scope of the Treaty" if its aim is sporting in nature, that aim is a necessary and inherent part of the sport *and* its economic effects are commensurate to that aim. Thus, rules which restrict eligibility for national sides to nationals of the particular state have an objective aim and are necessary to achieve that aim. Without such rules, international matches would lose their raison d'être. On the other hand, nationality rules restricting eligibility to play for club sides in European inter-club competitions, though similarly not necessarily economically motivated, are not necessary to achieve a pressing policy objective. Such matches would still have meaning and would still go ahead without such rules: Chelsea FC represents London even if it has more Italian and French-born players than London-born players.

---

[77] [1974] ECR 1405.
[78] See para. 129 of the Court's judgment.

4.61 Similar principles apply not only to players but also to other employees of sports teams such as managers, trainers and coaches. National sports federations sometimes impose rules as to the qualifications that must be possessed by such persons before they can be employed. Such rules might result in discrimination if they require, for example, that the person possesses a diploma granted by an institution of that state. Community law requires recognition to be given to equivalent qualifications attained in other member states. For some professions, such as the medical profession, there is specific Community legislation which achieves a degree of harmonisation of qualifications and describes what type of qualification a member state must treat as equivalent to its own.[79]

4.62 For physiotherapists, trainers, coaches and fitness consultants there are no specific harmonisation measures. However, the general principle of mutual recognition applies. This means that member states are under a duty to look at an applicant's existing qualifications and compare them to those required by the national rules to see if the applicant has the appropriate skills. If the comparison reveals that the applicant has only partially fulfilled the necessary qualifications, the member state must offer him or her the opportunity to demonstrate that he has the knowledge required. That can be achieved, for example, by taking a test or by a consideration of the applicant's practical experience, or both.[80] That a fair opportunity must be given to an applicant to demonstrate the equivalence of his qualification is demonstrated by *UNECTEF v. Heylens*.[81] That case concerned French rules providing that, in order to practise as a football trainer in France, a person must be the holder of a French football-trainer's diploma or a foreign diploma which has been recognised as equivalent by decision of the competent member of the government after consulting a special committee. Mr Heylens, a Belgian national and the holder of a Belgian football trainer's diploma, was employed by Lille Olympic Sporting Club as trainer of the club's professional football team. An application for recognition of the equivalence of the Belgian diploma was rejected by decision of the competent member of government, which referred to an adverse opinion of the special committee. The opinion of the special committee gave no reasons. The Court of Justice held that any decision refusing to recognise the equivalence of a diploma from another member state must be reviewable to see whether it is compatible with Article 48 (39).[82] Since Article 48 (39) is a fundamental right under the Treaty, a person seeking to secure effective protection of that right must be able to do so under the best possible conditions, including full knowledge of the relevant facts so that he or she can decide

---

[79] See Council Directive 93/16/EEC of 5 April 1993 to facilitate the free movement of doctors and the mutual recognition of their diplomas, certificates and other evidence of formal qualifications, OJ 1993 L165/1.

[80] See Case C–340/89 *Vlassopoulou* [1991] ECR I–2357 for a full discussion by the ECJ of requirements of mutual recognition of qualifications.

[81] Case 222/86 [1987] ECR 4097.

[82] See para. 14 of the Court's judgment.

whether there is any point pursuing a judicial remedy. Accordingly, the Court held that the national authority was required by Community law to inform Mr Heylens of the reasons on which its refusal was based.[83]

The upshot of this case is that, if sports associations wish to limit positions to   **4.63** those in possession of a particular qualification, they must carefully consider the degree to which qualifications gained in other member states are equivalent. Further, national law must provide the means for individual applicants effectively to challenge any determination of non-equivalence. In short, the *Heylens* case is a specific illustration of the general principle of effectiveness which requires national law to provide an effective means of enforcing Community law rights. How an applicant would frame a challenge to such a decision taken by an English association is an interesting question. The issue whether the body has failed to comply with Community law is one we consider most appropriately dealt with by way of an application for judicial review. However, as explained in chapter eight, judicial review is not normally available against sports governing bodies. A possible solution may be for the applicant to use restraint of trade as the free standing cause of action and argue that the restraint cannot be reasonable given that it is in breach of Community law. An alternative route would be to frame the action as a breach of statutory duty, the relevant statute being the European Communities Act 1972. More controversially, we can see the germ of an argument that, where a Community law right is at stake, the principle of effectiveness requires that judicial review be available against sports associations. At least that principle must require that the right of challenge should not fail for want of a procedural peg on which to hang it.

It is apparent, then, that Community law gives far reaching rights to employ-   **4.64** ees who fall within its scope, allowing them the same access to employment as nationals, and ensuring they receive equal treatment once that employment has commenced. The category of players who benefit from Community law comprises, for the main part, nationals of other member states of the European Union. However, spouses of EU workers may also fall within the scope of Community law even if they are not EU nationals themselves.[84] Further, nationals of states belonging to the European Economic Area (that is, Norway, Iceland and Lichtenstein) also benefit from similar rights.[85]

A slightly different issue is raised by a case currently pending before the ECJ,   **4.65** namely the extent to which sports organisations can stipulate the number of teams or athletes per country which may participate in European and international competitions.[86] In its observations to the Court, the Commission has submitted that such rules are of sporting interest only so long as they remain proportionate to their objective and do not fall to be considered under Articles

---

[83] *Ibid.*, para. 15.
[84] See Regulation 1612/68 and Case C–370/90 *Surinder Singh* [1992] ECR I–4265.
[85] The European Economic Area Act 1993.
[86] Case C–51/96 *Deliège*.

59 (49), 85 (81) or 86 (82). On the other hand, a regulation made by a sports organisation providing for or permitting the selection of athletes according to non-objective and/or discriminatory criteria, is likely to fall to be assessed under the provisions of the Treaty.

Immigration rules

4.66 Players who are not nationals of the European Union or European Economic Area need a work permit if they wish to join a club in the United Kingdom and not all will qualify. The Work Permit Scheme is administered by the Department for Education and Employment (Overseas Labour Service (OLS)) pursuant to the Immigration Acts of 1971 and 1988 and limits recruitment of non-EEA nationals to those whose presence in the UK is deemed to be "essential". In order to meet this requirement, players will have to show that they have performed at the highest level.

4.67 In 1994 the Department of Employment issued a guide on the issue of work permits to sports persons. This guide was still current at the time of writing. It states that the Work Permit Scheme for sports persons:

"enables current international performers of the highest standard who are able to make a significant contribution to the sports industry in the UK to work in this country while safeguarding the interests of the resident work force."

It goes on to explain that "work permits are issued only for top class sports persons whose employment will not displace or exclude UK or other EC workers". Such "top class" sports players must be "internationally established in the highest level in their sport" and be able to "make a significant contribution to sport in this country".

4.68 Both the Football Association and the Rugby Football Union have established criteria in conjunction with the OLS which give practical content to these guidelines. Thus, the OLS Document *Criteria for Football – 1997/98 Season* states as follows:

"Work permits will only be issued to current international players who have an acceptable international reputation. For example, players would be expected to have played in an international 'A' team for at least the past two seasons and to have participated in approximately 75 per cent of their country's competitive matches in that period . . ."

"Salaries offered to overseas players should be at the top end of the club's wage structure unless exceptional circumstances apply . . ."

"In determining whether or not to grant an extended work permit, the most important consideration will be the contribution the player has made to the game in this country. A player will be expected to have become a regular member of his club's first team, ie to have played in the region of 75 per cent of first team games.

The RFU *Notes for Guidance on the Work Permit Scheme* are less restrictive   **4.69**
than those for football. They provide that players must be full internationals and have played for their country within the last eighteen months. In deciding whether or not to grant an extension to an existing work permit, the most important factor will, again, be the contribution the player has made to the game in this country.

The case of *R v. Secretary of State for Education and Employment ex parte*   **4.70**
Portsmouth Football Club Ltd[87] makes clear that these criteria must not be applied too rigidly. Where there are relevant factors explaining why the criteria are not met by a player wishing to obtain a work permit, those factors must be taken into account by the OLS if its decision is to be lawful. Portsmouth FC wanted to employ a twenty four year old Australian international goalkeeper, Zeljko Kalac. The coach of the Australian national team regarded him as his first choice goalkeeper. However, the OLS refused to issue him with a work permit on the ground that he had not played in 75 per cent of Australia's competitive matches over the past two years. It reached this conclusion despite the fact that Portsmouth FC had pointed out that Mr Kalac had missed several competitive matches due to injury. McCullough J quashed the decision of the OLS. He found that it had erred in treating the 75 per cent test as determinative of whether the criteria as a whole were met. The 75 per cent test was merely an example – though no doubt an important one – of how the necessary ability could be demonstrated. Further, the OLS had erred in not taking account of the fact that Mr Kalac had been injured and, for that reason, missed a number of relevant matches. The judge held that this was plainly a material factor, stating:

> "If, for example, an English player of the highest reputation, who was invariably selected when fit to play, had a period of injury but for which he would have played in 75 per cent of his country's international matches over the two year period, but because of which he only played in 60 per cent of them, his reputation and standing in the game would stand as high as ever. The mathematics in that situation would not in the least diminish their reputation. . ."

> "No doubt in some cases it is too difficult to demonstrate that injury has been responsible for a player playing in fewer games than otherwise he might, but there is no reason in my judgment to say that, in every single case, injury, come what may, must be ignored."

This case is illustrative of the general principle that public bodies are obliged   **4.71**
to take account of all relevant considerations when exercising a discretion pursuant to statutory powers. Although the 75 per cent test may be a useful yardstick when measuring a player's international standing, it must not be

[87] *R v. Secretary of State for Education and Employment ex parte Portsmouth Football Club Ltd* [1998] COD 142, McCullough J.

treated as the only criterion and other material factors must be taken into account. Missing matches through injury will not be the only such factor. The judge in *ex parte Portsmouth* mentioned another possible factor, namely that Australia's geographical position meant that, for far distant matches, the Australian national team is sometimes chosen only from those based close to where the match is played. For this reason, Mr Kalac, who was based in Australia, was sometimes not chosen to play for Australia in Europe. There are a number of other factors which might be material in certain cases. For example, it is harder for goalkeepers than for outfield players to play in a high proportion of international matches. Outfield players can often play in a number of different positions, thus maximising their chances of selection.[88] This distinction may have played a part in Liverpool's successful appeal against the OLS's decision to refuse a work permit for the American goalkeeper, Brad Friedel, because he did not satisfy the 75 per cent test. Friedel had been sharing international duties with Leicester City's Kasey Keller.[89] Further, the 75 per cent test does not allow for the relative difficulty of gaining a place in certain national teams compared to others. A Brazilian player who has played in 25 per cent of his country's internationals over two years is likely to have attained a higher standard than a San Marino player who has played in 100 per cent of matches. The duty upon the OLS to take account of all relevant considerations applies, of course, not only to their decision whether or not to issue a work permit in the first place, but also at the stage of deciding whether or not to extend an existing permit.

The content of the player/club relationship

4.72 This section deals with some of the ways in which the relationship between player and club is regulated once the player has been employed by the club. First, we consider the extent to which some of the terms and conditions which might form part of a player's contract may be challengeable and, second, we address the issue of discrimination in sport. These are the areas where we consider that the particular context of sport throws up interesting questions. There are, of course, many other ways in which the relationship between players and their employers is regulated. There is a raft of employment legislation providing

[88] For example, Dion Dublin of Aston Villa, played for his former club Coventry City FC both in defence and as a striker. No doubt, this has been a factor behind his occasional selection for England squads.

[89] See M Whitehead, "Player Movement and the Work Permit Scheme", in *Sports Law Administration and Practice*, Vol, 5, issue No. 1, p. 5. Restrictions on foreign imports have recently been tightened. (*The Times 30 March 1999*). Prospective signings must normally have played in 75% of their country's competitive matches for the previous two years, while, over a similar time frame, FIFA ranking for the national side will be considered. The 75% test was waived in the case of Sheffield Wednesday's application for a permit for Dijan Stefanovic (*Sheffield Star: 20 October 1995*).

protection, for example in the event of unfair dismissal, redundancy, failure to pay wages. The interpretation of such legislation is not affected by the fact that an employee is a sportsperson. As it is a matter for general employment law, it goes beyond the scope of this book and is not dealt with here.[90]

Terms and conditions of work

As already noted, a term in a player's contract – or for that matter a federation **4.73** rule – which places restrictions on his or her ability to participate in their sport may well be unenforceable as an unlawful restraint of trade. An example is afforded by the *Greig v. Insole*[91] case in which the court found that ICC and TCCB rules preventing players taking part in test matches organised by a rival body went further than was necessary to protect the legitimate interests of the governing bodies and were, therefore, unenforceable as in restraint of trade.

Similar issues were raised in *Kemp v. New Zealand Rugby Football League*.[92] **4.74** Mr Kemp wanted to play rugby league for the Newcastle Knights in New South Wales but the New Zealand League refused "clearance" for Mr Kemp's transfer overseas with the consequence that the League in New South Wales would not authorise him to enter into the contract offered by the Newcastle Knights. The relevant rule gave the New Zealand League a complete discretion to grant or approve any transfer to an overseas league. Henry J decided that the New Zealand League had a legitimate interest to protect, and that public policy justified reasonable restrictions on overseas employment of players under the League's jurisdiction. However, he granted a declaration that the rule was void as an unreasonable restraint of trade. The rule was unlimited as to time and place and envisaged the possibility of being operated worldwide in a preventive way throughout the working life of a professional player. Such a wide power went beyond what was reasonable to protect the interests of the League.

Other rules limiting the conduct of players which have been struck down as **4.75** an unreasonable restraint of trade include a rule of the Australian Cricket Association providing for automatic disqualification of a player taking part in an unauthorised match[93] and rules of the Australian Rules Football Authority in Victoria which tied players to the club in the area in which they resided unless the club consented to their release.[94]

The restraint of trade doctrine is also relevant to terms dealing with the dura- **4.76** tion of a player's contract. In our discussion of transfer rules, we pointed out

---

[90] For a comprehensive guide to employment law see, *Harvey on Industrial Relations and Employment Law*, Butterworths.

[91] *Greig v. Insole* [1978] 1 WLR 302. See para. [4.52] *supra*.

[92] *Kemp v. New Zealand Rugby Football League Inc* [1989] 3 NZLR 463, HC.

[93] *Hughes v. Western Australian Cricket Association (Inc)* (1987) 69 ALR 660.

[94] *Hall v. Victorian Football League* [1982] VR 64. See also *Adamson v. West Perthshire FC* (1979) 27 ALR 475, *Blackler v. New Zealand Rugby Football League Inc* [1968] NZLR 547.

that clubs have attempted to mitigate the effects of the *Bosman* ruling by entering into longer term contracts with young players and, thereby, ensuring that they retain much of the player's value.[95] However, long term contracts themselves have a restrictive impact on a player's freedom, preventing them moving from one club to another in the event that they become dissatisfied with their employer. The question arises whether long term contracts in the context of sport may in principle be subject to the restraint of trade doctrine, and therefore subject to investigation by the courts as to their reasonableness. The courts have recognised that every contract may, in one sense, be said to restrict trade since by contracting with a particular party, a person is restricting himself from contracting inconsistently with someone else. However, it would be inappropriate for all contracts to fall within the restraint of trade doctrine. In attempting to provide a demarcation, the courts have in the past drawn a distinction between post-termination restraints which are subject to the doctrine, and restraints during the currency of employment which, the courts have said, are not. Terms governing the duration of a contract, *ex hypothesi*, fall into the latter category and so might be said to fall outside the restraint of trade doctrine. However, this approach has in recent years not found favour with the courts.[96]

4.77 The matter was discussed in *Watson v. Prager*[97] which concerned the duration of a contract between a professional boxer and his manager. The contract in question was in the form prescribed by the British Boxing Board of Control. It was of three years' duration, but contained a provision giving the defendant manager the option to extend the period for a further three years if the plaintiff should win one of several specified championships during the initial period. This did happen and the defendant exercised his option to extend the contract. The plaintiff became dissatisfied and sought to establish that the contract was unenforceable as an unreasonable restraint of trade. Scott J considered the attempts which had been made in the authorities to distinguish contracts subject to the restraint of trade doctrine and those which fell outside it.[98] He concluded that the contract in issue did fall within the scope of the doctrine because it was not negotiated freely but was prescribed by the governing body. It was not, in the judge's view:

> "satisfactory that an entity such as the board, which controls all aspects of professional boxing should be regarded as free from judicial supervision in so

[95] See para. 4.34 *supra*.

[96] See *Chitty on Contracts*, *supra*., n. 45 at para. 16–091: "It now appears probable that even restraints which operate during the currency of employment are subject to the restraint of trade doctrine, at any rate if they have as their objects the sterilising rather than the absorption of a man's capacity for work, or perhaps are such that one of the parties is so unilaterally fettered that the contract loses its character of a contract for the regulation and promotion of trade and acquires the predominant character of a contract in restraint of trade."

[97] *Watson v. Prager* [1991] 1 WLR 726.

[98] At 742F–745F.

far as its rules and regulations impose commercial restrictions on participators in the sport."⁹⁹

Scott J therefore went on to consider whether various restrictions contained in the contract were justified in the interests of the parties and the public. He held, as to its duration, that three years was reasonable, but that the manager's option to extend its duration for as long as three years was of doubtful reasonableness. Although there was an interest in ensuring that managers were able to take some share of the large financial rewards which would be available to a boxer if he won a major championship, this interest could be met by an option to extend the contract for eighteen months rather than three years.¹⁰⁰

Watson v. Prager establishes that restraints during the currency of a contract **4.78** in the context of sport may be subject to the restraint of trade principle. It only addresses the issue of terms governing duration of the contract where those terms have been imposed by the sport's governing body. However, authority in the context of the music industry suggests that, even where the rules of the governing body say nothing about duration and the parties have in principle been at liberty to negotiate freely, contracts of long duration may fall to be assessed for reasonableness under the restraint of trade doctrine in some circumstances. This will be the case where the courts perceive the contractual restrictions to be unnecessary or oppressive. Lord Reid put it this way in *Instone v. Shroeder Music Publishing Ltd*,¹⁰¹ a case in which the House of Lords held a ten year exclusive contract between a young songwriter and music publishers to be in unreasonable restraint of trade:

> "Any contract by which a person engages to give his exclusive services to another for a period necessarily involves extensive restriction during that period of the common law right to exercise any lawful activity he chooses in such manner as he thinks best. Normally the doctrine of restraint of trade has no application to such restrictions; they require no justification. But if contractual restrictions appear to be unnecessary or to be reasonably capable of enforcement in an oppressive manner, then they must be justified before they can be enforced."

---

⁹⁹ At 746C.

¹⁰⁰ The judge did not have to reach a final view on the reasonableness of the contract's duration as there were other restrictions which were more obviously offensive and which rendered the agreement as a whole unenforceable.

¹⁰¹ *Instone v. Shroeder Music Publishing Ltd* [19/4] 1 WLR 1308 at 1314G-H. The other Law Lords agreed. See, also *ZTT Ltd v. Holly Johnson* [1993] EMLR 6 in which the Court of Appeal held that a recording contract entered into by the parties was unenforceable as an unreasonable restraint of trade, and *Panayiotou v. Sony Music Entertainment (UK) Ltd*, *The Times* 30 June 1994, where George Michael failed to show that his contract with Sony was an unreasonable restraint of trade although Parker J accepted that the contract fell to be examined for reasonableness under the doctrine.

In reaching its conclusion, the House of Lords took account of the fact that the publishing house were not bound, under the contract, to publish or promote the songwriter's work if it chose not to. This might lead to him earning nothing and to the sterilisation of his talents contrary to the public interest.[102]

4.79   The courts are astute to prevent unfairness resulting from inequality of bargaining power and will invoke the restraint of trade doctrine, if necessary, to achieve this. We would submit that there is no difference in principle between a young sportsperson and a young musician without an established reputation. Both are often placed in a weak bargaining position against a large powerful organisation. Further, as was the case with the songwriter in *Shroeder*, a long term contract may lead to the sterilisation of a player's talents. One can envisage a young footballer signed up to a ten year contract with a rich club content to carry on paying him his weekly wage who never sees any first team play. For these reasons, we consider that the applicability of the restraint of the trade doctrine should be taken into account by clubs when negotiating contracts with players.

Discrimination

4.80 Arbitrary discrimination in some forms is arguably contrary to public policy in the common law and is prohibited on grounds of sex under the 1975 Sex Discrimination Act ("SDA"), of race under the Race Relations Act ("RRA") 1976 and of disability under the Disability Discrimination Act 1995 ("DDA") in areas within the reach of those respective Acts, and subject to the exceptions therein contained.[103] It is also prohibited under EC law on grounds of nationality and sex on the same basis.

Common law

4.81 In *Constantine v. Imperial Hotels*,[104] the famous West Indian cricketer bringing proceedings was awarded a mere five pounds damages for the refusal of an hotel to offer him accommodation on ground of his race, and then only because innkeepers were a "common calling". Exemplary damages were refused although Mr Justice Birkett found that there had been "unjustifiable humilia-

---

[102] See at 1313C–1314B.

[103] The standard textbook is C Bourn and J Whitmore, *Anti-Discrimination Law in Britain,* (Sweet and Maxwell 3rd ed., 1996). See also M J Beloff, *The Sex Discrimination Act 1975,* (Butterworths, 1976). The Human Rights Act ("HRA") will also make unlawful discrimination by public authorities in the exercise of Convention rights and freedoms on any ground such as sex, colour, language, religion, political or other opinion, national or social origin, association with a natural minority, property, birth or other status.

[104] [1944] KB 693.

tion and distress".[105] However, in *Nagle v. Fielden*[106] the Court of Appeal declined to strike out an action brought by the plaintiff based on the refusal of the Jockey Club to allow her a trainer's licence, holding it to be arguable that the practice of refusing a trainer's licence to women was void as contrary to public policy. Lord Denning MR said that "the Jockey Club's unwritten rule may well be said to be arbitrary and capricious. It is not as if the training of horses could be regarded as an unsuitable occupation for a woman like that of a jockey or speedway rider".[107]

It has been suggested that the common law protection of the right to work **4.82** may be engaged where a person is "deprived of the opportunity of exercising a profession on religious or political grounds that had no bearing on his competence in that profession".[108] For this purpose professional sport would presumably qualify as a profession. Further, a contract or rules with discriminatory effect may be in restraint of trade. Contracts in unreasonable restraint of trade are unenforceable as already discussed.[109] Discrimination may make the restraint unreasonable.

The anti-discrimination statutes

Discrimination can be direct or indirect. Direct discrimination occurs where the **4.83** prohibited ground was (objectively) the reason for the less favourable treatment.[110] An intention to discriminate is not a *sine qua non*. Indirect discrimination occurs where a criterion is applied for receipt of some benefit which is objectively neutral, but has a disproportionate adverse impact upon the protected class of which the victim is a member and which cannot be justified.[111] Section 1 of both the SDA and the RRA identify the two forms of discrimination. The DDA does not but both forms are apparently intended to be covered. The proper approach to the proof of direct discrimination in point of fact is now contained in *Glasgow City Council v. Zafar* where the importance of inference is stressed.[112] A case in which an inference was not drawn was *Saunders v. Richmond-upon-Thames BC*[113] in which the applicant (now MBE) failed in her claim that she had been refused a job as a golf professional on grounds of her sex even though the letter of acknowledgment was addressed "Dear Sir" and

---

[105] At p.708.
[106] *Nagle v. Feilden* [1966] 2 QB 633.
[107] See at 647C-E.
[108] *Chitty, supra.*, n. 45, Vol. I, 27–047.
[109] *Ibid.*, Chapter 16.
[110] The nature of less favourable treatment is discussed in *James v. Eastleigh BC* [1990] ICR 554. The Editorial in 1999 *Wisden* alleges racism in cricket, although the number of ethnic minority players in the English team casts doubt on the allegation.
[111] See generally on elements of indirect discrimination *Bourn and Whitmore*, above n. 112, paras. 2.40–2.59, pp. 66 and 82.
[112] [1998] 2 All ER 953 at p.998.
[113] *Saunders v. Richmond-upon-Thames BC* [1978] ICR 75, EAT.

seven out of nineteen questions related to her sex. It is submitted that the case would be decided differently today.

4.84 Examples in the field of sport where such discrimination was proved are provided by *Hassamy v. Chester City FC*[114] where the plaintiff relied on the fact that the manager had called him a "black cunt", and that he had subsequently been refused a professional contract.[115] In *Hargreaves v. FA*,[116] the successful female complainant was refused a coaching certificate by the FA when, out of fifteen hundred successful applicants, only two had been women and her performance on the advanced course outranked her victorious male rivals.[117]

4.85 Discrimination can occur vicariously.[118] Clubs will incur liability *qua* employers if they fail to protect players and other employees from racial harassment from other players or managers.[119]

Areas of discrimination

4.86 Discrimination in sport may occur in the area of employment.[120] This encompasses the discriminatory award of qualifications by governing bodies in circumstances where the qualification in fact facilitates employment.[121] In *Petty v. British Judo Association*[122] a female judo referee was granted a national referee certificate by the British Judo Association (BJA). However, she was told that she could not referee men's competitions at national level. As she was not an employee of the BJA, her claim relied on section 13 of the SDA. That renders it unlawful for authorities and bodies which can confer authorisations or qualifications which are necessary for or facilitate engagement in a particular profession or trade to discriminate on grounds of sex. The Employment Appeal Tribunal (EAT) found that, as the BJA both granted certificates and selected referees for matches, its conduct amounted to the granting of a certificate on discriminatory terms, ie on the terms that the applicant was not eligible to referee men's national events. In so holding, Browne-Wilkinson J said:[123]

"In our view section 13 covers all cases where the qualification in fact facilitates the woman's employment, whether or not it is intended by the authority or body which confers the authorisation to do so."

---

[114] *IT 2102426/97.*
[115] *SLB*, Vol. 1 No. 1, p. 4.
[116] IT Case 2320451/96.
[117] *SLB*, Vol. 1, No. 1, p. 4.
[118] Section 14 SDA, Section 32 RRA.
[119] See Welch, "The Potential Inclusion of Anti-Racism Clauses in Footballers' Contracts", in *SLB* Vol. 1, No. 1, p. 9.
[120] SDA Pt.II, RRA Pt.II, DDA Pt.II.
[121] SDA Section 13 RRA Section 12 but not the DDA.
[122] [1981] ICR 660.
[123] At 664.

Likewise the British Boxing Board of Control in *Couch v. BBBC*[124] and the **4.87**
FA, in respect of a coaching course[125] were held to be qualifying bodies but the
Kennel Club was not.[126]

Discrimination may also occur in the provision of goods, facilities and ser- **4.88**
vices.[127] These would include specifically "facilities for recreation".[128]

Single sex clubs (e.g. the MCC, which has now voluntarily changed its rules **4.89**
preventing the membership of women) are not within the reach of the discrimination statutes because to engage the Acts, the goods, facilities and services have
to be provided "to the public or a section of the public".[129] Nor are purely social
events. The PFA Dinner is for men only and the sole woman registered FIFA
agent, Mrs Rachel Anderson, who was ungraciously refused admission,[130] has
tested whether it was open to "a section of the public" in proceedings in the
Central London County Court heard in August 1999.

However, if the association has a public dimension, it may be covered. In **4.90**
Davis v. RFU,[131] the RFU was restrained from preventing Ms Davies from standing for election to their committee on grounds of her sex. After an interlocutory
injunction was obtained, the RFU changed its rules to permit women to be members of the Committee. In *Priestly v. Stork Margarine Social and Recreational
Club*, a social club open to all employees was held to be within the reach of
section 29 and, therefore, a "men only" rule for the snooker room was unlawful.

Justification

Direct discrimination is not justifiable under RRA and SDA, but is under **4.91**
DDA.[132] Justification requires "an objective balance to be struck between the

---

[124] IT Case No.2304231/97. See, " 'The Fleetwood Assassin' strikes a blow for female
boxers", in *SLB*, Vol. 1, No. 3 May/June 1998.

[125] *Hargreaves v. FA* IT Case 220651/96.

[126] *Nagle v. Kennel Club* (IT reference unavailable).

[127] SDA Section 29 RRA Section 20 DDA Section 19. See *Bourn and Whitmore*,
supra., Ch. 4.

[128] See *Bourn and Whitmore*, *supra.* n. 115 paras.8–25–8.28 (pp.274–276). See also
Prof. Carpenter "Gender Discrimination in Sport: Experience of Title IX" in *SLB* Vol. 1
No. 3 pp. 7–8 (no sex discrimination under federally-funded education programmes).

[129] SDA Section 29 RRA Section 20. See *Charter v. RRB* [1973] AC 885; *Dockers
Labour Club v. RRB* [1976] AC 285.

[130] The Independent 23 June 1998. See generally *Bourn and Whitmore*, *supra.*, n. 115,
para. 2.59–2.70 pp.76–82. Contrast: US decision that the PGA was not exempt from discrimination legislation *Martin v. PGA Tour Ltd* 1998 US Dist LEXIS 1980 (1998) coverage: *SLB* Vol. 1, No. 2, March/April p.2, 1998 J Gray). as it was a commercial enterprise
created to generate revenue for its members..

[131] (IT reference unavailable).

[132] See section 5(1)(b); 5(6); the reason is that whereas a person's race or sex is treated
as an irrelevant consideration for most areas concerned by the legislation the nature of a
particular disability may have to be taken into account.

discriminatory effect of the condition and the reasonable needs of the party who applies the condition".[133] It is not possible to visualise in the area of sport how indirect discrimination on grounds of race could be justified, and indirect discrimination on grounds of sex would either be exempted under SDA s.44 or not justified.

Exemptions

4.92 There is no relevant exemption for sport in RRA (nor does the law take any account of the hypothesis occasionally advanced that blacks have different and superior physiological qualities to whites[134]) and none is specifically enacted in DDA.

4.93 There is *an* exemption in SDA section 44:

"Nothing in Parts II–IV shall in relation to any sport, game or other activity of a competitive nature where the physical strength, stamina or physique of the average woman puts her at a disadvantage to the average man, render unlawful any act related to the participation of a person as a competitor in events involving that activity which are confined to competitors of one sex."

4.94 Section 44 SDA has been held not to apply to snooker since there was no evidence that a women's physique placed her at a disadvantage when playing snooker against men,[135] or to refereeing (as distinct from participating) in a judo bout as was held in *Petty v. British Judo Association*.[136] The EAT said in that case that:[137]

"we think that the words should be given their obvious meaning and not extended as to cover any discrimination other than provisions designed to regulate what is to take place in the contest as a competitor."

Further, section 44 does not apply to all women's sports such as all women's boxing[138] or wrestling[139] because the comparison has to be between the sexes. In *GLC v. Farrar*, the EAT said:[140]

"In a case where it is desired to exclude, for example, a girl from a mixed team, or to exclude girls from playing in teams against other boys or men, such an exclusion would not be unlawful for the purposes of the Act of 1975.

---

[133] *Hampson v. DES* [1989] IRLR 69 approved by HL in *Webb v. EMO Air Cargo (UK) Ltd* [1993] IRLR 27.

[134] "Black v. White in Sport" in *SLB* Vol. 1 No. 1, p. 12.

[135] *French v. Crosby Links Hotel* 7th May 1982 Great Yarmouth County Court.

[136] *Petty v. British Judo Association, supra.*, n. 122.

[137] At p. 665.

[138] *Couch v. BBBC, supra.*, n. 124.

[139] *GLC v. Farrar* 1980 ICR 266

[140] At p. 272.

But it seems to us that this section is dealing with situations in which men and women might both be playing the same game or taking part in the same physical strength, stamina or physique would become a relevant matter. It does not seem to us that this section is dealing with the situation where it is desired that a girl should play a game against a girl or where teams of girls are to play teams of girls.

Section 44 was held, however, to exempt the refusal to allow a twelve year old **4.95** girl to play football under FA auspices because of the reference to "average woman".[141]

There was little debate in Parliament on section 44 SDA, and several ques- **4.96** tions are unanswered. First, section 44 refers to "events" and it is unclear to what extent it applies to non-competitive facets of sport such as coaching or training sessions. Further, how does one measure the physical strength of the average woman or man? What link is required between physical factors and disadvantage – is it sport as a whole or specific games? Does it depend upon the role in a game? What if strength deficiency is compensated for by other factors such as, for example, style in ice-skating?

It has been contended that section 44 is inconsistent with the underlying prin- **4.97** ciples of the SDA, which requires persons to be treated as individuals, not as members of a group.[142] In *Couch* the Employment Tribunal held that the decision to prevent an all-women's boxing match was prompted solely by "gender based stereotypes and assumptions" about the relative risks posed by boxing to men and women. If a particular woman is strong enough to play a game on a basis of equality with men, why should she not be allowed to do so? The EOC's paper, "Equality in the 21st century", suggests that the exception in section 44 of the SDA should no longer permit the exclusion of young people of school age from competing in any sport, game or other competitive activity.[143]

Decency and privacy exemptions are built into the SDA: see section **4.98** 7(2)(b)(ii).[144] Single sex provision of facilities is permitted in circumstances of undress or other potential embarrassment (SDA s.35(1)(c)) or physical contact (SDA s.35(2))[145] or where the provision is by a voluntary body which caters for one sex only, i.e. a body carrying on its activities other than for profit and not set up under any enactment. Women's cricket clubs are lawful (s.34).

Much sport in the UK is organised via voluntary associations and clubs. In **4.99** order for the SDA to have a further reaching impact upon sport, it would be necessary to amend not only those sections of the SDA which permit certain single

[141] *FA v. Bennett* CA 28.7.98 (unreported).
[142] D. Pannick QC: Sex Discrimination in Sport (EOC 1983). M J Beloff QC, Paper to Bar Conference October 1998. *Bourn and Whitmore, supra.*, paras.8.63, pp.284–5.
[143] Published 1998. Available from EOC, p.175.
[144] See *Bourn and Whitmore, supra.*, para. 5.92.
[145] *Bourn and Whitmore, supra.*, n. 115, paras. 8.64–8.66, p. 285.

sex activities of voluntary bodies,[146] but also those which remove private clubs from the ambit of the Act.[147] The EOC report that two thirds of all complaints it receives concerning alleged discrimination in private clubs, relate to golf clubs.[148]

[146] Section 34 SDA.
[147] Section 29 SDA.
[148] "Misogyny on the Golf Course" in *SLB*, Vol. 1, No. 3, p. 12.

5

The Regulation of Play

Introduction

In the two preceding chapters we have considered the existence of rights to par- **5.1** ticipate in sport from two different standpoints. First, in chapter three we looked at direct rights of participation in sporting competition established by satisfying entry criteria. Second, in chapter four we examined the rights and duties of players (in a broad sense) and their clubs towards each other. In this chapter we move on to consider the extent and content of rights and obligations governing the conduct of sport itself. For the purposes of this chapter, our enquiry has passed the stage of ascertaining whether a right to participate exists at all, and, if it does, what are the pre-competition conditions subject to which that right may be exercised, and whether they have been fulfilled or not. Our account of sports law has now reached the stage of examining the content of sporting rights and obligations once all the pre-conditions for participation in a sporting competition have, from the perspective of the organisers of the competition, been satisfied.

It follows that, for the purposes of the current enquiry, we may assume that **5.2** the players are entitled and permitted to play; that the club they play for is eligible for the competition; and that no other objection to participation is forthcoming from the organisers of the competition. On those assumptions, we now look at the rules to which participation in sport is subject. Those rules are established, in part, by the organisers of the competition and, in part, by the general law of the state in whose territory the competition takes place. Their content may affect spectators as well as players and clubs. They include rules requiring safety measures to be taken, rules prohibiting criminal conduct in the course of sport and rules establishing the scope of liability, on the part of players and clubs, to others who may be participants, officials, spectators or indeed members of the public affected by a sporting event.

This rather amorphous collection of rules may, fairly loosely, be referred to **5.3** as rules regulating play. The notion of the regulation of play is considered, in our exposition, to denote rules which directly affect participation in sport and the organisation of sporting competition once eligibility to compete has been established. These rules are thus different in character from pre-competition eligibility rules of the type considered in chapter three. They also differ, conceptually, from rules governing relations between players and clubs which operate, so to speak, horizontally and do not, in principle, affect the actual conduct of sporting competition.

5.4   Rules which regulate play are also different, in their nature, from disciplinary rules which may apply to the course of the game itself but which are not operated until after the competition is over. Disciplinary regimes occupy an important position in sports law. Their functioning is discussed in chapter seven, and merits separate treatment. The operation of such disciplinary rules may require bodies exercising punitive jurisdiction to look backwards at events on the field of play, by way of post-mortem as it were. But such rules do not apply to play itself while the game is actually being played. The distinction is well illustrated by the example of a referee exercising the power to show a red card to a player, and thus sending him off for misconduct. The referee's power to do so arises in the course of the game, as it is a rule of the game that a player to whom a red card is shown must leave the field. This is a rule which regulates play and falls within the scope of our enquiry in this chapter. The same player may later face disciplinary charges as a result of having been sent off. These are applied to him *a posteriori*, and consequently do not fall within the scope of this chapter, but under the heading of disciplinary proceedings, considered in chapter seven.

5.5   Certainly in England and Wales, and it may be assumed in every country in the world, subject to any relevant special rules of law, the general principles of the criminal law and the law of tort or delict apply to participants in sport as they apply to everyone else. It goes without saying that the shooting of a player by another player during the game (as unfortunately happened once at a football match in El Salvador) is as much a crime as if it were committed anywhere else. Similarly, if a rugby player makes a dangerous tackle causing his opponent physical injury, the perpetrator may be guilty of a criminal offence such as common assault, or may be liable in tort for assault or negligence. It is not left solely to the laws of the game to penalise the perpetrator and to compensate the victim. And sporting rules empowering adjudicators to award compensation for dangerous play are rare or non-existent.

5.6   However, the application of common law principles in the context of sport throws up different issues to cases involving, say, a bar-room brawl or a road traffic accident. This is because in sport issues as to consent to physical contact frequently arise; so does the related issue of the standard of care in negligence in the course of a sport whose rules permit and envisage a greater or lesser degree of physical contact. Furthermore, statute may affect the manner in which sport is conducted. Match fixing would be unlawful as a criminal conspiracy at common law, and would almost certainly contravene the Theft Act 1968. Legislation requires measures to ensure safety and public order in some cases. And a raft of statutory provisions regulate betting on the outcome of horse races and other sporting competitions – as part of the specialist field of law relating to betting, gaming and lotteries.[1]

---

[1] See Smith, The Law of Betting, Gaming and Lotteries, Butterworths (1987) for a helpful account of that branch of the law.

It is beyond our purpose to give a comprehensive account of all rules regulating play, in the sense described above applicable in England and Wales; still less do we seek to describe fully those applying in other countries. Our aim is the more limited one of identifying the nature of such rules, subdividing them into categories which we estimate will be helpful, and giving a brief account of some of the more important legal developments within those categories. **5.7**

As a starting point, we ought just to pause to consider first what we mean by the notion of "play", when we speak of rules which regulate play. This requires us to consider, though only briefly, the nature of sport itself, and its limits. Immediately we are struck by the sheer variety of human activities which, down the ages, have been treated as sport. The founders of the Olympic Games in 776 BC[2] would probably have rejected synchronised swimming as inappropriate for inclusion in the Games. Those espousing the Corinthian ideal might have difficulty accommodating snooker and darts as sport; yet some purists, initially sceptically inclined, now accept them as legitimate sporting activity. Intellectual games such as chess are generally thought to test purely mental rather than physical prowess, but science now increasingly regards cerebral activity as physiological, so it may be that chess tests stamina as well as intellect.[3] **5.8**

This sort of musing is mildly entertaining but does not point in the direction of a precise legal definition of sport. Indeed in no legal system, so far as we are aware, has it been found necessary to embrace a conceptual approach to the nature of sport or to adopt a legal definition of the term – though in the familiar field of betting, gaming and lotteries the English courts have had to consider what is meant by a game of chance, and so forth. For the purposes of this book, we content ourselves with the easy proposition that sports law does not, or not yet, attempt to set limits to the definition of what a sport is. If we had to offer such a definition, we suggest that it would contain the following four elements: (i) an activity, human or animal (ii) in which one or more players, human or animal, compete against each other (iii) according to predetermined rules (iv) pursuant to which someone wins, and which determine who wins.[4] **5.9**

With those preliminary thoughts, we turn to consider the different types of rules regulating play. We began in chapter one with the premise that sports law is by nature international and non-governmental in character. In so far as rules regulating play are derived from the general law of the state in which a **5.10**

[2] Also the foundation date of the calendar based on recurrence of the Olympic Games every fourth year; see Bernard Knox, in the introduction to Homer's *Iliad* Penguin Classics (1996) p. 23.

[3] See *Chess – a Sport or Just a Game?* Sports Law Bulletin Vol. 2 No. 2 (March/April 1999) p. 16 recounting the British Chess Federation's efforts to get chess adopted as an Olympic sport and citing Michael Adams, Britain's number one chess player: "You need a lot of stamina . . . being in good shape helps to keep you focussed mentally . . . chess can be very draining". The same applies to legal practice, which however is *not* a sport.

[4] Cf. Grayson in All ER Annual Review 1987 at p. 239 ("The categories [of sport] are never closed").

competition is taking place, it is naturally a matter for the national law of that state to prescribe rules governing both the organisation of sports and liability arising from events in the course of play. The extent to which the general law of a particular state impacts on the conduct of sport, and the content of the relevant rules, will vary from sport to sport and from state to state. Our account of rules regulating play in this chapter is mainly specific to the law of England and Wales, though its common law content is also relevant in other common law jurisdictions across the world.

5.11 Before addressing the manner in which the law intervenes to regulate play, we consider a logically prior question with which the law is concerned: whether the game may be played at all.

Prohibited sports

5.12 The question here is whether the general law of the land, as opposed to the law governing relations between the parties involved in sport, permits the sport in question to be played. An answer to this question requires an account of prohibited sports. Under the mainly unwritten constitution of the United Kingdom, activities which are not specifically made illegal by statute or judicial precedent, may lawfully be undertaken. Under other written constitutions, sport is permitted by virtue of express constitutional guarantees of freedom of association. Chariot racing is therefore not banned in the United Kingdom, though it has lost some of its popular appeal.

5.13 A distinction must be drawn between sports which the state prohibits as such, and sports which are prohibited only if practised using unlawful means. For example, bear baiting, popular in Elizabethan times, would now by its very nature infringe legislation protecting animals against cruelty. So, probably, would dog fighting, which is known to have taken place clandestinely in recent times, in the East End of London. Professor Grayson's picturesque account of some of the legislation and litigation affecting rural and water sports, including hunting, shooting and fishing,[5] reminds us that our proposed definition of sport offered above excludes non-competitive sports pursued for pleasure. The current debate inside and outside Parliament over whether to ban stag or fox hunting[6] concerns an activity which some would call a noble and ancient sport while others would denounce it as mere barbarism masquerading as sport. We do not here enter that particular minefield except to observe that our conception of sports law concentrates on competitive sport with a clear winner and runner up at the end of the game.

5.14 Sports prohibited per se may also include sports in our sense of the term. Swordfights to the death between gladiators would infringe criminal laws ban-

[5] See Grayson, *Sport and the Law*, 2nd ed. (1994) pp. 112–7.
[6] See for example, *R v. Somerset County Council ex parte Fewings* [1995] 1 WLR 1037; *ex parte Scott* [1998] 1 WLR 226. The Prime Minister speaking in July 1999 on the BBC Programme "Question Time" suggested that Legislation to ban hunting with dogs was imminent.

ning offensive weapons, and probably amount to a common law conspiracy to commit grievous bodily harm or murder, and possibly to corrupt public morals as well. But martial arts and wrestling are not criminal by definition. Contact sports in this latter category are commonplace. The application to them of the criminal law is considered below.

Organisation and competition

Introduction

In the remainder of this chapter we consider how the law regulates the practical **5.15** organisation of and participation in sporting events. Jurisdiction over such activity is conferred in principally four ways: by statute, by the law of tort, by the criminal law and by the rules of the game itself. A fifth and extremely rare type of intervention consists in a challenge to the result of a game in a court of law, on the basis of applying the rules of the game. As to the latter, these include both primary rules determining how the game must be played (for example, the prohibition against handling the ball in association football, the rule that a cricketer is out if the ball is caught straight from the bat without bouncing, and so forth) and secondary rules conferring power on officials to disqualify a horse, to send a player off for misconduct, and so on. Such rules form a category narrower in scope even than that of rules which are "of sporting interest only" in the sense of developing Community law mentioned in chapter three and explained further in chapter four;[7] since that latter category includes some pre-competition eligibility criteria.

Jurisdiction conferred by the rules of the game is exercised summarily during **5.16** the game by the designated officials on the spot, and is virtually certain to be held non-reviewable by the courts. One could not realistically suppose that a court would ever overturn a decision to award try, or a penalty. The referee or umpire's exercise of discretion and judgment is beyond challenge, except to the extent that the rules of the game so provide, as they do in the case of an assistant referee in football whose provisional decision may be summarily reversed by the referee. The possibility of increased use of immediate video replay in refereeing may provide for summary appeal procedures in certain cases but, subject to that point, the risk of unfairness to a player is conclusively outweighed by the overwhelming sporting imperative of immediate certainty.

So obvious is the above proposition that one ought not to need authority to **5.17** support it; it simply goes without saying.[8] We need therefore look no

---

[7] See Case 38/74 *Walrave and Koch v. Association Union Cycliste Internationale* [1974] ECR 1405; Case 13/76 *Donà v. Mantero* [1976] ECR at 1333; Case 415/93 *Bosman* [1995] ECR I–5040; *AEK Athens FC and Slavia Prague v. UEFA* CAS arbitration 98/200, interim decision 17 July 1998.

[8] However there is authority to support the proposition: *Machin v. FA*, CA, unreported (1993) referred to at Grayson, Sport and the Law, 2nd ed., at p. 301 and 308;

further at summary jurisdiction over play exercised pursuant to the rules of the game. We turn next to the more substantial matter of legal intervention through statute, through the law of tort and under the criminal law.

Statute

5.18 The regulation of sport is not a matter in which the European Union legislature has become involved. At the March 1996 intergovernmental conference, the framing of the new Treaty of Amsterdam saw representations made by the European Olympic Committees and the European non-governmental sports organisations asking for an article in the Treaty whose effect would be to require sporting interests to be taken into account in the framing of new legislation by the European Union. The European Commission did not accept that there should be legally binding provisions in the new Treaty applicable to sport. The resulting compromise was soft law, in the form of a non-binding declaration attached to the Treaty in the following terms:

> "The conference emphasises the social significance of sport, in particular its role in forging identity and bringing people together. The conference therefore calls on the bodies of the European Union to listen to sports associations when important questions affecting sport are at issue. In this connection, special consideration should be given to the particular characteristics of amateur sport."

This falls far short of regulation of sport at Community level, and is only a very tentative step towards a sports policy in the European Union.[9]

5.19 It is therefore to national legislation that one must look to discern how sporting activity is regulated by statute. We include in our account some of the main statutes in England and Wales currently regulating the organisation of sports, which covers spectators as well as clubs and players. The claim of such legislation to form part of sports law properly so called, in our conception of the term, is a little doubtful, for legislative regulation of sport is undertaken by states primarily in support of non-sporting objectives, principally those of public safety and public order. However the legislation is of great practical importance to

---

Mendy, CAS Ad Hoc Division, Atlanta (1996), referred to in Beloff, Sport and the Law Journal Vol. 4 issue 3, pp. 5–9 at p. 8.

[9] See *The Path to a "Sports Policy" in the European Union*, Richard Parrish, Sports Law Bulletin, January/February 1998, Anglia Sports Law Research Centre. In May 1999 FIFA and UEFA announced that they would be making representations to the EU institutions with a view to procuring a limited legislative reversal of the effect of the *Bosman* decision. The measure sought is one permitting a minimum requirement that six nationals of the state in which a football club is located must be playing at any one time. In the UK, Wales, Scotland and Northern Ireland would be treated as different "states" for this purpose, so that Ryan Giggs would be treated as a "foreigner" at Manchester United.

sports administrators. It may be considered as meriting inclusion in this book on practical grounds and, for the purist theoretician, as a set of mere examples of statutory and judicial intervention in the course and context of sport rather than in or over sport itself.

In the United Kingdom statutory regulation intrudes relatively little into the **5.20** sporting world, even after a number of well publicised tragedies in recent times. It is fair to say that the legislature has reacted to those tragedies rather than anticipating them. Successive disasters at football stadia through this century at Wembley, Bolton Wanderers, Ibrox (Glasgow), Bradford and Hillsborough led to commissions of enquiry presided over by distinguished judges whose subsequent reports led to legislation. The most recent and authoritative reports are those of Mr Justice Popplewell[10] and Lord Justice Taylor.[11] A fuller account of legislative and administrative measures against football violence and in pursuit of safety can be found in Professor Grayson's *Sport and the Law*.[12]

The relevant legislative weapons in the state's armoury are, briefly, the fol- **5.21** lowing. The Safety of Sports Grounds Act 1975 enacted a regulatory regime whereby sports grounds designated by the Secretary of State required a safety certificate issued by the local authority in whose area the ground is located. Detailed provisions govern the power of the local authority to determine the terms and conditions for issue of such a certificate and the procedure for obtaining it.[13] Section 10 of the Act[14] empowers the relevant local authority to issue a prohibitive notice limiting the number of spectators who can lawfully be admitted to a particular ground, if the authority forms the view that admission of a greater number will involve a sufficiently high degree of risk to them to warrant such a limit until steps have been taken to reduce the risk to a reasonable level.

The 1975 Act marked the start of a general public supervisory function spe- **5.22** cific to sports grounds, over and above pre-existing regulatory powers applying to buildings generally, such as fire protection legislation. In 1987 the requirement for a safety certificate was extended specifically to stands at sports grounds holding 500 or more spectators.[15] The detailed procedure governing applications for such a safety certificate are prescribed by regulations.[16]

Parliament has also enacted legislation specific to sport for the purpose of **5.23** promoting public order, reacting to public concern about hooliganism. These

---

[10] Interim and final reports of the *Committee of Inquiry into Crowd Safety and Control at Sports Grounds*, Cmnd 9585 and 9710 respectively (Final Report November 1985)

[11] *Inquiry into Crowd Safety and Control at Sports Grounds*, Cmnd 962 (January 1990)

[12] 2nd ed. (1994) at pp. 125–144.

[13] See Sections 1–7 of the 1975 Act.

[14] As substituted by the Fire Safety and Safety of Places of Sport Act 1987 Section 23(1).

[15] Fire Safety and Safety of Places of Sport Act 1987 Section 26–30.

[16] The Safety of Places of Sport Regulations 1988, SI 1988/1807.

statutory provisions supplement the general law relating to public order, which applies in and around sporting events as it does anywhere else.

5.24 Thus the Sporting Events (Control of Alcohol etc) Act 1985 makes it an offence to cause or permit intoxicating liquor to be carried on a train or coach being used principally to carry passengers to or from a sporting event designated by the Secretary of State, which may be a sporting event abroad as well as in England and Wales.[17] Other offences of being drunk in a private vehicle adapted to carry more than eight passengers to or from such an event, or causing or permitting intoxicating liquor to be carried on such a vehicle, were added by a new section 1A of the 1985 Act the following year.[18] Section 2A made it an offence to possess, during a designated sporting event or while entering or trying to enter it, "any article or substance whose main purpose is the emission of a flare for purposes of illuminating or signalling (as opposed to igniting or heating) or the emission of smoke or a visible gas . . . [including] distress flares, fog signals, and pellets and capsules intended to be used as fumigators or for testing pipes, but not . . . matches, cigarette lighters or heaters".[19] An offence is also committed if the article carried is a firework.[20] Sections 6 and 7 of the Act give the police ancillary powers to close bars within a sports ground and to stop and search vehicles suspected of harbouring offenders under the Act. Other provisions in the same Act regulate licensing hours of premises concerned in selling alcoholic beverages within sports grounds.[21]

5.25 The Public Order Act 1986 contained wide ranging revisions to the general law of public order, including the creation of certain new offences not specific to sport but influenced by specific behaviour of, among others, individuals attending sporting events. Part IV of the Act also enacted provisions specific to football matches, empowering courts before which offenders are convicted of certain football related offences (as defined in section 31 of the Act) to impose exclusion orders prohibiting the offender from attending football matches. The provisions were made subject to prospective repeal by the Football Spectators Act 1989,[22] following the enactment of that Act which created a more wide ranging regulatory regime for football, including the concept of a national football membership scheme administered by a newly created Football Membership Authority, and a Football Licensing Authority with the function of issuing licences to organisers of designated football matches to admit spectators subject to such terms and conditions as the Authority should consider appropriate.[23]

[17] See Sections 1 and 9(3) of the Act.
[18] Section 1A was added by the Public Order Act 1986 Section 40(1) and schedule 1, Part I.
[19] Section 2A(3).
[20] Section 2A(4).
[21] See Sections 3–5D (Sections 5A-D added by the Public Order Act 1986 Section 44(1) and schedule 1 Part I).
[22] See Section 27(5) of the 1989 Act.
[23] See generally Sections 1–9.

However, the membership scheme has not been implemented. At the time of writing, the provisions relating to it not have not been brought into force and they are now unlikely to be.

The provisions relating to exclusion orders in the Public Order Act 1986, mentioned above, were replaced by similar powers to impose restriction orders which can apply to football matches outside as well as inside England and Wales. The added element was the duty on the offender to report to a specified police station on the occasion of designated football matches, so that the subject of the order cannot go to the match.[24] **5.26**

The Football (Offences) Act 1991 created an additional offence of throwing anything at or towards the playing area or any area where spectators or others are or may be present, at a designated football match.[25] Further offences were created by the same Act, of indulging in "chanting of an indecent or racialist nature";[26] and of going onto the playing area or an area adjacent to it.[27] **5.27**

Finally the Criminal Justice and Public Order Act 1994, which like the Public Order Act 1986 enacted various revisions to public order law generally, included a section creating a new offence of ticket touting at a designated football match, committed where a person unauthorised by the home club or the match organisers sells or offers to sell or exposes for sale a ticket, or something purporting to be a ticket, in any public place or place to which the public has access, or, in the course of a trade or business, in any other place.[28] **5.28**

Numerous regulations supplement the statutory regime outlined above, a detailed account of which is beyond the compass of this book. The recent legislation banning and restricting the sale and use of guns is likewise not described here. It is clearly a measure designed to enhance public safety, enacted without sporting considerations in mind and indeed in spite of them, for it has some impact on competitive shooting contests.[29] **5.29**

Tort and Sport

Generally

The obligations which arise out of contract are derived from the choice of the parties. The obligations which arise out of tort are derived from the law of the land. It is the sphere of the law of tort to determine in what circumstances, and with what consequences, one person may be liable for injury physical, psychological, psychiatric, financial or to reputation, which he has caused to another **5.30**

---

[24] Section 16 of the 1989 Act.
[25] Football (Offences) Act 1991 Section 2.
[26] See Section 3 of the 1991 Act.
[27] *Ibid*., Section 4.
[28] Section 166(1) of the Criminal Justice and Public Order Act 1994.
[29] Firearms (Amendment) Act 1997.

person, otherwise than under terms and conditions to which he has agreed. This is the subject matter of this part of this chapter.

5.31 The law of tort sometimes makes the standard of behaviour of the person who caused the injury determinative of whether liability arises. Assault and battery, respectively the threat of and the actual infliction of physical injury, require intent in the tortfeasor. Negligence requires the infliction of injury in circumstances where the person has no intent, but his action or omission falls short of an appropriate objectively set standard. The law of tort sometimes makes the nature of the action determinative of whether liability arises. Nuisance is constituted by an interference with another's enjoyment of land. These general propositions (which require elaboration and qualification) are applicable to all forms of human activity. Therefore tort applies to sport: Swift J in *Cleghorn v. Oldham* in giving judgment for the plaintiff who had been injured when struck by the defendant's golf club during a demonstration swing stated:

> "Games might be and [are] the serious business of life to many people. It would be extraordinary to say that people could not recover from injuries sustained in the business of life, whether that was football, or motor racing, or any other of those pursuits which were instinctively classed as games but which everyone knew quite well to be serious business transactions for the persons engaged therein."[30]

Negligence

5.32 Negligence is the dominant tort; indeed in the views of some it threatens to absorb or outflank almost every tort in the field. The tort of negligence has three elements: the plaintiff must establish that the defendant (i) owed him a common duty of care (ii) breached that duty (iii) damage resulted. The primary aspect of the common law duty of care which is relevant to sport is the need to avoid foreseeable risks which result in foreseeable physical injury.[31] Three main issues arise. First, whether there is a duty of care. Second, if so, what standard of care is required. Third, where the plaintiff is a participant, whether and – if so – to what extent such voluntary participation provides a defence.

5.33 As to the duty of care, it is elementary that a duty is owed to those who ought reasonably to be in contemplation as being affected by a particular act (the so-called "neighbour" principle). Further, the duty itself is to *take reasonable* care to avoid injury to another person or property. Finally, since both the identification of the individuals to whom the duty is owed and the existence and extent of the duty are substantially determined by conceptions of reasonableness, the facts of and relating to any given case will determine whether or not a duty is established and, if so, whether or not breach of such duty can be shown.

[30] 1927 43 TLR 465 at p.466.
[31] Duff, "Civil Actions and Sporting Injuries", 144 New LJ 639.

Duty of participants to each other

The existence of a duty of care between competitors in sports is now well estab- **5.34**
lished. It follows from the propositions adumbrated above that where a participant in a game or other sporting pastime is injured by the act or omission of
another participant, whether or not there exists a duty of care and, if so, to what
extent are both questions to be determined in the light of all the circumstances.
"Whilst the standard required of a sportsman has to take account of the competitive nature of sport, it would be misleading to regard the duty owed as being
any less than the duty of care".[32]

In *Rootes v. Shelton*,[33] the plaintiff was an experienced water skier tem- **5.35**
porarily blinded by spray and as a result he swung wider than usual so colliding
with a stationary boat. Kitto J said:

> "I cannot think that there is anything new or mysterious about the applica-
> tion of the law of negligence to a sport or a game. Their kind is older by far
> than the common law itself. And though water skiing may be slightly faster
> than chariot-racing it is, like every other sport, simply an activity in which
> participants place themselves in a special relation or succession of relations to
> other participants so that adjudication under the common law upon a claim
> by one participant against another for damages for negligence in respect of
> injuries sustained in the course of the activity requires only that the tribunal
> of fact apply itself to the same kind of question of fact as arises in other cases
> of personal injury by negligence."

> ". . . the conclusion to be reached must necessarily depend, according to the
> concepts of the common law, upon the reasonableness, in relation to the spe-
> cial circumstances, of the conduct which caused the plaintiff's injury . . . the
> tribunal of fact may think that in the situation in which the plaintiff's injury
> was caused, a participant might do what the defendant did and still not be
> acting unreasonably, even though he infringed the "rules of the game". Non-
> compliance with such rules, conventions or customs (where they exist) is nec-
> essarily one consideration to be attended to upon the question of
> unreasonableness; but it is only one, and it may be of much or little or even
> no weight in the circumstances."[34]

---

[32] And see Charlesworth and Percy on Negligence, 9th ed. (1997) at paras. 2–63 to
2–65.

[33] *Rootes v. Shelton* (1967) 41 ALJR 172, [1968] ALR 33, High Court of Australia. See
also *McComiskey v. McDermott* [1974] IR 75: where a racing car driver and his passenger are acting as a team, the duty of care owed by the driver to the latter was to drive the
car as carefully as a reasonably prudent competitive rally driver would be expected to
drive to win in the circumstances.

[34] At p. 387.

5.36   This approach was followed in the Court of Appeal in *Condon v. Basi*[35] where a foul tackle by the defendant, during a game of soccer, resulted in the plaintiff sustaining a fractured leg.[36] The Court concluded that the duty of care between players in competitive sports was a duty to take all reasonable care, taking into account the particular circumstances in which the completing players were placed. If one player injured another, because either he had failed to exercise the degree of care which was appropriate in all the circumstances, or because he had acted in a way to which the other could not have been expected to consent, he would be liable for damages in an action in negligence brought by the injured player.[37] In *Pearson v. Lightning*[38] the plaintiff recovered damages after being hit in the eye by the golf ball by the defendant. Sir Christopher Slade said "in any case concerning a golf course injuries must depend upon its particular facts".

5.37   The clear implication from *Condon v. Basi* is that, in the case of contact sports, such as football and rugby, it will be almost impossible to establish liability unless the actions of the defendant are outside the rules of the game. Indeed the Court of Appeal appeared to be saying that a breach of the rules is virtually a *necessary*, albeit not a *sufficient*, requirement for liability to attach. Again, there is nothing special about sports cases in this regard. In various fields, it has regularly been held that the rules and standards laid down by professional bodies provide a good guide as to the standards of reasonableness expected of those who operate in the fields governed thereby. Not every foul will constitute a tort: but something short of a foul will not do so.

5.38   What, then, are the relevant circumstances to be taken into account? These may, in our view, include the following. First, whether the sport is a contact or a non-contact sport. Different standards apply to boxing (where the object of the exercise is to engage in bodily contact) from rugby (where it is an incidental, but inevitable feature of the sport) to bowls (where such contact should not occur). Second, whether the accident is caused in the heat of the moment or in a

---

[35] *Condon v. Basi* [1985] 1 WLR 866.

[36] See Grayson "Revisiting the Field of Play" 136 New LJ 628; M.J.H. "Standard of Care in Competitive Sports" 4 Lit 337; Khan and Wolfgarten "Liability for Foul Play" 129 SJ 859; McEwan "Playing the Game: Negligence in Sport" 130 SJ 581.

[37] See *Ridder v. Thaler* 1997 unreported November 1990: Sports Law Bulletin ("SLB") Vol. 1, No. 1 (1998) p.3) (scrum half ordered to pay compensation for high tackle) also *McCord v. Swansea City AFC Ltd, The Times*, February 11, 1997, a tackle constituted "an error which was inconsistent with his taking reasonable care towards his opponent" (see also summary of cases of tackles settled out of court: Moore p.51). A "reckless disregard" test applies in USA in a player v. player situation. (*Nabozay v. Barnhill* 334 NE 2d. 258 (Illinois Appellate Court: 1975). The English test seems more stringent from the defendant's point of view. Recklessness necessarily involves negligence: but absence of recklessness does not disprove it: see GJBS: p.12 fn. 10. *SLJ* Vol 7. Issue 1. A. Duff "Reasonable Case v. Reckless Disregard".

[38] Unreported, CA, 1st April 1998.

quiet passage of play.[39] Third, the level of risk necessarily accepted as inherent in the sport. Fourth, as explained above, whether the rules of the game have been broken. Fifth, the cost and availability of precautions. Sixth, the level of risk involved.

5.39 These last two tests were applied in *Lewis v. Buckpool Golf Club*[40] where a high-handicap golfer was held to have been negligent in failing to wait before driving off the fifth tee. When he drove, he mis-hit the ball which struck and injured the pursuer, who was fully visible to him. The court stated that the mis-hit was something a reasonable man would have had in contemplation as a risk that was reasonably likely to happen i.e. more than merely possibly, but less than probably, and it was negligent to run such a risk in a situation where it could be avoided without difficulty, disadvantage or expense. This may be contrasted with *Feeney v. Lyall*[41] where the pursuer failed in a claim arising out of the circumstance that during a round of golf he was struck by a golf ball when he was in an unexpected fairway and invisible to the striker.

5.40 A controversial issue is whether different standards of care apply at different levels of the game, for example, depending on whether the game is professional or amateur. In *Condon v. Basi* it was stated: "The standard is objective but objective in a different set of circumstances. Thus there will of course be a higher degree of care required of a player in a First Division football match than of a player in a local league football match"[42] A contrary approach is, however, illustrated by *Elliott v. Saunders and Liverpool FC*[43] where Drake J. said:

> "The fact that the players are top professionals with very great skills, is no doubt one of the circumstances to be considered, but in my judgment the fact that the game is in the Premier League rather than at a lower level, does not necessarily mean that the standard of care is different."

[39] Where, during a motorcycle race, the sidecar passenger was injured when the machine crashed, which was caused partly by the failure of the rear brakes, as a result of a known defect that ought to and could have been rectified by its rider before the race began, his action for damages succeeded. It was held that the rider owed his passenger the normal standard of care and not the modified one, which usually applied to competitors in a sport, because the negligence had occurred in the relative calm of the workshop and not during the flurry and excitement of the race, at all: *Harrison v. Vincent* 1982 RTR 8. However, it was said in *Agar v. Canning* (1965) 54 WWR 302 at p.304 "The conduct of a player in the heat of a game is instinctive and not to be judged by standards suited to polite social intercourse."

[40] *Lewis v. Buckpool Golf Club*, [1993] SLT (Sh.Ct.) 43.

[41] *Feeney v. Lyall* [1991] SLT 156. *Leatherhead v. Edwards* 28.11.1998 (unreported). Where a defendant breached a safety rule at the heart and spirit of a game of uni-hockey, he was negligent when the high follow through of his stick caused the plaintiff to lose the sight of one eye.

[42] *Ibid.*, at 868, per Sir John Donaldson MR. Moore notes at p 48 in support of Sir John Donaldson MR, that "a variable standard of care is applicable in other areas of the law, most notably the medical profession"

[43] *Elliott v. Saunders and Liverpool FC* (unreported) 10 June 1994.

Moore also suggests that it would be anomalous if, when a professional team plays an amateur team (as sometimes occurs e.g. in the early rounds of the FA cup) differential standards of care apply to different teams.[44]

5.41   It may, however, be that the standard of care required in each case is the same, although the nature and level of the match in question (and, accordingly, the standards of skill to be expected from the players) would form part of the factual context within which such standard fell to be applied. From a practical point of view, sports injuries often raise evidential problems. In particular, it may be difficult to assess whether a player has breached the duty of care he owes another player given that this type of assessment will often involve analysing an occurrence whose duration can be measured in seconds.[45]

Duty of participants towards spectators

5.42   In *Woolridge v. Sumner*,[46] in which a horse ridden by the defendant collided with the plaintiff, Diplock LJ referred to "an almost complete dearth of judicial authority as to the duty of care owed by the actual participants to the spectators". The judgment sought to fill the vacuum. Diplock LJ's main points were as follows. First, Lord Atkin's statement of principle in *Donoghue v. Stevenson*

"does not purport to define what is reasonable care and was directed to identifying the persons to whom the duty to take reasonable care is owed. What is reasonable care in particular circumstances is a jury question and where, as in a case like this, there is no direct guidance or hindrance from authority it may be answered by inquiring whether the ordinary reasonable man would say that in all the circumstances the defendant's conduct was blameworthy . . . The law of negligence has always recognised that the standard of care which a reasonable man will exercise depends upon the conditions under which the decision to avoid the act or omission relied upon as negligence has to be taken."[47]

Second,

"if the course of a game or competition, at a moment when he has not had time to think, a participant by mistake takes a wrong measure, he is not to be held guilty of any negligence. . . In such circumstances something in the nature of a reckless disregard of the spectator's safety must be proved."[48]

Third, "the matter has to be looked at from the point of view of the reason-

[44] At p. 49.
[45] see Grayson p.74–75, *Woolridge v. Sumner* [1967] 2 QB 43 per Sellers LJ at p.52 and Diplock LJ at p.60.
[46] *Woolridge v. Sumner* [1963] 2 QB 43.
[47] At 66.
[48] At 67.

able spectator as well as the reasonable participant; not because of the maxim *volenti non fit injuria*, but because what a reasonable spectator would expect a participant to do without regarding it as blameworthy is as relevant to what is reasonable as what a reasonable participant would think was blameworthy conduct to himself".[49] Fourth, "a person attending a game or competition takes the risk of any damage caused to him by any act of a participant done in the course of and for the purposes of a game or competition notwithstanding that such act may involve an error of judgment or a lapse of skill, unless the participant's conduct is such as to evince a reckless disregard of the spectator's safety".[50]

There is in short a difference between a Carling colliding with a spectator and a Cantona kicking one. In *Wilks v. Cheltenham Homeguard Motor Cycle &* **5.44** *Light Car Club*[51] the plaintiffs were spectators at a motorcycle scramble and were watching the race lined up against the rope of the spectator's enclosure, when one of the competitors, riding at between 25 and 30 mph, suddenly left the track and plunged into them. It was held that a competitor in a race, who was going all out to win, owed a duty to spectators not to show a reckless disregard for their safety or (per Edmund Davies LJ) to cause injury "by an error of judgment which was a reasonable competitor being a reasonable man of the sporting world, would not have made" and which could not, in the stress of circumstances, reasonably be regarded as excusable.[52]

Duty of referees

In appropriate circumstances those refereeing or otherwise controlling dangerous sports may themselves be liable for any failure to display reasonable com- **5.45** petence resulting in injury to a player, including failure to implement relevant rules, designed in this instance to protect against injury. For example, in *Smoldon v. Whitworth*[53] the referee of a game of rugby was held liable to a player who was injured when a scrum collapsed dangerously.[54] The level of care required of an official towards a player was that appropriate in all the circumstances, taking full account of the factual context in which he was exercising his functions as referee. Lord Bingham LCJ declined to equate the duty owed by a referee to players with that owed by a participant to a spectator:

---

[49] At 67.

[50] At 68. Sellers LJ gave a judgment to the same effect.

[51] *Wilks v. Cheltenham Homeguard Motorcycle and Light Car Club* [1971] 1 WLR 668.

[52] At p. 674. See also *Payne and Payne v. Maple Leaf* (1949) 1 DLR 369 in which ice hockey players were held liable when they started a fight and injured a spectator with a hockey stick. For a useful list of negligence cases, see *Grayson* at pp. 178–180.

[53] *Smoldon v. Whitworth* [1997] ELR 249, CA.

[54] "The Liability of The Official" SLB 1998 Vol.1 No. 2 p. 8.

"In [the latter] cases it was recognised that a sporting competitor, properly intent on winning the contest, was (and was entitled to be) all but oblivious of spectators. It therefore followed that he would have to be shown to have very blatantly disregarded the safety of spectators before he could be held to have failed to exercise such care as was reasonable in all the circumstances. The position of a referee vis-à-vis the players is not the same as that of a participant in a contest vis-à-vis a spectator. One of his responsibilities is to safeguard the safety of the players. So, although the legal duty is the same in the two cases, the practical content of the duty differs according to the quite different circumstances."[55]

Lord Bingham LCJ then set out the way in which the duty of care was to be applied in this context:

"Full account must be taken of the factual context in which a referee exercises his functions and he could not be properly held liable for errors of judgment, oversights or lapses of which any referee might be guilty in the context of a fast moving and vigorous contest. The threshold of liability is a high one. It will not easily be crossed . . . [the learned trial judge] did not intend to open the door to a plethora of claims by players against referees, and it would be deplorable if that were the result. In our view that result should not follow provided all concerned appreciate how difficult it is for any plaintiff to establish that a referee failed to exercise such care and skill as was reasonably to be expected in the circumstances of a hotly contested game of rugby football . . ."[56]

Duty of coaches

5.46 Because a claim in negligence is founded upon the principle that the law requires the exercise of reasonable care to avoid injuring one's 'neighbour' and identifies one's neighbour as anyone who ought reasonably to be in contemplation as being affected by one's acts or omissions, it follows that coaches, other supervisors and the like will be expected to exercise reasonable care in imparting their knowledge and skills to their charges. It is submitted that a coach owes a duty to take reasonable care in all the circumstances to avoid physical injury but that a claim that deficient coaching resulted in economic loss (e.g. as a result of non-selection for a lucrative event) would only succeed if the coach had expressly undertaken that his protégé would achieve a particular standard of excellence.[57]

---

[55] At 256F-H.

[56] At 256E-F.

[57] "Should coaches take care?" (1998) Sport and the Law Journal Nov. p.11. New Law Journal: 12 Nov p.1598. See *Van Oppen v. Clerk to the Bedford Charity Trustees* 1990 1 WLR 235 where, in the context of an injury to a pupil on the rugby field, it was held that

Coaches may be liable for sins of omission as well as commission, for failing **5.47**
to give right advice as well as for giving wrong advice. Thus, for example, a
weightlifting coach who fails to advise as to the way in which to lift heavy
weights so as to minimise the risk of back injury may find himself exposed to liability when his charge sustains injury through the use of an unsafe technique.
Hence, a schoolboy who broke his neck when diving from a starting block into
the shallow end of a swimming pool succeeded in a claim for damages against
his PE teacher who had failed to give him appropriate instruction on how safely
to effect such a dive.[58] He also succeeded against the Amateur Swimming
Association for failing to issue (to instructors) appropriate warnings as to relevant dangers. Similarly, in *Hedley v. Cuthbertson*,[59] a professional mountain
guide was held liable for the death of his fellow climber because of his failure to
take adequate safety precautions when proceeding with a manoeuvre.

In a contact sport, where an adult coach participates in a demonstration or a **5.48**
practice game, his duty of care must take appropriate account of the difference
in size and strength between himself and his students.[60]

Duty of schools

The duty to take reasonable care is the same: the fact that those to whom the **5.49**
duty is owed are children intensifies its content.[61] In *Van Oppen v. Clerk to the
Bedford Charity Trustees*[62] where a schoolboy was injured by a rugby tackle but
not insured, it was held that there was no duty on the school to insure. Nor was
there a duty on the school to advise the boy's parents to arrange insurance.

the circumstances did not give rise to a duty on the school to have regard to its pupils'
economic welfare by advising on the dangers of rugby football or by taking out insurance
and that, in the absence of such a duty on the school it could not be said voluntarily to
have assumed a duty to advise parents on the question of insurance against injury.

[58] *Gannon v. Rotherham Metropolitan Borough Council*, 6 February 1991, unreported.

[59] *Hedley v. Cuthbertson*, Dyson J, 20 June 1997 (unreported).

[60] See for example, *Affutu-Nartoy v. Clarke* (1984) Times, 9 February.

[61] The particular duties of school and local authorities are discussed in Grayson
pp.103–108: see in particular, the valuable summary of relevant decisions at pp.105–107
which illustrates how courts have approached duties of supervision and guidance. See for
example, *Gibbs v. Barking Corpn* [1936] 1 All ER 115; *Ralph v. LCC* (1947) 111 JP 548;
Wright v. Cheshire County Council (1952) 2 All ER 789; *Conrad v. Inner London
Education Authority* (1967) 111 Sol Jo 684; *Fowles v. Bedfordshire County Council*
(1996) ELR 51 and *Thornton v. Trustees of School District No.57* (1976) 57 DLR (3d)
438. *A (A Minor) v. Leeds CC* (unreported) 2 March, Leeds Co. Court. Unstructured
gym activity negligent.

[62] [1990] 1 WLR 235.

Duty of Organisers/promoters

5.50 Organisers and promoters may be liable for injuries caused to spectators at a sporting event. The most likely cause of action is in negligence, and in addition under the Occupiers Liability Act 1957 (as amended by the 1984 Act of the same name), which imposes a statutory common duty of care not differing materially, as to the standard of care, from that which obtains in common law negligence. Whether or not the club or event organisers are liable for injury to spectators or others, such as officials, injured at the event naturally depends upon the facts. The authorities have tended to involve claims by spectators, but the principles should not differ according to whether the plaintiff is a spectator or an official or other person lawfully present at the game.

5.51 The Court of Appeal in 1932, the same year as the report of *Donoghue v. Stevenson*,[63] had to consider a case in which a car at a race track had careered over a barrier and struck a spectator.[64] The Court of Appeal reversed a jury's finding in favour of the plaintiff and entered judgment for the defendants. The court drew a distinction between exposure to the ordinary risks associated with presence at the event which the spectator must expect to run, and extraordinary perils to which he or she is additionally exposed in cases where the organisers or competitors act without proper regard to the safety of spectators. The latter, but not the former, will entail liability. Scrutton LJ described the test as applying generally to cases "where landowners admit for payment to their land persons who desire to witness sports or competitions carried on thereon, if these sports may involve risk of danger to persons witnessing them".[65] Thus he commented[66] that "those who pay for admission or seats in stands at a flying meeting run a risk of the performing aeroplanes falling on their heads"; and gave other more prosaic examples such as a spectator at Lord's or the Oval being hit by a cricket ball.

5.52 The principle has not changed, but has been applied on a number of occasions since. It is usually easy to predict the result of its application by using plain common sense. It is most unlikely that there will be liability unless the rules of the competition are breached, for compliance with them is the very thing which the plaintiff pays to watch. Such breach is a necessary but not a sufficient condition for liability. It is another matter altogether if safety is compromised by malfunctioning equipment provided by the event organiser, such as a collapsing grandstand at the Cheltenham Races.[67] In such a case no question arises of breach of the rules of the game. Indeed the cases only very rarely reveal exam-

---

[63] *Donoghue v. Stevenson* [1932] AC 562.
[64] *Hall v. Brooklands Auto-Racing Club* [1933] 1 KB 205, CA.
[65] [1933] 1 KB 205 at 209.
[66] *Ibid.*, at p. 213.
[67] *Francis v. Cockerell* (1820) 5 QB 501; see also *Brown v. Lewis* (1896) 12 TLR 455 (stand collapsed at Blackburn Rovers FC).

ples of liability being established where injury was caused through the actions of competitors. The defendants have been successful in cases where spectators were injured by a polo player on a pony running through a hedge,[68] a racing car leaving the track;[69] an ice hockey puck;[70] the winning horse at a horse show which collided with a photographer;[71] a motor-cycle at a scramble meeting[72] and a discus thrown at an athletics ground.[73]

But where ice hockey players started a fight and injured a spectator with a **5.53** hockey stick, the players were liable.[74] In one case competitors themselves recovered damages for injuries resulting from a defect in a race track controlled by a local authority, which caused horses and jockeys to stumble and fall.[75] And in *Cunningham v. Reading Football Club Limited*[76] Drake J held that the company which owned Reading Football Club was liable to police officers for injuries caused to them by football hooligans indulging in violence. The judge noted that the club's exoneration by a Football Association Commission of Inquiry was irrelevant to his finding that the common duty of care under the Occupiers Liability Act 1957 had been breached in circumstances where the visiting supporters were known to include an element with a propensity to violence.

It is also theoretically possible that promoters and organisers may be liable to **5.54** persons who suffer harm as a result of a sporting event even though they were not actually present at the ground. In *Alcock v. Chief Constable of South Yorkshire*,[77] a case arising out of the Hillsborough disaster where 96 football fans were crushed to death as a result of overcrowding in the stadium, the House of Lords considered whether a duty was owed to persons who suffered psychiatric injury as a result of the disaster. It was held that such a duty could be owed where a plaintiff fulfilled the following conditions. First, the plaintiff must have close ties of love and affection with the victim. Second, the plaintiff must have been present at the accident or its immediate aftermath. Third, the psychiatric injury must have been caused by direct perception of the accident or its immediate aftermath and not upon hearing about it from someone else. This test does

[68] *Piddington v. Hastings*, The Times, 12 March 1932.

[69] *Hall v. Brooklands Auto-Racing Club (supra).*

[70] *Murray v. Harringay Arena* [1951] 2 KB 529.

[71] *Wooldridge v. Sumner* [1963] 2 QB 43.

[72] *Wilkes v. Cheltenham Home Guard Motorcycle and Light Car Club* [1971] 3 All ER 369, CA.

[73] *Wilkins v. Smith* (1976) 73 Law Soc. Gaz. 938. However, organisers of a football match do not owe a duty of care to a spectator for its cancellation. *MacDonald v. FIFA/SFA* 1999 (Court of Session, Outer House). Unreported.

[74] *Payne and Payne v. Maple Leaf* (1949) 1 DLR 369.

[75] *Cook, Cochrane and Hampson v. Doncaster Borough Council*, The Sporting Life, 16 July 1993.

[76] The Times, 20 March 1991. For further cases on sport facilities management liability, see *Glenic v. Slair & Others* 1999 (unreported) (H. H. Graham Jones) *Davis v. Feasey* 14.5.99 (CA unreported); *Greening v. Stockton on Tees BC* (unreported 6.11.98).

[77] *Alcock v. Chief Constable of South Yorkshire* [1992] 1 AC 310.

envisage the possibility of a duty to a person who was not at the scene at the time the disaster happened.

5.55 However, it is in practice extremely difficult for a bystander to recover damages for psychiatric injury. This is demonstrated by the fact that, in *Alcock*, the House of Lords dismissed all the claims brought by relatives including the claim of a plaintiff who himself witnessed the scenes at the football ground where two of his brothers died. Further, in *White v. Chief Constable of South Yorkshire*[78] the House of Lords dismissed the claims brought be police officers who suffered psychiatric injury as a result of witnessing the tragic scenes.

Defences

Contributory negligence

5.56 There may well be occasions where the plaintiff, as an ordinary prudent participant in the game and calling upon his experience in the sport generally, will foresee dangers and will anticipate the likelihood of negligence of his fellow players. Just as in rescue cases, a court ought to make all proper allowances where the speed of the activity on the playing field has reduced the time available to the plaintiff to take stock of his situation and, hence, his opportunity to take evasive action either to avoid the accident or to reduce the degree of damage suffered. In *Feeney v. Lyall*,[79] during a round of golf, the pursuer had hooked his drive from the ninth tee on to the adjacent sixth fairway. In order to play his second shot he crossed over to the sixth fairway, where he was struck and seriously injured by a golf ball driven off the sixth tee by another golfer, who could not see the presence of the pursuer on that fairway. Liability in negligence was not established but, if it had been, the opinion was expressed that the pursuer would have been held 25 per cent contributorily negligent.

Volenti non fit injuria

5.57 The maxim *volenti non fit injuria* is used to describe a defence which operates where it can be shown that the plaintiff had consented to the breach of the duty of care alleged. Such consent may be express but it is usually implied from the particular circumstances of the case. There have been some cases concerning sport which have been analysed in terms of this defence or in which the court has commented on the potential availability of the defence. Thus, in *Lane v. Holloway*, where the defence was held not to apply, Lord Denning said as follows:[80]

> "I agree that in an ordinary fight with fists there is no cause of action to either of them for any injury suffered. The reason is that each of the participants in

[78] *White v. Chief Constable of South Yorkshire* [1998] 3 WLR 1509.
[79] *Feeney v. Lyall* [1991] SLT 156.
[80] *Lane v. Holloway* [1968] 1 QB 379 at 386, 387.

a fight voluntarily takes upon himself the risk of incidental injuries to himself. *Volenti non fit injuria*. But he does not take on himself the risk of a savage blow out of all proportion to the occasion. The man who strikes a blow of such severity is liable in damages unless he can prove accident or self-defence."[81]

5.58 Further, in *King v. Redlich*[82] the plaintiff, who was not yet wearing his protective helmet, suffered a severe head injury during the warm-up period prior to the start of an ice-hockey match. As the plaintiff was skating out from behind the goal the defendant, who had delayed his shot momentarily to enable the plaintiff to get clear, took a practice shot at goal but the puck hit the post and ricocheted, striking the plaintiff. The Court of Appeal of British Columbia held that the plaintiff should be deemed to have accepted the risk of injury in all the circumstances, because practice shots at goal during warm-up were a normal part of the game. Although the defendant had realised there was a higher risk in that he had seen the plaintiff, he had increased his level of care appropriately by the delay in making his shot and could not be expected to have foreseen that the puck would ricochet. Accordingly, the plaintiff's claim failed.

5.59 However, in our view the defence of *volenti non fit injuria* will rarely be of relevance in the context of sport. This is because the acceptance or risk by the participant or the spectator is already taken into account in determining the content of the duty of care. As shown above, the duty to exercise reasonable care to does not usually require the competitor, the referee or the coach to avoid risks which are inherent in the game itself. A court is unlikely to imply consent to risks which go beyond those inherent in the sport. It will only be in rare cases that a defendant is found to have acted in breach of his duty of care but is absolved of liability because of the consent of the plaintiff.

5.60 Thus in *Rootes v. Shelton*[83] a water skier brought an action against the driver of the towing speedboat, where he, one of a group of skiers which included the driver, was performing a complicated manoeuvre and was injured by a collision with a stationary obstruction of which the driver had given him no warning. It was held that the onus was on the driver to establish voluntary acceptance of a risk not inherent in the pastime. In another case, where a spectator did not know of the risk of injury caused by the failure of the organisers of a "jalopy" car race meeting to take proper safety precautions in roping off enclosures, it was held that the doctrine did not apply at all.[84] And in *Smoldon v. Whitworth*,[85] *volenti* was held inapplicable: there was no consent to a breach of duty by the referee. The Court of Appeal said:

[81] See also *R v. Coney* (1882) 8 QBD 534.
[82] *King v. Redlich* [1986] 4 WWR 567.
[83] *Rootes v. Shelton* (1967) 41 ALJR 172.
[84] *White v. Blackmore* [1972] 2 QB 652.
[85] *Smoldon v. Whitworth* [1997] ELR 249.

"... this argument is unsustainable. The plaintiff had of course consented to the ordinary incidents of a game of rugby football of the kind in which he was taking part. Given, however, that the rules were framed for the protection of him and other players in the same position, he cannot possibly be said to have consented to a breach of duty on the part of the official whose duty it was to apply the rules and ensure so far as possible that they were observed."

5.61   The scope of the defence in the context of sport was also addressed by Diplock LJ in *Woolridge* v. *Sumner*.[86] An experienced horseman, while taking part in a competition for heavyweight hunters at a horse show, galloped his horse called "Work of Art" so fast around a corner of the arena that centrifugal force caused it to follow a wide arc, sweeping out towards the edge of the course. The horse temporarily got out of control and plunged down a line of potted shrubs, bordering the arena, to a point where the plaintiff, a photographer, was standing. He, having no experience of horses, took fright, stepped back, stumbling into the path of the animal and was injured. Diplock LJ stated:

"The practical result of this analysis of the application of the common law of negligence to participant and spectator would, I think be expressed by the common man in some such terms as these: 'A person attending a game or competition takes the risk of any damage caused to him by any act of a participant done in the course of and for the purpose of the game or competition notwithstanding that such act may involve an error of judgment or a lapse of skill, unless the participant's conduct is such as to evince a reckless disregard of the spectator's safety'. The spectator takes the risk because such an act involves no breach of the duty of care owed by the participant to him. He does not take the risk by virtue of the doctrine expressed or obscured by the maxim volenti non fit injuria ... In my view, the maxim in the absence of expressed contract has no application to negligence simpliciter where the duty of care is based solely upon proximity or 'neighbourship' in the Atkinian sense. The maxim in English law presupposes a tortious act by the defendant. The consent that is relevant is not consent to the risk of injury but consent to the lack of reasonable care that may produce that risk, and requires on the part of the plaintiff at the time at which he gives his consent full knowledge of the nature and extent of the risk that he ran."

A competitor in a race 'is expected to go as fast as he can, so long as he is not foolhardy'.[87]

This modified standard of care did not apply unless the circumstances were such that the acts complained of were done in the flurry and excitement of the sport, for instance if a motorcycle rider missed changing his gear, when

---

[86] *Woolridge v. Sumner* [1963] 2 QB 43 at 68–9. The case was distinguished in *Quire v. Coates* [1964] SASR 294 and *Rootes v. Shelton* (1947) 41 ALJR 172.

[87] *Per* Lord Denning MR in *Wilks v. Cheltenham Homeguard Motor Cycle and Light Car Club* [1971] WLR 668 at 670.

approaching a hairpin bend in a race and crashed, having failed to get around the trace;[88]

However, the position is slightly different in relation to occupiers' liability. **5.62** The defence of *volenti non fit injuria* was always a defence available to the occupier, and section 2(5) of the 1957 Act expressly preserves it:

> The common duty of care does not impose on an occupier any obligation to a visitor in respect of risks willingly accepted as his by the visitor (the question whether a risk was so accepted to be decided on the same principles as in other cases in which one person owes a duty of care to another).

So where a visitor knowingly exposes himself, while on the premises, to a particular physical risk, the occupier may raise the defence against him. Thus in *Simms v. Leigh Rugby Football Club*[89] Wrangham J. held that a visiting rugby league football player willingly accepted the risks necessarily involved in playing on a field with a concrete wall running at a distance of seven feet three inches from the touchline, such walls being permitted under the rules of the game.

Of course, the *volenti* maxim only applies where the danger which causes his **5.63** injury is the one which the plaintiff willingly accepted – and this usually means that he must have known the precise risk in advance. Thus in *White v. Blackmore* it was held that the defence was not available against a spectator watching stock-car racing who was catapulted into the air by the safety ropes. The relevant risk did not arise from participation in a dangerous sport but from the organisers' failure properly to lay out the safety arrangements, a failure of which the plaintiff clearly did not knowingly take the risk.[90]

Nuisance

Members of the public in the vicinity of a sporting activity may sustain injury or suffer damage to their property as a result of the activity. Such persons may have **5.64** a cause of action in nuisance. Private law nuisance requires proof of interference with the reasonable use and enjoyment of land in which the plaintiff has a proprietary or possessory interest. Where such interest is lacking, the claim must be brought in public nuisance or negligence. Actions in public nuisance may arise from activity on sports grounds which causes danger on a highway nearby. Thus, where the hole of a golf course was placed adjoining the highway, so that players habitually drove out of bounds on to the road, that was held to be a nuisance, rendering the club liable to a person on the highway who was injured.[91]

---

[88] *Harrison v. Vincent* [1982] RTR 8, CA. See Kovats, 'Sportsman's Charter Revoked' 115 SJ 824.

[89] *Simms v. Leigh Rugby Football Club Ltd* [1969] 2 All ER 923.

[90] See also *Latchford v. Spedeworth International, The Times,* October 11, 1983; *Gillmore v. LCC* [1938] 4 All ER 331 and *Horton v. Jackson*, February 28, 1996, CA.

[91] *Castle v. St. Augustine's Links* (1922) 38 TLR 615. The player who struck the golf ball would also be liable if he had failed to take reasonable care to keep his ball from going where it did: wee *Cleghorn v. Oldham* (1927) 43 TLR 465.

That case should be compared to *Potter v. Carlisle and Cliftonville Golf Club Ltd*[92] where it was held that the playing of cricket on a ground, from which cricket balls were hit out of the ground on rare occasions only, was not a nuisance and the club was not liable to a person who was injured by a ball in the highway.[93]

5.65   An example of a claim brought in private nuisance is the case of *Miller v. Jackson*.[94] The law of private nuisance was applicable because the plaintiff's house adjoined a cricket ground. The Court of Appeal held that the defendants had committed a nuisance since their use of the land involved an unreasonable interference with their neighbour's use of their house and garden. However, Lord Denning MR and Cumming Bruce LJ refused an injunction on the basis that the public interests of the village in recreation should be preferred to the private interests of the plaintiff in his property. In *Kennaway v. Thompson*,[95] on the other hand, an injunction was granted against a water-sports club on orthodox principles that the discretion to award damages should only be exercised where the nuisance was "trivial and occasional".[96]

Assault

5.66   The tort of assault, sometimes called trespass to the person, is a further possible cause of action in sports injury cases. It requires the intentional or reckless infliction of injury, or the threat of it. It is therefore insufficient for this tort to prove merely negligent behaviour.[97]

Damages

5.67   It is not our intention here to deal in detail here with the principles governing awards of damages in tort cases involving sport. Those principles do not differ

[92] *Potter v. Carlisle and Cliftonville Golf Club Ltd* [1939] NI 114.
[93] See further *Bolton v. Stone* [1951] AC 850. *Calson Gillon v. Chief Constable of Strathclyde Police* 1996 The Times 22 November.
[94] *Miller v. Jackson* [1977] QB 966.
[95] *Kennaway v. Thompson* [1981] 1 QB 88.
[96] For other examples of claims brought in nuisance see: *Hilder v. Associated Portland Cement Manufacturers Ltd* [1961] 1 WLR 1434 (footballs regularly kicked out of field); *Lamond v. Glasgow Corporation* 1968 SLT 291 (liability established in circumstances where there were 60000 golf shots over fence in each year); *Lacay v. Parker and Boyle* (sued on behalf of Jordans Cricket Club) 1994 The Times May 15th (1994 144 NLJ 485) where an injunction was refused on the basis that the plaintiff came to the nuisance which is, however, no defence: *Miller*). See also *Sheler v. City of London Electric Lighting* (1895) 1 Ch. 287 and *AG v. Hastings Corporation* (1950) 94 Sol. Jo. 225.
[97] See *Letang v. Cooper* [1964] 2 All ER 929 and *Lane v. Holloway* [1968] 1 QB 379.

from the general principles applicable in cases of personal injury outside the sporting context. The measure of damages will, in the ordinary way, be that which is necessary to put the plaintiff in the position he would have been in – so far as money can do it – if the tort had not been committed. The award will cover cover pain and suffering, and any financial loss.[98]

Those representing participants in sport who are injured should bear in mind **5.68** the possibility of claiming damages for loss of chance.[99] In *Mulvaine v. Joseph*[100] the plaintiff, an American club professional golfer, suffered a hand injury as a result of a taxi driver's negligence. He was awarded damages for loss of the opportunity to compete in tournaments, the ensuing loss of experience and prestige which might have resulted in him becoming a tournament professional in America and loss of the chance of winning prize money. Arguably such loss is equivalent to the loss of the opportunity of competing at the Olympics and the loss of a chance of winning a medal, albeit these losses are more difficult to quantify. The principle in *Mulvaine* extends to loss of a chance to do something which attracts no monetary prize.

In assessing the value of the lost chance, the usual civil standard of the balance **5.69** of probabilities does not apply. In *Davies v. Taylor*,[101] Lord Reid said as follows:

"When the question is whether a certain thing is or is not true – whether a certain event did or did not happen – then the court must decide one way or the other. There is no question of chance or probability. Either it did or it did not happen. But the standard of civil proof is a balance of probabilities. If the evidence shows a balance in favour of it having happened, then it is proved that it did in fact happen. . . "You can prove that a past event happened, but you cannot prove that a future event will happen and I do not think that the law is so foolish as to suppose that you can. Sometimes it is virtually 100 per cent: sometimes virtually nil. But often it is somewhere in between. And if it is somewhere in between I do not see much difference between a probability of 51 per cent and a probability of 49 per cent."

Damages for loss of a chance are therefore to be assessed in proportion to that **5.70** chance, subject to the de minimis principle that no account is to be taken of possibilities which are very small, speculative or fanciful. The assessment process must take uncertain events into account. As a matter of fact, an athlete's chances of winning a competition would turn on many contingencies: his form at the time of the Olympics, the form of his competitors, avoidance of injury. It is

[98] *Watson v. Bradford* 1999 (unreported) (HC) almost £1 million damages awarded for a vicious tackle.
[99] See *Chaplin v. Hicks* [1911] 2 KB 786 CA; *Kitchen v. RAF Association* [1958] 2 All ER 241 CA. See also McGregor on Damages 16th ed., para. 385. Damages can be awarded for loss of opportunity to enjoy sport *Tsipoloudis v. Donald* CA, 11.12.98 (unreported).
[100] *Mulvaine v. Joseph* (1968) 112 SJ 927.
[101] *Davies v. Taylor* [1974] AC 207 at 213.

immaterial that such contingencies render the assessment of damages uncertain. In the leading case of *Chaplin v. Hicks* the plaintiff lost the chance of winning a prize. Vaughan Williams LJ said:[102]

> It was said that the plaintiff's chance of winning a prize turned on such a number of contingencies that it was impossible for anyone, even after arriving at the conclusion that the plaintiff had lost her opportunity by the breach, to say that there was any assessable value of that loss. It is said that in a case which involves so many contingencies it is impossible to say what was the plaintiff's loss. I am unable to agree with that contention. I agree that the presence of all the contingencies upon which the gaining of the prize might depend makes the calculation not only difficult but incapable of being carried out with certainty or precision. . . I do not agree with the contention that, if certainty is impossible of attainment, the damages for a breach of a contract are unassessable.

Practical issues arising in sporting injury claims

5.71 Apart from a sound grasp of the legal principles involved, the sports lawyer also needs a finely tuned understanding of the practical issues that are likely to arise when representing clients in such claims. Particularly difficult problems may confront a club which is sued in its capacity as employer of a player who injures another player. Take the straightforward case of a rugby player claiming in respect of injuries arising from an unlawful high tackle, contrary to the rules of the game. Liability may not be seriously in doubt, for example because the perpetrator is caught on video making a horrifyingly dangerous tackle long after the ball has been passed away. Suppose also that the culprit has immediately been shown a red card by the referee. So there is little doubt that the player is likely to be held liable.

5.72 But suppose, further, that the real issue in the case is whether the infliction of injury to the plaintiff was deliberate, reckless or merely negligent. If it was deliberate, the defendant player will be guilty of the tort of assault and it is most unlikely that the club would be held vicariously liable.[103] If, however, the injury was inflicted negligently or recklessly – in the sense that the guilty player showed reckless disregard for the safety of the victim, but without deliberate intent to injure him – the club will be vicariously liable on ordinary principles as the employer of the guilty player.[104]

5.73 The club may find itself in a difficult position. It may wish to stand behind its player, whom it may, for example, have defended in disciplinary proceedings subsequent to the incident. If it does that, it is likely to support the proposition that the injury was caused by accident, not design. However that outcome is

---

[102] at 791–792.

[103] See e.g. *Racz v. Home Office* [1994] 2 AC 45; *Makanjuola v. Commissioner of Police for the Metropolis* [1989] 2 Admin LR 214.

[104] See Clerk and Lindsell on Torts, 17th ed. (1995) at para. 5–20ff.

detrimental to the club's economic interests, since it will find itself liable. The club's financial position may be better served by "disowning" the player, and supporting the proposition that he deliberately inflicted the injury, with the consequence that the club is not vicariously liable. However as a matter of employee relations, that may not be a tenable position in practice.

One must add to the above equation the further practical considerations that (i) **5.74** the club is likely to have liability insurance under a policy which, typically, would cover liability for accidentally inflicted but not deliberately inflicted injury; and (ii) the governing body of the sport in question may take a dim view of a club which adopts inconsistent positions in, respectively, disciplinary proceedings and subsequent litigation. The relevant governing body may also be unimpressed with one of its member clubs taking a stance in litigation which appears to espouse a lenient view of, if not actually to condone, violence on the field of play.

We offer the above example as a convenient illustration of the application of the principle of vicarious liability in sports law, as well as an instance of the dif- **5.75** ficulties which clubs may face when seeking to reconcile sometimes divergent and conflicting interests.

The criminal law

Serious cases of sports injuries can lead to criminal prosecutions.[105] There are a **5.76** number of offences against the person which may be applicable in cases of violence on the sports field ranging from assault at one end of the spectrum to manslaughter at the other. We do not attempt here to provide a guide to the constituent elements of these offences. For that, the reader should consult a specialist criminal law textbook.[106]

However, one issue that is of particular relevance to sport is the defence of **5.77** consent. Consent provides a defence to the offences most commonly found in sport, for example common assault, battery and assault occasioning actual bodily harm contrary to section 47 of the Offences Against the Person Act 1861.[107] Consent will not be a defence in the absence of "good reason". Thus, in *R v. Brown*,[108] the House of Lords held that the defence did not avail the defendants who had consensually engaged in sado-masochistic practices as the satisfaction of sado-masochistic desires does not constitute good reason.[109] In *Attorney-*

---

[105] See Grayson at pp. 161–165 for a useful list of criminal prosecutions for sporting violence on the field of play between 1878–1994.

[106] Such as *Archbold* or *Smith and Hogan, Criminal Law* 9th ed., 1999.

[107] Though not to the more serious offences against the person.

[108] *R v. Brown* [1994] 1 AC 212, HL.

[109] In *Laskey, Jaggard and Brown v. UK* 24 EHRR 39, the European Court of Human Rights ruled that the conviction of the defendants was an interference in their private lives which was "necessary in a democratic society" and was therefore not contrary to Article 8 of the European Convention on Human Rights.

General's reference (No 6 of 1980)[110] Lord Lane, the then Lord Chief Justice, in addressing the question of whether persons engaged in a fight outside the context of the sport could avail themselves of the defence of consent and concluding that most fights will be unlawful regardless of consent, emphasised that:

> "nothing which we have said is intended to cast doubt upon the accepted legality of properly conducted games and sports."

5.78   Thus, consent to injury deriving from the fact of participation in a sport will be consent for "good reason". However, this does not mean that every injury inflicted in the course of sporting activity is lawful. Whether a participant can be taken to have consented to the risk of an injury will depend on the nature of the sport, the type of injury and the manner in which it was inflicted. A common sense approach must be taken to this type of assessment. The nature of the sport will often be determinative. Take the case of boxing. Its very purpose is to "assault" one's opponent and each competitor will be taken to have consented to the level of injury which is inherent in the sport itself. Compare that to a tennis match in which there is no physical contact between competitors. No defence of consent will be available to the tennis player who leaps over the net and hits his opponent.

5.79   Apart from the nature of the sport, the issue whether or not the injury has been inflicted within the rules of the games will also be important. Thus, even in the context of a boxing match, there are types of injury to which the participants cannot be said to have consented because they are not envisaged by the rules of the sport. The biting by Mike Tyson of Evander Holyfield's ear is a case in point. The intention of the aggressor is also important. A sportsperson can be said to have consented to the risk that a contact sport may have unintended effects of such severity that they may amount to a serious injury not envisaged by the rules of the game. However, the law does not permit that type of injury to be inflicted deliberately or recklessly.[111]

5.80   The criminal law has been used increasingly in recent years to resolve disputes on the field of play. In Scotland, the Lord Advocate has issued a series of *Instructions* to Chief Constables which provide guidance on when and why the police ought to take action.[112] These *Instructions* state, for example, that the Lord Advocate wishes the police to investigate in circumstances "where the violence used by the participant goes well beyond that which would be expected to occur during the normal run of play and which the rules of the sport concerned are designed to regulate. In deciding which incidents to investigate the police should pay particular regard to incidents where the violence or disorderly

---

[110] *Attorney-General's reference (No 6 of 1980)* [1981] QB 715.

[111] See *R v. Brown* (above) and Kuldip Singh QC, *Consent to Violence in Sport* (1994) 2 Sport and Law Journal 7; and the Law Commission's Consultation Paper No 134, *Consent and Offences Against the Person*; Simon Gardner, *The Law and the Sports Field* [1994] Crim LR 513.

[112] See, Gardner, *Touchlines and Guidelines: The Lord Advocate's Response to Sportsfield Violence* [1997] Crim LR 41.

conduct has occurred after the whistle has blown and whilst the ball is dead and to incidents where the violence or disorderly behaviour has occurred in circumstances designed or liable to provoke a disorderly or violent response from spectators". The Lord Advocate's intervention followed a number of high profile prosecutions in Scotland involving violence on the field. These included the conviction of Duncan Ferguson, then of Glasgow Rangers FC, for an assault by headbutting John McStay of Raith Rovers FC.[113]

Litigation determining the outcome of a game

5.81

We conclude this chapter by explaining, lastly, a particular and unique form of regulation of play consisting of an actual legal challenge in a court to the result of a match. The astonishing result was that the identity of the winning side was determined by a judge in a court of law, long after the game was over; though in the event he upheld the award of the victory to the team which both sides and the umpire on the day regarded as having won.

5.82

The case emanated from the Caribbean island of Barbados where cricket arouses high passions. A local encounter between St Catherine's and the Police Sports Club, under the auspices of the Barbados Cricket Association saw the first two days of the three day two innings match rained off. The captains agreed to limit the first innings of each team to one over. After each team had batted for one over, the Police team was one run ahead. In the second innings St Catherine's were all out for 75, which score the Police team attained for the loss of only five wickets. Both clubs regarded the Police team as the winner. The Association challenged the result, which would have taken the Police team to the top of the table. After an inquiry the Association's board of management declared the result void.

5.83

A rule purported to make the board "sole authority" for the interpretation of its rules, but Williams CJ in the High Court held that the two clubs' joint allegations of procedural unfairness and reasonable suspicion of bias were matters of law for the court, not the Association. These complaints were upheld. So, significantly, was the further complaint that, contrary to the Association's view, the rules on their true construction did allow the captains to agree to shorten the first innings. Consequently the court granted a declaration that the Association's decision was void, and that the Police team had validly won the

---

[113] Duncan Ferguson was sentenced to three months in prison and received a 12 match ban from the Scottish Football Association. The increasing number of criminal prosecutions in sport has been a feature throughout the UK. See, for example, *R. v. McHugh* (1998) unreported 20 February. McHugh was convicted of causing grievous bodily harm under section 20 of the Offences Against the Person Act when he kicked an opposing player, Darren Smith, in the head causing him severe injuries: Sports Law Bulletin: Vol.1, No.2, March/April 1998, p. 3.

match.[114] The unique feature of the case is that the identity of the winning side depended not on the court interpreting *ex post facto* disputed versions of what had occurred on the field of play, which would clearly be impermissible. The result depended purely on the legal question of construction of the relevant rules in question, which is *par excellence* a matter for the court, as we have already seen in chapter 3.

5.84   Most unusually, the rules at issue were the actual laws of the game of cricket, not, as is usually the position, disciplinary rules or rules governing eligibility to compete. This is the only known instance in authority of a court deciding the result of a match. Such "outcome litigation" differs conceptually both from "eligibility litigation" of the type described in chapter 3 above, and from disciplinary litigation examined below in chapter 7, in that it entails the regulation by the court of play itself. On the facts of *Griffith v. Barbados Cricket Association*,[115] both teams agreed with the court's decision, and that of the umpire, as to which was the winner. The challenge to the result emerged after a complaint to the Association by a third party team, which led to the Association wrongly upholding the complaint and thereby becoming the defendant in the proceedings.

5.85   But we leave this chapter with the thought that, according to the logic of *Griffith*, a losing team could equally challenge in court the proposition that it had lost, claiming a declaration against the winning team, seeking to substitute itself as the winner. Such a claim would fail in the vast majority of cases where the identity of the winner depends on the non-reviewable judgment of the referee or umpire as to whether a goal is offside, whether a cricketer is out LBW, and so forth. But in the rare case where the winner's identity depends on a pure question of construction of the rules, there is no reason *a priori* why a loser should not become a winner through the intervention of a judge after the event.

---

[114] *Griffith v. Barbados Cricket Association* [1990] LRC (Const) 786. On the construction issue, the court applied *Lee v. Showmen's Guild of Great Britain* [1952] 2 QB 239, CA.

[115] Supra.

6

Broadcasting, Marketing and Competition Law

Introduction

This chapter is concerned with selling sport to the public. The manner in which   **6.1**
sport is sold is undergoing a rapid transformation and sport, as an industry, is
growing in stature. Sports sponsorship generates US$ 15 billion per year, the sale
of broadcasting rights US$ 42 billion and the sale of tickets US$ 50 billion.[1] An
illustration of the growing importance of broadcasting and marketing to a large
sports club may be given by a breakdown of Manchester United's revenues in
the financial year 1997–8. While ticket sales were still the largest overall earner,
accounting for 34 per cent of revenue, merchandising earned the club 27 per cent
of its revenue, television 19 per cent, sponsorship and royalties 13 per cent and
conference and catering activities 7 per cent.[2] In other words, two thirds of
Manchester United's earnings come from activities not directly connected with
attracting people to the ground to watch football. As it also announced plans to
open up to one hundred and fifty franchised retail outlets in Ireland,
Scandinavia and East Asia, it looks likely that non-ticket earnings are going to
account for an ever increasing proportion of the club's income, and this is a
trend reflected across professional sport.

Broadcasting

Introduction

The value of broadcasting rights to sport has been an important part of its grow-   **6.2**
ing commercialisation. Sports events draw bigger television audiences than anything else. It was estimated that 27 million viewers in the UK watched Argentina
eliminate England from the World Cup in a penalty shoot-out on 30 June 1998.
Other than state occasions, no other type of event has the capacity to draw such
a large audience. This has obvious economic repercussions. Not only is it
extremely lucrative to market sport through television, it is also attractive to
use that medium to market other products by associating them with sport.

---

[1] Stephen Townley, "Finding the Right Balance in Sport", *Sportvision*, January 1998.
SLB Vol. 2, No. 3 Fraser Reid "Investing in a Sports Event".
[2] *The Financial Times*, September 29 1998, p. 30.

Deregulation and the introduction of new technology mean that broadcasting services are undergoing rapid development which further enhances its enormous commercial potential. In particular, digital technology, pay-TV and pay-per-view services, providing additional broadcasting time and capacity, allow for ever-increasing consumer choice. Viewers will, for example, be able to opt for theme channels, have improved picture quality and be able to view a particular event from the perspective of their choice.

6.3 For years, prices for television rights to sports events were kept relatively low. However, increased competition for those rights and an enhanced appreciation of their commercial value has meant that prices have risen considerably within a short period of time. For example, the fee for the Eurovision rights paid by the European Broadcasting Union to the International Amateur Athletics Federation for the World Athletics Championships rose from US$ 6 million for the Tokyo championships in 1991 to $ 91 million for the Stuttgart and Gothenburg championships in 1993 and 1995. The fee for the summer Olympics rose from $90 million dollars for the Barcelona games in 1992 to $250 million for the Atlanta games in 1996. Television rights to the Sydney games have been sold for $705 million in the USA.

What are broadcasting rights?

6.4 Organisers of sporting events may spend significant resources in making them happen. Likewise, a club with a large support base will need to make a considerable ongoing investment in maintaining and increasing its popularity. Where a sporting event is televised, are the organisers automatically entitled to the television revenues? Where a match between popular clubs is televised attracting a large audience, are those clubs entitled to share in the proceeds? The issue at the root of these questions is the extent to which the law recognises a "right", akin to a property right, in a sporting event.

6.5 Different legal systems take very different approaches to this fundamental question.[3] In the United States, quasi-property rights in sporting events are recognised as part of the doctrine of commercial misappropriation. In an early case a radio station was sued for broadcasting play-by-play commentaries of Pittsburgh Pirates games. The necessary information was obtained from observers that it paid to watch the games from premises that the radio station leased and which overlooked the ball park. The Court held that the plaintiff, Pittsburgh Athletic Co, had a property right in the news disseminated by the defendant and the right to control that news for a reasonable period following each game. This "right" derived from the fact that the plaintiff organised the games and controlled the ball park. The defendant's conduct constituted unfair

---

[3] For a helpful summary of US and Commonwealth case-law see Aaron N. Wise "A 'Property Right' in a Sports Event: Views of Different Jurisdictions", (1996) *Sport and the Law Journal* (SLJ), issue 3, p. 63.

competition and an interim injunction was granted to the plaintiff to restrain radio broadcasts of the games.[4] Essentially, the test for intervention by the courts seems to be whether a third party is "free-riding" on the plaintiff's efforts. In a recent case involving the legality of transmitting data about basketball games in progress via Motorola's "Sportstrax" device, the Second Circuit Court of Appeals reversed the District Court's finding that Motorola had misappropriated the National Basketball Association's (NBA) "property right" in NBA games, holding that the NBA had failed to show that the defendants were "free-riding" on its efforts.[5] In France, the organisers of some sports events own statutory rights enabling them to exploit those events. In Italy, there is case-law recognising that a sports event organiser has a "right" in the event and in Germany and Japan, though no such right is recognised as a distinct legal concept, nonetheless broad unfair competition laws usually have the effect of protecting the organiser of an event against appropriation of the benefits by a third party.[6]

In English law there is no property right in sports events, nor does it recognise **6.6** a tort of unfair competition which prevents third parties exploiting the business developed by others. Thus, someone who had bought supposedly exclusive rights to photograph a dog show was unable to prevent others from taking and publishing their own photographs, the Court of Appeal holding that the promoters of the dog show had no property right capable of assignment.[7] Nonetheless, "broadcasting rights" in sports events are routinely negotiated and sold. Since such rights do not exist as such, what is it that is actually sold? The answer is that the ability to broadcast is often dependent upon a recognised proprietary right. For example, if a match is to be held at a cricket ground, a television company will require a licence from the owner of the ground in order to enter it and film the event. If such a licence is granted, the company may loosely be described as owning a "broadcasting right" in respect of the match in question.

---

[4] *Pittsburgh Athletic Co v. KQV Broadcasting Co*, 24 F Supp 490. On the misappropriation doctrine generally, see the decision of the US Supreme Court in *International News Service v. Associated Press* 248 US 215.

[5] *The National Basketball Association and NBA Properties Inc v. Motorola Inc and Sports Team Analysis and Tracking Systems Inc* 931 F Supp 1124, 17 USC §102(a).

[6] Wise and Meyer, *International Sports Law and Business*, Part IV "Broadcasting and Sports in Selected Jurisdictions", para. 5.9.1.A, (Kluwer Law International).

[7] *Sports and General Press Agency Ltd v. 'Our Dogs' Publishing Co Ltd* [1917] 2 KB 125, CA. Most Commonwealth jurisdictions take a similar approach. Thus, the leading Australian decision on the issue is *Victoria Park Racing and Recreation Grounds Company Ltd v. Taylor* (1937) 58 CLR 479 in which the plaintiff racecourse sought to prevent the defendant from broadcasting a radio commentary of a race by using a scaffolding erected on the defendant's own property near the racecourse. The plaintiff argued that it had a quasi-property right in the races. The Australian High Court rejected this argument, holding that "a spectacle cannot be owned".

6.7   Ultimately then, where the ability effectively to televise an event is dependent upon access to the sports ground where the event is held, the owner of that ground may be said to own broadcasting rights which it may sell to television companies either on an exclusive or non-exclusive basis. Practically, however, market power may well lie not with the owner of the ground but with the organiser of the event or with the teams competing. Thus, a company wishing to organise a high profile international athletics meeting in the UK will have a choice of venue at which to stage it. Conversely, owners of the available venues will compete for the contract to hold the event. An important part of the selection and negotiation process will undoubtedly be the issue of broadcasting rights. Where there are many potential venues, the event organiser will be in a powerful position to negotiate a favourable agreement in respect of television rights. Thus, though a broadcasting right stems from a licence to enter property, as a matter of commercial reality its value derives from the event itself and it is the organiser of or participants in that event that will usually gain most of the profit. Broadcasting rights are, therefore, a commercial rather than a legal concept.

6.8   Where sports clubs are members of a league, it is common to find that the rules of the league deal expressly with the sale of broadcasting rights. Often such rules provide that the league will be responsible for selling rights to broadcast matches played within the league structure. The rules of a league are generally contractually binding upon clubs and this means that clubs subject to such a rule have no latitude to sell rights to their own matches individually to the highest bidder. Thus, though Manchester United can undoubtedly command larger television audiences than, say, Charlton Athletic or Southampton, it is precluded by the Premier League Rules from capitalising on that by individually selling broadcasting rights to its games at a higher price. This type of joint selling has competition law implications which are discussed below.[8]

Copyright over broadcasts

6.9   Broadcasting rights should be distinguished from copyright in television broadcasts. Copyright is a property right which subsists in works including broadcasts.[9] The first owner of the copyright in a broadcast is the person who makes the broadcast.[10] Broadly, the owner of the copyright has a monopoly over it and is able to prevent others copying the broadcast, issuing copies to public – for example, video recordings, showing the broadcast in public – for example in a cinema or including it in a cable programme service.[11] All of these acts are prohibited where they are carried out in relation to the broadcast as a whole or a

---

[8] See paras. 6.56–6.63 infra.
[9] Section 1(1) of the Copyright, Designs and Patents Act 1988.
[10] Sections 6(3), 9(2)(b) and 11(1) of the 1988 Act.
[11] Sections 16–20 of the 1988 Act.

substantial part of it.[12] "A substantial part" means a substantial part qualitatively rather than quantitatively. Thus, a clip showing the wickets taken in a cricket match or goals scored in a football match would constitute a "substantial part" of a broadcast of the entire match because they are the most significant and newsworthy element.

However, it is important to note that, even when the "substantial part" point **6.10** has been passed, "fair dealing" with a broadcast for the purpose of recording current events does not infringe any copyright in it.[13] This means that, within reasonable limits, a television company may use part of a broadcast of a sports event made by another company in order to report a news story. This is illustrated by the case of *British Broadcasting Corporation v. British Satellite Broadcasting*.[14] The BBC owned the copyright in its broadcasts of the 1990 World Cup. BSB showed, in its sports news programmes on Sky Sports, excerpts taken from BBC broadcasts of some of the football matches. The excerpts were between fourteen and thirty seven seconds long and were used over the period of twenty four hours following the match in question. They concentrated on one or two significant events such as the scoring of a goal or a near miss and were accompanied by a verbal report of the incident and by an acknowledgment of the source of the film. The BBC brought an unsuccessful copyright infringement action. Scott J held that BSB were entitled to rely on the fair dealing defence under section 30(2) of the 1988 Act. In so holding, he rejected the BBC's argument that that defence should be limited to the reporting of current events in general news programmes, finding that the BSB programmes were genuine news reports, albeit confined to news of a sporting character. They were not programmes of football analysis or review.[15] The judge found that BSB's use of the excerpts was fair dealing. In assessing this, it was important to look at both the quality and quantity of the broadcast. The excerpts at issue were short. Though they showed the highlights of the match, this did not take them outside the scope of the defence as it was such a normal and obvious means of illustrating a news report on the World Cup.[16]

Following this case, the main broadcasters formulated and subscribed to a **6.11** Sports News Access Code of Practice covering the volume of sports footage that may be lifted and used in news programmes. It was agreed that compliance with the Code would amount to a "fair dealing" defence under section 30(2).[17] The Code covers only general news and regional news programmes and does not permit the use of material in specialised sports review or sports news programmes. Although the *BBC v. BSB* case does establish that the "fair dealing"

---

[12] Section 16(3) of the 1988 Act.
[13] Section 30(2) of the 1988 Act.
[14] *British Broadcasting Corporation v. British Satellite Broadcasting* [1992] Ch 141.
[15] See at 159B-E.
[16] See at 158C-G.
[17] The Sports News Access Code of Practice has now expired.

defence extends to news programmes concerned solely with sport, the judge was careful to make the point that the programmes at issue in that case were not programmes of football analysis or review. It therefore seems likely that the defence will not extend to use of excerpts in programmes of that nature.

6.12   Copyright in the broadcast of a sports event can, of course, be assigned or licensed. Thus, the party which "owns" the broadcasting rights may require the television company to which it sells them to assign the copyright in the broadcast back to it. In that way it would be able to control future exploitation of the material, for example, use in video compilations or end of year sports review programmes. Similarly, the television company is likely to require the copyright to be licensed back to it so that it may use the footage again for certain purposes. Such agreements may themselves be subject to restraints imposed by competition law. This is dealt with below.[18]

How are broadcasting rights regulated?

6.13   In common with other commercial agreements, broadcasting contracts must comply with competition law. This impacts upon the content of such contracts, affecting issues such as exclusivity and joint selling. Second, broadcasting relationships must comply with the statutory framework which is in place to regulate broadcasting. Before moving on to discuss the limitations imposed by competition law, the main subject of this chapter, it is appropriate to make some brief observations about statutory regulation.

Statutory regulation

6.14   The regulatory scheme for television broadcasting is contained largely in the Broadcasting Acts of 1990 and 1996. These are intended to implement and, therefore, should be interpreted as necessary in accordance with the Television without Frontiers Directive.[19]

6.15   It is not the purpose of this book to provide a general survey of the manner in which television broadcasting is regulated by these statutes. Suffice it to say that the Independent Television Commission ("ITC"), established pursuant to section 1 of the 1990 Act to regulate the commercial broadcasting sector, has wide-ranging powers and functions. Those include responsibility for granting and controlling broadcasting licences[20] as well as a general regulatory function in respect of issues such as sponsorship and advertising[21] and the content of programmes.[22]

---

[18] See paras. 6.70–6.76 below.

[19] Council Directive 89/552/EEC as amended by Directive 97/36/EC.

[20] See Part I of the Broadcasting Act 1990.

[21] See sections 8 and 9 of the 1990 Act as well as the ITC Advertising and Sponsorship Codes.

[22] See sections 6 and 7 of the 1990 Act and the ITC Programme Code.

Sports broadcasting is subject to the regulatory scheme in the same way as **6.16** any other broadcasting. However, it is singled out for special treatment by Part IV of the Broadcasting Act 1996 which is entitled "Sporting and Other Events of National Interest". The concern addressed by this Part of the Act is the limitation placed by the growth of satellite and other forms of subscription television on the general accessibility of popular sporting events. This concern was underlined by a general resolution passed in 1996, in which the European Parliament declared that it "considers it essential for all spectators to have a right of access to major sporting events" and that

> "exclusive broadcasting rights for certain sports events which are of general interest in one or more Member States must be granted to channels which broadcast in non-encrypted form so that these events remain accessible to the population as a whole."[23]

To this end, Article 3a(1) of the Television Without Frontiers Directive as **6.17** amended expressly permits member states to take measures

> to ensure that broadcasters under its jurisdiction do not broadcast on an exclusive basis events which are regarded by that member state as being of major importance for society[24] in such a way as to deprive a substantial proportion of the public in that member state of the possibility of following such events via live coverage or deferred coverage on free television.

The provision goes on to state that, if member states choose to take such measures, they shall draw up a designated list of such events.

Accordingly, section 97 of the 1996 Broadcasting Act provides for the **6.18** Secretary of State to draw up and publish a list of sporting or other events of national interest. The Secretary of State also has the power to revise or cease to maintain the list. Before exercising any such power he must consult.[25] Sections 98–101 then protect the general accessibility of listed events by declaring void any contract purporting to grant a broadcaster exclusive rights to a listed event. Indeed, section 101 goes further and requires rights to carry listed events to be granted to both a free to air and a pay-TV broadcaster, unless permitted otherwise by the ITC.[26]

The current listed events are divided into two groups, the difference being **6.19** that those in Group B can be shown live on pay-TV as long as there is adequate coverage, such as edited highlights or delayed coverage, on free to air television.

---

[23] European Parliament Resolution of 22 May 1996, 1996 OJ C166/109.

[24] Recital 18 to the Directive gives as examples the Olympic games, the Football World Cup and the European Football Championships.

[25] See subsection (2).

[26] Cf the position in Italy where the government has passed a decree which limits pay-TV operators to 60 per cent of the broadcasting rights to Serie A football matches from next year. If there is only one bidder for the rights, then the contract will hold for a maximum of three years: *The Financial Times*, 1 February 1999 and *Il Sole 24 Ore*, 2 February 1999.

The revised list published in January 1999 is as follows. In Group A are the Olympic Games, the FIFA World Cup Finals Tournament, the Scottish FA Cup Final (in Scotland), the Grand National, the Derby, the Wimbledon Tennis Finals, the European Football Championship Finals Tournament, the Rugby League Challenge Cup Final, the Rugby World Cup Final. In Group B are cricket test matches played in England, non-finals play in the Wimbledon tournament, all other matches in the rugby world cup finals tournament, Five Nations rugby tournament matches involving home countries, the Commonwealth Games, the World Athletics Championship, the finals, semi-finals and matches involving home nations' teams in Cricket World Cup, the Ryder Cup and the Open Golf Championship.

Competition law

An introduction

6.20 It is convenient to discuss at this juncture the application in general terms of competition law to sport.[27] This section is of relevance not only to the substantive issues of broadcasting dealt with in this chapter but also to access to competitions which forms the subject of chapter three, employment rights (chapter four) and discipline (chapter seven).

6.21 This section discusses EC competition law, ie. Articles 85 and 86 (now Articles 81 and 82) of the Treaty of Rome. These provisions are directly applicable in the UK. The UK has also now adopted competition rules modelled on Articles 85 and 86 (81 and 82) which are contained in the Competition Act 1998, which reformed UK competition law to reflect Community law as far as possible. The UK equivalent to Article 85 (81) is to be found in Chapter I of the Act; Article 86 (82) in Chapter II and these are referred to respectively as the Chapter I and Chapter II prohibitions[28]. Given that there is a large substantive (though

---

[27] For a comprehensive commentary on competition law see, Bellamy and Child, *Common Market Law of Competition* (Sweet and Maxwell 1993, 4th ed.), and Green and Robertson, *Commercial Agreements and Competition Law* (Kluwer, 2nd ed. 1998).

[28] There is no statutory or case law exemption for any sport from application of either EU or UK competition law, although a declaration to the Treaty of Amsterdam does emphasise the social significance of sport and urge special consideration for it in policy making. M. J. Beloff QC "The Sporting Exception in EU Competition Law" *European Current Law* (forthcoming 1999) analyses the extent to which restraints of sporting interest only are outwith the reach of the Treaty provisions. See also SLB Vol. 2, No. 2, Parrish "Steering a Middle Course in European Union Sports Policy" The European Model of Sports Consultation Document of DGX. In the US, professional baseball has long held a case law based exemption from antitrust law: *Federal Base-ball Club of Baltimore v. National* League 259 U.S. 200 (1922, Sp. Ct.), *Toolson v. New York Yankees Inc* 346 U.S. 356 (1953, Sp. Ct.), but this has been held by the Supreme Court to be "an aberration . . . rest[ing] on a recognition and an acceptance of baseball's unique characteristics and needs": *Flood v. Kuhn* 407 U.S. 258, 282 (1972, Sp. Ct.). No other sport had any exemption from antitrust law; see however the Curt Flood Act 1998.

not procedural) coincidence between the two regimes, all discussion in this book of the substantive application of Articles 85 and 86 (81 and 82) to sport can also be taken as demonstrating the probable application of UK law. There is one significant jurisdictional difference between the two regimes. In order for EC law to apply, an effect on inter-state trade must be demonstrated; the same restriction does not apply in respect of UK law.

Article 85 (now Article 81)

Article 85 (81) of the EC Treaty provides as follows: **6.22**

1. The following shall be prohibited as incompatible with the common market; all agreements between undertakings, decisions by associations of undertakings and concerted practices which may affect trade between member states and which have as their object or effect the prevention restriction or distortion of competition within the common market, and in particular those which:

(a) directly or indirectly fix purchase or selling prices or any other trading conditions;

(b) limit or control production, markets, technical development, or investment;

(c) share markets or sources of supply;

(d) apply dissimilar conditions to equivalent transactions with other trading parties, thereby placing them at a competitive disadvantage;

(e) make the conclusion of contracts subject to acceptance by the other parties of supplementary obligations which, by their nature or according to commercial usage, have no connection with the subject of such contracts.

2. Any agreements or decisions prohibited pursuant to this Article shall be automatically void.

3. The provisions of paragraph 1 may, however, be declared inapplicable in the case of:

– any agreement or category of agreements between undertakings;

– any decision or category of decisions by associations of undertakings;

– any concerted practice or category of concerted practices;

which contributes to improving the production or distribution of goods or to promoting technical or economic progress, while allowing consumers a fair share of the resulting benefit, and which does not:

(a) impose on the undertakings concerned restrictions which are not indispensable to the attainment of these objectives;

(b) afford such undertakings the possibility of eliminating competition in respect of a substantial part of the products in question.

Thus, for Article 85(1) (81(1)) to apply, the following features must be present. First, there must be an agreement, decision or concerted practice between undertakings. Second, it must affect competition within the common market. **6.23**

Third, there must be an effect on inter-state trade. Even if these factors are all present, the agreement may benefit from exemption pursuant to Article 85(3) (Article 81(3)). In order for it to do so, the parties must notify the agreement to the Commission which has sole jurisdiction to grant exemptions. If the agreement does fall within Article 85(1) (Article 81(1))and is either not notified or is not exempted, then Article 85(2) (Article 81(2)) renders the agreement, subject to possible severance, automatically void. Other consequences may also ensue. The parties are likely to be fined by the Commission and may be liable to actions in damages brought by injured third parties. These constituent elements of Article 85 (81) and their particular application to the context of sport are discussed in turn below.

Undertakings, associations of undertakings

6.24 The term "undertaking" has been construed broadly to extend to any entity, regardless of legal form, which carries on an economic activity. As explained in chapter four above, Community law takes a broad view of what constitutes an economic activity. It includes the provision of services as well as the supply of goods. Thus, it is well-established that entities which transmit television broadcasts are undertakings within the meaning of the competition rules.[29] Further, it is immaterial whether or not the undertaking is profit-making.

6.25 Professional and semi-professional sports clubs will almost always be "undertakings". Even if their main purpose is sporting, they will generally be engaged in economic activities such as the sale of tickets for matches, sports merchandise such as replica shirts, television broadcasting rights and advertising.

6.26 The status of sports' governing bodies was considered by the Commission in *Distribution of Package Tours During the 1990 World Cup*.[30] At issue were agreements between FIFA, the Italian Football Association and the local organising committee. All three entities were held to be "undertakings" for the purposes of Article 85 (81). The Commission noted that although FIFA carries out sporting activities, it also carries out activities of an economic nature, for example, the sale of advertising and television broadcasting rights.[31] Similarly, the Italian Football Association was responsible for the organisation of the World Cup and, for the purpose of financing its expenditure, had a share in the net profits of the competition.[32]

6.27 It may be that sports governing bodies are better described as associations of undertakings in that it may be more accurate to view them as amounting to the sum of their participant clubs rather than an independent structure in their own

---

[29] See, eg, Case 155/73 *Sacchi* [1974] ECR 409, [1974] 2 CMLR 177.

[30] OJ 1992 L326/31, [1994] 5 CMLR 253.

[31] See paras. 47–9 of the Commission's decision.

[32] See paras. 50–3. See, also, Case T–46/92 *Scottish Football Association v. Commission* [1994] ECR II–1039 in which the Scottish FA did not dispute before the CFI the power of the Commission to rely against it on Regulation 17/62 implementing Articles 85 and 86 (81 and (82).

right. As far as the application of Article 85 (81) is concerned, it makes no real substantive difference whether a governing body is found to be an undertaking in its own right or an association of undertakings as both are caught. However, the characterisation of a governing body may be of tactical significance to a potential plaintiff as it may well have an impact upon the choice of defendant. Thus, where a league has engaged in an anti-competitive practice and a plaintiff wishes to proceed against an individual club rather than against the body itself, then it will be in that plaintiff's interest to argue that the league comprises an association of undertakings and is not itself an indivisible undertaking. The choice of defendant will of course dictate whether it is the club or the governing body which is fined or liable in damages if the plaintiff's action is successful. The second consequence flowing from this type of characterisation relates to Article 86 (82). If a governing body is found to be an undertaking in its own right, it may be subject to that provision if it holds a dominant position in the market place.[33] Though it should be said that even if a governing body is an association of undertakings, those undertakings might be linked economically such that they are jointly dominant and therefore subject to Article 86 (82) in any event.[34]

Agreements, decisions, concerted practices

Agreements, decisions and concerted practices overlap and are treated fluidly by **6.28** the courts. No formality is required; the concept of "concerted practices" covers informal cooperation not recorded in any agreement or decision. The Court of Justice (ECJ) has defined "concerted practice" as:

> "a form of co-ordination between undertakings which, without having reached the stage where an agreement properly so called has been concluded, knowingly substitutes practical co-operation between them for the risks of competition."[35]

Thus, any form of co-operation between undertakings falls within Article 85(1) (Article 81(1)) if it significantly affects competition and has an affect on trade between member states.

As far as associations of undertakings are concerned, Article 85 (81) covers all **6.29** activities which produce anti-competitive effects and have an impact on interstate trade. So, although Article 85 (81) expressly refers to decisions, nothing will really turn on the precise form of the measure taken. This is particularly important to appreciate in the context of sports law given that associations in the form of leagues and governing bodies are common in the sports sector. Thus, agreements between such associations may be caught by Article 85(1) (Article 81(1))[36] and so may their rules, constitutions and statutes.

---

[33] See para. 6.44 below.
[34] See para. 6.44 below.
[35] Case 48/69 *ICI v. Commission* [1972] ECR 619, [1972] CMLR 557, at para. 64.
[36] Case 71/74 *Frubo v. Commission* [1975] ECR 563, [1975] 2 CMLR 123, para. 30.

Prevention, restriction or distortion of competition

6.30 An agreement is caught by Article 85(1) (Article 81(1)) if its object or effect is to prevent, restrict or distort competition. Nothing turns on which of these three expressions applies to a particular agreement.[37] The effect on competition must be appreciable.[38] Conceptually it is difficult to define what constitutes the necessary effect of competition. The text of Article 85(1) (Article 81(1)) itself contains examples but these are far from exhaustive. It is important to appreciate that a restriction on conduct will not necessarily amount to a restriction on competition.

6.31 Commercial agreements may be horizontal (ie. between undertakings at the same level of supply in the market) or vertical (ie. between undertakings at different levels, eg. manufacturers and retailers). Common examples of horizontal agreements caught by Article 85(1) (81(1)) are price-fixing and market-sharing agreements. The Commission and European Courts view price-fixing and market-sharing-agreements as anti-competitive by their very nature so they will almost certainly be caught by Article 85(1) (81(1)).[39]

6.32 Examples of vertical agreements which may fall within Article 85(1) (81(1)) are exclusive distribution, exclusive purchasing and trade mark licensing agreements. Broadly, the effect on competition of agreements of this type must be assessed with regard to the whole economic context of the agreement.[40] For example, in assessing whether an exclusive purchasing beer-tie agreement restricted competition, the ECJ held that it was necessary to examine the extent of other barriers to entry or to growth for participants on the market and consider the cumulative effect of the agreement and others like it.[41] Similarly, the Court has held that where restrictions are objectively necessary for the performance of a particular type of contract, for example provisions protecting a franchiser's intellectual property rights, then they may fall outside Article 85(1) (81(1)).[42] However, where restrictions in a vertical agreement have the effect of preventing imports or exports between member states of the EU or otherwise

[37] In this text these expressions are used interchangeably.

[38] See Case 5/69 *Völk v. Vervaecke* [1969] ECR 295, [1969] CMLR 273. The ECJ held that "an agreement falls outside the prohibition in Article 85 when it has only an insignificant effect on the markets, taking into account the weak position which the persons concerned have on the market of the product in question."

[39] In a similar way to which some agreements are *per se* illegal under the US Sherman Act 1890.

[40] Similar to the US "rule of reason" approach.

[41] Case C–234/89 *Delimitis* [1991] I ECR 935, [1992] 5 CMLR 210.

[42] See for example, Case 161/84 *Pronuptia v. Schillgalis* [1986] ECR 353, [1986] 1 CMLR 414. Further, where the commercial risk taken on by a distributor, licensee or franchisee is so great that they will only enter the market if some degree of exclusivity is conferred on them, then the relevant restrictions are also likely to fall outside Article 85(1): see Case 258/78 *Nungesser v. Commission* [1982] ECR 2015, [1983] 1 CMLR 278.

segregating the market, then such restrictions by their nature are likely to be caught by Article 85(1) (81(1)).

It is important at this stage to make the point that, although the competition **6.33** rules of the Treaty undoubtedly apply to sport in so far as it constitutes an economic activity, sport has a characteristic which differentiates it from other industries and which may justify a somewhat more sensitive application of the competition rules. That characteristic is that it is not in a sports participant's interest to eliminate its rivals from the market. A sports event depends on there being several competitors. Whereas in other industries the elimination of inefficient businesses from the market is an aim of effective competition, the same is not the case in the sports sector. The elimination or economic weakening of its rivals is not in a sports club's interests because it could lead to less even-handed competition on the sports field, and therefore present less of an attraction to spectators. Thus, measures which tend to restrict competition between sports undertakings *may* be justifiable as necessary to the maintenance of sporting competition whilst analogous measures would be unlawful in other industries.

Effect on inter-state trade

This is a threshold test. Articles 85 (81) and 86 (82) of the Treaty will not apply **6.34** unless there is an appreciable effect on trade between member states. The test, as consistently laid down by the ECJ, as to whether an agreement has the requisite effect is as follows:

> ". . . it must be possible to foresee with a sufficient degree of probability on the basis of a set of objective factors of law or fact that it may have an influence, direct or indirect, actual or potential, on the pattern of trade between member states . . ."[43]

The term "trade" is construed broadly and covers the activities of profes- **6.35** sional sports bodies. In *Bosman*[44] UEFA argued that the transfer of players did not amount to "trade". Advocate General Lenz disagreed stating that "trade" "is not restricted to trade in goods but covers all economic relations between the member states".[45] This is consistent with the Court's case-law which shows that the test is a relatively easy one to satisfy. Thus, agreements between sports leagues (or clubs) located in different member states would certainly affect inter-state trade. So too might an agreement which determines the manner in which a sport is organised in one member state if this in turn affects the ability of clubs to participate in competitions with clubs from other member states. However, in such a case, if the possibility of clubs playing in European competitions is remote then the inter-state trade hurdle will not be surmounted. In *Stevenage*

---

[43] Case 56/65 *Société Technique Minière v. Maschinenbau Ulm* [1966] ECR 235, [1966] CMLR 357.

[44] Case C–415/93 [1995] ECR I–4930.

[45] Para. 261 of AG Lenz's opinion.

Borough FC Limited v. The Football League Limited,[46] Stevenage argued at first instance that the League rule preventing its promotion from the Vauxhall Conference to the League was contrary to Article 85 (81) and that there was an effect on inter-state trade because entry into the League enabled it to compete for a place in one of the UEFA competitions. This argument was rejected on the ground that this eventuality was unlikely.

6.36   The significance of the existence or otherwise of an effect on inter-state trade is now reduced given that the provisions of the Competition Act 1998 apply where there is no such effect. This means that the Chapters I and II prohibitions of the Act which are equivalent to Articles 85 and 86 (81 and 82) can be enforced in the UK.

Article 85(3) (now Article 81(3))

6.37 An agreement which falls within Article 85(1) (81(1)) may nonetheless be exempted pursuant to Article 85(3) (81(3)). Exemptions take two forms: individual and block exemptions. In order to gain individual exemption, agreements must be notified to the Commission which has exclusive power to grant exemptions and will do so if the applicant undertaking satisfies each of the four conditions set out in Article 85(3) (81(3)).[47] These are, that the agreement produces a benefit; a fair share of that benefit will accrue to consumers; the agreement contains no restrictions which are not indispensable and that there is no substantial elimination of competition.

6.38   Because the Commission has exclusive jurisdiction to grant exemptions, and limited resources, significant delays can sometimes be experienced. For this reason it may be more efficient to draft an agreement to fit within one of the available block exemption regulations. These are drafted by the Commission to allow for exemption on a generic basis and obviate the need individually to notify an agreement. The most significant block exemptions currently in force cover exclusive purchasing, exclusive distribution, technology transfer agreements and franchising. In the context of sport, the exclusive distribution and purchasing block exemptions may be relevant in relation to sports merchandising. These two block exemptions are due to expire at the end of 1999 and will be replaced by a single block exemption covering distribution.[48]

Enforcement

6.39 If restrictions are caught by Article 85(1) (81(1)) and are not exempt, they are automatically void pursuant to Article 85(2) (81(2)). Whether or not the remain-

---

[46] *The Times*, 1 August 1996.

[47] If, upon notification of an agreement, the Commission considers that it does not fall within Article 85(1) (81(1)) it will grant negative clearance.

[48] See European Commission's *Communication on the application of EC Competition Rules to Vertical Restraints*, COM (98)544 final.

der of the agreement remains in force depends upon whether the offending restrictions are capable of being severed.[49]

There are two ways in which Articles 85 (81) and 86 (82) may be enforced. **6.40** The first is by the Commission which possesses sophisticated powers of investigation and enforcement against private parties.[50] The Commission may fine parties acting in breach of the competition provisions. This includes an agreement caught by Article 85 (81) or an agreement caught by Article 85(1) (81(1)) which does not fall within any of the block exemptions and has not been notified in order to obtain individual exemption. The second means of enforcement is by way of private action. Thus, persons harmed by an anti-competitive agreement may bring an action in the English courts for an injunction or in damages. Recent Court of Appeal authority establishes that it is never open to one party to an agreement to bring an action in damages against another party even in circumstances where the plaintiff was in a much weaker negotiating position than the defendant.[51] Whether this is correct must be open to some doubt given that it precludes an entire category of person from enforcing Article 85 (81) and is therefore arguably inconsistent with the Community law principles that Community law rights must capable of effective enforcement.

Article 86 (now Article 82)

Article 86 (82) provides: **6.41**

"Any abuse by one or more undertakings of a dominant position within the common market or in a substantial part of it shall be prohibited as incompatible with the common market in so far as it may affect trade between member states. Such abuse may, in particular, consist in:

(a) directly or indirectly imposing unfair purchase or selling prices or unfair trading conditions;

(b) limiting production, markets or technical development to the prejudice of consumers;

(c) applying dissimilar conditions to equivalent transactions with other trading parties, thereby placing them at a competitive disadvantage;

(d) making the conclusion of contracts subject to acceptance by other parties of supplementary obligations which, by their nature or according to commercial usage, have no connection with the subject of such contracts."

An undertaking acts in contravention of Article 86 (82) if (i) it occupies a **6.42** dominant position on the market place, and (ii) it abuses that dominant position

---

[49] See *Chitty on Contracts* (27th ed.) vol. 1 at paras. 16–164 to 16–172.
[50] These powers are found in Regulation 17/62.
[51] *Gibbs Mew v. Gemmell* [1998] EuLR 588, affirmed in *Trent Taverns v. Sykes* [1999] EuLR.

by acting anti-competitively. It is important to emphasise that occupying a dominant, ie. monopolistic, position does not of itself constitute an infringement of Article 86 (82). The dominance or otherwise of an undertaking can only be assessed in the context of a defined market. Careful market definition is crucial. The more narrowly a market is defined, the more likely the conclusion that a particular undertaking is dominant in it. Conversely, the same undertaking is less likely to be found dominant in a widely construed market.

Market definition

6.43 There are two principal elements to market definition: the product market and the geographical market. Regard must be had to the twin concepts of demand and supply substitutability. This means the extent to which other products are deemed to be substitutable for that under consideration from the point of view of consumers and suppliers respectively. The Commission has stated that:

> "Basically, the exercise of market definition consists in identifying the effective alternative sources of supply for the customers of the undertakings involved, in terms both of products/services and of geographic location of suppliers."[52]

The retail of replica football shirts affords a good example of how these tests are applied. To assess whether a particular shirt manufacturer is dominant, the market must first be defined. Is the market the retail of Manchester United shirts or is it the retail of football club shirts generally? There is likely to be almost no demand substitutability. In other words, Manchester United fans would not switch to Liverpool shirts if there was a change in their respective price. Supply substitutability is more complicated. At first sight it might be thought easy for manufacturers of other shirts to start producing Manchester United shirts. However, football clubs enter into exclusive contracts with one shirt manufacturer. Furthermore, shirts bear at least three trade marks: those of the club, shirt manufacturer and sponsor. Manchester United is therefore able to prevent other shirt manufacturers producing its replica kit. This is not to say that a shirt manufacturer does not face any competitive pressure; once its contract with the club has expired it must compete with other manufacturers for another contract. However, it does seem that supply substitutability is fairly limited. The Commission has stated that where, as in this example, supply substitutability would entail time delays, it will not be considered at the stage of market definition.[53] Instead, it will be relevant, once the position of the undertaking in the

---

[52] Commission Notice on the definition of relevant market for the purposes of Community competition law, 1997 OJ C372/5 at para. 13.

[53] Commission Notice on the definition of relevant market for the purposes of Community competition law, para. 23: "When supply-side substitutability would entail the need to adjust significantly existing tangible and intangible assets, additional investments, strategic decisions or time delays, it will not be considered at the stage of market definition."

market has been established, to determine whether action complained of is anti-competitive.

Dominance

The test is whether an undertaking enjoys a position of economic strength such **6.44** that it can behave to an appreciable extent independently of its competitors and ultimately of consumers.[54] In most markets, market share will provide a good indication of whether an undertaking is dominant. In the context of sport, however, the issue of dominance will arise mainly in relation to governing bodies. As discussed above, depending on the precise facts, governing bodies may be analysed either as single undertakings or as an association of their members. If a governing body is a single undertaking, the question of whether it is dominant will generally be straightforward as there is normally only one such governing body operating in a particular "market". It is less likely that individual clubs will be found to be dominant. The possibility cannot be excluded, however, and in making the assessment the relevant market must be borne in mind. It seems to us that clubs may compete in a number of different markets simultaneously, for example the broadcasting market, the merchandising market, the market for players. One can envisage, for example that in the broadcasting market, a club might find itself dominant in the market for the sale of broadcasting rights if it were owned by the dominant purchaser of those rights.

Abuse

The dominant position itself is not prohibited by Article 86 (82); only abuse of **6.45** that position contravenes the provision. Essentially, conduct is abusive where it distorts competition. The ECJ has explained it as follows[55]:

> The concept of abuse is an objective concept relating to the behaviour of an undertaking in a dominant position which is such as to influence the structure of a market where, as a result of the very presence of the undertaking in question, the degree of competition is weakened and which, through recourse to methods different from those which condition normal competition in products or services on the basis of transactions of commercial operators, has the effect of hindering the maintenance of the degree of competition still existing on the market or the growth of that competition.

In the context of sport, conduct which is potentially abusive includes collec- **6.46** tive selling of television rights (discussed below), the application of non-objective entry criteria to leagues or competitions, charging unfairly high prices for merchandise and selling tickets only as part of expensive package holidays.

---

[54] See, Case 322/82 *Michelin v. Commission* [1983] ECR 3461, [1985] 1 CMLR 282, para. 30 of the Court's judgment.
[55] Case 85/76 *Hoffmann-La Roche v. Commission* [1979] ECR 461, [1979] 3 CMLR 211.

Broadcasting and competition law

6.47 Broadcasting contracts in the context of sport, in common with other commercial agreements, must comply with Article 85 (81). The growing commercial importance of sport and technological developments in the broadcasting sector have given this area of competition law a high profile. The Commission is actively involved in developing policy and has recently adopted some preliminary guidelines on the application of the competition rules to the sports sector.[56]

6.48 There are various characteristic features of broadcasting agreements and, sports broadcasting agreements in particular, which invite particular scrutiny under Article 85 (81). These are dealt with below. However, the compatibility of any such agreement with the competition provisions will largely depend on the market definition adopted. It is only by defining the market that it is possible to identify an undertaking's competitors and potential competitors and then assess whether competition is being restricted.

The relevant market in sports broadcasting cases

6.49 Defining the market and assessing market share in sports marketing depends principally upon four issues. First, is it appropriate to consider television generally or to draw a distinction between pay-TV and ordinary television for which no subscription is necessary (free to air TV)? Second, does the sport in question form its own separate market or is it part of a broader market for sports coverage generally? Third, are there separate markets for live and recorded sports? Fourth, what is the relevant geographic market? These issues are discussed in turn below.

(i) Type of television

6.50 Broadcasters fall into two principal categories. Traditionally, television has been broadcast "free to air"; that is to say, anyone with a television set and aerial was free to receive it, subject to payment of any government licence fee. Free to air broadcasters obtain revenue from either government funding, advertising or both. More recently, pay-TV broadcasters have entered the market, broadcasting scrambled or "encrypted" signals which require decoding through an appropriate piece of equipment, often referred to as a "set-top box". The right to decode has to be paid for by the viewer through a subscription. With analogue (wave) signals, pay-TV could be broadcast through encrypted signals from satellite or by cable; now the latest digital technology has enabled pay-TV also to be broadcast terrestrially, capable of reception through normal roof top aerials.

6.51 While pay-TV and free to air broadcasters clearly compete with each other for the attention of the viewing public, do they compete in the same market? The

[56] Press release dated 24 February 1999. Final conclusions are to be drawn up after a process of consultation with the sports sector launched at the initiative of Commissioner Oreja. See also SLB Vol. 2 No. 1 Parrish, "Sports Broadcasting and European Competition Policy"; ibid. Anderson "The Regulation of Sports Broadcasting in the US."

UK's Office of Fair Trading (OFT) came to the conclusion in its *Review of BSkyB's Position in the Wholesale Pay TV Market*[57] that they did not. The analysis of whether two types of broadcasters compete, as with all issues of market definition, essentially depends upon whether they are in price competition with each other; a lack of price competition is a strong indication (in the absence of a cartel) of separate markets.[58] While BSkyB, the dominant pay-TV broadcaster in the UK was constrained to some extent in the level of prices it charged for its subscriptions by the existence of free to air television, the evidence suggested that neither its retail prices to its satellite viewers, nor its wholesale prices to cable companies selling on to their customers, were set at a competitive level and this indicated that BSkyB operated in a separate market. This conclusion was supported by significant differences between pay-TV and free to air services: pay-TV offered subscribers the option to view a far greater quantity of programming at any one time, and some sports and films were not available or only available on a limited basis on free to air TV. The European Commission had previously reached the same conclusion in its merger decision *MSG Media Service*.[59] On the other hand, the OFT did not think, albeit on the basis of very limited practical experience at that date, that pay-per-view TV formed a separate market; it was in reality only likely to be a segment within the overall pay-TV market.[60]

(ii) Type of sport

Whether there is a market for sports broadcasting generally, or whether it can **6.52** be further broken down similarly depends on the presence or otherwise of price constraints. It seems clear that across Europe top flight football is, to use BSkyB's turn of phrase, the "battering ram" for pay-TV. Football is the only sport which has been able to generate the demand for pay-TV in a sufficiently large proportion of the population, and along with the screening of first run Hollywood films, has been responsible for the success of pay-TV. The fact that viewers are prepared to pay a premium for watching football rather than other sports indicates a separate market in football broadcasting. From broadcasters' perspective in the UK, even popular sports such as rugby or cricket are not substitutes for football, and thus do not constrain the price that can be demanded by those selling the rights to broadcast football.

Sports other than football may also have a premium quality to them which **6.53** would indicate a separate market. The fact that a premium can be charged for

---

[57] OFT Report, December 1996. See, on market definition, paras. 2.3–2.7 and chapter four.

[58] Commission Notice on the definition of relevant market for the purposes of Community competition law, OJ 1997 C 372/5, para. 13.

[59] *MSG Media Service*, OJ 1994 L 364/1, para. 32.

[60] OFT's Review of BSkyB's Position in the Wholesale pay-TV Market (1996), para. 2.6.

boxing on pay-per-view TV[61] to those who already have a pay-TV subscription may indicate that there is a separate market in boxing coverage. There may also be a market in non-premium sports generally, such as cricket, golf and snooker whose main attraction to broadcasters lies in the fact that they generate many hours of low cost sports broadcasting to fill in the gaps between premium events, but for which viewers are not prepared to pay premium prices. To conclude, it should be borne in mind that, at present, the generalist nature of sports coverage means that further defining the market by sport has not been an issue of great importance. However, with digital technology enabling the introduction of specialist channels dedicated to particular sports, this question may receive more attention than hitherto.

(iii) Live and recorded sport

6.54 Once again, price is the indicator of a separate market for live sport. One, if not the key, element in interest in sporting events lies in their unpredictability, whereas recorded sport has only apparent, not real, unpredictability. BSkyB's success in using live football coverage to sell pay-TV subscriptions indicates that comprehensive highlights programmes such as *Match of the Day* do not constrain their pricing ability for live football. It should be added that in pay-TV it is not only sport which has this element of timeliness, leading to the creation of separate markets. The market in Hollywood movies also splits into the various time windows of cinema first run, video release, (possibly) pay-per-view release, pay-TV first run and then re-runs on TV,[62] and the acquisition of first run Hollywood movies has been an important part in showing pay-TV to form a separate market.

(iv) Geographic market

6.55 TV is for linguistic and cultural reasons split along largely national lines through Europe and elsewhere. Although sport may at the highest level transcend both language and culture, its broadcasting remains subject to largely national trends of demand and supply. This means that it will often be the case that an agreement or practice relating to sports broadcasting will only have an effect on one member state, thus precluding the application of Articles 85 (81) and 86 (82)[63] and rendering the matter one for the relevant national competition law (the Chapters I and II prohibitions in the UK under the Competition Act 1998).

[61] At the time of writing, boxing promotions had accounted for nearly all the pay-per-view events shown on pay-TV in the UK.

[62] OFT's Review of BSkyB's Position in the Wholesale pay-TV Market (1996), paras. 2.22–2.24.

[63] For factors which the Commission may take into account in deciding whether there is an effect on inter-state trade, see the Commission's paper "Broadcasting of Sports Events and Competition Law", *Competition Policy Newsletter No 2*, June 1998, para. 4.

Collective selling

It is currently very common for television rights to all matches played by teams **6.56** in a league to be marketed centrally by that league rather than individually by its member clubs. Many leagues and associations contain a rule to this effect. The Commission takes the view that collective selling may affect competition in several ways. First, it may restrict competition between clubs themselves; second, it may restrict competition between broadcasting companies; third, it may constitute an abuse by a league or association of its market power; and fourth, the Commission takes the view that collective selling may be the source of other competition problems relating to broadcasting sports events.[64] Each of these issues is considered separately below.

As a preliminary issue it can be observed that collective selling is potentially **6.57** challengeable under Article 85 (81) and Article 86 (82). Thus, as stated above, many league rule books contain a rule providing for collective selling. Generally speaking, the members of a league agree to be bound by its rules and so such a rule would constitute an agreement between clubs within the meaning of Article 85 (81). However, it may also be possible to characterise a league as an undertaking in its own right. If the commercial (and sporting) reality is that clubs wishing to take part in a particular sport at a certain level have no choice other than to join a particular league, then that league has market power and probably enjoys a dominant position on the market within the meaning of Article 86 (82). If the league imposes, as a condition of membership, a collective selling rule on clubs then, unless objectively justified, that may constitute an abuse of its dominant position contrary to Article 86 (82). The potential effects on competition discussed below will be relevant to the determination of whether there has been a breach of the competition rules regardless of whether collective selling is analysed according to Article 85 (81) or Article 86 (82).

First, collective selling may restrict competition between clubs *inter se*. In the **6.58** absence of a collective selling rule, clubs which are members of a league may decide that it is in their interests to sell rights to their matches on an individual basis. Thus, a football team such as Manchester United or Arsenal will clearly attract larger television audiences for its matches than many smaller less popular clubs in the Premiership. However, because the Premiership collectively sells broadcasting rights to all matches, that advantage in the popularity stakes cannot be translated into greater broadcasting revenues. There is therefore a distortion in the competition between clubs.

Further, collective selling rules have an impact on competition between **6.59** broadcasting companies. In the absence of collective selling, a greater number of individual rights are available for broadcasters meaning that more broadcasters have the possibility of entering the market. Collective selling, on the other hand,

---

[64] "Broadcasting of Sports Events and Competition Law", *Competition Policy Newsletter No 2*, June 1998.

acts as a means of foreclosing the market to potential entrants by tying rights up together. The issue of whether there is market foreclosure depends on the correct market definition.[65] To take the collective sale of rights to live transmission of Premiership football matches, if one defines the market as the market in live broadcasts of Premiership football matches, then the collective sale of those rights will inevitably foreclose entry to the market. If, however, the market is defined more broadly then the question becomes more difficult. Thus, it might be said that the correct market definition is the market in sports broadcasts in the most general sense. If that is right then the collective sale at issue is less likely to result in market foreclosure.

6.60 The Commission has stated that collective selling can be the source of other competition issues related to the broadcasting of sports events. Such arrangements are likely to affect the functioning of the market because they permit only periodic transactions, restrict output and bundle the products offered. Further, collective selling can facilitate other restrictive practices, such as gaining a long duration of exclusivity. It could also hinder the development of other sports or other participants in the same sport which, in consequence of preferential treatment for some classes of participants, are not able to obtain satisfactory television exposure or attract sponsors.

6.61 It must be concluded that, subject to affecting inter-state trade, joint selling arrangements will normally fall within Article 85(1) (Article 81(1)). This has certainly been the approach of the Commission and Courts when they have considered joint selling in the context of sectors other than sport.[66] The next question then is whether they are likely to be exempted pursuant to Article 85(3) (81(3)). In most joint selling cases it has had to consider, the Commission has refused an exemption.[67] However, the Commission has indicated that in the context of sports broadcasting, the assessment whether collective selling agreements meet the four criteria for exemption of Article 85(3) (81(3)) "should not be based on purely commercial considerations" and should take account of "the special characteristics of sport".[68] It went on to state that such characteristics:

> "could include, for example, the need to ensure 'solidarity' between weaker and stronger participants or the training of young players, which could only

---

[65] This is addressed at para. 6.43–6.55 *supra*.

[66] See Bellamy and Child at para. 4–096 and, eg. *Floral* OJ 1980 L39/51, [1980] 2 CMLR 285; *Centraal Stikstof Verkoopkantoor* OJ 1978 L242/15, [1979] 1 CMLR 11; *Bayer/BP Chemicals* OJ 1988 L150/35, [1989] 4 CMLR 24, *Hudson's Bay Co/Dansk Pelsdryavlerforening* OJ 1988 L316/43; *Ansac* OJ 1993 L152/54.

[67] One exceptional case in which the Commission granted an exemption was *UIP* [1990] 4 CMLR 749 which concerned a film distribution joint venture between three film producers. The key to the decision seems to have been that there was a declining market and this was an attempt to rationalise distribution.

[68] "Broadcasting of Sports Events and Competition Law", *Competition Policy Newsletter, No 2*, June 1998 at p. 26.

be achieved through redistribution of revenue from the sale of broadcasting rights."

Such aims would, of course, have to be a genuine and material part of the objectives and ones which could not be achievable through other, less restrictive arrangements. In expressing this view, the Commission is acknowledging that, in the context of sport, different competition considerations apply. Clubs which are members of a league can only compete against each other commercially to a certain degree. It is not in a club's interests to eliminate other clubs from the market since this would deprive it of its source of sporting competition and hence of income.[69] Therein lies a significant difference from the competitive relationship between undertakings in other markets.

6.62 The Commission has not up until now issued any decision on the matter of collective selling of sports broadcasting rights though several cases concerning collective sale are currently pending before it at the time of writing. These include the collective sale of the television rights to the Formula 1 Championship,[70] football championships and rugby tournaments. UEFA has notified the Commission of its arrangements for the central marketing of the commercial rights to the Champions League and has requested a negative clearance or, alternatively, an exemption.[71] A similar arrangement was notified to the Commission in August 1998 by the Deutscher Fussball-Bund. Further, a complaint was lodged in March 1998 by various professional rugby clubs in England. The complaint is directed against rules of the International Rugby Federation and the Rugby Football Union which give those federations exclusive rights to organise cross-border matches and tournaments and to sell the broadcasting rights to those tournaments.

6.63 The issue has been raised before national competition authorities of the UK, the Netherlands and Germany. In Germany, the Bundesgerichsthof concluded that the central marketing of broadcasting rights to European Cup football matches by the national football association was a cartel for which exemption was not justified. In the UK, the FA Premier League's collective selling of the television rights of its member clubs has been referred to the Restrictive Practices Court.[72] The issue has also come before the US courts, which have

[69] See para. 227 of AG Lenz's opinion in *Bosman*.

[70] The governing body of world motor-racing, the Fédération Internationale de l'Automobile (FIA) has complained about the four and a half year delay by the European Commission in determining the competition issues (including those relating to broadcasting) arising from its statutes: *The Financial Times*, 16–17 January 1999.

[71] The Commission has published a Notice stating that, on a preliminary examination, it finds that the notified rules could fall within the scope of Regulation 17 and inviting interested third parties to submit observations: 1999 OJ C99/23.

[72] The Restrictive Practice Court issued its decision shortly before publication of this book. The judgment and its effect are summarised in a note at the end of this chapter.

struck down league rules or restrictions on broadcasting games on a number of occasions as contrary to the Sherman Act.[73]

Collective purchasing

6.64 Broadcasting companies sometimes join forces in order to acquire the rights to televise sports events. One of the reasons why this may be attractive is that collective selling is currently commonplace. It gives sellers of rights strong bargaining strength, thus often making television rights expensive to buy. Moreover, in addition to the cost of the rights, sports programmes may be costly and risky to broadcast. As the Commission has noted, the cost of production of the television signal is high. This applies in particular to tournaments or championships which take place over a number of days with several events taking place at the same time. While only a fraction can be broadcast, most if not all must be covered in order to be able to offer a meaningful selection. Further, the broadcasting of sports events may be risky in that rights must be acquired well in advance of the event but its appeal to audiences may change considerably depending, for example, on how a particular team performs. The expense and risks are reduced if several television companies contribute to the purchase of rights.[74]

6.65   The Commission used to take the view that joint purchasing agreements always fall within Article 85(1) (81(1)) although they may merit exemption under Article 85(3) (81(3)) if they do not prevent market access to competitors.[75] More recently, however, and in line with its increasing readiness to take an economically realistic view of what constitutes a restriction of competition, the Commission has stated that some agreements of this type may not be caught by Article 85(1) (81(1)) at all. Rather, whether it does so depends on all the circumstances of the case.[76] Thus, joint purchasing agreements will almost certainly fall within Article 85(1) (81(1)) if the parties are important competitors with strong positions in the market. However, if the agreement is between a number of small broadcasters in circumstances where none would be able to acquire the rights in question individually, then the agreement might well fall outside Article 85(1) (81(1)). Also relevant will be the scope of the agreement, its duration, and whether the rights are exclusive. Thus, an agreement between small broadcasters to jointly acquire the rights to a one-off sporting event on a non-exclusive basis is likely to fall outside Article 85(1) (81(1)), whereas an

[73] See for example, *NCAA v. Board of Regents* 468 U.S. 85 (1984, Sp Ct) (college basketball); *Chicago Professional Sports Ltd Partnership v. NBA* 961 F. 2d. 667 (7th Cir 1992), applied at 874 F. Supp. 844 (N.D. III, 1995) (professional basketball). See also *US v. NFL* 116 F. Supp. 319 (E.D. Pa, 1953) (American football).

[74] See, *EBU/Eurovision System*, OJ 1993 L179/23 at paras. 17–18.

[75] 20th Report on Competition Policy (1990), point 82.

[76] See "Broadcasting of Sports Events and Competition Law", a Commission orientation document, *Competition Policy Newsletter No 2* June 1998. For the approach of the ECJ to collective purchasing generally see Bellamy and Child para. 4–088 et seq.

agreement between the same broadcasters to acquire the exclusive rights to, for example, European football matches for an extended period is very likely to be caught by it.

A collective purchasing agreement which is caught by Article 85(1) (81(1)) **6.66** may nonetheless be exempted under Article 85(3) (81(3)) where its purpose is pro-competitive and where it does not have the effect of excluding competitors from the market. The Commission has given as an example an agreement, the purpose of which is to maintain a broadcasting sector with limited resources faced with competing against the "big four" broadcasters, BskyB, Canal Plus, Bertelsmann and Kirch for the procurement of broadcasting rights.[77]

This, indeed, was the approach adopted by the Commission when it adopted **6.67** its decision in *EBU/Eurovision System*.[78] The European Broadcasting Union ("EBU"), an association of public broadcasting companies facing increasing competition from commercial broadcasters, notified its statutes and rules to the Commission. These provided, amongst other things, for the joint acquisition of rights to international sports events. In particular, television rights for international sports events were normally acquired jointly by all interested members who then shared the rights and the fee between them. Whenever EBU members from two or more countries were interested in a specific sports event, they requested coordination from the EBU. As a result, negotiations were carried out on behalf of all interested members either by a member or by the EBU itself. Once negotiations for Eurovision rights had been commenced and until they had been formally declared to have failed, members were required not to engage in separate negotiations for national rights. Where rights were jointly acquired, then coverage was normally carried out by a member of the country where the event was taking place if the event was within the Eurovision area, and the signal would be offered free of charge to other EBU members on the understanding that in return it would receive corresponding offers from other members in respect of events taking place in their respective countries.[79] The Commission held that this arrangement did distort competition within the meaning of Article 85(1) (81(1)). Although members from different countries normally acquired rights only for those respective countries and so did not compete directly with each other, competition between them was nevertheless restricted because (i) some countries had more than one EBU member which would normally compete with each other for coverage of international sports events, and (ii) there was an increasing number of members broadcasting via satellite and cable into each other's countries who would, therefore, normally have to acquire the rights for those countries in competition with the national members. Further, competition with commercial channels was distorted, since those channels were disadvantaged in not being able to participate in the rationalisation and cost

[77] Commission orientation document, Section VI, see note 76 *supra*.
[78] OJ 1993 L 179/23, [1995] 4 CMLR 56.
[79] See para. 27–40 of the Commission's decision.

savings that joint purchasing permitted. The Commission held that there was an effect on trade between member states in that the Eurovision system concerned cross-border acquisition and use of television rights. The impact on competition and trade was appreciable given that sports programmes are indispensable for any generalist channel; they cannot be totally replaced by any other type of programme. However, the Commission went on to hold that the agreement merited exemption under Article 85(3) (81(3)). It provided a number of benefits. In particular, it led to an improvement in purchasing conditions by, for example, reducing the transaction costs which would be associated with a multitude of separate negotiations and guaranteeing that the negotiations were carried out by the most competent negotiator. Further, the exchange of the television signal resulted in considerable rationalisation and cost saving and provided smaller countries with coverage which they would otherwise find very difficult to afford. Consumers received these benefits in that the system enabled EBU's members to view more and higher quality sports programmes than they would otherwise be able to do. The money saved could be used for the acquisition of other attractive programmes. The Commission went on to find that the arrangement contained no restrictions which were not indispensable to its purpose. Finally, EBU's rules did not allow participating members to eliminate competition for a substantial part of the products in question as the joint negotiation rules concerned only international and not national events which constituted the majority of sports on television.

6.68   The Commission's decision was, however, annulled by the Court of First Instance (CFI) on appeal, an appeal brought by private commercial television companies that were not entitled to membership of the EBU.[80] One of the restrictions of competition identified by the Commission was that "competition vis-a-vis purely commercial channels, which are not admitted as members, is to some extent distorted" by the EBU's membership rules since those channels cannot participate in the rationalisation and cost savings achieved by the Eurovision system. In order for Article 85(3) (81(3)) to apply, the restrictions of competition caused by the membership rules must be indispensable. The CFI found that the Commission had not adequately considered this issue. In particular, it had failed to examine whether the membership conditions were "applied in an appropriate, reasonable and non-discriminatory way".[81] The CFI found further that it was a misinterpretation of Article 85(3) (81(3)) to treat fulfilment of a particular public mission as a criterion for granting exemption; this was a

---

[80] Joined Cases T–528/93, T–542/93, T–543/93 and T–546/93 *Metropole Television SA v. Commission* [1996] ECR II–649.

[81] See paras. 94–103 of the CFI's judgment. The reference to uniform and non-discriminatory application of membership criteria is drawn from the jurisprudence of the European Courts on selective distribution, as indeed is expressly acknowledged by the CFI at para. 95 of its judgment with its reference to Case 26/76 *Metro v. Commission* [1977] ECR 1875, [1978] 2 CMLR 1.

factor relevant to Article 90(2) (now Article 86(2))[82] of the Treaty and not Article 85(3) (81(3)). The Commission has appealed against the CFI's decision to the ECJ; the appeal has not yet been decided.[83]

Currently being considered by the Commission is the notification[84] of a joint **6.69** venture agreement for the exploitation of broadcasting rights to the Spanish football league and cup. The agreement provides for four Spanish television enterprises jointly to broadcast Spanish football matches from 1998 until 2003.

Exclusivity

The sale of exclusive rights to broadcast sports events is an accepted commer- **6.70** cial practice. From the point of view of the sports organisers, the price paid for exclusivity by one broadcaster is probably higher than the sum of the amounts that would be paid by several broadcasters for non-exclusive rights. For the broadcaster, it represents the best way of realising the value of the purchase of expensive broadcasting rights. Further, exclusive rights bring to the broadcaster greater opportunities to gain advertising or sponsorship revenue as it will be ensured of a particular audience. For pay-TV channels, exclusivity of rights to very popular sports events is crucial in order to be able to attract new subscribers.

Despite the paucity of authority directly on point, there is much to suggest **6.71** that, in determining whether the sale of exclusive rights is compatible with Article 85 (81), the Commission and Courts will take an economically analytical approach and will not take the view that it falls *per se* within Article 85(1) (81(1)).[85] Parallels can be drawn between the sale of exclusive broadcasting rights and the grant of exclusive copyright licences, and it is likely that a similar approach would be taken to the former as to the latter. The case law on exclusive copyright licencing is, therefore, instructive. The permissive approach taken by the European institutions to this practice is demonstrated by the judgment of the ECJ in *CODITEL II*[86] which concerned the grant of an exclusive licences to the copyright in films. The Court held in that case that:

"the characteristics of the cinematographic industry and of its markets in the Community, especially those relating to dubbing and subtitling for the

---

[82] Article 90(1) makes public undertakings subject to the competition rules and Article 90(2) provides a defence for undertakings charged with the operation of services of general economic interest.

[83] Case C–320/96P. Following the ruling of the CFI, the EBU amended the wording of its membership rules and the Commission is currently examining its application for exemption.

[84] In April 1997.

[85] See for example, "Broadcasting of Sports Events and Competition Law", Commission orientation document, *Competition Policy Newsletter No 2*, June 1998. For a general survey of the law see Fleming, "Exclusive Rights to Broadcast Sporting Events in Europe" [1999] ECLR 143.

[86] Case 262/81 *CODITEL II* [1982] ECR 3381, [1983] 1 CMLR 49.

benefit of different language groups, to the possibilities of television broadcasts, and to the system of financing cinematographic production in Europe serve to show that an exclusive exhibition licence is not, in itself, such as to prevent, restrict or distort competition."

However, the Court went on to say that the exercise of such a right may, depending on the circumstances, result in a restriction of competition.

6.72   The Commission considered exclusive copyright licences in its *Film Purchases by German television stations*[87] decision. The Commission held that the grant of licences to an association of German television stations giving it the exclusive right to broadcast MGM films for a period of fifteen years did fall within Article 85(1) (81(1)) but nevertheless merited exemption under Article 85(3) (81(3)). In finding that the exclusive licence restricted competition within the meaning of Article 85(1) (81(1)), the Commission observed that the stock of suitable feature films cannot be increased at will and that therefore large quantities of films must not be withdrawn from the market as a result of long-term ties. The films at issue, though representing only 4.5 per cent of the total stock available worldwide, constituted a particularly popular selection and so had an importance which went a long way beyond their numerical quantity. Further, exclusivity was conferred for a long period of time. In granting exemption, the Commission took the view that the agreement enhanced distribution because it enlarged the number of films available on the market and permitted more films to be dubbed into German. These benefits were passed on to consumers since more films were shown in German than would otherwise be the case. Further, the exclusivity was necessary in order to allow the television stations a fair return from the relevant investments such as the licence fee, dubbing costs and administrative costs. The agreement did not eliminate competition in a substantial part of the common market since the licence period for groups of films were staggered, thus ensuring that some films remained available to other television stations at all times. Moreover, other stations had access to non-MGM films.

6.73   Thus, it seems likely that agreements providing for the sale of exclusive rights to broadcast sports events will not *per se* fall within Article 85(1) (81(1)) though they may do so if they restrict the access of rival broadcasters to the market. This is really the key issue; it is particularly important for those operating payTV channels which may require sports broadcasting rights in order to lure people into buying a subscription. The extent to which exclusivity operates to foreclose the market does, of course, depend on the market definition adopted. If there is a separate market in the live broadcast of the Wimbledon tennis tournament, then the grant of an exclusive right to carry out that broadcast for a number of years will operate to foreclose that market. However, the market is highly unlikely to be defined so narrowly.

6.74   Having said this, it remains the case that the Commission is currently interested in exclusivity in the sports broadcasting sector and has recently announced

---

[87] *Film Purchases by German television stations*, OJ L248/36.

that it is likely to investigate all agreements which grant exclusive broadcasting rights for longer than one year.[88] Agreements between the BBC, BskyB and the FA for the exclusive coverage of football matches for the 1988–9 to 1992–3 football seasons have been considered by the Commission.[89] The agreements related to all national and international matches organised by the FA, namely FA Cup and Charity Shield matches and matches involving the England national team. The BBC and BskyB which had bid jointly for the rights, shared them between themselves by alternating transmission. The Commission took the view that the exclusivity granted to the BBC and BskyB was caught by Article 85(1) (81(1)). Such contracts should, in principle, be restricted to one season in order to allow all channels a fair chance to obtain access to major football matches. However, the Commission decided that in this particular case an exemption was justified since BskyB, which only started operating in 1990, required a longer term contract in order to facilitate its entry into the developing market for satellite broadcasting. Originally the agreements also gave the BBC and BskyB the exclusive right to televise football matches from abroad, which under Article 14 of the UEFA Statutes was subject to the prior permission of the FA. At the Commission's request this clause was removed from the agreements in 1992, and the FA undertook not to discriminate between the BBC and BskyB on the one hand and other broadcasters on the other as regards the sale of rights for these matches. Following notification of a new agreement made between the two channels and the FA Premier League in 1994, providing for an extension of the exclusive agreement for five seasons, the Commission sent an administrative letter of incompatibility. This agreement and its extension to the year 2001 are currently the subject of proceedings brought by the OFT in the Restrictive Practices Court.[90]

6.75 The Commission has also considered an agreement between the Dutch Football Association and Sport 7, a new sports channel in the Netherlands, whereby the former granted to the latter the exclusive right to televise Dutch football league matches for a period of seven years. The Commission considered that this period was too long and also rejected a renewal clause which favoured the channel in the invitation to bid procedure provided for upon expiry of the contract.[91]

6.76 The Commission is currently considering the sale of exclusive broadcasting rights to the Formula One Grand Prix Championship. The Fédération Internationale de l'Automobile (FIA), the world governing body for international motor sports, appointed Formula One Administration (FOA) as the

---

[88] "Brussels gets tough on TV deals", *The Guardian*, 25 February 1999. See also *The Financial Times*, 25 February 1999. This is not to say that all such investigations will lead to a conclusion that the agreement falls within Article 85(1).

[89] XXIIIrd Report on Competition Policy (1993), Annex III, p. 459.

[90] See the endnote to this chapter.

[91] There has been no formal decision in this case.

holder of the commercial rights to the Championship events. As a condition of their participation in the Championship, teams assign to FIA on an exclusive basis any media rights they may have in relation to the Championship events. FIA then arranges for FOA to exploit those rights and enter into agreements with participating teams setting out the allocation to teams of the television payments made to FOA each year. Thus, television rights are collectively sold through FOA which has entered into broadcasting agreements with sixty broadcasters worldwide. For each Grand Prix, FOA contracts with a broadcasting company in the host country which is responsible for filming the event and making its signal available to non-host broadcasters transmitting the event in their territories. All events in each year's Championship are sold as a package to each broadcaster which is obliged to televise every event in the Championship. Some of the broadcasting agreements provide for a discount of 33 per cent on the price paid by the broadcaster if it agrees not to broadcast any "open wheeler racing" other than Formula One. Contracts are typically granted with one broadcaster per territory and certain limited exclusivity is granted. The Commission appears to have taken the view that these arrangements are caught by Article 85(1) (81(1)), stating that, on a preliminary examination, it considers that the agreements affect the organisation and televising of the Formula One Championship and other motor sports.[92] As described above, the agreements contain a number of features which are potentially anti-competitive: joint selling, exclusivity, "full-line forcing" in that broadcasters are compelled to buy and broadcast every Grand Prix race within a particular Championship year, and exclusive purchasing in that broadcasters are offered a significant financial incentive not to broadcast competing motor sport events.[93] The Commission has not yet indicated which of these features render the agreements anti-competitive.

Other anti-competitive practices

6.77 It is important to appreciate that the three common features of broadcasting agreements discussed above do not represent the only forms of commercial practice likely to be found anti-competitive. Broadcasting agreements may contain other clauses which fall to be considered under the competition provisions. The touchstone is whether a particular feature of a broadcasting contract has an effect which is anti-competitive; that assessment can only be made after defining the market in the context of which the agreement is made. An agreement may have an anti-competitive effect because it tends to foreclose the market to potential entrants. On the other hand, an agreement may operate anti-competitively vis-à-vis competitors already in the market. Thus, it is likely that this is the Commission's concern about the Formula One broadcasting agreements which offer broadcasting companies a financial incentive not to broadcast any com-

---

[92] Notification of agreements relating to the FIA Formula One World Championship, OJ 1997 C 361/05.
[93] For example, Indycar racing.

peting motor sport events. The organisers of motor sport events compete with each other in the exploitation of those events including the sale of broadcasting rights. If there is a single, worldwide market in the sale of rights to broadcast motor sports championships, then the type of restriction referred to above may make it more difficult for competitor organisers, such as Indycar, to find a television market. However, against that it can cogently be argued that the proliferation of television companies means that competitor events will encounter little problem in finding an alternative purchaser of its broadcasting rights in most countries.[94] If, on the other hand, the market is regional rather than worldwide in nature, then this restriction could be characterised as contributing to market foreclosure (as opposed to restricting competition between actual competitors already in the market) in that it helps prevent Indycar entering the market in various European states where its championship is not broadcast.

Marketing

The same competition law principles that apply to the broadcasting of sports   **6.78** also apply to the ways in which sports may be marketed. Most obviously, sports are marketed directly to the public through ticket sales to view the actual sporting event as it takes place and, in that sense (although treated separately here because of its overriding economic importance), broadcasting is no more than a means of marketing an event. Increasingly importantly, sports are marketed through sales of sports related merchandise to the public. That merchandise may capitalise upon the image of a club, a player or even a league. These forms of marketing are considered in the following sections. However, as a general comment, it can be observed that, in contrast to broadcasting, there is less case law, probably because sale of tickets and merchandise does not depend upon a few distributors in a position to control access to the consuming public. However, if there is consolidation in these forms of sports marketing, leading to a concentration of market power, competition law would come to play as important a part in regulation as it currently does in relation to sports broadcasting.

Ticket Sales

A ticket for a sporting event is, essentially, a licence to occupy a place on the sta-   **6.79** dium owner's property for a limited period of time and, usually, restricted to a particular part of that property. Normally, the main problems encountered in relation to ticket sales are touting and counterfeiting. Both are dealt with in the UK under the criminal law, the former being the subject of a specific criminal prohibition.[95]

---

[94] See paras. 6.2–6.3 *supra*.
[95] Section 166, Criminal Justice and Public Order Act 1994; see para. 5.28, *supra*.

6.80   However, for major sporting events, it is also important to ensure that distribution arrangements comply with competition law. Two football World Cups have come under European Commission scrutiny in this regard.

6.81   In *Distribution of Package Tours During the 1990 World Cup*[96] the European Commission investigated and condemned under Article 85 (81) ticket distribution arrangements for the 1990 World Cup in Italy. The international governing body for football, FIFA, had appointed the Italian Football Association (the Federazione Italiana Gioco Calcio or "FIGC") as organiser of the World Cup and jointly they set up a local organising committee for the event. The organising committee granted a joint venture, set up by two Italian travel agencies, for exclusive worldwide rights to sell tickets for matches as part of package tours. These tickets accounted for at least 30 per cent of the total capacity of the grounds used in the tournament. Otherwise tickets were to be sold through national football and sport associations, UEFA, the tournament sponsors and an Italian bank, and under those arrangements were not to be resold. A Belgian travel agent complained to the Commission that it could not obtain tickets for sale as part of package tours it wished to sell for Italia 90, and the Commission upheld this complaint under Article 85 (81). It held that the grant of exclusive rights to sell tickets as part of package tours distorted competition between tour operators. The Commission refrained from imposing fines due to the (then) novelty of some of the legal issues involved.

6.82   The principal justification advanced in defence of the exclusive arrangements was that of safety. It was claimed that the separation of spectators within grounds by nationality and the need for safety around the grounds meant that only one tour operator could be authorised to put together the package tours comprising entrance tickets for sale at world level. This was rejected by the Commission on the ground that restriction of ticket sales through one operator was a disproportionate means of achieving this objective. There were other less restrictive means of ensuring spectator segregation. Indeed, evidence was given by a representative of the local organising committee that the computerised ticketing arrangements operated by one of the main distributors within Italy, an Italian bank, could with the appropriate co-ordination have enabled the selection of "two, fifteen or twenty" tour operators.[97] However, it is important to understand the limits of this decision. It did not establish a principle that any tour operator was entitled to tickets for a major sporting event. The Commission acknowledged the need for ticketing arrangements to ensure crowd safety and stated that:

> "the Commission considers it justified that travel agencies not controlled by the organisers, such as the agency which has brought the complaint in this

---

[96] OJ 1992 L 326/31, [1994] 5 CMLR.
[97] *Ibid.*, para. 115.

case, should not have been able to acquire blocks of entrance tickets with a view to putting together package tours that would have been sold in a way that was not controlled.[98]

However, it stressed that those particular exclusive arrangements were unnecessarily restrictive, disproportionate and therefore contrary to EC law.

Despite the problems identified in ticket distribution in Italia 90, further dif- **6.83** ficulties were encountered when ticket distribution for the France 1998 World Cup was entrusted to the organising committee, the Comité Français d'Organisation de la Coupe du Monde de Football 1998 ("CFO"). It is not clear whether the agreements that the CFO entered into with tour operators and others restricting the supply of tickets, which were almost certainly caught by Article 85(1) (81(1)) of the Treaty of Rome, had in fact been fully notified to the European Commission; a cryptic reference on the CFO's web site suggested at the time that they were, although no formal exemption has been granted.

What was rather more controversial was the CFO's decision to restrict sales **6.84** of 60 per cent of the tickets for the World Cup to people with a verifiable French address[99] which led to a high profile European Commission investigation from the competition directorate DG IV. This was clearly discriminatory against non-French EU citizens. As such, whether or not it was part of distribution arrangements falling foul of Article 85(1) (81(1)), it seemed to constitute both an abuse of a dominant position contrary to Article 86 (82) and an unlawful restriction on free movement of services contrary to Article 59 (49), particularly when those provisions are read in conjunction with the prohibition in Article 6 (now Article 12) of the Treaty on discrimination based upon nationality. The outcome of that investigation was a symbolic fine of 1,000 euros, a decision which outraged the British tabloid press. The pitfalls which the affair highlights for ticket distribution are clear. A ticket distribution policy should not be based on criteria which discriminate as between EU citizens on the basis of nationality or equivalent tests such as residence. Whatever the need to ensure crowd segregation, a restriction on sales of tickets cannot be permitted which offends the fundamental EC principle of non-discrimination on the grounds of nationality.

Merchandise sales

As already indicated, merchandise can exploit the image associated with a club, **6.85** players, competitions in which they take part, and associated sponsors. Thus club replica strips exploit a club's image, particularly through the design of the

---

[98] *Ibid.*, para. 118.

[99] In *Italia 90*, it appears that some 50 per cent of tickets were distributed in Italy; it is not clear from the Commission decision whether there was a requirement of a particular address. The complaint in that case did not concern any nationality requirement. See OJ 1992 L 326/31, [1994] 5 CMLR, para. 27.

strip and the application of the club's crest or other logo, but adding a player's name and number also enables his or her image to be exploited as well. Other types of merchandise, not specifically related to the field of play, may bear a club or league logo or a player's photograph or signature or some other form of endorsement. For the most part these images will be protected by trade mark, in the UK either by registered trade mark or under the law of passing-off. In addition, drawings and photographs may also be protected by copyright. Therefore, in order to produce sports related merchandise, a manufacturer or supplier will require a trade mark or copyright licence. An unlicensed supplier of products will be likely to be committing a trade mark infringement, actionable under possibly both the Trade Marks Act 1994 and the tort of passing-off, and also committing a breach of copyright contrary to the Copyright Designs and Patents Act 1988. Similar rights exist throughout Europe and North America and indeed in all developed jurisdictions.[100]

6.86 The terms of a merchandise licence agreement need to be examined for their compatibility with competition law. The example given above of replica shirt contracts shows that a competition problem might arise if a shirt supplier were to tie a club into an unreasonably long shirt supply contract that prevented other shirt suppliers getting into the market. While it is unlikely that one such agreement could have that effect, were a shirt supplier to have a number of similar agreements, an anti-competitive effect could begin to emerge, contrary to Article 85 (81) EC and its domestic equivalent.

6.87 Further, an agreement between a league or competition organiser on behalf of all participating clubs to use only a particular supplier's kit would almost certainly have such an effect and be prohibited. This illustrates the point that an agreement between a league and merchandiser is inherently more likely to have an anti-competitive effect because of the way in which a league normally represents all clubs to whom competing merchandisers or suppliers would seek to have access.[101] In the *Danish Tennis Federation* case,[102] the DTF's tennis ball sponsorship arrangements were investigated by the European Commission for their compatibility with the EC competition rules. The DTF had been in the practice of nominating a particular tennis ball supplier as its official supplier and requiring all tournaments to obtain their balls only from that supplier's official outlets in Denmark. Following Commission intervention, these arrangements

[100] On trade mark and copyright issues, see Cornish's *Intellectual Property* (Sweet and Maxwell, 3rd ed., 1996), parts IV and V.

[101] The collective selling need not necessarily be through a league. In Italy, the football players' professional association has the right to license copyright in players' photographs. A collective licence by this association of players' images exclusively to Panini for an Italian footballers sticker collection was struck down as anti-competitive under the Italian domestic equivalent of Article 85 by the Italian Monopolies Commission in 1996 (subsequently overturned on appeal).

[102] European Commission Press Release IP/98/355, 15 April 1998.

were amended to require the DTF only to award the sponsorship contract after an objective tender procedure open to all suppliers, to award the contract for no more than two years at a time, to allow the nominated balls to be bought any-where throughout the EU and, surprisingly from a competition point of view, to cease describing the nominated balls as "official" DTF balls, because consumers were being misled into thinking that term denoted superior quality. However, a rule banning a particular type of equipment for purely sporting reasons would not be caught.[103]

The fact that agreements relating to the distribution of sports products must **6.88** be assessed against Article 85 (81) in exactly the same way as distribution agree-ments covering any other products was underlined by the fines imposed by the Commission in *Dunlop Slazenger International*.[104] The infringement of Article 85 (81) consisted of the imposition of an export ban in order to protect the com-pany's exclusive distribution network.[105]

Note on the judgment of the Restrictive Practices Court in the FA Premier League case

The Restrictive Practices Court ("RPC") handed down its judgment in *Re the FA Premier League* on 28 July 1999, rejecting an application by the Director General of Fair Trading ("DGFT") to have the broadcasting arrangements entered into by the FA Premier League ("FAPL") with BSkyB and the BBC declared void as contrary to the public interest under the Restrictive Trade Practices Act 1976 ("RPTA"). While the judgment concerns only the compati-bility of broadcasting arrangements which expire at the end of the 2000/2001 season with the RTPA which is to be replaced by the Competition Act 1998 in March 2000, the judgment does have implications for future scrutiny of sports broadcasting under EC competition law as well as the 1998 Act.

The FAPL's broadcasting arrangements under scrutiny by the RPC, initially entered into with BSkyB and the BBC for five seasons, from 1992/93 to 1996/97, and which were then extended on broadly the same terms for a further four sea-sons until the end of the 2000/2001 season, involved collective exclusive selling. First, the football clubs comprising the FAPL agreed only to sell broadcasting rights through the FAPL. Secondly, the FAPL agreed to allow only BSkyB to broadcast live matches and to allow only the BBC to broadcast recorded

[103] A challenge under antitrust law in the US courts to a ban on double strung tennis rackets failed in *Gunter Harz Sports Inc v. US Tennis Association*, 511 F. Supp 1103 (D. Neb, 1981). A challenge to the ban imposed by the cricket authorities on Dennis Lillee's infamous aluminium cricket bat would doubtless similarly have failed.
[104] OJ 1992 L131/32; appeal dismissed by CFI in Case T–43/93 *Dunlop Slazenger International v. Commission* [1994] ECR 2441.
[105] See also, *Tretorn*, Commission Decision of 21 December 1994, 1994 OJ L378/45.

highlights. Live broadcasts were restricted to 60 out of the 380 Premier League games played each season.

The DGFT contended that the FAPL's broadcasting arrangements deprived viewers of the greater live and recorded coverage of Premier League matches that would otherwise occur in the absence of collective exclusive selling. The FAPL, BSkyB and the BBC argued that television presentation of the Premier League as a competition rather than allowing clubs to sell rights to individual games increased the total financial return to the FAPL and its member clubs, as well as being the only viable way of ensuring the FAPL's broadcasting rights maintained their value, as viewers were generally interested in the competition as a whole, rather than just the fortunes of individual clubs.

The RPC rejected the DGFT's application. It held that prohibiting collective exclusive selling would deny the public "specific and substantial benefits or advantages" and as a result the broadcasting arrangements passed the test (traditionally known as the gateway) under section 19(1)(b). As regards the FAPL and its clubs, the FAPL would be unable to sell the rights in the product that viewers wanted, the Premier League Championship as a whole. FAPL member clubs would consequently suffer a loss of income, with consequent adverse effects for stadia, facilities and squad improvement. The FAPL would lose its ability to divide broadcasting income equitably between clubs, thus diminishing the ability to maintain or improve competitive balance. Finally, the ability of FAPL clubs to pass on benefits to football outside the Premiership would be limited. As regards the broadcasters, the RPC found that the availability of exclusive rights promoted competition for them between broadcasters.

The RPC's judgment decides conclusively that the FAPL broadcasting arrangements are compatible with the RTPA. However, the effect of that clearance may be short-lived and not only because the broadcasting arrangements themselves are due to expire at the end of the 2000/2001 season. The RPC's judgment does not preclude further investigation by the European Commission (or indeed litigation by third parties) under Articles 85 and 86 (now 81 and 82), as the RPC did not have jurisdiction to consider arguments based upon EC law. It is understood that the European Commission has written to the FAPL and its clubs as a first stage in considering whether to open an investigation under Article 85 (81).

Moreover, the RTPA will be fully replaced in the UK by the Competition Act 1998 in March 2000. Although the arrangements cleared by the RTPA may not be challenged under the 1998 Act, whose transitional provisions provide a five year immunity for arrangements approved by the RPC, it would seem that the new arrangements after the end of the 2000/2001 season would not also be regarded as cleared (unless it might be argued that it would be an abuse of process to challenge any new arrangements if not significantly different from those approved by the RPC). It is therefore open to the DGFT to investigate any new arrangements under the 1998 Act.

There are grounds for believing that an investigation by the European Commission under Article 85 (81) may have a greater prospect of success than the DGFT's application to the RPC. The RPC found in its judgment that the FA Premier League's broadcasting arrangements do restrict competition. It therefore follows that, assuming there is an affect on inter-State trade, those arrangements are caught by Article 85(1) (81(1)) and would require exemption under Article 85(3) (81(3)) to avoid being void under 85(2) (81(2)).

If the broadcasting arrangements were to be notified for exemption, the Commission would require the parties to the broadcasting arrangements to demonstrate that they only include such restrictions as are strictly necessary under Article 81(3) EC. The RPC, by contrast, had no power to consider alternative arrangements, as it regarded itself as constrained by the RTPA to comparing the broadcasting arrangements with what would happen if collective exclusive selling were completely prohibited.

It would, therefore, be unsafe to conclude from the RPC's judgment in *Re the FA Premier League* that collective exclusive selling of sports broadcasting will comply with EC and UK competition law, particularly where agreements are entered into for more than one season. The RPC's judgment has done more to highlight the inadequacies of the RTPA than to throw light on how sports broadcasting agreements will be treated under Articles 85 and 86 (81 and 82) and their new equivalents under the Competition Act 1998. Agreements in this area will still have to be considered carefully under those provisions and, if collective exclusive selling is involved, a notification to both the European Commission and the DGFT may well be necessary and will almost always be advisable if only on a fail safe basis.

7

Disciplinary Proceedings in Sport

Introduction: disciplinary proceedings in sport generally

As we have explained in chapters two and three, our courts have frequently professed themselves reluctant to intervene in sporting disputes and, generally, are only prepared to do so at a relatively high threshold, where confronted with a clear case of unfair or otherwise unlawful operation of the domestic machinery for the resolution of sporting disputes. In chapter three we looked at the validity and effect of rules determining eligibility to participate in sporting competition. As we saw, the aspiring entrant seeking to satisfy entry criteria, or to persuade a court that he or it has done so, may or may not be in a pre-existing contractual relationship with the sporting body charged with applying and enforcing those criteria. **7.1**

Self-evidently, disciplinary proceedings occupy an important place in sports law, for without them it would be unfair to punish wrongdoing by those involved in sport, and it is essential that misconduct should be visited with appropriate punishment where it is proved, unless we are prepared to run the risk of violent behaviour, cheating and unfair sporting advantage being tolerated. That would be as unacceptable in sport as in other forms of social life, but except in cases of serious criminal conduct it is usually sufficient for sport to manage its own disciplinary régime, without involving the general law enforcement machinery of the state.[1] **7.2**

In this chapter we shall consider the nature and scope of the punitive jurisdiction exercised by sporting organisations over sportsmen and women and clubs subjected to such jurisdiction and accused of violating disciplinary rules applying to the sport practised by the accused.[2] Such a person or club, accused in disciplinary proceedings, must necessarily have a prior legal relation of some sort with the body exercising disciplinary jurisdiction. Without such a prior **7.3**

---

[1] However, two notorious ear biting cases of recent times show that there must be limits to the principle of self-regulation in sport. One involved rugby in England, the other boxing in the United States. These cases fell close to the line. Both led to the imposition of severe disciplinary sanctions following oral – or aural – hearings, and both could have entailed criminal proceedings.

[2] See generally Parker, "Disciplinary Proceedings from the Governing Bodies' Point of View"; Bitel, "Disciplinary Procedures from the Point of View of the Individual"; Wearmouth, "No Winners on the Greasy Pole; Ethical and Legal Frameworks for Evaluating Disciplinary Processes in Sport"; Stewart, "Judicial Control of Sporting Bodies in Scotland", all in *Sport and the Law Journal (SLJ)* (1995) volume 3, issue 3.

relationship there would be no foundation for the sporting body's punitive powers, with the consequence that any disciplinary proceedings and any penalty
imposed, would be wholly void in the same way as would be a "trial" of an
alleged burglar detained by a self-appointed group of vigilantes, conducted in
the back garden of one of them.

7.4   However, disciplinary jurisdiction exercisable by a sporting body does not
necessarily exist by virtue of a direct contractual relationship between that body
and the accused. The relationship may be indirect, in the sense that the accused
may have contracted with his club to submit to the jurisdiction of the governing
body within the sport concerned; and the club may in turn have contracted with
the governing body that its players will abide by the disciplinary regime established by that body from time to time. Thus in *Haron bin Mundir v. Singapore
Amateur Athletic Association*[3] the Court of Appeal of Singapore had no difficulty in entertaining a private law action brought by an athlete disciplined by the
Singapore Amateur Athletic Association which had suspended him for pre-
maturely returning from a training trip to Japan.

7.5   The athlete won his action (other than his claim for special damage) in that
the Court of Appeal upheld the decision of the High Court to quash the
Association's decision to suspend him.[4] Mr Mundir achieved his victory without being a member of the Association, which was made up of several sports
clubs and had no individual members at all. In the event, the High Court held
that an ad hoc contract should be implied, and based its decision on contract. It
is not clear from the brief report whether the Court of Appeal upheld that aspect
of the reasoning of the court below. We do not, for our part, consider that implication of a direct contractual nexus between the accused and the adjudicating
body is a necessary pre-requisite of the latter's obligation to act fairly, or of its
other common law obligations examined further below.[5] In most cases there
will be, at least, an indirect legal relation between the parties, both of which are
likely to have a contract with another body, usually the club or other organisation of which the accused is a member and which, in its turn is a member of the
disciplining body.

7.6   But even without any element of contract at all, where a sporting body asserts
control over a particular sport or particular competitions, and the accused is a
participant, or potential participant, in that sport or in such a competition, the

---

[3] [1994] 1 SLR 47, CA

[4] See *Haron bin Mundir v. Singapore Amateur Athletic Association* [1992] 1 SLR 18;
Commonwealth Law Bulletin, April 1992 p. 444, and April 1994 p. 437.

[5] Our view is also supported by the decision of Pilcher J in *Davis v. Carew-Pole* [1956]
2 All ER 524, who held that contractual relations are not necessary to found the jurisdiction of the court to grant a declaration or injunction in a case where an association
exercising disciplinary jurisdiction (the Stewards of the National Hunt Committee over
a livery stable keeper) exceeds its jurisdiction; but decided in the event that an ad hoc contract could be implied from submission to the association's jurisdiction.

accused ought in principle to be entitled to, at least, a declaration to enforce the duties of fairness, and the other common law obligations, of the disciplining body by virtue of its control over the sport or competition concerned, and its subjection of participants to disciplinary rules applying to the activity in question. A person or club entitled to take part in sporting competition has a stronger right to such a declaration than a mere stranger seeking to gain entry, in the circumstances examined above in chapter three. *A fortiori*, therefore, in the disciplinary context a remedy ought to be available, irrespective of the separate question, which we consider in chapter eight, whether the nature of the right allegedly infringed is such that it properly arises in private or public law. Subordination to a disciplinary regime, with or without contract, is itself, in our view, a sufficient pre-existing legal relation between accuser, accused and adjudicating body.

We are concerned in this chapter to give a brief outline of the content of the **7.7** law governing the exercise of punitive jurisdiction by domestic sporting bodies over individuals or clubs. Our account will, inevitably, overlap to some extent with the discussion in chapter three of rights of access to competitions, since the punitive measures open to the disciplining body may include imposing a ban from taking part in a particular competition, or over a particular period. But we observe here the distinction between ineligibility and expulsion: the latter, imposed as a disciplinary measure, presupposes the prior fulfilment of entry criteria, which, by contrast, in a case of alleged ineligibility as discussed in chapter three, is the very question under consideration. This chapter deals with the content of the law, not with the ways in which breaches of it may be enforced, which is the subject of chapter eight below.

An intellectually rigorous approach to the subject of disciplinary proceedings **7.8** in sport does not involve treating particular types of misconduct separately. Thus doping cases, which occupy a large part of the sporting jurisprudence in this area, are not conceptually distinct from cases involving other types of misconduct such as swearing at a referee or failing to play a scheduled fixture. Nevertheless, the CAS has developed principles in doping cases which, though capable of application outside that field, are particularly relevant within it, and can be seen as an important step towards the creation of an international *lex sportiva*. In recognition of the practical importance of doping cases and of the work of the CAS in balancing the twin objectives of aiding the fight against drugs and safeguarding the right to fair treatment, we end this chapter with a short separate summary of those principles.

We begin our general account with the following observations. Sporting dis- **7.9** ciplinary bodies, like other domestic tribunals, are not required to conduct themselves as if they were amateur courts of law. This proposition is the traditional starting point for any exposition of their obligations. They are not bound by the strict rules of procedure and evidence which apply in courts of law (but, frequently and increasingly, not in statutory tribunals), except to the extent that their rules so provide. However, they must not misinterpret the meaning of the rules they are applying; nor must they conduct themselves other than in conformity with well recognised principles of fairness. Examples of unlawful conduct in the course of disciplinary proceedings, of the type examined more closely below, include:

(1) Finding guilt on the basis of a defective charge; defective because what it accuses of is not a disciplinary offence at all. An extreme example would be a charge of ingesting aspirin where aspirin is not a banned substance under the relevant rules. Another, less extreme, example drawn from our own experience in a case which confidentiality prevents us from explaining more fully, is that of a charge of failure to report certain wrongdoing where the rules in play place no duty on the accused club to report such wrongdoing, but only on individuals.

(2) Misconstruction or misapplication of the disciplinary rule being applied; as in a case where the disciplining body purports to find the accused guilty of a disciplinary offence on the basis of findings of fact which do not amount to such an offence. For example, where a player is charged with knowingly receiving an illegal payment, it would be unlawful for the disciplining body to find him guilty where its finding of fact was that the payment was made into his bank account without his knowledge.[6]

(3) Making a finding of fact which is unsupported by any evidence at all. An example, again rather extreme, would be a case where an athlete is charged with deliberately taking a banned steroid, and the tribunal finds that he has done so in the teeth of unanimous expert evidence agreed upon by all the scientists in the case, that the substance found in his body was not a steroid at all but a permitted substance.

(4) Acting in bad faith: for example, making a finding of guilt without genuine belief in its rectitude, in order to achieve an ulterior purpose unrelated to the exercise of disciplinary jurisdiction. An example would be a ban imposed on a racing driver for a disciplinary offence predominantly for the purpose of leaving the field clear for a rival competitor. Such a decision would be tainted by bad faith, if that predominant purpose could be proved, whether or not the disciplining body regarded the driver as guilty; but if it did not, the case would be the more heinous.

(5) Deciding a disciplinary case without hearing the accused, in breach of the celebrated duty to comply with natural justice, or, as it is now more commonly known, the duty of fairness.[7] Other lesser forms of unfairness, drawn from myriad case law on the subject, would include the making of a decision on the basis of information undisclosed to the accused, and the giving of insufficient time to prepare a defence.

---

[6] Various instances of this type of error can be found in Beloff, "Pitch, Pool, Rink . . . Court ? Judicial Review in the Sporting World", [1989] *PL* 95, at p. 98.
[7] *Ibid.*, p. 101 for a number of examples.

(6) The adjudication of a disciplinary case in which the decision-making body, or an individual sitting on it, has an interest, financial or otherwise, in the outcome, to an extent giving rise to a real danger of bias against the accused.

(7) Cases in which the disciplining body purports to impose a penalty for a disciplinary offence outside the range of sanctions open to it. A very simple example would be imposition of a £10,000 fine where the rules provide for a maximum fine of £5,000. More difficult cases arise where the body seeks to impose a penalty said to be impliedly outside the range of available sanctions, where the rules are silent or confer ostensibly unfettered discretion. Clearly a sporting body cannot impose a prison sentence on a sprinter for leaving the blocks early. Nor could it (drawing again from our experience of a confidential case raising this question) order an individual found guilty of receiving illegal payments to leave his wife or to have his head shaved.

The validity and meaning of disciplinary rules; jurisdiction of disciplinary panels

A familiar refrain in sporting circles in recent times is the complaint made by **7.10** administrators in sport that they and the bodies they administer are over susceptible to legal attack. This concern, which is in principle a perfectly legitimate one, explains why conferences in the sporting field often include discussion about ways of fortifying such bodies against legal challenge. Indeed, some such bodies, particularly international ones, would wish to be immune from such challenge in the courts altogether, which explains certain provisions in the rules of international sporting bodies (which no English court would enforce) purporting to prohibit recourse to the law at all, and seeking to confine all disciplinary jurisdiction within the sporting arena. However, as already observed in chapter two, any attempt in this country to oust the jurisdiction of the courts is necessarily doomed to fail, for the constitutional right of access to the courts cannot be removed or bargained away except by Parliament. Sports administrators therefore have to lower their sights somewhat and concentrate not on immunising their governing bodies from legal attack, but fortifying them against challenges, recognising that such challenges cannot be stopped but seeking to ensure that, if made, they will not succeed.

The first question which, logically, may confront a sporting body in a disci- **7.11** plinary case, may be the question whether the disciplinary rules which it is applying are valid in law or not. It may seem surprising at first blush that a domestic tribunal should be put in the position of adjudicating upon the validity of the very rules which it is its task to apply. It is sometimes thought that a submission emanating from the accused that a rule relevant to his case is void, is incompetent. But that is not correct. There is no theoretical difficulty in the adjudicating body accepting the jurisdiction to rule on the validity of its own rules. Indeed it could be an instance of unfairness to abdicate responsibility for

adjudicating upon a submission of invalidity. A body exercising punitive jurisdiction must act in accordance with the rules constituting it. If one or more of
those rules is in law void, then the disciplining body may not apply that rule. It
follows, logically, that the body must decide whether to apply it and, in order to
do so, must decide whether it is valid or not.

7.12   It is not fanciful to envisage accused athletes, clubs or other sportsmen and
women making such a submission to a body entertaining disciplinary proceedings against them. Indeed, the authors are aware of at least one example where
a sporting body (chaired by one of them) was specifically invited to treat as
wholly void a rule providing for an automatic two year ban for a first doping
offence, and an automatic life ban for any subsequent offence. The basis of the
submission was that such a rule would be in unreasonable restraint of trade,
according to the principles discussed above in chapters three and four. In the
case in question it was unnecessary for the tribunal to decide the point. Where a
sporting disciplinary tribunal does decide such an issue, its decision will be subject to review in point of law by a court or other tribunal in which a subsequent
challenge is brought, as we shall see in chapter eight.

7.13   The following are examples of some of the arguments that could be deployed
by an accused in support of a case of invalidity affecting the rules of a sporting
body. First, it might be contended that the rules in play had not been properly
adopted and were consequently unconstitutional. If the argument were well
founded, the disciplining body would have no jurisdiction to hear the case at all,
and its decision would be of no more effect than that of any member of the public; the resulting decision would simply be a nullity. Next, there can be cases in
which the panel is improperly constituted. Such an argument may go to the
heart of the jurisdiction of the disciplining body, as in a case where that body
assumes a jurisdiction which it does not possess. A simple example would be a
hearing conducted, and a penalty imposed, by committee A where the rules vest
in committee B the power to conduct the hearing and impose penalties.[8] In such
a case, self-evidently, committee A will have to rule on the accused's objection
to its jurisdiction to hear the case and, if it did hear the case, it would be found
to have impliedly ruled against the accused whether or not it gave an express ruling on the point.

7.14   Another example would be an argument that the body concerned is "making
up the rules as it goes along"; in other words that it is seeking to enforce rules of
its own invention which have not been properly adopted under the constitu-

---

[8] As in the *Anderlecht* case: the CAS quashed the decision of the UEFA Executive
Committee to ban Royal Sporting Club Anderlecht from UEFA competitions for one season in consequence of revelations of corruption of the referee in respect of a cup tie
between Anderlecht and Nottingham Forest in the 1983–4 season. The decision was
taken without jurisdiction because UEFA's rules vested disciplinary powers exclusively
in its juridical organs, not its Executive Committee; see CAS Press Release of 19 May
1998 on "l'Affaire Anderlecht".

tional instruments of the body concerned. For instance, if that body's constitution required disciplinary rules to be adopted by a two-thirds majority at an annual meeting, then a disciplinary tribunal could not lawfully apply disciplinary rules which, on a vote at the last annual meeting, had obtained only one-third support of the membership. Such was one of the successful arguments of Mr Henry Andrade in his contest against the Cape Verde National Olympic Committee which was arbitrated by the CAS at Atlanta in July 1996.[9] His National Olympic Committee had purported to remove his accreditation at the Atlanta Olympic Games, with the consequence that he was prohibited from entering the heats of the 110 metres hurdles. The Committee had purported to impose this penalty by way of a disciplinary measure on the ground that Mr Andrade had disrupted the organisation, questioned the authority of its President and Secretary General and, in particular, carried the flag at the opening ceremony contrary to a decision of the Committee that the flag bearer would be the Chef de Mission of the Committee.

The panel applied the relevant rules promulgated for the occasion of the 1996 **7.15** Olympics by the International CAS, the Swiss Private International Law Act of 1987 and the Olympic Charter. It noted that Article 17 of the ICAS rules required the panel to apply those legal provisions and "general principles of law and the rules of law, the application of which it deems appropriate". Having done so the panel held that the decision to exclude Mr Andrade was void for want of consent of the International Olympic Executive Board. It went on to hold once again a few days later that the decision was void even though the consent of the International Olympic Committee (IOC) had been obtained in the interim, because Mr Andrade had not had an opportunity to make any representations prior to his exclusion, in breach of the duty of fairness discussed further below.

As already mentioned, an accused person or club might argue that a discipli- **7.16** nary rule is void as an unreasonable restraint of trade. This point was taken in the High Court in *Gasser v. Stinson*,[10] although there is no suggestion that the point was taken, as it could have been, by way of submission to the International Amateur Athletic Federation (IAAF) prior to that body's announcement of Miss Gasser's two year ban. The rule in that case operated by way of ineligibility rather than as a disciplinary measure, so that there appears to have been no hearing at which Miss Gasser could have sought a ruling (which she failed to obtain in court afterwards in any event) that the relevant rule was void. In principle, such a contention could be advanced before a disciplinary panel in relation to disciplinary penalties imposed for misconduct, such as the automatic bans already mentioned.

There is no reason why the restraint of trade doctrine should not be applied **7.17** to such rules, although harsh penalties for doping offences will be easily

---

[9] *Andrade v. Cape Verde NOC*, CAS Ad Hoc Division, Nos. 002 and 005.
[10] Unreported Scott J, 15 June 1988, discussed in chapter three above.

justified by the need for a level playing field and the grave mischief of drug taking in sport. Allied to the restraint of trade doctrine as a potential ground of invalidity is the broader principle that a domestic tribunal may not impose a penalty so radically out of proportion to the offence charged as to be irrational, or so manifestly excessive that it is outside the permitted range of discretionary responses to the offence.[11] It follows from that principle that a disciplinary rule providing for a manifestly perverse penalty necessarily out of all proportion to the seriousness of the offence to which it applied, would itself be void on public policy grounds. That consideration appears to have influenced the recent decision of the IAAF to reduce from four years to two years the length of its mandatory ban for serious doping offences.[12]

7.18   We consider it likely that a rule purporting to reverse the traditional onus of proof in a sporting disciplinary context, so as to require the accused to prove his innocence, rather than the other way round, would be regarded by an English court as invalid by reason of public policy as informed by our criminal law and indeed the principle that in civil proceedings also the party asserting a fact must, generally, prove it. Such a rule must be distinguished sharply, however, from the commonplace provision in the rules of sporting bodies creating a presumption, in doping cases, that ingestion of a banned substance was voluntary unless the athlete should prove the contrary. Such a provision is unobjectionable since it does not, in truth, require the athlete to prove innocence: the onus of proving the presence of the banned substance in the athlete's body remains on the accuser and is not placed on the accused.

7.19   Similarly, rules making positive test results prima facie evidence of the presence of a banned substance in the body, are not open to objection on policy grounds. A more difficult case is that of a rule purporting to render a positive test result "conclusive" as to the presence of the substance in the body. Such a rule might be justified on the basis of the need for certainty and the mischief of drug taking in sport, by analogy with *Gasser v. Stinson*. But we incline to the

[11] See *R v. Barnsley MBC ex parte Hook* [1976] 1 WLR 1052; *R v. Brent LBC ex parte Assegai, The Times*, 18 June 1987; *R v. Secretary of State for Transport ex parte Pegasus Holdings (London) Limited* [1988] 1 WLR 990 at 1001; *R v. General Medical Council ex parte Colman* [1989] 1 Admin LR 469 at 489; and note the well publicised outcome of the arbitration proceedings in *Tottenham Hotspur v. Football Association*, briefly reported in Grayson, All ER 1994 *Annual Review* p. 389.

[12] See *The Independent*, 1 July 1997, referring to restraint of trade legislation in Germany, Russia and Spain, and to successful applications for reinstatement by German Athletes half way through four year suspensions. In *Blalock v. Ladies Professional Golf Association* (1973) 359 F. Supp.1260 the Atlanta Division of the US District Court (District Judge Moye) held that an agreement to suspend a professional golfer from the Association for one year for alleged cheating was an unlawful restraint of trade and illegal under the Sherman Anti-Trust Act in that the suspension had been imposed in the exercise of the Association's unfettered subjective discretion, as was evident from the fact that it had initially imposed only probation and a fine, and had subsequently, without hearing from the golfer, decided to impose the one year suspension.

view that recent reports of unreliable testing procedures, even in accredited laboratories,[13] might induce an English court to strike down on policy grounds such a rule if it were operated in a manner which left no possibility of an athlete submitting that the sample tested was not hers at all. One can envisage a hard case in which an athlete might prove in court that a positive test result occurred in consequence of manifest mistaken identity. It is difficult to contemplate an English court upholding a ban imposed on an innocent athlete by a disciplinary body determined to apply a literal interpretation. But such a case has yet to come before an English court, and it may be that testing procedures will improve sufficiently to justify such a rule.

Assuming, then, that the rules in question are valid and therefore fall to be **7.20** applied by the disciplining body, the next question is what they mean on their true construction. Again, the interpretation of valid rules is a matter, in the first instance, for the sporting body applying them, but always subject to the non-excludable power of the court to review the correctness of that body's interpretation.[14] The body considering the meaning of the rules it is applying, must arrive at the correct interpretation of them, on pain of correction by a court. It follows that such a body must necessarily entertain submissions as to the true meaning of its disciplinary rules. This can create difficulty in cases where that meaning is opaque and the tribunal lacks a legally qualified member or access to legal advice, while the athlete may be legally represented or, if not, may nonetheless be advancing submissions formulated by a lawyer.

Thus in *Stewart v. Judicial Committee of the Auckland Racing Club Inc.*[15] the **7.21** question arose whether, in a three tier system with two successive rights of appeal, the function of the appellate bodies was confined to reviewing the fairness of the initial hearing, or whether the appeals, or either of them, should proceed as a full re-hearing and if so, whether they should receive fresh evidence. Hillyer J held that the rules must be construed so as to accord fairness to the accused overall and that, in view of time constraints preventing full examination of the issue at the initial hearing, any appeal should be by way of re-hearing and not merely review. In consequence he set aside the decisions of all three domestic bodies, the effect of which was to impose a three month ban on a jockey for failing to ride a horse on its merits. Incidentally, the relevant rule also empowered the stewards to disqualify the horse, which seems harsh as the duty was imposed on the rider only.

---

[13] Arising from e.g. the Diane Modahl case forming the backdrop to *Modahl v. British Athletic Federation Limited*, 28 July 1997, CA; see generally *The Diane Modahl Story: Going the Distance*, (Hodder and Stoughton, 1998). However, the House of Lords rejected as unarguable Ms Modahl's claim that the British Athletic Federation could be liable to her on the basis of an implied term that drug tests would only be carried out in a duly accredited IOC laboratory (TLR, July 23 1999). Doping controls should anyway be construed *contra preferentum*. Determination of BAF Drug Advisory Committee in the case of Douglas Walker 1999, para. 4.5.

[14] See *Lee v. The Showmen's Guild of Great Britain* [1952] 2 QB 329, CA.

[15] [1992] 3 NZLR 693.

7.22   The case is a striking illustration of a domestic body having to rule on a procedural submission by the accused. He sought to introduce two affidavits not available at the initial hearing which had taken place shortly after the finish of the race. The first appeal body refused to admit the affidavits and declined even to read them. Had its role been confined to a review of the fairness of the initial hearing, that position would have been tenable and correct. But the court subsequently held that the initial hearing was too cursory to warrant interpretation of the rules governing appeal in that restricted way. Not for the first time a sporting body fell into the error of interpreting its own rules less favourably to the accused than was consistent with fairness.

7.23   A more straightforward example of a sporting tribunal misunderstanding and misapplying its own rules occurred in *Jockey Club of South Africa v. Forbes*.[16] The Transvaal and Orange Free State Stipendiary Stirrups Board had charged a racehorse trainer with being party to the administration of a prohibited substance to a horse. An alternative, less serious charge, was being the trainer of a horse in respect of which an analytical test disclosed the presence of the prohibited substance. Under what the court described as "an elaborate system of inter-meshing measures", the rules provided for urine samples taken from the horse to be split into two. The trainer could insist on analysis of one of the two samples at a laboratory selected by him so that the rules made the analyst's certificate conclusive proof of the result of the analysis. But no such "conclusive proof" provision applied to the other sample which it fell to the Board's scientists to analyse.

7.24   Both specimens were apparently found to contain Naproxen, a banned substance. But the Board's decision to convict of the more serious offence of being party to the administration of a banned substance, was quashed. The court observed that in the case of the more serious offence, the correctness of the analysis of the sample had to be proved, and the Board could not rely on the conclusiveness of the certificate provided by the analyst nominated by the trainer, as it could have done to support a conviction for the lesser offence. The court was sympathetic to the trainer's contention that he had been charged under the wrong rule and that as a result the Board had not considered the substance of his defence, namely his denial that the specimens contained Naproxen. The result may seem favourable to the trainer, but the principle is sound. The difference between knowingly administering a banned substance to a horse, and unwittingly training a horse to which someone else has administered a banned substance, may mean the difference between destruction of a livelihood and reputation, and mere technical liability. If the Board had accepted the certificate of its scientists as merely prima facie, rebuttable evidence instead of regarding it as conclusive, the trainer might well have been in grave difficulty in refuting the proposition that the samples did indeed contain Naproxen.

---

[16] (1993) (1) SA 648; the Appellate Division of Witwatersrand said that the tribunal had "fundamentally misconceived the scope of the inquiries and hearings to be conducted", per Kriegler AJA at 633.

prohibited substance. Such was the conclusion of the CAS in the case of a French swimmer, Mlle Chagnaud, who appealed against a two year ban imposed by the international federation (FINA) of which the French Swimming Federation was a member. The relevant anti-doping provision contained an explicit definition unmistakably couched in the language of strict liability.[22] The CAS approved the use of strict liability rules irrespective of any question of guilty intent.[23] Despite this the CAS construed the rules in favour of the swimmer, relying on previous flexibility exercised by FINA in applying them. There was evidence that FINA had previously allowed a swimmer to adduce exculpatory evidence disproving fault, deliberately ignoring the letter of its rules. Accordingly the CAS would have allowed Mlle Chagnaud to rebut the presumption of deliberate ingestion, but held on the facts that she had failed to do so.

7.31 The previous case which the CAS had in mind related to another swimmer, Samantha Riley. Ms Riley had escaped with a warning after testing positive for propoxyphene metabolite. FINA instead imposed a two year ban on her coach, a Mr Volkers, who admitted giving Ms Riley the analgesic painkiller which caused her positive test. The ban was then shortened to one year. Mr Volkers appealed against it. The CAS applied "the rules of FINA and . . . general principles of law" having heard citations of Swiss and Australian law in argument. It decided that the rule created strict liability for a coach as well as a swimmer, and dismissed Mr Volkers' appeal against FINA's finding of guilt.[24] The decision is difficult to square with that in *Chagnaud*. The former case is best seen as an interesting example of the effect which prior custom and practice may have on the correct interpretation of disciplinary rules. FINA's failure to discipline Ms Riley on the basis of strict liability was invoked in support of a construction favourable to the swimmer and at odds with the plain meaning of the words creating a strict liability offence. Similarly, in English law, the interpretation of contractual terms, including disciplinary rules, may be informed by past custom and practice, but only to the extent that the meaning of the words in question is unclear or ambiguous.

7.32 To complete this account of the CAS jurisprudence we must lastly mention another aquatic asthmatic case, *Cullwick v. FINA*,[25] this time concerning a New Zealand water polo player who tested positive for salbutamol at Dunkirk in July 1995 and appealed against a two year ban, again on the basis of ingestion by inhalation pursuant to medical necessity. The CAS considered Mr Cullwick's submission that prior notification to a relevant authority of the medical necessity to inhale salbutamol, was a free standing obligation but not a precondition of the swimmer's right to invoke the exception to the ban on salbutamol. But the

---

[22] See *Chagnaud v. FINA*, CAS 95/141, para. 4, p. 7: "the identification of a banned substance . . . in a competitor's urine or blood sample will constitute an offence . . .".

[23] Citing Dallèves, Conférence Droit et Sport, CAS 1993, p. 26.

[24] *Volkers v. FINA*, CAS 95/150

[25] CAS 96/149, presided over by one of the authors.

submission was rejected in favour of a purposive construction which drew inspiration from the *Quigley* case. The *Lehtinen* case was held distinguishable in that there had been evidence in that case of prior written notification to the relevant authority by the athlete's doctor.[26] So we may conclude that strict liability doping offences are acceptable and indeed regarded as appropriate by the highest international sporting judicial authorities. But those same authorities are loath to allow such rules to operate unfairly so as to punish the innocent in a case where the rules themselves are unclear or their applicability to the facts of the case doubtful.

Evidence and proof in disciplinary proceedings

7.33 In the first part of this chapter we have looked at the legal requirement that the rules operated by a disciplining body must be valid, and that the body must interpret them correctly. In this next section, we consider upon what factual material a sporting tribunal exercising punitive jurisdiction may lawfully rely in support of a finding of guilt. In some cases disciplinary tribunals have sought to make findings of guilt and impose penalties in consequence, on the basis of evidence whose nature and sufficiency is subsequently put in issue in a legal challenge before the courts.

7.34 The starting point here is the proposition that the disciplinary tribunal, like all domestic tribunals, must have some evidence before it supporting a finding of guilt, if such a finding is to be lawful; but that the weight to be placed on such evidence is a matter for the tribunal and not the court.[27] English law insists on autonomy of decision making for domestic tribunals, including those concerned with discipline in the sporting field, provided the tribunal has some evidence before it to support its finding, and provided (as explained above) it applies valid rules correctly interpreted.

7.35 Nor is such a tribunal bound by the strict rules of evidence which apply in English courts. This has the consequence that a sporting disciplinary tribunal may accept hearsay evidence without the procedural requirements of the Civil Evidence Acts 1968 and 1995, and of rules of court.[28] Thus the tribunal may generally receive evidence in written form without cross-examination, even in the case of expert evidence. However, the latitude allowed to such disciplinary

[26] *Ibid.*, paras. 5.7 and 5.9, pp. 19 and 20; evidencing the growth of an incipient body of precedent in the CAS jurisprudence. See now *Mrs Michelle Smith de Bruin v. FINA* CAS 98/211.

[27] *Dawkins v. Antrobus* (1881) 17 Ch Div 615, CA, per James LJ at 626–8; Brett LJ at 630, 633; Cotton LJ at 633–4; *Faramus v. Film Artistes Association* [1964] AC 925 at 941–2 per Lord Evershed, and at 944–8 per Lords Hodson and Pearce; Josling and Alexander, *The Law of Clubs*, 5th ed., pp. 32–3; *Lee v. The Showmen's Guild of Great Britain* [1952] 2 QB 329, CA, per Denning LJ at 342–4.

[28] See the former Order 38 of the Rules of the Supreme Court 1965, now Civil Procedure Rules Part 33.

tribunals is always qualified by the duty to act fairly. If the nature of evidence received and relied upon by the tribunal is such as to compromise the duty of fairness, the resulting decision could later be set aside in court; for example, where evidence relating to the scientific appropriateness of laboratory procedure in a doping case is given by a secretary at the laboratory with no scientific qualification.

Expert evidence is particularly important in doping cases, but can also bear **7.36** on other issues, such as that recently given in criminal proceedings by Mr Bob Wilson, the famous broadcaster and former Arsenal goalkeeper, on the issue whether video footage supported the contention that another goalkeeper had or had not deliberately failed to save certain goals. Any expert called on to give evidence before a sporting disciplinary tribunal should bear in mind the guidance recently given by Cresswell J on the duties of an expert: to be and be seen to be independent; to provide an objective unbiased opinion; to state the facts or assumptions on which that opinion is based; to volunteer material facts which detract from his opinion; to delineate clearly his area of expertise and identify any issue falling outside it; to distinguish between concluded opinions and provisional ones; and to communicate to the other side any change of view on a material point, arising, for example, from availability of new material.[29]

The practicalities of obtaining expert evidence are of vital importance to both **7.37** sides in sporting disciplinary proceedings. The duty of the tribunal to act fairly and impartially, and to decide the case on the evidence before it, may mean that the absence of any, or of adequate, expert evidence leads to the acquittal of the guilty or, worse, the conviction of the innocent. In a doping case, for instance, expert evidence may be necessary to determine whether a sample has been taken properly so as to exclude the risk of contamination from outside; or to establish whether subsequent testing procedures are scientifically adequate. Expert evidence is not, however, necessary to establish whether a sample subsequently tested is that of the accused athlete at all. That issue can be determined by examining the chain of custody of the sample and, if the chain is a long one and the sample has passed through several hands, the absence of a lay witness through whose hands it has passed, may be telling. Among the disciplines involved in doping cases we may find chromatography, mass spectrometry, pharmaceutical science, toxicology and steroid endocrinology. Such narrowly focussed specialisms require great care in the choice of expert.

The next question which may arise is which party bears the onus of proving **7.38** guilt, or of proving a particular factual point relevant to guilt? We have already commented that an outright reversal of the presumption of innocence, written into the rules of a sporting body, would be unlikely to survive a judicial challenge in English law. We now look more closely at the incidence of the burden of proof in sporting disciplinary proceedings. The starting point is the normal

---

[29] *The Ikarian Reefer* [1993] 2 Lloyds Rep 68 (reversed on appeal on an unrelated point). On video evidence see SLB Vol. 2 No. 1 Gardiner "The Third Eye: Video Adjudication in Sport".

rule that a party asserting the existence of a particular fact bears the onus of proving that fact. But that rule may be modified or displaced by the effect of disciplinary rules creating presumptions or reversing the onus of proof on a particular issue, provided that the effect of any such modification is not to create a presumption of guilt. Thus in a doping case, the onus must be on the association bringing the case to prove the presence of a banned substance in the athlete's body. But the association's disciplinary rules may also require that ingestion of the substance occurred voluntarily and/or with intent to gain advantage, so that the case is not one of strict liability. In that event, the rules may also create a presumption that ingestion occurred voluntarily and with intent to gain advantage, arising on proof of the presence of the substance in the body, unless the athlete can show the contrary – for example, by producing a witness who says he "laced" the athlete's drink, or similar evidence.

7.39   English law does not find objectionable the placing on the accused of the onus of proving a specific factual defence.[30] Nor, as already explained, need the rules afford such a defence at all. The IAAF has apparently established that its rules create a strict liability doping offence.[31] The Federation, in its argument in support of a strict liability construction, assured that if an athlete was bound and gagged and forcibly injected with a prohibited substance, the Federation would not prosecute. However, if the knowledge and intention of the athlete are truly irrelevant, and if the justification for strict liability is the gaining of unfair advantage, then it is difficult to see why an "innocent" athlete in whose body the prohibited substance is present, should not suffer disqualification on the authority of *Gasser v. Stinson*.[32]

7.40   At the International Symposium on Sports Law held in Berlin and Potsdam on 19 November 1997, Lauri Tarasti, a Justice of the Supreme Administrative Court of Finland and former Chairman of the Arbitration Panel of the IAAF, observed[33] that the principle *nulla poena sine culpa* (which we have already mentioned in chapter one) was global but subject to exceptions. He distinguished four types of doping offence under the IAAF rules: (1) presence of a prohibited substance; (2) use of a prohibited substance; (3) admission of use of a prohibited substance; and (4) failure or refusal to submit to doping control. He went on to state that as to (3), no issue of liability arises; the case is determined by the admission. As to (2), use implies *mens rea*.[34] As to (4) mere refusal is sufficient, but could itself be the product only of intent or negligence.[35] As to (1) presence of the substance suffices; there is no need for the IAAF to prove that the

---

[30] *Phipson on Evidence*, 14th ed. (Sweet and Maxwell, 1990) paras. 4–16. *Wilander v. Tobin* (No. 1) CA (unreported) 1998.

[31] *Re Capobianco*, Arbitration Award of 17 March 1997.

[32] Unreported, Scott J, 15 June 1988; see chapter three, *supra*.

[33] See Tarasti, "Strict Liability in Doping Cases in the Light of Decisions made by the Arbitration Panel of the IAAF" (conference paper, 1997).

[34] See IAAF disciplinary proceedings against *Katrin Krabbe* (Case no. 1).

[35] See IAAF disciplinary proceedings against *John Ngugi*.

drug has assisted performance. But, controversially, he said that presence indicates intent or negligence so that, if there is no such intent or negligence, the offence is not committed.[36] However we respectfully submit that Judge Tarasti was in error in his interpretation of rule (1). Presence is a question of pure fact; thus an IAAF panel dealing with the issue of presence stated without any misdirection that "no mental element of intent or negligence has been taken into consideration".[37]

The importance of the question where the onus of proving a particular point lies **7.41** is not confined to doping cases. It was illustrated recently in a case where a football club of high repute in England had admitted cancelling a fixture with another club, which constituted a disciplinary offence under the relevant rules unless there were "just cause" for cancelling the match. The gist of the offence was cancellation of the fixture, which the association would have to prove in the normal way. In the event it did not have to do so since cancellation of the match was admitted by the club. The question at issue was whether there was "just cause" for the cancellation. On that issue the onus clearly lay on the club to show just cause, though the rules in question did not explicitly say so. It was because the club was asserting "just cause" that it had to prove it. It was not for the association to show lack of "just cause" for cancelling the fixture. The club's attempt to discharge the onus upon it failed and it suffered a penalty in consequence.[38]

The discussion above shows how great is the practical problem in doping **7.42** cases for an athlete faced with a positive test result. If he or she has no means of challenging the validity of that test result, and if the rules allow him to establish a defence of innocent ingestion, the question then arises, how can that be done? Merely to deny knowingly taking a banned substance is unlikely to cut much ice in the face of an unassailable test result. Unless there is a witness available ready to admit surreptitiously causing the athlete to take the substance, the only likely defence is accidental contamination.

This issue has arisen recently in more than one case in which an accused **7.43** athlete has pointed to contaminated meat as the source of innocently ingested

[36] This was Judge Tarasti's interpretation of the 1996 *Bevilacqua* case, concerning an Italian high jumper, where the panel held that the athlete had "not done enough to ensure that no prohibited substance has entered her body tissues or fluids".

[37] *Re Capobianco*, Arbitration Award of 17 March 1997, *supra.*, n. 31. However Judge Tarasti's view has support from a CAS arbitrator, Denis Oswald; see his "Doping Sanctions: Guilty or Innocent", FISA No. 6 (1995) pp. 2–3. A Wise argues that strict liability rules are intrinsically illegal, e.g. in his article in *Defensor Legis*, No. 1 (1997) pp. 119–133. See further on the drugs issue M. J. Beloff QC "Drugs, Sport and the Law" *Per Incuriam,* March 1991. Young "Problems with the Definition of Doping: Does Lack of Fault or the absence of performance enhancing effect matter?" (available from Holmes, Roberts and Owen, Colorado Springs USA); SLB Vol. 2, No. 2 Fraser Reid "Drugs and Doping"; SLB Vol. 2 No. 1 reports on the IOC World World Conference on Doping in Sport in 1999.

[38] *Middlesbrough FC Limited*, Premier League disciplinary proceedings and appeal, 1997; in which two of the authors were involved; see also the *Lehtinen* case, *supra.*, n. 19, CAS 95/142, in which the athlete accepted the onus of rebutting the prima facie case against him arising from his admission of a positive test.

banned steroids in his body. Expert evidence has been deployed to support the assertion that unscrupulous meat producers sometimes illegally inject animals, destined for slaughter, with the very same banned steroids in order to increase the yield of meat from the animals. Scientists responsible for testing samples taken from athletes accept that illegal contamination of this kind is not unknown, but regard the prospect of innocent contamination as infinitesimally small. Consequently they discount such a defence even where meat of a type known to be susceptible to illegal contamination is shown to have been on the menu shortly before the test. Other scientists, instructed on behalf of athletes, dispute the statistical improbability of innocent contamination and have given evidence that it cannot be discounted. The issue remains a live one. Another argument advanced in respect of female athletes is that an unnatural amount of testosterone can be the product of hormonal disorder; thus in the United States the Olympic runner Mary Decker-Slaney was acquitted of a doping offence before the United States Amateur Athletic Federation Panel on the basis of this defence. The case has recently been heard before the IAAF Panel in Monte Carlo.[39]

7.44   Finally on this topic, we should mention one other point. The concept of the onus of proof is not wholly apt in the context of bodies which exercise inquisitorial, as opposed to adversarial disciplinary jurisdiction. Some sporting bodies' rules make provision to the effect that a committee of enquiry shall enquire into the matters alleged and may, if of the view that they are well-founded, impose appropriate sanctions. Other bodies' rules provide for the classical English adversarial model of proceedings, with a "prosecutor" and a "defence". Even where the latter form of provision is made, the tribunal's freedom from the strictures of formal rules of evidence and procedure may enable it to exercise its punitive jurisdiction in a quasi-inquisitorial manner, leading from the chair and taking the initiative in defining issues and questioning witnesses. To the extent that such a tribunal conducts itself in an inquisitorial manner, in the tradition of the civil law jurisdictions, the utility of the concept of onus of proof may be undermined. A fact finding body conducting an enquiry as to the truth of matters under investigation will decide for itself where the truth lies, and may do so without necessarily engaging in a comparison of the relative strengths of the cases presented by each party. Thus it may decide the issue without recourse to the question of onus at all. Subject always to the duty to hear both sides, there is nothing objectionable in such an approach.

7.45   The next question to consider is that of the standard of proof, a question which arises whether the body concerned is conducting itself adversarially, inquisitorially or somewhere between the two. Here the position in English law is tolerably clear. Unless the relevant rules provide otherwise, the standard of

---

[39] *In Re Mary Decker-Slaney* IAAF Tribunal 26.4.99 which indicates the proper approach to the IAAF (and BAF) rule on testosterone cases at paras. 19–28. Also Dennis Mitchell, IAAF Tribunal 3.8.99, para 9. An IAAF panel has held that an athlete is entitled to the benefit of the doubt where a metabolite of a prohibited substance could also come from an allowed substance, such as a contraceptive drug: see *Akpan* case (IAAF, 1995).

proof under disciplinary or other rules administered by sporting bodies is the normal civil standard, that is to say, proof on the balance of probabilities or, to put it another way, that it is more likely than not that the factual state of affairs in question obtains. The standard of proof before a domestic tribunal in proceedings governed by English law, including proceedings before sporting disciplinary or other tribunals, is not the criminal standard of proof beyond reasonable doubt. The contrary view appears to have some currency[40] and may have some validity outside England, but is inconsistent with the decision of the Court of Appeal in *Hornal v. Neuberger Products.*[41]

Application of the criminal standard of proof is unnecessary; the view that **7.46** fairness calls for the criminal standard confuses the standard of proof with the weight of evidence required to meet that standard. In English law, the courts accept the proposition that the more serious the misconduct alleged, the greater the weight of evidence required to meet the civil standard of proof and thus to discharge the onus of proof. That proposition, which represents English law, is also no more than common sense and fairness personified, for it is inherently less likely – or so we must hope – that a person will commit a grave wrong than a trivial wrong. The practice of the civil courts in England of recognising a connection between the gravity of the charge and the weight of the evidence required to prove it on the balance of probabilities, has on occasion led to the fallacious proposition that the criminal standard of proof must be met even in civil proceedings (which sporting disciplinary proceedings are) where the conduct of which the accused stands charged is a criminal or other gravely wrongful act.

The civil standard of proof on the balance of probabilities is a measure, in **7.47** proceedings conducted adversarially, of the standard required to discharge the onus of proof. To the extent that the proceedings are conducted in an inquisitorial manner, the civil standard of proof is a measure of the standard imposed by the disciplinary tribunal on itself. From time to time the standard has been formulated in other ways; for example, in one of the cases heard by the ad hoc division of the CAS at Atlanta in 1996, the CAS referred to a requirement of "comfortable satisfaction" as the standard necessary to establish commission of a doping offence of which two Russian athletes stood charged. The CAS went on to reiterate the proposition that the more serious the allegation, the greater the degree of evidence required to achieve "comfortable satisfaction".[42] This is

[40] See for example, Morton-Hooper, "Sporting Disciplinary Proceedings in Practice – the participant's view", Sports Forum 1996, conference paper, at pp. 15–17; cf. *Phipson on Evidence, supra.,* n. 30, para. 4–39.

[41] [1957] 1 QB 247, CA; see also *Phipson on Evidence, supra.,* n. 30, para. 4–36 and the cases therein cited, including *R. v. Hampshire County Council ex parte Ellerton* [1985] 1 WLR 749, CA (civil standard of proof applies to proceedings before disciplinary tribunal subject to any contrary provision in the relevant rules).

[42] *Korneev and Russian NOC v. IOC; Gouliev and Russian NOC v. IOC*, reported in Mealey's *International Arbitration Report*, February 1997, pp. 28–9; applied in *Wang*

perhaps more than just a reformulation in other language of the normal civil standard of proof applicable in English law. But to the extent that the concept of "comfortable satisfaction" denotes a higher standard of proof than that of the "balance of probabilities", English law does not require such a high standard.

7.48 We noted above that the civil standard of proof applies unless the relevant rules provide otherwise. The rules of the IAAF do indeed include a provision requiring proof beyond reasonable doubt in doping cases. That provision led Athletics Australia, a member of the IAAF, to acquit Mr Dean Capobianco of a doping offence in July 1996, shortly before the Atlanta Olympics where he was due to compete. Athletics Australia dismissed the charge despite a positive test result, because of defects in the chain of custody of the relevant samples. The national tribunal held that it had not been shown beyond reasonable doubt that a doping offence had been committed.

7.49 However, following a reference to arbitration by the Federation, the arbitrators found (in the light of certain fresh evidence not previously available) that the chain of custody was complete and that there was no reasonable doubt that a doping offence had been committed. As the offence was one of strict liability, there was no room for the athlete to mount a defence of innocent ingestion through contaminated products. The Federation relied in addition on the English law principle embodied in the Latin maxim *omnia rite praesumuntur esse*, otherwise known as the presumption of regularity, which holds that official acts are deemed to have been properly carried out unless the contrary be shown.[43] However, the applicability of the presumption to official acts of an international sporting association is open to doubt and is not established authoritatively in English law.

7.50 One other question remains to be considered: what if the sporting association in a disciplinary case is able to prove the primary fact constituting the offence (for example, presence of a banned substance in an athlete's body), but the accused seeks to discharge the onus of proving facts constituting a defence (for example, innocent ingestion of the banned substance in a non-strict liability case)? To what standard must the athlete prove the facts constituting his defence? The logical answer would seem to be that he must meet the same standard as that required to prove the prima facie offence, namely that of the balance of probabilities.[44] The importance of the point is evident, for an athlete may be able to show a *possibility* of innocent ingestion, yet be quite unable to prove that this possibility was anything more than just that, i.e. that innocent ingestion is more likely than not to be the explanation for a positive test result. The point arose, but was not tested fully on the facts, in *Wang Lu-Nuyeta v.*

and others v. FINA, CAS 98/208 (22 December 1998), para. 5.6, describing the standard as "less than criminal standard, but more than the ordinary civil standard". Also *Mrs Michelle Smith de Bruin v. FINA* CAS, 98/211 adopts *Korneev* test at 10.2 especially where manipulation is alleged

[43] See *R v. Inland Revenue Commissioners ex parte P C Coombs and Co* [1991] 2 AC 283, per Lord Lowry at 300 C-F.

[44] See also to the same effect *Phipson on Evidence*, *supra*, n. 30, at paras. 4–36 et seq.

FINA.[45] Chinese swimmers who had tested positive for triamtarene, a banned substance, appealed to the CAS against a two year ban imposed by FINA, contending, *inter alia*, that a health food called actovegin could have been responsible for a false triamtarene reading.

Rule DC9.3 of FINA's doping control rules provided that a finding of a **7.51** banned substance present in the body "shall shift to the competitor the burden of establishing why he or she should not be sanctioned . . .". The majority of the CAS, applying Swiss law but with power to find the facts as well as the law and thus with "its main focus . . . on evidence before it", found that the evidence as to laboratory procedure was unimpeachable and that the swimmers could not raise a reasonable doubt that the substance detected might, in truth, be a substance other than triamtarene such as actovegin not containing triamtarene. The panel found that the presence of the banned substance was established beyond any reasonable doubt. The next question was whether triamtarene could actually be present in actovegin and thus be present as a result of innocently ingested actovegin (whose manufacturers denied that it contained triamtarene). As to that question, the onus lay on the swimmers, but the panel held that rule DC9.3 was relevant to penalty, not to liability, and that in any case the swimmers would have to prove the point on the balance of probabilities, i.e. they would have to show it was more likely than not that the presence of triamtarene in actovegin was the explanation for the positive test. On the facts, they failed to discharge this onus.

Disciplinary procedures – the content of procedural fairness

Our account of the law relating to disciplinary procedures in sport continues **7.52** with a brief exposition of the content of the rules of natural justice, or the duty of procedural fairness.[46] We have observed already that this duty can inform and influence the interpretation of disciplinary rules, which generally must be construed in conformity with the duty of procedural fairness and not in conflict with it, where the words so permit. If a disciplinary rule is itself, on its correct construction, inconsistent with the duty of fairness – for example, a rule which explicitly provided that an accused should have no right to be heard before determination of the charge against him – the rule would probably be held invalid by an English court on the basis that the rule making body could not lawfully and constitutionally adopt unfair rules.

However the point is not entirely clear cut, since disciplinary rules, as already **7.53** explained, take effect as contractual terms. A duty of fairness is implied into contracts containing such terms, yet in the field of employment no such duty is

[45] CAS 98/208, 22 December 1998.
[46] See generally Parpworth, "Sports Governing Bodies and the Principles of Natural Justice; an Australian Perspective", *SLJ* (1996) Vol. 4, issue 2, p. 5.

implied, and, as a general rule of English contract law, implied terms may be displaced by express ones. It follows that, in order to preserve the integrity of the duty of fairness in the context of disciplinary rules to which sportsmen and women are subjected, the law must regard such rules not merely as contractual terms but as quasi-legislative in character. This approach protects the duty of fairness and accords with the celebrated analysis of Lord Denning MR in a seminal dissenting judgment.[47]

7.54   Putting aside the unlikely case of an attempt expressly to exclude the implied duty of fairness, we consider next what the true scope of that duty is. In an interlocutory appeal, the Court of Appeal has recently declined to give a definitive answer to that difficult question, but contemplated that the answer to it would vary according to the surrounding factual circumstances, including the rules of the body in question.[48] The celebrated athlete Diane Modahl sued the British Athletic Federation for damages of about half a million pounds after samples she had given were reported to contain an impermissibly high ratio of testosterone to epitestosterone. She was initially suspended, subsequently banned following a hearing before a disciplinary committee of the Federation, but thereafter in 1995 her appeal was allowed by an Independent Appeal Panel and the ban was lifted. She alleged wrongful use of an unaccredited laboratory to test the samples, and bias on the part of two members of the disciplinary committee; and she claimed the expenses incurred in connection with the disciplinary hearing and the subsequent appeal, and loss of earnings during the period of her allegedly wrongful suspension from competition.

7.55   As Ms Modahl had been successful in her appeal, the Federation was able to argue that the disciplinary system had functioned correctly in protecting an athlete whose guilt could not be proved, the Independent Appeal Panel having accepted, on the basis of evidence not before the disciplinary committee, the possibility of degradation of the samples. The Federation applied on that ground, among other grounds, to strike out the claim. The question what term should be implied to give effect to the duty of fairness was among the points at issue. The federation contended for a term to the effect that disciplinary proceedings would only be flawed if the proceedings as a whole, including the appeal, were unfair. On that basis there could not be a breach in view of the athlete's successful appeal. The athlete, however, advanced an implied term that the members of the disciplinary committee would act in good faith and would not be biased, a term she alleged was breached in the course of the initial hearing, the unfairness of which she submitted could not be cured by an appeal.

7.56   Lord Woolf MR mentioned the well known case law establishing the proposition, in public as well as private law, that an appeal can cure defects in earlier proceedings if the result of the appeal is that the process, taken as a whole, was

---

[47] *Breen v. Amalgamated Engineering Union* [1971] 2 QB 175, 189–191.

[48] *Modahl v. British Athletic Federation Limited*, CA transcript 28 July 1997, per Lord Woolf MR at pp. 20–26; per Morritt LJ at pp. 36–9; and per Pill LJ at pp. 43–4.

fair;[49] and the general reluctance of the English courts to become embroiled in sporting disputes.[50] His Lordship strongly hinted (in our respectful view correctly) that the Federation was correct in submitting that the court will not imply a term which goes beyond requiring the disciplinary process to be fair as a whole. He pointed to the structure of the Federation's rules, and those of the International Federation to which it was affiliated. It was inherent in that structure that an innocent athlete might suffer suspension between an initial disciplinary hearing and a successful appeal from its outcome. He noted the lack of any financial remedy under the rules, and contrasted that with the contention that the alleged implied term could found such a financial remedy. Finally, he observed that if the claim had been sustainable in public law[51] damages would not be available, only the setting aside of the decision which would be otiose as the appellate body had already done so. But as this was an interlocutory application and not a trial, he felt unable to strike out the claim on that issue, accepting as arguable the proposition that each step in the disciplinary process must be individually fair. Morritt LJ regarded as "well arguable" the existence of the implied term for which the athlete contended. The tenor of his judgment, and of Pill LJ's, is more positive in favour of the athlete's contention, and it remains to be seen which way the case will go if it proceeds to a trial.

The approach of the Master of the Rolls is, in our respectful view to be pre- **7.57** ferred, for it avoids an artificially sharp differentiation between private and public law approaches to decisions of sporting bodies. As we explain in chapter eight, we do not regard as sound the rationale for denying (in all but the rarest of cases) a public law remedy to challenge decisions of sporting bodies. There is strong support in principle and in authority[52] for the view that the result of a claim should not differ according to whether it is available by way of private or public law procedure. In public law, damages for unlawful administrative action are only recoverable in a case of misfeasance, which requires a finding of bad faith, in the sense of conduct going beyond bias or an appearance thereof in the form of a predisposition against the athlete, but without malice, arising from a genuinely held belief in her guilt. The athlete's argument in *Modahl* entails a dilution of the strong requirement of malice or bad faith necessary to recover damages in public law, but in circumstances not conceptually different from a

[49] *Calvin v. Carr* [1980] AC 575, PC; *Lloyd v. McMahon* [1987] 1 AC 625, HL.

[50] Citing *Cowley v. Heatley, The Times*, 24 July 1986; *McInnes v. Onslow-Fane* [1978] 1 WLR 1520, 1535. See too *British Wheelchair Sports v. British Paralympic Association*, 5 November 1997, Scott V-C ("What is unnecessary and to be avoided if my judgment is spending scarce resources of these charitable associations in conducting litigation when a solution that can be lived with by all concerned can surely be reached by sensible discussion.")

[51] I.e. by application for judicial review, a remedy not currently available as English law stands, as we explain in chapter eight below.

[52] See for example, Carnwath J's judgment in *Stevenage Borough FC Limited v. The Football League Limited*, transcript 23 July 1996.

public law claim. We therefore consider that Lord Woolf's provisional view as correct and that the scope of the implied term as to fairness should, absent any specific term modifying it, be the narrow one advanced by the Federation in *Modahl*: that the disciplinary process taken as a whole must be fair, but nothing more.

7.58 It can be objected that, according to that view, damages can in any event be recovered for breach of the overall duty of fairness even without bad faith in the strong sense of malice required in a public law misfeasance claim. We agree that the objection is sound, and we consider that the only satisfactory answer lies in treating athlete's rights under disciplinary regimes as not arising primarily in private law at all, but in public law. That view does not at present represent English law, but we are far from alone in believing that it should.[53] Until the controversy over the juridical nature of rights asserted by sportsmen and women challenging decisions of sporting bodies is resolved, anomalies are inevitable and the law will not be on a sound footing. An appeal to their Lordships' House is needed to clarify the point, but opportunities for such an appeal rarely arise and the likelihood of one is diminished by the fact that most sporting associations prefer, for some reason, the current position in which they must face private law proceedings but are rarely at risk of judicial review of their decisions.

7.59 To conclude our comments on the general nature of the duty of fairness, we should observe that its existence should not be seen as detracting from the wide discretion enjoyed by sporting tribunals as to the manner in which they may, without unfairness, conduct their proceedings. Thus in *Justice v. South Australian Trotting Control Board*,[54] the Supreme Court of South Australia refused an application for review, under a form of public law procedure not available in England, alleging injustice in the conduct of disciplinary proceedings following which the plaintiff had been suspended for five weeks for failing to take all reasonable and permissible measures to ensure that his trotting horse was given full opportunity to win or obtain the best possible place in the field. The Court rejected the submission that the investigating stewards must be available for cross-examination by the accused, pointed to the wide discretion of a domestic tribunal as to the manner of its proceedings and the lack of any obligation to adopt the formalities of a court of law, and found no other form of unfairness made out.

7.60 That authority does not appear to have been cited to Ebsworth J in *Jones v. Welsh Rugby Union*,[55] in which Her Ladyship found arguable the proposition that unfairness had tainted disciplinary proceedings against a rugby player

---

[53] See for example, D. Pannick QC, "Judicial Review of Sports Bodies" [1997] JR 150; Beloff and Kerr "Why Aga Khan is Wrong", [1996] JR 30.

[54] (1989) 50 SASR 613.

[55] Unreported, transcript 27 February 1997, upheld on appeal, *The Times*, 6 January 1998, CA.

because the system was one which "in effect prohibits a party from challenging by question or by evidence the factual basis of the allegations against him".[56] The judge's approach was unusually interventionist in that the proposition she found arguable was, in effect, that an adversarial system was necessary to comply with the duty of fairness, and that an inquisitorial one could not do so unless it included the adversarial elements of live evidence and cross-examination. This approach goes beyond previous authority in circumscribing the discretion of the disciplinary body as to the conduct of its proceedings. Much has been made of the decision but it was only an interlocutory application which required the judge to apply tests that can make the law appear more favourable to the plaintiff than it actually is.[57] Thus Ebsworth J described the issue as whether the association had applied its rules with undue rigidity and whether the rules themselves were unfair. She did not have to resolve that issue but was impressed by the contention that it was unfair for the disciplining body to view a video of the incident in question in private, despite a specific request to the contrary.

7.61 To summarise the position thus far, uncertainty remains in our law both as to the definition of the duty of fairness, and as to the extent of procedural discretion required to comply with it in a particular case. In one sense, this is as it should be, since questions of natural justice always turn on the facts of the particular case. But the development of the law has been unnecessarily hampered by the intrusion of orthodox contract law thinking into a field which ought rather to be governed by principles derived from the jurisprudence of administrative law. The recent success of some plaintiffs in achieving findings, albeit sometimes only provisional findings, of unfairness, makes it surprising that some sporting bodies remain rather wedded to their traditional reluctance to entertain full adversarial procedure, even though it is more convenient to do so than to face a lawsuit afterwards.

7.62 Our next task is to focus more closely on some of the individual characteristics of the duty of fairness. These can be readily identified despite the prevailing uncertainty about the overall scope of the duty. The first is the well known proposition that an accused has the right to be informed in clear terms of the allegations against him or her. In practice this may mean that the sporting association must accede to a request by the accused for further and better particulars of the allegations, before they are considered by the body exercising punitive jurisdiction. It would not be fair merely to allege that a sportsman or woman had engaged in conduct likely to bring his or her sport into disrepute, without condescending to inform the accused when, where and how he or she is alleged to have committed that conduct. If those particulars could be shown to be already well known to the accused and the request for them merely tactical,

[56] Ebsworth J, transcript 27 February 1997, p. 20. In the Court of appeal Potter I.J remarked "In the days of professional sport now upon us, the requirements of natural justice in relation to disciplinary proceedings may well require further development".

[57] This is because of the low threshold required of a plaintiff in interlocutory injunction applications on the authority of *American Cyanamid v. Ethicon* [1975] AC 396, HL, and *Leisure Data v. Bell* [1988] FSR at 367, CA.

then doubtless no relief would be available from a court in respect of failure to provide them; but as so often in this field, the sporting association is usually best advised to opt for caution and provide more information than necessary, rather than less.

7.63   Equally well known and now only rarely disregarded by sporting bodies is the right of an accused to make representations by way of defence against the charge, or if the charge is admitted, by way of mitigation of the penalty.[58] As an established principle, this right requires no elaboration, but we will consider further below the extent to which the exercise of the right may include the making of representations in a particular way in certain cases.

7.64   The next, likewise very well known, aspect of the duty of fairness is the rule against bias which, broadly, requires the adjudicating tribunal to be free from any predisposition against the accused, and free from any vested interest, particularly a financial interest, in the outcome of the proceedings in which it is adjudicating. The modern law is now to be found in the speech of Lord Goff in *R v. Gough*.[59] The question is whether there is a real danger of bias arising from the facts, which include the composition of the adjudicating body and any statement made by any prospective member of it before the adjudication.

7.65   The rule against being "judge in one's own cause",[60] makes it most unwise for sporting bodies to appoint to disciplinary panels persons who have had prior involvement with the matter, especially if they have been involved in formulating charges or have expressed a view, on or off the record, as to the merits of a disciplinary case. The expression of such views may be extremely tempting in a case where there appears to be no conceivable defence to the charge, where its existence has already received wide publicity and the press are clamouring for a reaction from the sporting body responsible for determining the charge. It is understandable that a sporting association, faced with such position, should feel the need to send strong signals to others at once, without waiting for the case to be completed. Indeed the body may risk criticism for failing to speak out against the conduct with which the accused is charged. The two cardinal rules to follow are first, to ensure that any such statement condemns the conduct complained of only in general terms and with the caveat that no reference is being made to the individual case in question, which has yet to be determined; and second that any such statement should emanate from a person who will have no part to play in

---

[58] Examples of outright failure to hear the sportsman in his defence are found in *Keighley Football Club v. Cunningham*, *The Times*, 25 May 1960 (rugby player sent off the field and subsequently suspended without notice either to him or his club); and *Angus v. British Judo Association*, *The Times*, 15 June 1984 (judoka banned after positive drug test not allowed opportunity to explain that the prohibited substance was found in a sinus decongestant taken under a lawful medical prescription).

[59] [1993] AC 646, HL; see also in relation to a decision of their Lordships' House itself the celebrated case concerning the former dictator of Chile: *In re Pinochet*, speeches delivered on 15 January 1999, reported in *The Times*, 18 January 1999.

[60] Or, for those who prefer Latin, the maxim *nemo iudex in causa sua*.

the subsequent disciplinary process. If these rules are carefully followed, allegations of bias engendered by considerations of public relations, can be avoided, for bias is not established by showing a predisposition against the conduct complained of, which ex hypothesi is unlawful under the relevant rules, as distinct from a predisposition against the person charged with that conduct.

Cases in the sporting field in which allegations of bias have been aired mainly **7.66** predate the decision of the House of Lords in *R v. Gough*. But it is unlikely that they would have been decided differently following the shift of emphasis from a "real likelihood" of bias to a "real danger" of bias. Thus in 1979 members of a tribunal of the Football Association who had spoken critically of the former England team manager, Don Revie, before hearing charges against him, were held by Cantley J to have acted unlawfully in subsequently imposing a ten year ban from football activities on Mr Revie.[61] By falling into the trap of speaking out, they had demonstrated a likelihood of bias. The plaintiff had objected to the constitution of the tribunal, but the members had refused to stand down. The result would be no different today.

For well over a century English law has regarded any person with a direct **7.67** pecuniary or proprietary interest in the outcome of proceedings, as disqualified from adjudicating in such proceedings.[62] But if such an interest is merely indirect and tenuous, the person concerned may not be disqualified, a proposition best illustrated by the case of the judge who was held not disqualified from trying a defendant alleged to have robbed a bank in which the judge held shares.[63] A notable illustration of the principle in the sporting field is found in *Barnard v. Jockey Club of South Africa*,[64] an alleged horse doping case in which a member of one of the disciplinary bodies which found against the accused horse trainer fatally impaired the validity of the proceedings by declining to recuse himself after being invited to do so by the accused. His good faith was not impugned, and he had very properly disclosed that he was a partner in the firm of attorneys representing the respondent Jockey Club. His apparent financial interest, which was not contradicted by evidence, arose by inference from the fact of being a partner in that firm, and the drafting of the reply to the grounds of appeal to the body on which he sat, drafted by another partner in the same firm. Gordon J went on to hold that the same evidence also established a very real likelihood of bias which should have disqualified the partner concerned irrespective of his financial interest. But this latter conclusion might have been overcome by adducing evidence of an effective "Chinese wall" between the two partners.

---

[61] *Revie v. Football Association*, The Times, 14 December 1979.

[62] *Dimes v. Grand Junction Canal Co. Proprietors* (1852) 3 HLC 759; and the useful account in de Smith, Woolf and Jowell, *Judicial Review of Administrative Action*, 5th ed., (Sweet & Maxwell, 1995) at pp. 528–530.

[63] *R v. Mulvihill* [1990] 1 WLR 438.

[64] (1984) 2 SALR 35 (W).

7.68   Needless to say, personal hostility against the accused will readily lead a court to apprehend a real danger of bias.[65] But the cases may go either way as the question is one of fact and degree, and the courts are particularly reluctant to hold that the judgment of professionals is likely to be impaired by personal motives. It is beyond our purpose to give a full account of the myriad case law on the subject. Reference should be made to specialist works.[66]

7.69   Moving away from the composition of the tribunal, another question which frequently arises is whether the accused may insist on exercising his right to make representations in his defence through a solicitor or counsel, rather than on his own or with help from a friend or colleague. Disciplinary rules frequently make provision as to representation; often it is explicitly permitted, particularly in serious cases where the accused's livelihood may be at stake. In other instances, it is explicitly prohibited or limited, for example by allowing representation but not by a solicitor or, it may be, not by counsel. Such rules presumably reflect varying perceptions as to the utility of a contribution from lawyers, or from lawyers of a particular type. In an intermediate category of cases, the rules in question are either silent on the point or confer a discretion on the adjudicating body to permit or prohibit legal representation, or legal representation of a particular type, as it thinks fit.

7.70   English law does not require the rules of sporting bodies to confer an absolute right to legal representation of a person accused of a disciplinary offence. If the rules do confer such a right, then obviously it will be irregular to deny representation. If the rules are silent, the adjudicating body necessarily has a discretion arising from the general proposition that it may regulate its own proceedings in such manner as it thinks fit. Lord Denning MR has pithily pointed out that in domestic tribunals "justice can often be done . . . better by a good layman than a by a bad lawyer".[67] But there may be cases in which the charge is so serious that it would be a wrong exercise of discretion and unfair to disallow representation, for example in a doping case or, but more doubtfully, in a case arising from a fracas on the field of play.[68]

7.71   A closely related question to that of legal representation is whether the right to make representations may include the right to call witnesses and, often more importantly, the right to cross-examine witnesses appearing for the other side. Rights to the attendance of witnesses to give oral evidence may be more valu-

[65] See, e.g. *Taylor v. National Union of Seamen* [1967] 1 WLR 532; *Roebuck v. National Union of Mineworkers* [1977] ICR 573.

[66] The best recent account is in de Smith, Woolf and Jowell, *supra.*, n. 62, see at pp. 521–548.

[67] *Enderby Town FC v. The Football Association Limited* [1971] 1 All ER 215, CA, at 218.

[68] See, as to the former, *Pett v. Greyhound Racing Association Limited No.2)* [1970] 1 QB 46, CA (sometimes colloquially known as the "unruly horse" case); and as to the latter, *Jones v. Welsh Rugby Union, supra.*, n. 55, at pp. 9 and 20 of the transcript.

able if the accused has the services of a qualified lawyer to put questions to those witnesses. These difficult questions raise again the tension between adversarial and inquisitorial procedure, between formality and informality in disciplinary proceedings, and between traditional judicial abstentionism and recent interventionism corresponding to higher stakes in an increasingly professionalised sporting world. In *Jones v. Welsh Rugby Union* the court was invited to grant an injunction, *inter alia*, on the basis of denial of legal representation. The argument was that rugby union football was now a professional sport and consequently representation could not lawfully be denied, livelihood being at stake. The practice of the Union was not to allow representation, but to allow a "shoulder to lean on", which in the particular case was a distinguished Queen's Counsel who, at one point, was allowed to speak for the accused uninterrupted for a period estimated variously from ten minutes to twenty minutes. Ebsworth J, granting the injunction, did so apparently not in reliance on denial of legal representation, but because of the Union's refusal to allow viewing of a video of the incident by the parties and representations on it, and refusal to allow cross-examination of the referee or the calling of witnesses. The judge made copious reference to sport having become "big business" from which many people now earn their living, and commented that it would be "naive to pretend that the modern world of sport can be conducted as it used to be not very many years ago".[69]

While the learned judge's observations are, in themselves, correct, they do not **7.72** differentiate between a merely temporary effect on the livelihood of a sportsman, of which Mr Jones was in jeopardy; and utter destruction of his livelihood, for example through a life ban for drugs offences or horse doping. There will be cases falling somewhere in the middle; a two year ban on a professional footballer may or may not in practice snuff out his career and, on any view, is serious enough. But the true principle ought to be that enunciated by Lord Denning MR in the *Pett* case, namely that it is a question of fact, having regard to the seriousness of the charge, whether natural justice requires a right to legal representation. The same logic must dictate that a parallel principle applies where the right to call or cross-examine witnesses is at issue. The *Jones* case, which was only an interlocutory application, ought not to be regarded as authority supporting an absolute right to call and cross-examine witnesses, still less an absolute right to legal representation, in every case where the outcome may have an economic impact on the accused. For example, a professional footballer facing a possible ban after receiving one too many yellow cards, should not expect to succeed in restraining the Premier League or the Football Association from proceeding with a hearing without allowing him to be represented by counsel and to call a panoply of witnesses.

A related issue, which has arisen from time to time, is whether a third **7.73** party with an interest adverse to the accused should be allowed to appear at a

---

[69] Transcript, 27 February 1997, p. 25.

disciplinary hearing to speak against the accused. A rule conferring a right on such a third party would not be objectionable in principle. If the rules are silent, the discretion as to the manner of conducting disciplinary proceedings is broad enough to allow an appearance by an adversely interested third party. The objection that an accused ought not to face "two prosecutors" or, in relation to penalty, a "plea in aggravation", is not compelling, and was recently rejected in a disciplinary case involving Middlesbrough Football Club in which Blackburn Rovers Football Club was allowed to appear by leading counsel to argue in support of Middlesbrough's guilt, and in support of a particular form of punishment – forfeiture of the match and award of the points to Blackburn – favourable to Blackburn's interest. As has since been remarked, to say that an accused faces two prosecutors is a vivid phrase, but does not mean the accused faces more than one case to answer.

7.74 The law does not require, necessarily, that there should even be an oral hearing of a disciplinary charge at all. For example, in *Currie v. Barton*[70] the Court of Appeal held that an amateur tennis club did not breach its duty of fairness when its committee decided to ban a player from the amateur county team for three years, for refusing to play a match and walking off the court, without inviting him to appear before the committee in person. He had learned from press reports that he might be facing a ban, and had written a long letter to the secretary giving his side of the story. His ban from the county team did not affect his livelihood earned from coaching, sponsorship and professional tournaments. The restraint of trade doctrine was therefore not engaged. In *USA Shooting and Quigley v. Union Internationale de Tir*,[71] a case of alleged doping, the UIT had held a meeting of its executive to decide Mr Quigley's fate. Neither Mr. Quigley nor his national association were permitted to attend that meeting despite requests to do so. However a detailed written presentation on Mr Quigley's behalf was submitted and considered by the executive. The relevant rules provided that the accused person should have the right to present evidence, comment on the accusation, defend himself and be represented. In the event, the CAS did not need to rule on his alternative contention that he had not received a fair hearing, since he was successful in establishing that the offence was not one of strict liability. However the CAS commented that it was obvious Mr Quigley's argument would have failed, since the right to be heard does not include a right to an oral hearing. The CAS added that even if the procedure had initially been insufficient to comply with natural justice, "as long as there is a possibility of full appeal to the [CAS] the deficiency may be cured".[72]

7.75 It appears to be frequently assumed in the jurisprudence relating to the conduct of sporting disciplinary proceedings, that the right to a fair hearing has some existence independent of contract. If the right were a pure creature of con-

[70] *The Times*, 12 February 1988, CA.
[71] CAS 94/129.
[72] *Ibid.*, paras. 74–80; cf. *Calvin v. Carr* [1980] AC 574, PC.

tract, it could be excluded by an express term in the contract. However, as we have commented above, we do not believe such a term would be upheld by an English court. This is because the right to fairness is regarded as more than contractual in the context of disciplinary proceedings before a domestic tribunal; the rules of a sporting association are quasi-legislative in nature and, particularly where livelihood is at stake in professional sport, the right to fairness is at least partly public in character, even though public law remedies are not available to enforce it. The question is difficult because in the English law of employment, an employee has no implied right under his contract of employment to be treated fairly by his employer; he only has statutory rights subject to procedural conditions.

Thus the courts in England have stopped short of implying a term in an **7.76** employment contract generally requiring the employer to observe the tenets of natural justice in the conduct of disciplinary proceedings. Statute is required to create such a right. But sportsmen and women do not enjoy comparable statutory rights except to the extent that they are employees themselves. Consequently the common law is astute to prevent unfair treatment. In *Jones v. Welsh Rugby Union*[73] the suggestion that the rules being applied could themselves be unfair, and, presumably, unenforceable as a result, treats such rules as par excellence legislative in character. Ebsworth J's judgment in effect treats subjection to unfair rules as an infringement of a right apparently arising independently of contract and, we would argue, arising at least in part in public not private law. Indeed in *Stewart v. Judicial Committee of the Auckland Racing Club Inc.*[74] the High Court in Auckland, New Zealand, entertained a motion for statutory review, which is a public law form of proceeding, in respect of a challenge to the fairness of certain disciplinary proceedings in which a jockey was accused of failing to ride his horse on its merits. Hillyer J set aside a three month suspension, inter alia, on the ground that the appeal body had declined to receive two affidavits in support of the defence, without looking at them. But in *Justice v. South Australian Trotting Control Board*,[75] the plaintiff trainer and driver of trotting horses failed to establish unfairness in the conduct of a quasi-inquisitorial process in which the stewards enquired into whether the plaintiff had failed to give his horse a full opportunity to win or obtain the best possible place. Among the contentions rejected by O'Loughlin J was that the stewards were investigating and giving evidence at the same time, but had not been subject to cross-examination, and that this was unfair. The judge noted that they were available for questioning and that Mr Justice had to some extent questioned them, but they were not required to present evidence formally and be cross-examined on it.

---

[73] Unreported, 27 February 1997.
[74] [1992] 3 NZLR 693.
[75] (1989) 50 SASR 613.

7.77   Our brief survey of some of the case law delineating the scope of the duty of
fairness shows that each case depends upon its own facts. This is consistent with
the well known administrative law proposition that there is no such thing as a
technical breach of natural justice. Running through the case law, however, is a
consistent tension between traditional latitude and autonomy afforded to
domestic tribunals, encouraging an abstentionist judicial line; and a more modern formalist approach evincing a growth of legalism in sport coinciding with
the growth of professionalism. This tension was very marked in *Jones v. Welsh
Rugby Union* in which the respective parties' submissions reflected the
traditional and the modern approach. Ebsworth J attempted to steer a course
between the two, but gave a fillip to the modern formalist approach in a dictum
which may mark a departure from the courts' policy of non-interventionism:

> "There are likely to be many people who take the view that the processes of
> the law have no place in sport and the bodies which run sport should be able
> to conduct their own affairs as they see fit and that by and large they have
> done so successfully and fairly over the years. It is a tempting and attractive
> view in many ways, particularly to those (and I almost said those of us) who
> grew up on windy and often half deserted touchlines. However, sport today
> is big business. Many people earn their living from it in one way or another.
> It would, I fear, be naive to pretend that the modern world of sport can be
> conducted as it used to be not very many years ago."

7.78   Whatever the limits of permissible informality in sporting disciplinary proceedings, there is as yet no clear duty on a sporting disciplinary body to give reasons for its decision, unless the relevant rules so provide. In *Dundee United
Football Club Ltd. v. Scottish Football Association*[76] Dundee United purported
to terminate the contract of a player who appealed to the appeals committee of
the Scottish Football League. The League upheld the appeal but did not give reasons. Dundee appealed to the Scottish FA appeals committee, which dismissed
the appeal. Dundee then petitioned for judicial review of that decision, seeking,
inter alia, a remission to the League appeals committee for an explanation of the
reasons for its decision. The Outer House held that since the League appeals
committee had been represented before the Scottish FA appeals committee, the
former committee was able to provide in that forum whatever explanation was
necessary for its decision. The court noted that while a right of appeal was a
strong indication that reasons should be given for a decision that could be
appealed, the existence and scope of any duty to give reasons was a question of
fact dependent on the circumstances in which the decision is made, and the rules
under which it is made.

7.79   In English administrative law, a general duty to give reasons has not yet developed but a limited implied obligation on administrative bodies to give reasoned
decisions may exist in some circumstances, and absence of cogent reasons may

---

[76] [1998] SLT 1244.

sometimes ground an inference that a decision is flawed in some other way.[77] In the sporting context, as in other contexts, it is a salutary discipline on those who discipline others to provide an explanation for their decisions. There is no doubt that having to give reasons concentrates the mind and is likely to improve the quality of decision making. But it cannot be said that in the English law relating to sport there is necessarily any duty on a sporting disciplinary body to give reasons.

In cases where reasons are not given, their absence could be relied upon in **7.80** support of a submission of unfairness of some other kind, such as wrongful exclusion of relevant material from consideration, or even bias. But this is merely an evidential question. Where reasons are given, they likewise can be analysed and used to support a case for setting aside an allegedly unlawful decision, if the reasons given are thought to disclose a misapplication of the rules, or unfair treatment of the accused. While it would not be a good thing for the law to encourage decision makers exercising disciplinary jurisdiction in sport deliberately to refrain from giving reasons in order to protect themselves against subsequent criticism of the reasons they give, the absence of a general duty to give any does mean that decision makers in sport are sometimes better protected against legal challenge in cases where their reasons are either non-existent or extremely brief, than in cases where they are set out in full and detailed form.

We should not leave the subject of the content of procedural fairness in sports **7.81** disciplinary proceedings without referring to the Human Rights Act 1998.[78] Article 6 of the European Convention on Human Rights is, on the entry into force of the Act, to become part of English law to the extent provided by the Act. It covers criminal as well as civil proceedings. Its first paragraph provides as follows:

"1. In the determination of his civil rights and obligations or of any criminal charge against him, everyone is entitled to a fair and public hearing within a reasonable time by an independent and impartial tribunal established by law. Judgment shall be pronounced publicly but the press and public may be excluded from all or part of the trial in the interest of morals, public order or national security in a democratic society, where the interests of juveniles or the protection of private life of the parties so require, or to the extent strictly necessary in the opinion of the court in special circumstances where publicity would prejudice the interests of justice."

The relevance of Article 6 to sports disciplinary proceedings lies in the possi- **7.82** bility, even probability, that in some circumstances sports disciplinary bodies will make a "determination of [the] civil rights and obligations" of those who stand accused before them. This would be likely to lead the law in the direction of articulating obligations on those conducting such proceedings to meet the

[77] See generally de Smith, Woolf and Jowell, *supra.*, n. 62, pp. 457–73.
[78] A general exposition in briefest outline of the probable effects of the Act in the English law relating to sport appears in chapter eight, below; see paras. 8.29–8.33.

standards set by Article 6(1), whether directly by treating as "public authorities" within the Act some of the bodies which exercise disciplinary jurisdiction in sport or indirectly, by developing the law of contract so as to imply such obligations into contracts conferring disciplinary jurisdiction. It is therefore relevant to consider briefly the Strasbourg jurisprudence dealing with Article 6(1) in so far as applied to disciplinary proceedings.

7.83 To engage Article 6, there must be a "determination" of civil rights and obligations. This has been interpreted to mean that there must be a dispute or (in French) "contestation", not merely an administrative or legislative determination affecting property rights[79] or a statutory immunity from liability in tort.[80] The proceedings in question must be decisive of the relevant rights or obligations, even if the decision is not the main purpose of the proceedings.[81] If there is a "determination", it must be of "civil rights and obligations". In *H. v. Belgium*[82] the European Court of Human Rights held that disciplinary proceedings against a lawyer were covered by Article 6. It follows that Article 6 covers proceedings before a plethora of statutory or non-statutory bodies exercising punitive or regulatory jurisdiction. It is possible that disciplinary and other domestic tribunals established under the rules of sporting bodies and members' clubs are also covered. As we have seen, in England such bodies normally owe their existence to contract and (as we shall see in chapter eight) their decisions are rarely if ever amenable to judicial review in English law.

7.84 Incorporation of Article 6(1) into English law may have profound implications for development of the content of the duty of fairness owed by such bodies.[83] Carnwath J in *Stevenage Borough FC Limited v. The Football League*

[79] *James v. UK* A 98 para. 81 (1986) (no Article 6 issue where applicant deprived of property rights through tenants' statutory right to acquire properties).

[80] *Powell and Rayner v. UK* A 172 (1990) (statutory immunity against trespass or nuisance claims through aircraft flying overhead did not raise an article 6 issue; *aliter* if a state should "remove from the jurisdiction of the courts a whole range of civil claims or confer immunities from civil liability on large groups or categories of persons": *Fayed v. UK* A 194-B para. 65 (1994)); cf. *Osman v. UK*, *The Times*, 5 November 1998, European Court of Human Rights (successful challenge to police immunity from negligence claims in prevention or suppression of crime); *X. and others v. UK*, pending before the Court (challenge to social workers' immunity from negligence claims arising from performance of statutory functions in respect of children in their care).

[81] *Ringeisen v. Austria* A 13 (1971) (administrative permission required for purchase and sale of land for non-agricultural purpose); *Le Compte v. Belgium* A 43 (1981) (decision of medical disciplinary tribunal directly decisive of doctors' right to practise medicine).

[82] A 127 (1987); *semble*, *Le Compte v. Belgium*, A 43 (1981) (medical disciplinary proceedings held within article 6(1) protection).

[83] Thus cases such as e.g. *Jones v. Welsh Rugby Union*, Ebsworth J, 27 February 1997, and CA, *The Times*, 6 January 1998, could, post-incorporation, involve consideration of the facts against Article 6(1) standards. SLB Vol. 1 No. 6 Wood "Sports Governing Bodies and the Human Rights Act 1998" suggesting that Article 6(1) fair trial provisions may apply to Sports Governing Bodies.

Limited[84] has said that it is difficult to see why different tests should apply in private and public law challenges to decisions such as those of a sporting body. Lord Woolf MR in *Modahl v. British Athletic Federation*[85] made a similar observation. The obligation of the courts in England to observe Convention rights[86] could well lead them to infuse with the standards set by Article 6(1) a contract giving such a body the power to determine civil rights and obligations, and consequently to construe it as by implication of law requiring compliance by the disciplining body with the Article 6(1) rights of the accused.

Thus the right of a party to be personally present when his or her civil rights   **7.85** and obligations are determined, in cases where the party's manner of life or (perhaps) conduct is directly in issue[87] could be of importance in sporting disciplinary proceedings. If Article 6(1) applies to such proceedings before sporting and other domestic tribunals as well as disciplinary bodies with statutory underpinning, the rules of some sports bodies may have to be amended to provide for oral hearings[88] instead of consideration of written representations. By parity of reasoning, some disciplinary rules may require amendment to conform with Article 6(1) by giving the accused in such a case the option of a public hearing.[89] Some sporting disciplinary bodies provide in their rules for publication of the outcome, but do not provide for publicity in relation to the hearing itself. The purpose is often protection of the interests of the accused, not just those of the body dispensing disciplinary justice.

The same point applies to the right to a hearing within a reasonable time,[90]   **7.86** and before an independent and impartial tribunal. As to independence and impartiality, the test for compliance with Article 6(1) derived from Strasbourg case law[91] may be slightly easier to satisfy than the common law test of a "real

---

[84] Transcript, 23 July 1996.

[85] See CA transcript, 28 July 1997, at pp. 20F–21C.

[86] Human Rights Act 1998 Section 6(3)(a) and (b).

[87] *Håkansson v. Sweden* A 171-A para 66 (1990); *Fredin v. Sweden (No. 2)* A 283-A para 21 (1994).

[88] Cases involving an assessment of a party's conduct may also entail a right to personal attendance, but this is not wholly clear; see e.g. *Muyldermans v. Belgium* A 214-A (1991) Com Rep para. 64.

[89] *Fredin v. Sweden (No. 2)* A 283-A para. 21 (1994).

[90] See among many Strasbourg cases, e.g. *Casciaroli v. Italy* A229-C para. 18 (1992).

[91] *Belilos v. Switzerland* A 132 para. 64 (1988); *Ettl v. Austria* A 117 para. 38 (1987) (civil servants); *Engel v. Netherlands* A 22 (1976) (armed forces); *Eccles v. Ireland* 59 DR 212 (1988); *D v. Ireland* 51 DR 117 (1986) in which the judge owned shares in one of the parties; cf. *Dimes v. Grand Junction Canal Co.* (1852) 3 HL Cas. 759 and *In re Pinochet*, HL, *The Times*, 18 January 1999; *Langborger v. Sweden* A 155 (1989) (breach of Article 6(1) where lay tribunal members were linked to organisations with an interest in removal of tenancy clause they were empowered to remove, despite equal number of impartial judges on panel, one of whom had casting vote; cf. *Le Compte v. Belgium* A 43 para. 58 (1981) (no breach of Article 6(1) where medical members of medical disciplinary

danger" of bias, viewed from the standpoint of the court;[92] particularly in cases in which members of disciplinary tribunals are appointed ad hoc to hear particular cases such as doping allegations against athletes, in which they may be required to sit in judgment on the adequacy of the procedures of the organisations they govern.

Penalties in disciplinary proceedings

7.87 We consider next the jurisdiction of disciplinary bodies to impose penalties on those whom they have lawfully found guilty of misconduct. The jurisdiction to penalise is derived from the relevant rules. It is usual for there to be a provision setting down the powers of the disciplining body to impose sanctions. Among the powers commonly found in the rules of sporting associations are powers to impose fines, suspend from particular competitions or for a particular period; powers of expulsion from the association and the ubiquitous power to impose such other penalty as the tribunal shall think fit. As we have already noted, punitive powers, though derived from contract, may not constitute contractual terms directly binding the accuser and the accused. Each may contract with another body to abide by the outcome of the exercise of those punitive powers.

7.88 From time to time the question arises whether a disciplining body has gone beyond the powers of punishment possessed by it in a case where it has lawfully found an accused guilty. In other cases, a penalty imposed partly in respect of findings of guilt validly reached, and partly in respect of invalid findings of guilt which are erroneous in law, may be successfully challenged on the basis that the disciplining body took into account the invalid as well as the valid matters, resulting in an excessive penalty. It is desirable, therefore, for a disciplinary tribunal to indicate, when passing sentence, which punishment corresponds to which offence, lest a court should subsequently overturn the decision, not being able to sever any unobjectionable parts from the objectionable parts of the sentence.

7.89 A contractual power to penalise a person must, naturally, be exercised in accordance with the true meaning, scope, spirit and intent of the power. In a case where the rules provide an apparently unlimited discretion, the discretion must be exercised in a manner which is rational and within the range of reasonable sanctions with which the misconduct found may be visited. In the context of association football, an open-ended power to penalise does include a power to deduct points previously earned by winning or drawing matches. This was the fate suffered by Middlesbrough Football Club when it wrongly cancelled a

committee had interests close to defendant's; equal number of judges, one of whom had casting vote).

[92] Articulated by Lord Goff in *R. v. Gough* [1993] AC 646. A direct pecuniary or proprietary interest always disqualifies the decision maker.

fixture in late 1996 without just cause.[93] We understand that in mainland Europe the award of a notional 2-0 win in favour of the other club is common-place in cases of wrongful cancellation of a fixture.

However, the obligation to exercise powers of punishment rationally and in **7.90** accordance with the spirit and intent of the power, may mean that an exercise of penal power can be set aside, in an extreme case, even where the penalty imposed is one which is within the scope of the power on the true construction of the rule in play. Thus deduction of points from a football club's total may be within the range of penalties open to the relevant association where its rules allow it to impose such penalty as it thinks fit in respect of a particular trans-gression. *Non sequitur* that the association's disciplinary organs may validly deduct any number of points, however great, in respect of any misconduct, how-ever venial. The discretion must be exercised within the four walls of the rule so as to give effect to their purpose. The protection of the discretion against subse-quent interference by a court, though great, is not absolute; there must be some relationship of proportionality between the offence and the penalty with which it is visited. This principle flows from the normal approach to the interpretation of contractual terms. They are presumed to bear a meaning in harmony with, and not at odds with, the inferred intention of the parties. A similar principle applies to the imposition of disciplinary penalties pursuant to statutory or other non-contractual powers of punishment or sanction.[94]

The principle is clear; applying it in a particular case may be more difficult. **7.91** The view of a court subsequently considering the validity of a penalty imposed by a sporting body, will necessarily depend to an extent on the outlook of the particular judge. The court will not substitute its view for that of the disciplining

---

[93] An eccentric sequel to the Middlesbrough case was a county court action, *Arnolt v. Football Association* (unreported, 2 February 1998) in which the plaintiff Boro supporter unsuccessfully argued that he was deprived of Premier League football by the deduction of three points, which in the event propelled the club into the relegation zone at the end of the season, giving Coventry City FC a windfall reprieve and condemning Middlesbrough to a season in the First Division.

[94] See *R v. Barnsley MBC ex parte Hook* [1976] 1 WLR 102; *R v. St Albans Crown Court ex parte Cinnamond* [1981] 2 WLR 681 at 684, DCQB; *R v. Tottenham Justices ex parte Dwarkados Joshi* [1982] 1 WLR 631, 634, DCQB; *R v. Home Secretary ex parte Benwin* [1984] 3 WLR 843 at 846; *R v. Secretary of State for Transport ex parte Pegasus Holidays (London) Limited* [1989] 2 All ER 481 at 490h-j. Cf. Mummery J's decision in *Swindon Town FC v. The Football Association Limited*, the Times, 20 June 1990. Note the possibility that a court which is subject to the Human Rights Act may have regard, post-incorporation, to the civil law doctrine of proportionality in relation to penalties imposed by sporting bodies, particularly in cases with the potential to engage Convention rights, such as that of freedom of expression under Article 10; cf. the case of an Olympic coach who risked disciplinary proceedings by calling for the use of perfor-mance enhancing drugs to be allowed in British sport, reported in *The Independent*, 22 February 1998.

body on the question whether the penalty imposed was right or wrong provided it is within the range of responses open to a rational disciplinary body acting within its powers. But the court will have to form a view of where the upper and lower limits of that range lie in order to determine whether the sanction imposed falls within the range or outside it. To that extent, the court cannot avoid engaging in an assessment of the gravity of the misconduct found. Thus Tottenham Hotspur Football Club was able to achieve restoration of its rights to compete in the 1995–96 FA Challenge Cup, and restoration of twelve points which an appeal panel of the Football Association had purported to deduct from its premiership tally.

7.92   The CAS has also had occasion, from time to time, to consider the validity of a sanction imposed for misconduct. In *National Wheelchair Basketball Association v. International Paralympic Committee*,[95] the US paralympic basketball team had been disqualified and ordered to forfeit its gold medal gained by beating Spain in the 1992 Barcelona Paralympics, in consequence of a doping offence by one of its members. The CAS, applying Swiss law, upheld the decision to find misconduct proved, since it construed the rule as one imposing strict liability (as already explained above). The CAS went on to consider the contention that the penalty of withdrawal of the gold medals from the entire team was grossly disproportionate to the infringement by one member of it (who was also personally banned for six months). It held that an infringement by one team member necessarily must lead to forfeiture of the match, competition or event during which the infringement took place, by the entire team. It was able to leave open the separate question whether the rule in play conferred discretion to apply the forfeiture only to the match following which detection of the infringement takes place, or whether the rule automatically applied to the entire competition leading up to the point of the infringement. The difference between these two interpretations was that according to the former, the US team might have been able to have the silver medals instead of the gold; whereas on the latter, the team would get nothing at all. In the event the CAS did not have to decide this subsequent issue of interpretation since the team abandoned its alternative case that it should be declared the silver medallists.

7.93   In *Chagnaud v. FINA*,[96] the CAS dealt with a two year ban in a case of doping by a swimming coach without the swimmer's knowledge. The CAS explained the tension between the need for strict anti-doping measures, and the unfairness of a system that fails to differentiate between athletes doped without their knowledge and those who deliberately dope themselves. It came down in favour of a compromise position somewhere between the two extremes. It considered that automatic disqualification from the competition in question should follow without any opportunity to disprove intent or fault. However, as to suspension from competitions over a period, the CAS stressed that the rules on

[95] CAS 95/122.
[96] CAS 95/141.

sanctions should make allowance for "an appreciation of the subjective elements in each case . . . in order to fix a just and equitable sanction".[97] Thus the athlete should be presumed guilty where the banned substance is found present, but should be allowed to provide exculpatory evidence showing lack of fault or knowledge, in mitigation of the penalty to be imposed. The CAS pointed out that another swimmer had previously escaped with a strong warning in a similar case, and relied upon this precedent as showing that the Federation itself had refrained in the past from applying its doping rules strictly and rigidly. The rule in question merely stated: "sanction recommended is 2 years for the first offence".

7.94

The CAS therefore went on to consider whether Mlle Chagnaud had succeeded in rebutting the presumption of fault on her part, and found that she had not done so. Nevertheless it intervened to shorten the length of the ban from two years to a period of some thirteen and a half months ending with the date of the hearing. The panel commented that the penalty was not in proportion to the circumstances of the case and pointed to the evidence of the "excellent morality and exemplary conduct" of Mlle Chagnaud in general.[98] The CAS was prepared to substitute its own penalty for that of the Federation whose decision it overturned, rather than remitting the matter back for reconsideration by the Federation as an English court would do. But that was because the rules of the Federation provided for the CAS to hear the matter by way of appeal and not merely as a reviewing tribunal. Thus the CAS was able, in effect, to substitute its own view of the appropriate penalty. It did not, in the *Chagnaud* case, appear to confine its role strictly, as an English court would do, to consideration of the limits to the broad range of penal responses open to the Federation's disciplinary organs. Such freedom to interfere must be found, if it is to exist at all, in the relevant rules providing for an appeal or other form of subsequent recourse for the accused.

7.95

In *Cullwick v. FINA*[99] a division of the CAS presided over by one of the authors entertained an appeal in a yet further doping case and held the offence to be one of strict liability of which the athlete was guilty in a technical sense only and without fault on his part. The power of the CAS under its regulations was a "full power to review the facts and the law".[100] In considering what sanctions to impose, the panel pointed out that since the offence was committed, the rules of the Federation had been amended so as to provide for a maximum two year suspension for a first offence, rather than – if such were previously the correct interpretation – a mandatory two year suspension for a first offence. The panel went on to invoke the doctrine of *lex mitior* which, in the civil law jurisdictions, permits a disciplinary tribunal to apply current sanctions to the case

---

[97] *Ibid.*, para. 4(d) at p. 9.
[98] *Ibid.*, para. 5 at p. 12.
[99] CAS 96/149.
[100] CAS Regulations as amended on 22 November 1994, regulation R57.

before it, if those current sanctions are less severe than those which existed at the time of the offence.[101] The offence being technical only, the upholding of the Federation's finding of liability was sufficient penalty in itself. No further penalty was imposed. The *lex mitior* concept is not familiar to common lawyers versed in the practice of the English speaking jurisdictions of the world. Whether our courts might be willing to import it remains to be seen. We see no reason why such a felicitous doctrine should not be allowed to take root here, since it is in harmony with the benevolent common law tradition of leaning in favour of the accused in procedural matters arising from the exercise of punitive

7.96 power.

We have already observed above, in chapter three, that powers to impose automatic or lengthy bans for certain types of misconduct can, in principle at least, be the subject of a challenge on the ground of restraint of trade. Such challenges would be unlikely to succeed before the English courts, unless the penalties provided for were so manifestly excessive and disproportionate as to go beyond all reason. Automatic life bans for a first offence without possibility of mitigation or exculpation, applying in a case of innocent ingestion without fault or intention to gain, might be regarded as so harsh as to merit being struck down. But strict and severe penalties short of that may be expected to be upheld, for the English courts would be loath to hand down rulings which would undermine the fight against drugs in sport.

Costs in disciplinary proceedings

7.97

This subject may be briefly disposed of. Rules of sporting bodies may or may not provide for awards of costs. In the absence of such provision the tribunal concerned will not have any power to make an award of costs, so that each party will bear its own legal costs, if any. However rules of sporting bodies frequently do confer a discretion on their disciplinary tribunals to make awards of costs if they think fit. The regulations of the CAS also provide for jurisdiction to award

7.98 costs.[102]

The duty on domestic tribunals to act fairly does not require there to be a jurisdiction to award costs. Indeed, as we have already seen, there are cases in which representation need not be allowed, even where it is provided at the expense of the represented party.

---

[101] See for example, Article 2 para. 2 of the Swiss Penal Code, and cf. Article 2 of the Italian Penal Code; applied in *International Cycling Union and Italian National Olympic Committee*, CAS advisory opinion, February 1995, CAS 94/128, para. 33, pp. 48–9.
[102] See regulation R65.3; however the CAS has a marked tendency to let costs lie where they fall.

Appeals in disciplinary proceedings

Likewise, it is not necessary, as part of the duty of fairness, for the rules of a **7.99** sporting body, or its practice in disciplinary matters, to allow for an appeal, whether internally or to an external independent body, against the determination of a properly constituted disciplinary body established under the association's rules. Whether such an appeal lies will depend entirely on the content of the rules in play.[103]

Naturally, if the rules do provide a right of appeal and the appeal itself, or the **7.100** hearing leading to the decision appealed against, is conducted in an unlawful manner, then the accused may be entitled to relief from the court, subject to the possibility of an initial defect being cured by means of an appeal, in accordance with the principles established by the Privy Council in *Calvin v. Carr*.[104]

The practical management of disciplinary issues

We conclude our general treatment of disciplinary proceedings in sport by offer- **7.101** ing our brief views on certain practical points that are likely to arise when managing disciplinary issues. In doing so, we draw on the practical experience of the authors of representing sportsmen, women and clubs and sporting associations in disciplinary tribunals, and of sitting as members of disciplinary panels in the sporting field. We venture the view that, subject always to questions of cost, sporting bodies are now better served by taking legal advice frequently and above all, before not after the event, than by seeking to exclude lawyers from sporting affairs. We appreciate that this view is, by its nature, one that members of the legal profession might be expected to espouse. However, a saving of legal costs early on may result in a greater outlay of legal costs later, since good legal advice is an effective form of insurance.

Moreover, for good or ill, it is simply no longer possible to do without **7.102** lawyers in sport, now that we are in the age of Rupert Murdoch, transfer fees running to many millions of pounds, satellite broadcasting, cable television, business sponsorship and the inexorable growth of professionalism. Disciplinary issues in sport are particularly likely to give rise to legal controversy. The accused in disciplinary proceedings is usually no less, and sometimes more, in need of good legal support as his, her or its accuser. For example, many athletes faced with a positive test for a banned substance, may feel at a loss as to the options open to them. Should they accept a long period of suspension, even if they have not consciously taken anything stronger than cough medicine for

---

[103] See *Jones v. Welsh Rugby Union*, transcript 27 February 1997 at p. 21, applying *Ward v. Bradford Corporation* (1972) LGR 27, CA. The IAAF rules and ITC rules permit (unusually) an appeal by the Governing body itself; in the former case for the perceptible purpose of checking that national tribunals do not give "home town" decisions in favour of their own athletes.
[104] *Supra.*, n. 72, [1980] AC 574, per Lord Wilberforce at 592–6.

bronchitis? Is the positive test conclusive evidence? Is the offence committed without knowledge, intention or fault? These are issues which could bemuse any intelligent lay person.

7.103 In the case of sporting bodies, legal advice is relevant at the following stages:

(1) the drafting of rules; many sporting associations have rules which have not been drafted or even vetted by lawyers. Drafting by lawyers, or scrutiny by lawyers of draft rules, ought not to mean, if the lawyers are good, that the rules become more complicated and technical. On the contrary, rules should be simple, drafted in plain English (or whatever is the language of the association) and free from technicality, but should avoid legal pitfalls so that they can survive robust consideration by a court or arbitration panel in the event of challenge.

(2) The composition of adjudicating bodies, and the administrative arrangements for disciplinary hearings or other potentially contentious matters, including procedures for selecting participants for particular competitions, which may in some cases engage the duty to act fairly.

(3) The conduct of domestic disciplinary hearings, including the exercise of discretion as to procedural matters. If a lawyer is not sitting on the panel, adjournments to obtain advice quickly may be preferable to the risk of a legal mistake by a lay tribunal member, when reacting to, for instance, a request to be allowed to call a particular witness, or to be granted access to confidential documents about the case.

(4) Consideration of the function of the adjudicating body in deciding on guilt or innocence; for example, whether a particular finding is open to the tribunal on the basis of the evidence, or on the basis of the correct construction of rules at issue.

(5) Consideration of the merits of any dispute as to the conduct of disciplinary matters after their conclusion but before the issue of proceedings to challenge the outcome. As we shall see shortly, sporting bodies can be protected against successful claims even after they have made mistakes of law or treated a sportsman or woman or a club unfairly.

(6) Finally, advice on the prospects of success of proceedings to challenge the outcome of a disciplinary case, and if necessary representation as an advocate in such proceedings.

7.104 One obvious way of achieving good legal decision making in the conduct of disciplinary proceedings is to appoint one or more lawyers to sit as a member of the disciplinary panel. This already happens in many cases. An alternative is to ensure that the rules provide for or permit the presence of a lawyer to act as an adviser to the disciplinary panel. In the latter case it is important to ensure that the lawyer does not stray beyond his or her brief by becoming involved in the factual merits, as opposed to the legal issues, in the case.

7.105 Good practical management of disciplinary issues by a sporting body requires experience and legal knowledge. In the case of the accused, the objective will be to assert procedural rights so as to prevent any risk of prejudice, and in order to allow presentation of the defence, and if necessary mitigation, at its strongest. Experience shows that the sporting body is generally best advised to produce a document, drafted or approved by its lawyers, for use as a framework within which the disciplinary proceedings will be conducted. A major purpose of this document is to record matters of agreement and, where possible, avoid later factual disputes about what actually happened during the disciplinary process. A further purpose is to isolate matters of disagreement in point of law so as to enable legally unimpeachable rulings on points of procedure, evidence and construction to be given before, or in some cases during, the substantive hearing of the factual disciplinary issues.

In drawing up a procedural framework document, it is useful to state in its **7.106** introductory first paragraph that its contents constitute provisional views about the forthcoming hearing and are subject to consideration of any submissions by the parties at the hearing. It can also usefully contain a brief account of the anticipated procedure, to assist the parties, for example under the following headings, which may be useful as a check list:

(1) The constitution of the disciplining body; the basis for its decision, i.e. whether unanimous or majority;

(2) the role of the disciplining body; inquisitorial, adversarial or hybrid;

(3) the role of any adviser to the panel, making clear the distinction between the adviser and the members;

(4) the question of time to prepare for the hearing, and whether the accused agrees that it has been adequate;

(5) whether the disciplinary offence charged is admitted, denied or admitted in part;

(6) the nature of the hearing, i.e. whether it is an initial hearing or an appeal, whether, if an appeal, it is by way of rehearing *de novo* or by way of review only;

(7) the onus of proof in relation to each issue, under the rules, or at common law, to the extent that onus is relevant, i.e. particularly in an adversarial procedure;

(8) the standard of proof: the balance of probabilities unless the rules provide otherwise, but subject to the point that graver charges require stronger evidence to meet the standard;

(9) the contents of the bundle of relevant documents, and any outstanding requests for documents;

(10) the procedure for the giving of evidence orally (if applicable) at the hearing;

(11) the order in which the parties will make closing submissions at the conclusion of the evidence;

(12) deliberation by the disciplining body in private following closing submissions, without involvement of any other person in consideration of the factual merits;

(13) the means by which the decision will be announced; whether orally, or in writing; and whether in a reserved or *extempore* decision, if yet known;

(14) the position as to costs, i.e. whether there is jurisdiction to award them; if not it is as well to warn the parties that each side will bear their own whatever the outcome;

(15) the range of penalties open to the disciplining body in the event of a finding of liability in whole or in part; but this may only be appropriate where there is an exhaustive list of available penalties; if not, the discretionary provision should be referred to;

(16) any rights of further appeal from the decision of the disciplining body, for example, to the CAS.

7.107   Needless to say, a record should be kept, as accurately as possible, of the oral hearing of a disciplinary issue. Involvement of an independent person as a member of a disciplinary panel may or may not be provided for in the rules. The inclusion of such a person helps to ensure the exercise of independent judgment which minimises the risk of procedural or other unfairness to the accused and consequential legal challenge. The avoidance of prior discussion of the merits by any panel member, is an essential discipline. So is the avoidance of any appearance of bias or the risk of bias, such as may be even innocently conveyed by private discussions held in corridors during a hiatus in a hearing.

7.108   In some cases it may be desirable, in addition, to draw up a "list of issues" arising in the hearing. The objective is to focus everybody's mind on that which is relevant and away from that which is irrelevant. The following is an example of issues that could arise in a doping case: (i) did the sample tested contain a banned substance? (ii) if so, was the sample tested the same sample as that provided by the athlete? (iii) if so, was the athlete aware of the presence of a banned substance in his body? (iv) if not, is the offence of doping nevertheless made out? (v) if so, what penalty may be imposed?

7.109   Where documents of the type just suggested are available, it is a useful discipline to invite each party or representative to indicate to what extent they are in agreement as to the points set out in the procedural framework document, and to what extent they are in agreement that the list of issues truly states the relevant issues. A procedure document along the lines suggested above, intended to secure agreement to procedural matters, will be very difficult for a party to challenge in any subsequent legal proceedings, if no challenge to what it records is made at the time of the hearing. Unnecessary later disputes arising from no more than simple misunderstanding in a tense atmosphere, may frequently be avoided by these simple expedients.

7.110   If a contentious procedural issue arises at a hearing before a disciplining body, of a type which might later become the subject of a legal challenge, then it is advisable to give clear, brief and legally correct rulings on those points, recorded on tape or in note form. An example would be a brief ruling on the panel's interpretation of a particular rule; or on whether an adjournment should be granted to allow more time to prepare; or on whether the accused should be allowed to cross-examine a laboratory technician who packed certain samples which later tested positive. It is desirable that such rulings should include brief reasons, but it is important that the rulings should be sound in law, and that the reasons given should be good and not unlawful, since the record of the decision and the reasons for it will be admissible in any later court proceedings.

A vexed question which quite frequently arises in legal challenges to discipli- **7.111** nary proceedings, is whether a party who has omitted to take a particular objection, or who has actively acquiesced in a particular procedural course, is precluded from subsequently taking the objection not previously taken, or from resiling from his acquiescence to the particular course. For the accused's representative, a dilemma may arise between wishing to reserve the accused's position for a later legal challenge in the event of a disagreement with the disciplining body on a particular procedural issue, and the risk that the disciplining body may look with ill favour upon such a reservation of the accused's position, perceiving it as an expression of less than full confidence in the disciplining body's ability to conduct itself properly. For the sporting association, and the disciplinary panel established under its rules, the objective is normally to achieve something as close as possible to finality. The steps mentioned above constitute an important safeguard against later legal proceedings. But given the constitutional impossibility of immunising sporting bodies against proceedings, the next best thing is to ensure that any proceedings taken will fail; a precaution which will confer de facto immunity unless the other party is badly advised.

The extent to which a party has, or has not, availed himself of his right to take **7.112** a particular objection at a disciplinary hearing, or has acquiesced in a certain course later challenged, is always relevant to the exercise of the court's discretion as to the grant of relief, a subject to which we shall return in the next chapter on remedies. A more difficult question concerns the circumstances in which a court will hold that a party is barred from advancing a contention at all by reason of having taken a previous inconsistent position. In *Modahl v.British Athletic Federation Limited*[105] the plaintiff alleged, among other things, bias against two members of the disciplinary committee which initially found her guilty of a doping offence, though her subsequent appeal was successful. On the assumption that the appeal had not cured any defect arising from such bias (which was assumed but not at that stage proved), the Court of Appeal went on to consider whether it was open to the plaintiff to complain in court of bias on the part of one committee member, to whose presence on the panel objection had been taken prior to the hearing but not at the hearing. In so far as reliance was to be placed solely on that member's alleged bias, Lord Woolf MR held[106] that her claim for breach of contract would have failed because her failure to

---

[105] Transcript, 28 July 1997, CA.
[106] Transcript p. 28.

object was a representation by silence which prevented the disciplinary committee considering the basis of her objection, i.e. alleged bias. Morritt LJ considered that Ms Modahl's conduct in forbearing to object to the particular panel member at the hearing, was capable of creating an estoppel of the type exemplified in *Central London Property Trust Limited v. High Trees House Limited*,[107] or a waiver as described by Lord Denning MR in *W.J. Alan & Co v. El Nasr Export*.[108] However, the Court of Appeal declined to strike out the allegations of bias because they included a further, different objection of which the plaintiff athlete had, on the assumed facts, been unaware at the time of the hearing when she failed to make her objection.

7.113 Likewise in *Jones v. Welsh Rugby Union*,[109] Ebsworth J, on an interlocutory application, stated that the omission of the plaintiff rugby player's accompanying friend to request specifically leave to question witnesses, "cannot estop the plaintiffs from complaining of the unfairness of the procedure".[110] The reasoning in support of that proposition is not elaborated in the judgment. In the same case, the judge considered an argument advanced by the Union that Ebbw Vale Rugby Football Club had acquiesced in the procedural disciplinary rules of which it was complaining in court by omitting to take any constitutional step to alter them in a general or special meeting of the Union which had promulgated them, of which the Club was a member. On that point, the judge reserved her conclusion to trial, holding that the question of acquiescence was a matter of factual dispute on which it would be wrong to draw conclusions on affidavit evidence. At best, such an argument is likely to influence the exercise of a court's discretion to grant relief, rather than fulfilling the stricter requirements of estoppel or waiver.

7.114 Even in a case where unfairness has tainted disciplinary proceedings, for example owing to failure to take into account exculpatory material relevant to the defence, there remains still the possibility of a further hearing curing the defect and preventing the other party from obtaining a remedy from the court which, as always, it is open to the court in the exercise of its discretion to refuse. If the conduct of the proceedings has been fair overall, taking into account the curative effect of any appeal, then relief may well be refused. If the rules of the body concerned provide no mechanism for an internal appeal, that is in itself no bar to a sporting body deciding voluntarily to revisit a decision which it believes may otherwise be challenged in court – whether successfully or otherwise (and even an ill-founded challenge has nuisance value and may generate irrecoverable cost). It is often overlooked that reconsideration of a disputed or contentious ruling can be undertaken by means of a rehearing, or some other form of renewed and further consideration of the matter, perhaps by a differently con-

---

[107] [1947] KB 130.
[108] [1972] 2 QB 189, CA at 213.
[109] Transcript, 27 February 1997.
[110] *Ibid.*, at p. 19 of the transcript.

stituted body, and perhaps using a more rigorous procedure. There is no effective doctrine of *functus officio* in contract law, unless the contract itself so provides. Once a sports disciplining body had changed its allegedly unfair procedure it was perfectly at liberty to hold a second hearing and impose a new suspension.[111]

However, one inhibiting factor is the consideration that the sporting body **7.115** may not want to be seen to admit any failing in its prior handling of the matter of which complaint is made. It need not make any such admission, since further consideration of the matter can take place on the basis that this will occur without prejudice to the body's contention that the handling of the matter to date has been impeccable.[112] The other party, if well advised, is likely to respond by agreeing to such further consideration, but without prejudice to the contention that the first consideration of the matter was invalid and unlawful; and that any subsequent reconsideration is not admitted to be capable of curing the defect.

Postscript: general principles of CAS case law especially in doping cases

Under rule R45 of its rules the CAS decides disputes according to the rules of law **7.116** chosen by the parties, or in the absence of such a choice, according to Swiss law. However the CAS has shown flexibility and creativity within such a framework.[113] The principles are summarised below under two heads: those which can be applied to non-doping cases and those specific to doping cases, the major CAS diet at any rate in terms of importance. Many of the cases mentioned below have already been referred to in our general account.

General principles

Judicial self-restraint in sporting matters

Courts or panels should abstain from reviewing technical decisions or standards **7.117** of referees or umpires (as distinct from alleged violation of particular legal provisions, social rules or general principles of law): *Mendy* (CAS Atlanta Arb. No.006) (boxing low blow).

The right to be heard

The elementary rules of natural justice and due process (e.g. fair play) are **7.118** applicable to disputes between athletes and governing bodies: *Andrade v. Cape*

---

[111] See *Jones v. Welsh Rugby Union* in the Court of Appeal, *The Times* 6 January 1998 (appeal from Potts J).

[112] See *McKenzie v. NUPE* [1991] ICR 155, QBD.

[113] A digest of CAS awards including those of its ad hoc panel, edited by Matthieu Reeb: *Recueil de Sentences du TAS; Digest of CAS Awards 1986–1998*, ed. M. Reeb (Stämpfle Editions SA, Berne, 1998).

Verde NOC, Atlanta Arb. No. 005. A particular illustration is provided by the following unusual situation. The International Equestrian Federation (FEI) notified a rider of the positive results of a urine analysis of his horse and gave him two deadlines: the first for requesting a confirmatory analysis; the second (ten days later) to supply written explanations and evidence, and to request a personal hearing before the FEI. The rider had to choose between these two possibilities, taking into account the fact that the results of the confirmatory analysis would not be known before the expiry of the second deadline. The CAS considered that the rider had the right to request a confirmatory analysis and a personal hearing if necessary. On receipt of the positive result of the confirmatory analysis, the FEI should have formally notified the rider, setting a new deadline for giving explanations and written evidence as well as for the purpose of seeking a personal hearing.[114]

Unbiased tribunal

7.119 In the composition of a tribunal, justice must not only be done, but be seen to be done. A person appearing against a party as an advocate in one matter cannot be an arbitrator where that same party is involved even in a completely separate matter.[115] There must be "the absence of any appearance of presumption". However an objection to an arbitrator must come from a party, not a co-arbitrator: *Wang Lu-Nuyeta v. FINA*.[116]

Good faith

7.120 In *Cullwick v. FINA*[117] a water-polo player tested positive for salbutamol, which is a substance allowed by the rules of the International Swimming Federation (FINA) on condition that its use be declared prior to the doping test. The water-polo player forgot to make this declaration and was sanctioned by FINA. During the proceedings, the athlete demonstrated that his national federation had given him a list of all the banned substances and some permitted substances; salbutamol was mentioned on this list as a permitted substance, without any other indication or conditions. The CAS was of the opinion that an athlete should be able to trust the information given by his national federation, and annulled the sanction.

7.121 A governing body is under an obligation to make full disclosure of material evidence which may bear on an athlete's decision whether, and, if so, how to make use of procedures designed to ensure a fair resolution of a doping charge.[118]

---

[114] CAS 91/53.
[115] *Celtic plc v. UEFA* CAS 98/201.
[116] CAS 98/208.
[117] CAS 96/149.
[118] *Cooke v. FEI* CAS 98/184, paras. 11.15–11.20.

The benefit of the doubt

In another horse doping case[119], jars containing urine samples for analysis were **7.122**
not sealed after a doping test in accordance with the FEI regulations. Indeed, it
would have been possible to slide the seal placed on the jars and introduce a foreign substance. As it was impossible formally to exclude the possibility of
manipulation and contamination of the jars, the CAS considered that this was
an element of doubt which had to benefit the rider.

Rules and guidelines

The CAS has made clear in several awards that only the provisions contained in **7.123**
the statutes, rules or regulations of sports bodies can be considered texts of reference, and that the provisions contained in any accompanying guidelines
should be used only as a means of interpreting these texts. Rules, however,
whose breach may result in severe sanctions, especially where strict liability is
involved, must be adopted according to proper procedures, unambiguous in
their meaning, consistent in their application.[120] For example, the gold medal
winner of the Olympic snowboard giant slalom competition at Nagano was not
punished for admitted use of cannabis, which did not feature on the list of prohibited substances.[121]

Legitimate expectation

Where rules governing entry to a competition have been flexibly applied, it is **7.124**
unfair to apply them strictly and without notice to an individual athlete.[122]
Where a sporting organisation, in particular circumstances, chooses to depart
from its established rules of selection procedure and to nominate in advance a
particular athlete as its selected choice for a particular event and, in doing so,
creates expectations in and obligations upon that individual, then it should be
bound by its choice unless proper justification can be demonstrated for revok-
ing it.[123]

Principles specifically related to doping

Strict liability

The CAS applies the principle of strict liability in cases of doping. Once a **7.125**
banned substance is discovered in the urine or blood of an athlete, the burden
being on the association to prove presence in the body to the standard of the
panel's "comfortable satisfaction . . . having regard to the seriousness of the

---

[119] CAS 91/56.

[120] *Quigley v. UIT*, CAS 94/129, para. 55; *Cullwick v. FINA*, CAS 96/149 para. 59.

[121] *Ross Rebagliati IOC* (OG Nag: 002). However an athlete will not be excused for a
failure to read clear rules *Hall v. FINA* CAS 98/218, para. 24.

[122] *US Swimming v. FINA* CAS At. Arb.No.001.

[123] *Watts v. Australian Cycling Federation Inc* CAS 96/153.

allegation which is made"[124] this athlete is presumed to have committed a doping offence. In such cases, the CAS considers that the general principle of law *nulla poena sine culpa* ("no punishment without guilt") must not be applied too literally. Indeed, if for each case the sports bodies had to prove the intentional nature of an act in order for it to be deemed an offence, the fight against doping would become virtually impossible.[125] With this principle, the subjective elements of the case are not examined: the guilt of the athlete is presumed and she or he does not have the right to supply exculpatory evidence save in relation to mitigation.[126]

Anti-technicality

7.126 While adherence to stipulated procedures is always desirable, departure from them is not fatal where the evidence otherwise convincingly establishes a doping offence.[127]

Sanctions

7.127 Disqualification is mandatory. It would be unfair to other athletes to include in the ranking someone who had used artificial means of performance enhancement if the rules are sufficiently clear. This includes disqualification of a team where one individual only has committed a doping offence.[128] Disciplinary sanctions are additional, e.g. suspension. If the rules of the association permit discretion, the seriousness of the offence is reflected in the seriousness of the penalty. Subjective elements should be appreciated in each doping case. The *lex mitior* doctrine involves applying the penalty range in force at the time of adjudication, if more benign than that in force at the time of the offence.[129]

[124] *Korneev* At. Arb. 003–4.

[125] *Volkers v. FINA*, CAS 95/150 para. 53; *Chagnaud*, CAS 45/141 para. 4C.

[126] *Wang v. FINA* CAS 98/208, para. 535; *Chagnaud v. FINA* CAS 95/41 para. 5(a); *Cullwick v. FINA* CAS 96/149, para. 6.5 and 6.6.1; *Volkers v. FINA* CAS 95/150, paras. 40, 44; *Foschi v. FINA* CAS 95/156, para. 15.

[127] *Cooke v. FEI* CAS 98/184 paras. 11.12–11.13.

[128] *National Wheelchair Basketball Association v. International Paralympic Committee* CAS 95/122. See eg. *ITC v. Korda* CAS 99/223.

[129] CAS Advisory opinion 94/128, para.33: *Cullwick, supra.*, n. 126, para.6.4.

8

Remedies: The Resolution of Legal Disputes in Sport

Introduction

Our task in this final chapter is to provide a brief account of the law governing **8.1** the availability of particular remedies sought by parties to legal disputes arising in the sporting field. However we do not here deal with the operation of purely domestic machinery within that field. We have already, in the previous chapter, considered the functioning of domestic bodies exercising disciplinary jurisdiction over sportsmen and women, and over clubs. The following account proceeds on the basis that internal domestic remedies provided for under the rules of a sporting body, including any right of internal appeal within such a body, have been exhausted. The purpose of this chapter is to explain the functioning of the machinery used to resolve legal disputes, sometimes including disputes of fact, in so far as that machinery provides for dispute resolution by a body wholly separate from, as well as independent of, the players, clubs, and sporting associations involved in the dispute in question.

The rules of some sporting associations provide for a right of recourse to an **8.2** external body such as an independent panel of arbitrators, or the CAS based primarily in Lausanne. For example, the rules of several associations responsible for promoting individual Olympic sports, including for example the Fédération Equestre Internationale (FEI), provide for a right of final appeal in doping cases to the CAS.[1] The rules of the Football Association make provision for disputes between members and clubs, or between clubs, to be referred to arbitration. Such referrals are not always confined to cases in which a sportsman or woman,

---

[1] However in *Korda v. ITF*, the Times, 4.2.99, transcript 29.1.99, Lightman J held that a rule of the International Tennis Federation's Anti-Doping Programme providing that "any dispute arising out of any decision made by the Anti-Doping Appeals Committee shall be submitted exclusively to the Appeals Arbitration Division of the Court of Arbitration for Sport" did not entitle the Federation to appeal to the CAS against a sentence it considered too lenient. The Programme also provided that the Appeal Committee's decision shall be the "full, final and complete disposition of the appeal and will be binding on all parties". However the arbitration provision would have entitled the player to challenge the enforceability of the Committee's decision on the ground of error of law or procedural unfairness: "What that formula does not preclude is a dispute as to the rights and obligations of the parties to which a decision of the [Committee] gives rise" (transcript at page 7, para 13). The Court of Appeal allowed ITC's appeal against the decision, and the case duly went before CAS (CAS 99/223).

or a club, wishes to appeal against an adverse ruling. The International Amateur Athletic Federation (IAAF) has the power under its rules to submit to arbitration, by way of appeal, cases in which a tribunal established by a national member association "in the conclusions of the hearing misdirected itself and reached an erroneous conclusion".[2]

8.3 In England, as in most other countries, supervisory jurisdiction over decisions of sporting bodies is exercised ultimately by the ordinary courts of law. There is no statutory or other specialist judicial body exercising general jurisdiction in the field of sport. The existence of that ultimate supervisory jurisdiction is assured by the constitutional principle that the courts' jurisdiction over matters of law cannot be ousted. However the English court is not, in the sporting field, a court of merits in cases where the function of finding the facts is entrusted to officials under domestic sporting rules. In such cases, the court will not entertain a challenge founded on the contention that the sporting body came to an erroneous conclusion in point of fact, unless such conclusion was based on no evidence at all or was otherwise irrational. The court will not otherwise substitute its own view of the facts for that of the designated official or body charged with their ascertainment. As the jurisdiction is supervisory, not original, a plaintiff seeking to impugn a decision must show that it was wrong in point of law, or tainted by some other vitiating factor rendering it legally objectionable.

8.4 A distinction must therefore be drawn between cases where the rules of a sporting body confer jurisdiction over disputes on a judicial body of some sort, and cases where that is not the position. In the latter category of case, where rules conferring powers of adjudication are not in play, the courts in England retain their traditional function of exercising original jurisdiction over sporting matters in the same way as they do over other legal matters coming before them. In such a case, a plaintiff will have to show, just as any other citizen would have to show, that his or her rights have been infringed in a manner cognisable as a legal wrong under the ordinary law of the land. An example of the latter type of case would be a personal injury claim arising from participation in sport, of the type described in chapter five.

8.5 Our consideration of remedies in the law relating to sport does not, in this chapter, extend to a detailed account of the ordinary remedies available to a plaintiff in a case, such as a personal injury claim, where no supervisory jurisdiction is being exercised. The remedies available to such a plaintiff do not differ from those applicable to ordinary claims brought daily by plaintiffs from all walks of life and comprising the standard fare of our courts. Thus, a libel action may be brought by one sportsman against another, as in a case in which Ian Botham sued Imran Khan (and lost). Likewise, the proprietor of a football club

---

[2] See IAAF Rule 21.3(ii). The second limb has been interpreted to include reaching an erroneous conclusion by reference to material which was not open, or even unavailable to, the national tribunal; see e.g. *Re Capobianco*, Arbitration Award of 17 March 1997, discussed in chapter seven.

may bring proceedings against a building contractor for failing to complete stadium refurbishment works on time or to the required standard. Such claims do not differ, as to the remedies available, from other such claims outside the sporting field, any more than they differ as to the rights being asserted. Consequently, the remedies available in litigation of this type do not merit separate treatment in the sporting field from that which they have received in a vast legal literature on the subject of remedies generally, to which reference can be made as necessary.

We therefore concentrate here mainly on the supervisory jurisdiction of the **8.6** English courts and on the remedies available before arbitral tribunals in the sporting field, other than the ordinary courts. The supervisory character of the jurisdiction arises from our law's insistence on autonomy of decision making by domestic and public bodies alike, provided they act within their rules and otherwise lawfully in accordance with the principles of fairness, legality and good faith expounded in the previous chapter, and provided they do not seek to become the final arbiter on questions of law and construction.[3]

We have already looked at the various ways in which disciplinary and other **8.7** tribunals exercising original first tier jurisdiction over questions of fact may also have to deal with submissions of law, or of mixed fact and law, such as whether a life ban for a first doping offence would be in unreasonable restraint of trade. Likewise, such bodies commonly have to deal with submissions as to the true meaning of the rules they are applying. Generally, further redress in a court of law or other tribunal is only available if the primary tribunal makes a mistake other than in relation to a question of fact. However some independent and external appellate tribunals, such as the CAS, may have jurisdiction expressly conferred upon them by relevant domestic rules over questions of fact as well as questions of law; and over questions as to the severity of the penalty properly to be imposed in disciplinary cases. Such an arbitral body differs conceptually from a court in that its jurisdiction arises not from the general law of the land, but from the content of the rules establishing its constitution and powers.

We consider below, separately, the types of remedy potentially available in, **8.8** respectively, the courts and other bodies exercising judicial functions. Rights of redress before the institutions of the European Union (EU), i.e. the Commission, the Court of Justice (on a reference from a national court under Article 234, formerly Article 177, of the Treaty of Rome) and the Court of First Instance, may be of prime importance in sporting disputes which have an international impact

---

[3] See *Dawkins v. Antrobus* (1881) 17 Ch Div 615, CA; *Lee v. The Showmen's Guild of Great Britain* [1952] 2 QB 329, CA, per Denning LJ at 324–4; *Faramus v. Film Artistes Association* [1964] AC 925 at 944–8 (per Lord Pearce); Josling and Alexander, The Law of Clubs, 5th ed. (1984) pp. 32-3; and in Scotland, *St Johnstone FC Ltd v. The Scottish Football Association Ltd.* (1965) SLT 171, in which Lord Kilbrandon predictably held that a rule requiring the consent of the Scottish FA Council to litigation against the Scottish FA would be void as contrary to public policy.

within the European Union. We have touched on these separately in chapters four and six and do not deal with them in this chapter except in passing.

Court proceedings – remedies in public law

8.9 In this next section we consider the scope for obtaining public law remedies in litigation concerning decisions of sporting bodies. It is not our purpose here to provide a comprehensive account of the nature and purpose of applications for judicial review. Reference should be made to the several excellent specialist works on the subject.[4] We can begin by observing pragmatically that, in the current state of English law, public law remedies are for the most part unavailable. We are of the view that this state of affairs is unsatisfactory. We will consider further below the prospects for a future change in the law that would open the way for judicial review of the decisions of sporting bodies. Other common law jurisdictions already recognise the public law nature of legal challenges to decisions of sporting bodies, taking the view that sport engages public as well as private law rights.

8.10   We start by explaining why the question need arise at all. The fact that our law regards most sporting litigation, and in particular challenges to the validity of decisions made by sporting associations, as a matter arising in private law and not public law, might be thought of little consequence since there are perfectly good remedies available to the aspiring plaintiff in our private law. Why should a player, club or sporting body be concerned about whether the body's decision, if overturned by a court, is overturned by means of an order of *certiorari* quashing it (a public law remedy), or by a declaration that it is void and of no effect (a remedy common to both private and public law), or by the more draconian method of an injunction restraining the body from acting upon it (again, a remedy common to both private and public law) ? It might well be said that the effect is the same in each case, namely that the decision does not stand and may be ignored. But the question is of more than academic interest for a number of reasons.

8.11   First, public law remedies cannot be obtained unless proceedings are brought within a very short time of the decision challenged,[5] while private law remedies founded on contract are, in principle, available for up to six years from the date

---

    [4] See, in particular, de Smith, Woolf and Jowell, *Judicial Review of Administrative Action*, 5th ed. (Sweet and Maxwell, 1995); *Wade on Administrative Law*, 7th ed. (OUP, 1994); Fordham, *Judicial Review Handbook*, 2nd ed. (John Wiley and Sons); Supperstone and Goudie, *Judicial Review*, 2nd ed. (Butterworths, 1997) *Craig on Administrative Law*, 4th ed.
    [5] Supreme Court Act 1981 Section 31(6); RSC Order 53 r. 4.

of the alleged breach[6]. In practice, however, the urgency of sporting cases and the prejudice to a plaintiff's position if he delays in seeking an injunction make it imperative to begin the proceedings promptly. Six years is manifestly too long to keep a sporting body in suspense, not knowing whether a decision it has taken is valid or not. An injunction claim will usually fail unless the proceedings are brought promptly, as we shall see below. Judicial review proceedings must, normally, be brought promptly and in any event not more than three months from the date when grounds for the challenge first arose.[7] In an urgent case, with an expedited hearing on the basis of affidavit evidence only, i.e. without oral evidence and cross-examination, the court is able to deliver a considered and final ruling within months or even weeks of the decision challenged.

Second, the nature of the remedy available can impact on the procedure **8.12** which the challenger must adopt in order to achieve any remedy at all. Lawyers with practical experience of challenging sporting bodies' decisions are aware of the tactical differences between judicial review and writ procedure. Because judicial review is usually available more swiftly than a private law remedy, the court's determination in judicial review is, more frequently than in private law proceedings, made on a final basis without the need for any hearing for consideration of interim relief. In private law proceedings, by contrast, the court is more likely to give an interim or interlocutory determination based not on its final view of the merits of the claim, but on its perception of the balance of justice at the date of the initial hearing. Normally such an interim hearing will take place within a very short time of the decision under challenge even though the plaintiff has – in theory – six years in which to bring the claim, since urgency is inherent in most disputed sporting decisions – the matter cannot await a full trial; the effect of the decision is usually immediate and serious, requiring the court to respond quickly.

Thus, a decision challenged by means of a private law action may be treated **8.13** as not susceptible of final resolution on the basis of affidavit evidence alone, while the same decision may be resolved finally and quickly if judicial review is available. The private law speedy trial procedure is more cumbersome and less easy to yield a quick result because of the state of the court lists. Its hallmark has traditionally been oral evidence and cross-examination, which are only necessary if there are genuine and material disputes of fact. More often than not in sporting disputes there are not. In private law, the procedural starting point is the assumption that evidence will be heard orally and that any preliminary ruling on affidavit evidence will be a temporary holding operation not based on a final view of the merits. In public law cases the presumption is in favour of a swift final hearing on affidavit evidence, on the footing that findings as to

---

[6] Limitation Act 1980 section 5; see generally on limitation periods in public and private law, Beloff, "Time, Time, Time, is on my Side, Yes it Is", Essays in Honour of Sir William Wade QC, ed. Christopher Forsyth (OUP, 1998).

[7] RSC Order 53 rule 4(1).

disputed fact are not required. The procedural rules are in both cases capable of adaptation and flexibility to meet the needs of the particular case, particularly since the advent of the Civil Procedure Rules in force from 26 April 1999; but the form of the proceedings nevertheless frequently influences the way in which, and the speed with which, they are disposed of.

8.14   Thirdly, the characterisation of a juridical right as one arising in public law or, it may be, in private law, can – perversely, some would say – actually influence the substantive content of the right asserted, and may thereby determine the result of the case. The tests for obtaining interim relief in private law proceedings are easier for a plaintiff to satisfy than the tests for obtaining final relief in substantive judicial review proceedings, or after a full trial in private law proceedings. There is some evidence in recent High Court decisions of distortion in the development of sports law resulting from the application of principles developed in the private law jurisdiction to grant interlocutory injunctions, which, superficially, can make the law appear more favourable to plaintiffs than it actually is.[8] Conversely, defendant sporting bodies have fared better in cases disposed of by means of a full trial – usually a speedy trial owing to the urgency of the matter.[9] We regard it as unsatisfactory that the development of this critical area of sports law, and indeed the practical outcome of individual cases, should be influenced by questions of forum and procedure.

8.15   With that introduction, we return to the starting point of the discussion, which is the observation that judicial review is, in English law, rarely if ever available as a remedy to challenge the decision of a sporting body. That is the practical effect of the decision of the Court of Appeal in *R v. Disciplinary Committee of the Jockey Club ex parte Aga Khan*.[10] It is often said, inaccurately, that a particular body is or is not amenable to judicial review. However, the availability or otherwise of judicial review depends in the final analysis not on the body whose decision is challenged,[11] nor even on the nature of the decision under challenge (though both these elements are significant), but on the nature of the right allegedly infringed. Thus the actual decision in the *Aga Khan* case was that the rights which the Aga Khan sought to enforce against the disciplinary committee of the Jockey Club were private rights enforceable by a private action founded on the contract subsisting between him and the Jockey Club. In theory, the decision leaves open the possibility that other decisions of other sporting bodies, or even of the Jockey Club itself, could infringe rights arising in public law which would be challengeable by – indeed, exclusively by – judicial review. But in practice the Court of Appeal's decision is rightly per-

---

[8] See for example, *Jones v. Welsh Rugby Union*, Ebsworth J, 27 February 1997, and CA, *The Times*, 6 January 1998.

[9] See for example, *Stevenage Borough FC Limited v. The Football League Limited*, Carnwath J, 23 July 1996, and CA (1997) 9 Admin LR 109.

[10] [1993] 1 WLR 909.

[11] See Pannick, "Who is Entitled to Judicial Review in Respect of What", 1992 *PL* 1.

ceived as throwing an insurmountable roadblock in the path of any player or club wishing to bring judicial review proceedings against a sporting body, unless and until the House of Lords plots a different approach.

The Court of Appeal had previously held that a decision of the National **8.16** Greyhound Racing Club stewards to suspend a trainer's licence could not be judicially reviewed as the matter was governed by a contract between the trainer and the club.[12] That decision has been treated by the judges, sometimes with considerable reluctance, as binding authority for the non-reviewability of decisions of sporting bodies even in the absence of a remedy in contract. Before the *Aga Khan* case itself, the Divisional Court had applied the greyhound case to preclude judicial review of decisions of the Jockey Club to remove a man's name from the list of chairmen of panels of stewards[13]; and to refuse to allow a company to run race meetings at a new racecourse in Telford.[14]

But there is a difference between exclusion of judicial review on the ground **8.17** that the decision challenged does not affect public rights, and its exclusion in the exercise of the court's discretion on the narrower ground that a private law remedy in contract is available on the facts. In the case law, those two distinct grounds for excluding judicial review have become confused. Whether a decision affects public rights should be determined by applying the criteria in the seminal Court of Appeal decision in *R v. Panel on Takeovers and Mergers ex parte Datafin*,[15] in which the ambit of judicial review was recognised as extending beyond the decisions of bodies whose powers had been conferred by statute or the royal prerogative. Emphasis was placed on the argument that the regulatory powers of the body concerned should not be conferred merely by consensual submission to jurisdiction, as under a contract.

However, the *Datafin* decision in 1987 did not persuade the courts in England **8.18** to countenance judicial review of sporting bodies' decisions. A football club was similarly unsuccessful in obtaining judicial review of the Football Association of Wales' decision to refuse it permission to join a particular lower league.[16] And in the Football League's celebrated challenge to the Football Association's decision to set up the Premier League, Rose J held that the court had no power to

[12] *Law v. National Greyhound Racing Club Ltd* [1983] 1 WLR 1302,CA.

[13] *R v. Disciplinary Committee of the Jockey Club ex parte Massingberd- Mundy* [1993] 2 All ER 207.

[14] *R v. Jockey Club ex parte RAM Racecourses Limited* [1993] 2 All ER 225. Powers exercised pursuant to contract are sometimes regarded as necessarily private functions, but the touchstone should be the nature of the function not its source. The better view is that contract may bar discretionary relief in judicial review, but because it provides an alternative remedy, not because – fallaciously – contract is said to negate public rights. In the sporting sphere there is often no contract and no alternative remedy, leading to injustice.

[15] [1987] QB 815, CA.

[16] *R. v. Football Association of Wales ex parte Flint Town United Football Club* [1991] COD 44, DC.

review that decision, on the basis that the FA was not a public law body.[17] In the *Aga Khan* case itself, the decision to disqualify the horse whose urine was found to contain a prohibited substance was held to be outside the scope of judicial review. Sir Thomas Bingham MR accepted that the Jockey Club exercised de facto monopoly powers over horse racing in this country, and that government would be driven to intervene if the Club did not exercise those powers. Nevertheless submission to its jurisdiction was said to be consensual, presumably because horse racing enthusiasts could choose not to engage in the sport.

8.19   That reasoning is unsound; it applies to all forms of voluntary activity subject to a licensing regime. Any applicant for a statutory licence could be said to submit "voluntarily" to the jurisdiction of the licensing authority, in the sense that the applicant could choose not to engage in the regulated activity and would not then need to apply for a licence. Even if the public character of sport is not accepted *a priori*, the tests serving to identify a public law right derived from the *Datafin* case[18] ought to have led to the conclusion that the decision of the Jockey Club's disciplinary committee engaged a right arising in public law. The upshot of these unsatisfactory precedents is that judicial review is likely to be a non-starter for any player or club wishing to challenge the decision of the sporting body, unless and until the House of Lords reconsiders the position, or other jurisprudential developments overtake the existing case law.

8.20   We have argued elsewhere that many decisions of sporting bodies are, on a correct analysis, ones which affect public and not merely private rights, and that English law took a wrong turn in the *Law* case in 1983, from which it has not yet recovered.[19] A number of senior judges, as well as practitioners, agree that sports bodies should be susceptible to judicial review. It is notable that in the *Massingberd-Mundy* and *RAM Racecourses* cases the following judges, now in the Court of Appeal, would, if freed from the constraints of precedent, have allowed judicial review of the Jockey Club: Neill LJ, Roch LJ, Stuart-Smith LJ and Simon Brown LJ.[20] Others favour the status quo. The debate is part of a broader one over the nature of public law functions in general, not confined to the realm of sport. It would go beyond our purpose to delve more deeply into that broader debate here.

8.21   We should however observe that in the overseas common law jurisdictions, the courts have frequently showed themselves willing to entertain public law

[17] [1993] 2 All ER 833.

[18] [1987] QB 815, CA

[19] See Beloff and Kerr "Why Aga Khan is wrong", [1996] JR 30; see also to similar effect Pannick, "Judicial Review of Sports Bodies" [1997] JR 150.

[20] Simon Brown J (as he then was) in the *RAM Racecourses* case [1993] 2 All ER 225 said at p. 245 that he "disagree[d] with the conclusions of the court in *ex p. Massingberd-Mundy*" in so far as the court's decision in that case rested on the broad ground "that the Jockey Club can never be reviewable in regard to any of their decision-making functions".

challenges to sporting bodies' decisions, in cases not always cited before the English courts. In New Zealand, a string of cases has seen judicial review used to resolve disputes in association football, rugby union, rugby league and racing.[21] In *Western Australian Turf Club v. Federal Commissioner of Taxation* the High Court of Australia, by contrast, held that the Turf Club was not a "public authority constituted under any Act or State Act" and consequently was not exempt from income tax.[22] The court noted that although certain public powers and functions had been conferred on the Turf Club by statute, its principal functions were the ordinary private ones involved in running a racing club. The Club derived its revenue from those activities, to which its non-income producing public law functions were merely incidental.

Yet the Supreme Court of Australia in *Justice v. South Australian Trotting* **8.22** *Control Board*[23] was prepared to entertain applications for the public law remedies of certiorari and mandamus in view of the Board's statutory function of regulating and controlling the sport of trotting in South Australia. And in *Jockey Club of South Africa v. Forbes*[24] the Club, taking the opposite line from its English counterpart, argued that a challenge to its disciplinary decision should have been brought by the South African equivalent of judicial review procedure. The court was prepared to assume that that procedure "extends to decisions of domestic tribunals and does not apply only to breaches by officials of duties imposed on them by public law".[25] The court went on to hold that the use of a private law procedure was not fatal to the application, even on that assumption.

Only in the English courts has procedure triumphed over substance to the **8.23** extent of denying any remedy at all to a party unable to rely on contract as the foundation for a challenge to a sporting body's decision. A private law cause of action for a simple declaration, even in the absence of contract, may rescue the aspiring plaintiff;[26] but such a course has its own difficulties, which we look at further below.[27] The root of the difficulty in this jurisdiction is the decision in

[21] *Simpson v. NZ Racing Conference* 24 June 1980, High Court, Wellington A531–79; *Johnson v. Appeal Judges* CA 117/96, 16 July 1996; *Lower Hutt City AFC v. NZ Football Association*, 13 March 1993, High Court, Auckland M335/93; *Loe v. NZ RFU* 10 August 1993, High Court, Wellington CP209/93; *Otahuhu Rovers RLC v. Auckland Rugby League Inc*. 12 November 1993, High Court, Auckland M818/93; *La Roux v. NZ RFU* 14 March 1995, High Court, Wellington CP346/94; noted in "Judicial Review in the Commercial Arena", paper and lecture given on 15 November 1996 by Paul Walker in Wellington, New Zealand.

[22] (1978) 19 ALR 167.

[23] (1989) 50 FAR 613.

[24] (1993) (1) FA 649.

[25] *Ibid*., at p. 659E, per Kriegler AJA.

[26] See further below, and see e.g. *Stevenage Borough FC Limited v. The Football League Limited*, *supra*., n. 9.

[27] For a further review of Commonwealth authority, see Beloff and Kerr "Judicial Control of Sporting Bodies, the Commonwealth Jurisprudence", Sport and Law Journal Vol. 2, issue 1 (1995), p. 5.

O'Reilly v. Mackman[28] establishing the so-called procedural exclusivity rule whereby a decision must be characterised as arising in public or private law, and the corresponding procedure adopted on pain of dismissal of the proceedings.[29] The eventual demise of the procedural exclusivity rule has been widely predicted, for it is regarded as unsatisfactory that the tail of procedure should wag the dog of substance. If and when the rule is reconsidered and departed from, our courts will be as free as those of South Africa to adjudicate on challenges to decisions of sporting bodies using the swiftest and most efficient and economical procedure available.

8.24   In England, we consider judicial review to embody such a procedure. We draw support from the remarks of Carnwath J in *Stevenage Borough FC Limited v. The Football Limited*.[30] The case took the form of a private law challenge to a decision of the Football League to deny admission to Stevenage after it had won the Vauxhall Conference. The case proceeded by way of speedy trial, with oral evidence and cross-examination, within three months of issue of the writ. The judge analysed the divide between public and private law and remarked:

> "... the procedural distinctions are not obviously justifiable. Rose J's concern that extension of judicial review to such bodies as the Football Association, would result in excessive pressure on judicial time, is not borne out by the evidence of the present case. In spite of the efforts of the parties, and the economy of presentation, the writ procedure, with pleadings, discovery and oral evidence, inevitably is more elaborate, time consuming and expensive than judicial review. Most of the facts in the present case were uncontentious, and little emerged in the process of oral evidence which could not have been adequately dealt with by affidavit and examination of documents. Under the judicial review procedure, if properly conducted, the case for each party can generally be set out in one main affidavit on each side, supported only by relevant documents; rather than, as in this case, in some 16 witness statements, 15 files of documents and transcripts of 5 days of oral evidence."[31]

He went on to observe that it was:

> "... difficult to see any reason in principle why the tests applied to the exercise of discretion by such regulatory bodies [as the Football League], acting in good faith, should be materially different to those applied to bodies subject to judicial review."[32]

---

[28] [1983] 2 AC 237, HL.

[29] Subject to the power of the High Court in an application for judicial review to order that the proceedings be treated as if began writ; see Order 53 Rule 9(5).

[30] Unreported, transcript 23 July 1996.

[31] *Ibid.*, pp. 36–7.

[32] *Ibid.*, p. 38. See also Lord Woolf MR in *Wilander v. Tobin* [1997] 2 Lloyds 293, CA, at pp. 299-300 ("If the Appeals Committee does not act fairly or if it misdirects itself in

Earlier in the same judgment, Carnwath J commented that the dividing line **8.25**
between governmental and non-governmental functions in the case law is not
only difficult to draw, but difficult to justify. He referred to academic writing
suggesting that the extension of judicial review to non-statutory bodies such as
the Takeover Panel has a "common law root" in cases dealing with the exercise
of monopoly powers.[33] Thus examination of the substantive rights in play in
this field throws doubt on the validity of an approach which proceeds from a
sharp divide between decisions affecting private and public rights. If, as
Carnwath J's analysis suggests, there is an organic link between decisions of
public bodies and those of domestic tribunals, the justification for separate procedural treatment appears to vanish.

Moreover, in *Modahl v. British Athletic Federation Limited*,[34] where the **8.26**
plaintiff athlete claimed damages for breach of contract arising from a wrong
finding that she was guilty of doping which was subsequently reversed in a
domestic appeal, Lord Woolf MR commented that it was wrong to suggest that
public law principles governing judicial review have no relevance in domestic
disciplinary proceedings. He went on to observe that the test of fairness should
be the same whether the claim lies in private or in public law. He pointed out
that the procedural differences in the respective regimes ought not to impact on
the scope of any substantive right to damages, which would not be obtainable
in a public law claim but could be in a private law claim. Again, the point was
that the tail (classification of the claim for procedural purposes) should not wag
the dog (content of substantive rights). The *Modahl* case shows that arguments
about remedies should not be used to prop up arguments about the scope of
rights.

Our brief survey of the impact of the public/private law divide on challenges **8.27**
to decisions of sporting bodies demonstrates that the strong preference of the
latter for being treated as private entities has, so far, found favour with the
courts in England, though not in all other jurisdictions, where the public/private
law divide is not as rigid in any event. The conclusion is that, from the perspective of a player or club wishing to mount a challenge, pursuit of a public law
remedy is most unlikely to be advisable in this country. But we venture to question whether sporting bodies are better protected from judicial intervention
than they would be if treated as bodies with a public element whose decisions

---

law and fails to take into account relevant considerations or takes into account irrelevant
considerations, the High Court can intervene. It can also intervene if there is no evidential basis for its decision.") See also Dawn Oliver, "Administrative Decision Making;
Common Law; Natural Justice" [1997] *PL* 630.

[33] *Ibid.*, p. 36, referring to Forsyth (1996) CLJ 122; *Alnutt v. Inglis* (1810) 12 East 527,
in which it was held that the London Dock Company which owned the only warehouses
in which wine importers could bond their wine had a correlative duty to charge only reasonable hire.

[34] CA transcript, 28 July 1997.

could be challenged by judicial review. The tests for intervention by the courts do not differ greatly in substance. But the rules governing the grant of interlocutory injunctions in private law are more favourable to plaintiffs, generally, than to defendants.

8.28   Ultimately, the argument that sport is by nature more a public than a private activity proceeds from an *a priori* judgment about its nature. We regard sporting activity as more public than private, and we form that view as commercial lawyers as well as administrative lawyers. This is because sporting endeavour is – and should be – undertaken for more than commercial gain. Clubs and players should be seen to represent themselves, their clubs, or their country, more than they represent the commercial sponsor whose logo temporarily adorns their shirts. Clubs in team sports have geographical roots which can never be completely destroyed by an increasingly international trade in players' services, however developed that market becomes. In principle, the injection of private capital into sport should not detract from its public character, any more than the function of managing a prison should be regarded as a private function merely because it happens to be entrusted to a private company.

Remedies under the European Convention on Human Rights

8.29 Before leaving the subject of public law remedies entirely, we must mention the possibility of a remedy under the European Convention on Human Rights which, at the time of writing, is shortly to become available through the Human Rights Act 1998 in the English domestic courts and tribunals, as well as before the European Court of Human Rights in Strasbourg. The general significance to sports law of this momentous constitutional development in the longer term cannot yet be assessed and will have to await a future edition of the book. For present purposes we confine ourselves to the following brief observations. First, in England, the incorporation into domestic law of nearly all the rights and freedoms guaranteed by the Convention could encourage the English courts towards a relaxation of the rigid distinction between the public and private aspects of the rights enforced in legal proceedings. Second, sportsmen and women and clubs, like others, will be able to invoke Convention rights directly in the English courts, instead of having to bring a claim against the United Kingdom before the Court of Human Rights at Strasbourg. However, sports cases have not predominated at Strasbourg in the forty five years or so that the Convention has been in force.[35]

8.30   The evolution in domestic law of rights derived from the Convention still lies in the future at the time of writing. The Human Rights Act 1998 will

---

[35] The Convention was adopted in 1950 and came into force on 1 September 1953. The United Kingdom adopted the right of individual petition to the Court of Human Rights in 1966.

oblige"public authorities", defined so as to include courts and tribunals, not to act in a manner incompatible with the incorporated Convention rights, unless primary or secondary legislation compels them to do so.[36] Domestic courts and tribunals will be required to interpret legislation, where possible, in conformity with those rights, and to take account of jurisprudence emanating from the European Commission of Human Rights, the Court of Human Rights and the Committee of Ministers of the Council of Europe.[37] The higher courts, which in England will mean the High Court and above, will have power to declare legislation incompatible with a Convention right.[38] Convention based rights may be invoked in any proceedings, civil or criminal, whether as the basis for a claim or as a defence. Damages for breach of a Convention right may be awarded if the court or tribunal normally has jurisdiction to award them.[39]

We have already observed in chapter seven the effect that incorporation of **8.31** Article 6, in particular, could have in relation to disciplinary proceedings in sport, on the basis that such proceedings may constitute the determination of civil rights and obligations within the meaning of the first paragraph of that Article. Under the Human Rights Act 1998, however, the definition of a "public authority" which must observe Convention rights, expressly excludes, in relation to a particular act, a person who is performing a private act.[40] This means that a sportsman or woman wishing to allege that a disciplinary body has acted in breach of rights under Article 6 by denying a fair hearing, could be prevented from doing so on the basis that the disciplinary body is performing a private act when exercising its disciplinary function, even though it is determining the sportsman's "civil rights and obligations" within Article 6 at the time.

The basis for such reasoning can be found in the jurisprudence emanating **8.32** from the Commission and the Court of Human Rights in Strasbourg, which equates "civil rights and obligations" with those arising in "private law", in the autonomous Convention sense of that term, which is however very different from the English law sense. Under the 1998 Act in England, the continuing effect of the *Aga Khan* case, unless and until reconsidered, could lead our domestic courts to conclude that such disciplinary bodies are performing private acts within section 6(5) of the 1998 Act and are therefore not public authorities within section 6(1) and (3). In our view, that would be a pity. It is preferable that English law should use the opportunity provided by incorporation of the Convention to re-assess its notions of private and public rights in the sporting field (which are flawed in any event for the reasons given above), than that it should invoke the 1998 Act as a ground for entrenching the existing divide. The English courts will be obliged to take into account the Strasbourg jurisprudence

---

[36] Section 6(1), (2) and (3) of the 1998 Act.
[37] Human Rights Act 1998, sections 2(1) and 3.
[38] *Ibid.*, section 4.
[39] *Ibid.*, section 8.
[40] See section 6(5) of the 1998 Act.

but will not be required to follow it to the letter, particularly in so far as it proceeds from a concept of private law very different from our own.

8.33   If the latter course is, contrary to our view, adopted, the effect would be that a challenge to the validity of the disciplinary process relying on Article 6 of the Convention, would have to proceed, as now, by way of private law action by issue of a writ, rather than by a free standing judicial review of the disciplinary body's decision, under section 7 of the Act. In that event, the court before which the proceedings are brought will itself be under an obligation to respect the plaintiff's rights under Article 6 of the Convention, with the consequence that contractual obligations pursuant to which punitive jurisdiction is exercised, may become infused with the rights which Article 6 guarantees, as explained in chapter seven.

Court proceedings – remedies in private law

8.34   In English private law, the remedies available in a sporting dispute depend upon the nature of the right asserted by the plaintiff, and on the circumstances in which it is asserted. The remedies available are those available generally to litigants in private law proceedings. English law remedies have developed historically, under the influence of the historic division of the courts between those exercising common law jurisdiction, and those – presided over by the Lord Chancellor – exercising jurisdiction in equity. It is not proposed here to give an exhaustive account of all the remedies open to plaintiffs at common law and in equity; only of those that are most important in the sporting field. The common law traditionally leans towards the primacy of damages as a remedy.

8.35   Yet, in the field of sport, with notable exceptions such as the recent litigation involving the athlete Diane Modahl,[41] monetary compensation is not the remedy uppermost in the mind of the plaintiff. Sporting disputes which develop into litigation, more often than not, arise at short notice and in circumstances where the swiftness of the court's ruling is as important as the result itself. This is because legal disputes often concern forthcoming competitions for which the date has been set, or which recur annually. Most litigation, unless deliberately expedited with the parties' timetable in mind, takes more than a year from claim to judgment. Often the question is whether a sportsman or woman should be permitted to take part in a particular tournament. Damages may occupy a place in the background thinking of the parties, usually as a remoter consequence of failure to achieve the right to participate in a competition. But the immediate priority, in most sporting litigation, is likely to be the obtaining of an injunction. The remedy of injunction is often coupled with a claim for a declaration regulating the respective rights of the parties for the future. We therefore consider first the non-pecuniary remedies of declaration and injunction.

[41] See *Modahl v. British Athletic Federation Limited*, CA, transcript 28 July 1997; HL transcript 22 July 1999.

Declarations

A declaration[42] is a highly effective weapon in the hands of a sporting litigant, **8.36**
which enables both parties to know their rights and obligations, which the court
declares at the end of the case. Two types of declaration concern us particularly
in the context of sporting litigation.[43] The first is a declaration of contractual
rights. Obviously there must be contractual relations between the parties in
order for the court to declare what their contractual rights are. However, occasionally cases arise in which one party asserts the existence of a contractual
right, for example to compete in a particular competition, while the other party
denies its existence. In such a case, the court's role is to declare whether the contractual right exists or not and, it may be, how far it extends if it does exist. Thus
in *Watson v. Prager*[44] a professional boxer successfully claimed a declaration
that a particular clause in his contract with his manager, which was in a form
prescribed by the British Boxing Board of Control, was in unreasonable
restraint of trade and therefore unenforceable. The same success was achieved
by a professional rugby league player as against his club in relation to the retention and transfer system then obtaining in New South Wales.[45]

The second type of declaration is less well known and occasionally over- **8.37**
looked. It is a declaration in the absence of contract, sometimes referred to as a
declaration simpliciter. This remedy has already been mentioned in chapter 3
where we observed that an aspiring entrant to a sporting competition may lack
a contractual right to enter it even though he fulfills the organising body's criteria for entry. Judges have recognised that there may be circumstances in which
it would be unjust to deny a plaintiff declaratory relief usual in the absence of a
contractual right, if his private rights are affected by unlawful conduct of the
defendant. Thus, contrary to what is sometimes supposed, the law does recognise a right to a declaration as against a party with whom the plaintiff is not in
a contractual relationship or other recognised legal relationship, where that
party's actions affect or may affect the plaintiff in his private rights.

As already noted in chapter three, this principle assisted George Eastham **8.38**
with his troublesome transfer from Newcastle United to Arsenal.[46] Examples of

[42] See generally Zamir and Woolf, *The Declaratory Judgment*, 2nd ed. (Sweet and
Maxwell, 1993).

[43] The Court of Appeal currently regards the scope for granting declaratory relief as
narrower in private law than in public law proceedings; see e.g. *Meadows Indemnity Co.
v. Insurance Corporation of Ireland* [1989] 2 Lloyds 298; *Trustees of the Dennis Rye
Pension Fund v. Sheffield City Council* [1998] 1 WLR 840; *Link Organisation v. North
Derbyshire Tertiary College*, CA, transcript 14 August 1998.

[44] [1991] 1 WLR 726, Scott J.

[45] *Buckley v. Tutty* (1971) 125 CLR 353 (High Court of Australia).

[46] *Eastham v. Newcastle United FC* [1964] Ch 413 at 443, per Wilberforce, J; see
also Zamir and Woolf , *The Declaratory Judgment* 2nd ed., *supra.*, n. 42 above, at

cases in which it has been conceded or held that a right to a declaration can exist as a free standing cause of action, without a need for a contractual peg on which to hang it, are now quite numerous. It is therefore surprising that recognition of the *declaration simpliciter* as an independent right of action is not more widely recognised. Even in 1966 the Court of Appeal thought it arguable that a female trainer of horses had a right to a declaration where her only ground for relief, in the absence of a contract, was her assertion that rules which discriminated on the ground of her sex were void as contrary to public policy.[47] The existence of the jurisdiction to grant free standing declaratory relief has been recognised many times in subsequent case law, particularly in the sporting field[48] but also – especially in restraint of trade cases – outside it.[49]

8.39 The court has a discretion whether to grant or refuse a declaration. It cannot be assumed that one will automatically be granted even if the plaintiff succeeds in establishing the primary case. But in the sporting context the courts have generally been willing to assist those with legitimate complaints against their regulatory bodies. It seems likely that the court would also be prepared to assist a commercial body adversely affected by unlawful regulatory action, as was contended in *R v. Jockey Club ex parte RAM Racecourses Limited*.[50] The applicant company wished to establish a new racecourse but was turned down by the Jockey Club. It sought to bring a claim by way of judicial review. The Divisional Court considered the case on its merits and the applicant company lost on the merits. The court would have been prepared to grant a declaration if the decision under challenge had been shown to be unlawful, and subject to the difficulty over the claim having been brought by application for judicial review.[51]

8.40 We should not leave the remedy of declaration without pointing out one substantial drawback: it has in the past only been available as a final order at the

pp. 203–211; *Greig v. Insole* [1978] 1 WLR 302 (Slade J); cf. in the Antipodean jurisdictions *Finnigan* [1985] 2 NZLR 1959; *Adamson* (1991) 103 ALR 319.

[47] *Nagle v. Feilden* [1966] 2 QB 633, CA.

[48] See inter alia *McInnes v. Onslow-Fane* [1978] 1 WLR 1520; *Buckley v. Tutty* (1971) 125 CLR 353; *Gasser v. Stinson*, transcript 15 June 1988 (Scott J) at pp. 24–5; *Newport AFC Limited v. Football Association of Wales Limited* [1995] 2 All ER 1987 (Jacob J); *Lennox Lewis v. Frank Bruno and The World Boxing Council*, transcript, Rattee J, 3. November 1995 (claim dismissed on other grounds); and *Stevenage Borough FC Limited v. The Football League Limited* (1997) 9 Admin. LR 97, CA.

[49] *Pharmaceutical Society of Great Britain v. Dickson* [1970] AC 403, HL.

[50] [1993] 2 All ER 225 DC.

[51] Stuart-Smith LJ noted at p. 244 e-g that the court had the power under RSC Order 53 rule 9(5) to order that the proceedings continue as if they had begun by writ. More recently the Court of Appeal has observed that the scope for granting declarations is narrower in private law matters than in public law matters: *Link Organisation plc v. North Derbyshire Tertiary College*, CA transcript 14 August 1998, citing *Meadows Indemnity Co. v. Insurance Corporation of Ireland* [1989] 2 Lloyds Rep 298 and *Trustees of the Dennis Rye Pension Fund v. Sheffield City Council* [1998] 1 WLR 840.

conclusion of proceedings. An interim declaration, unlike an interim injunction, could not be obtained. This has serious ramifications for the practical utility of the remedy, since speed is often of the essence as already noted. The suggestion[52] that interim declarations could be available in cases where due to the sensitivity of the circumstances, the courts cannot grant injunctive relief, is attractive but is contrary to the authority of *International General Electric Co. of New York v. Commissioners of Customs & Excise.*[53] However in the Civil Procedure Rules, Part 25.1(1)(b) an "interim declaration" is listed among interim remedies available. It is questionable whether such a procedural rule is capable of affecting the scope of the availability of the remedy as a matter of substantive law.[54]

Injunctions

Injunctions are probably the most useful remedy in sporting disputes. An **8.41** injunction can compel an unwilling competition organiser to permit an eligible entrant to compete in the competition, though it could not compel an unwilling competitor to compete. Injunctions probably best represent the capacity of the law to aid the weak against the strong, and to give vivid expression to the concept of equality before the law, redressing the imbalance of power between modest individuals and mighty institutions (or, occasionally, the other way round).[55] Again, it is not our purpose to expound the historical development of the equitable remedy of injunction, nor to give a full account of its scope. Reference should be made to specialist works for that purpose.[56] We confine our account to injunctions as used in the sporting context.

The principal relevance of the remedy is at the interim stage of proceedings, **8.42** i.e. usually very near the beginning. In most sporting litigation played out in the courts, the objective of obtaining an injunction is the plaintiff's main and often only goal. An applicant for an interim injunction must include in the relief sought a claim for an final injunction, which the court would be asked to grant in the event that the matter went to a full trial, albeit that a full trial rarely happens. Subject to the discretion of the court, a plaintiff who can establish a legal wrong is normally entitled to a final injunction to restrain repetition of the wrong and, sometimes, to require the defendant to put it right. This is all well

---

[52] In Zamir and Woolf, *The Declaratory Judgment* 2nd ed., (*supra.*, n. 42 above), para. 3.092.

[53] [1962] Ch 784 per Upjohn LJ at 789–790; see also *R v. IRC ex parte Rossminster* [1980] AC 952 per Lord Diplock at 1014 E-F and Lord Scarman at 1027 C-E.

[54] Cf. *St. George's Healthcare NHS Trust v. S* [1998] 3 All ER 673 at 700C-D; and see Neenan [1999] JR 6, at p. 7, noting that as the CPR are procedural in nature by virtue of the Civil Procedure Act 1997 (esp. sections 1 and Schedule 1 para 2), Part 25.1(1)(b) of the CPR may be *ultra vires*.

[55] Lord Denning, *The Discipline of Law* (Butterworths, 1979), at p. 140 cites the words of Thomas Fuller over 300 years ago: "Be you never so high, the law is above you".

[56] See for example, Spry, *The Principles of Equitable Remedies*, 5th ed. (1997).

trodden ground for lawyers. What is less well known to sportsmen and women is that, other than in rare cases, a plaintiff who seeks an interlocutory injunction must be prepared to offer an undertaking in damages and, if necessary, prove that he is in a position to honour it by supplying evidence that he is of sufficient financial substance.

8.43 Two simple examples will serve to illustrate the point. Suppose that a hockey club wishes to prevent one of its players from entering into a lucrative advertising contract to promote certain sportswear. The club alleges that to do so would be contrary to the player's obligations under his contract of employment with the club, which obliges the player not to promote any product save one endorsed by the club and its commercial sponsor. The player alleges that this term in his employment contract is void as an unreasonable restraint of trade. The club seeks an interim injunction to prevent the player appearing in a national television advertisement scheduled for screening in a week's time. The player counterclaims for a declaration that the restrictive term in his contract with the club is void. The club, in that example, must give an undertaking in damages to the player that in the event of the court later deciding the substantive case in favour of the player, the club must pay to the player such damages, if any, as the court shall decide it ought to pay to compensate him for the loss occasioned by the granting of an interim injunction against him. If any question arises as to the club's ability to honour the undertaking, it will have to produce its accounts or other financial evidence to show its worth. If the club takes the form of a small subsidiary of a large company, the latter may have to give the undertaking as it might otherwise be worthless.

8.44 In the second example, suppose the facts are the same but that instead of seeking an interim injunction against the player, the club reports him to the league of which the club is a member. The league serves notice on the player not to appear in the television advertisement or otherwise contract with the sportswear manufacturer, on pain of punitive action. The player, fearing to lose his lucrative television appearance the following week, urgently consults with lawyers who advise him to seek an injunction restraining the league from instituting disciplinary action against him on the basis of a restrictive obligation in his contract which he alleges is void. An urgent court hearing is hurriedly arranged, just before the scheduled television appearance. The player must give an undertaking in damages to the league and produce evidence of financial worth to support it. Continuing with the example, one may suppose that at the hearing the league's counsel produces a letter from another, rival, sportswear manufacturer threatening to pull out of a proposed lucrative sponsorship arrangement with the league, should the plaintiff player appear in the television advertisement the following week. The player's undertaking in damages may or may not be sufficiently backed by financial worth to persuade the court to grant him his injunction.

8.45 The risk of a high financial price for an interlocutory injunction is apparent from the two examples. They serve to emphasise the importance of an undertaking in damages and the peril of overlooking it. They also should encourage the parties to sporting disputes to settle their differences if they can. The plaintiff in both the above examples faces a difficult decision to be taken under heavy time pressure. With that practical introduction, we look next at some of the main features of injunctions in sports law. The test which the courts in England apply is well known. Provided there is a serious issue to be tried, the court looks at the adequacy of damages as a remedy for either party, and the balance of convenience, or the balance of justice, in deciding whether to grant or refuse the injunction. Without an undertaking in damages, as explained above, the court is unlikely to grant one. In a case where a final trial is impracticable because the whole of the issue between the parties turns on an event, for example a cup final, scheduled imminently, the court will look beyond the question whether there is merely a serious issue to be tried, to a fuller appraisal of the merits. This may be difficult as hurriedly garnered affidavit evidence, without cross-examination, is not the best factual basis on which to assess merit.

The application of these well established principles in the sporting field was **8.46** illustrated in *Jones v. Welsh Rugby Union*.[57] A rugby union player obtained an interim order restraining the Welsh Rugby Union from implementing a four week ban on the basis of arguable procedural defects in the disciplinary procedure applied to him following an altercation on the field of play. Ebsworth J was "concerned with whether or not the plaintiffs can establish a case for interim relief on the usual principles applicable . . .".[58] She commented that "the practical reality requires the suspension to be lifted until the issue is determined between the parties", saying she hoped that interlocutory relief was a "just and workable compromise . . . that the suspension . . . shall not be enforced until the trial of this matter or further order".[59] The *Jones* case went to appeal, following a further interlocutory skirmish in which Potts J held that the defendant Union was precluded by Ebsworth J's initial order from imposing a subsequent suspension pursuant to further disciplinary proceedings. The Court of Appeal held that the initial discretionary decision of Ebsworth J could not faulted, even though the Union's arguments on the merits might well succeed at trial, but upheld the Union's contention that the judge's order had not precluded it from holding a second disciplinary hearing and imposing a penalty in consequence.[60]

As already noted, regulatory bodies in sport usually fare better at final trial **8.47** than they do in interlocutory injunction applications, because the low threshold which a plaintiff must attain, coupled with inadequacy of damages as a remedy for a sportsman or woman with a short career span and a vital need to create and maintain a reputation in a short time, make it difficult for the sporting asso-

[57] Transcript, 27 February 1997.

[58] *Ibid.*, p. 3, referring sub silentio to *American Cyanamid v. Ethicon Limited* [1975] AC 396, HL.

[59] *Ibid.*, pp. 28–9.

[60] *The Times*, 6 January 1998.

ciation to show a balance of justice in its favour. The susceptibility of such associations to negative injunctions restraining the implementation of disciplinary penalties, is now beginning to be exploited by plaintiff players in an increasingly professional climate. Their professional associations, the equivalent of trade unions in industry, can assist in the matter of undertakings in damages, if their club is not supporting them and they are insufficiently wealthy on their own account.

8.48   The interlocutory injunction is also a powerful weapon in the hands of a plaintiff seeking to prevent implementation of a rule alleged to be in unreasonable restraint of trade, according to principles discussed in previous chapters. A recent example is *Newport AFC Limited v. The Football Association of Wales Limited.*[61] Jacob J commented that if an interlocutory injunction were not granted to prevent the Welsh FA imposing sanctions on the plaintiff club, the latter might well simply cease to exist, rendering worthless its chances of success at trial.[62] More recently, two distinguished rugby union football clubs in Wales, Cardiff and Ebbw Vale, succeeded against the Welsh Rugby Union in obtaining an interim injunction preventing the Union from implementing a decision that all clubs which wished to be part of it had to commit themselves to membership for a ten year period. The matter was too urgent for a full trial as the effect of the decision would have been to prevent the plaintiff clubs from playing in European competition the following season and from playing in the Premier League. The judge's order granted the injunction for one playing season or a year, but not so as to extend to the 1998/99 season.[63] He did not accept that the very future of the clubs was imperilled, but granted a limited order on orthodox principles, holding that there was a triable issue as to whether the decision under challenge was an unreasonable restraint of trade, that damages would not be an adequate remedy for the plaintiffs in view of the incalculable effect of loss of exposure to high level competition; and that the defendant Union was adequately protected by the plaintiffs' undertaking in damages. He pointed out[64] that if the clubs were to join the Union for the ten year period and then lose the case at full trial, they would be locked in against their will without the opportunity to withdraw after the four or five years which they would have accepted as reasonable.

8.49   In our brief survey of interim injunctions in sporting litigation, the next point which arises is the thorny problem of jurisdiction to grant an interim injunction in a claim for a *declaration simpliciter*. There is some doubt as to whether the jurisdiction exists. The point is of considerable importance in view of the

---

[61] [1995] 2 All ER 87.

[62] See at p. 98e-f. The club eventually won at trial before Blackburne J (unreported, transcript 12 April 1995) and obtained a declaration that the resolution of the Welsh FA was void as an unreasonable restraint of trade.

[63] *Williams v. Pugh*, transcript, 23 July 1997, Popplewell J.

[64] *Ibid.*, pp. 13–14.

absence of contract, generally speaking, between a player and the league of which his club is a member. In *Newport AFC Limited v. The Football Association of Wales Limited*[65] the point arose directly. Newport Football Club had no contract with the defendant Association, having resigned from it and joined its English counterpart. The Association contended at the interlocutory stage that the court lacked jurisdiction to grant an interlocutory injunction as a remedy ancillary to a *declaration simpliciter* on the basis that a bare right to a declaration does not entail any actionable wrong by the defendant, and injunctions can only be granted in cases where there is a potential actionable wrong. The judge rejected that argument,[66] commenting that a right to a declaration is a sufficient cause of action on which to found jurisdiction to grant an interlocutory injunction.[67]

We respectfully agree with the reasoning and conclusion, but unfortunately a **8.50** passage throwing doubt on the existence of the jurisdiction was not cited to the court in the *Newport* case. In *R v. Disciplinary Committee of the Jockey Club ex parte Aga Khan* [68] Hoffmann LJ said:

> ". . . in cases in which power is exercised unfairly against persons who have no contractual relationship with a private decision-making body, the court may not find it easy to fashion a cause of action to provide a remedy. In *Nagle v. Feilden* [1966] 2 QB 633, for example, this court had to consider the Jockey Club's refusal on grounds of sex to grant a trainer's licence to a woman. She had no contract with the Jockey Club or (at that time) any other recognised cause of action, but this court said that it was arguable that she could still obtain a declaration and injunction. There is an improvisatory air about this solution and the possibility of obtaining an injunction has probably not survived *Siskina v. Distos Compania Naviera SA* [1979] AC 210.[69]

We hope that if that passage had been cited to Jacob J in the *Newport* case, he would nevertheless have held that he did have jurisdiction to grant the interim injunction sought. The passage from Hoffmann LJ's judgment quoted above was not necessary for the decision in the case before him, and the *Siskina* case, which arose in a very different context, does not compel the conclusion he draws from it. As Jacob J recognised, in the case before him, unless the plaintiff were protected at the interlocutory stage from the defendant's unlawful act, it could not be protected from it at all.

There are, however, areas in which the law will not assist a plaintiff by **8.51** injunction. As already explained in chapter three, the court will not enforce by

---

[65] [1995] 2 All ER 87.

[66] See *ibid.* at pp. 91j–93b

[67] He drew support from *Buckley v. Tutty* (1971) 125 CLR 353, per Barwick CJ at 380, and Wilberforce J in *Eastham v. Newcastle United FC Limited*, *supra.*, n. 44.

[68] [1993] 1 WLR 909, CA.

[69] See the *Aga Khan* case at 933 A-C.

injunction a claim to membership of an association unwilling to accept the new member, as observed by Carnwath J in *Stevenage Borough FC Limited v. The Football League Limited.*[70] Nor would a court in normal circumstances compel by injunction a player unwilling to play for his or her club to do so, even if the refusal to play is a plain breach of contract. The normal principle would apply, namely that the law does not – absent special circumstances unlikely to be relevant in sport – compel by injunction performance of an employee's obligation to serve under a contract of employment, nor indeed other contractual obligations to render personal service or bringing the parties into a personal relationship requiring close cooperation between them.[71]

8.52   English law recognises the distinction between mandatory and prohibitory injunctions. As a general proposition, it is easier to obtain a negative or prohibitory injunction than a positive, or mandatory one. The distinction is sound in principle. A negative injunction requires the defendant to refrain from doing something; a positive injunction requires him to do something. The distinction can have particular relevance to sporting disputes. Generally, the jurisdiction to grant a mandatory injunction is exercised sparingly, only where the plaintiff shows a very strong probability that grave damage will occur to him if it is not granted.[72] The plaintiff will have to meet a higher standard at the interim stage in relation to the strength of his case than in the case of a prohibitory injunction.[73] In *Jones v. Welsh Rugby Union* Ebsworth J treated the application before her as "for essentially a mandatory injunction".[74] With respect, it is not clear what was mandatory about it. Mr Jones was asking the court to prevent the Welsh Rugby Union from implementing its four week ban on him playing matches. The Union did not have to do anything to comply with the order except sit back and let him play.[75] Perhaps that is why the judge observed that to do what was required of it under the order "will not cost the defendants money or reputation".[76] The observation about reputation, incidentally, may appear somewhat innocent in view of the subsequent media coverage of the case.

8.53   As that case shows, one must not read too much into the distinction between mandatory and prohibitory injunctions. On the facts, the practical relevance of

---

[70] Unreported, transcript 23 July 1996; and see the cases cited to Carnwath J, noted at para. 3.13 *supra*.

[71] See *Snell's Equity* 29th ed. (Sweet and Maxwell, 1990) pp. 685–7; Spry, *The Principles of Equitable Remedies*, 5th ed. (Sweet and Maxwell, 1997) pp. 119–125.

[72] *Morris v. Redland Bricks Limited* [1970] AC 655, HL.

[73] *Leisure Data v. Bell* [1988] FSR 367, at 368.

[74] See transcript at p. 25.

[75] In extreme cases the court will intervene, not merely to prevent implementation of a disciplinary penalty likely to have unlawfully imposed, but even to restrain unlawful disciplinary proceedings before they are heard: *Esterman v. NALGO* [1974] ICR 625, Templeman J; cf. *Longley v. NUJ* [1987] IRLR 109, CA, and the other cases cited in *Harvey on Industrial Relations and Employment Law*, at M[2715].

[76] Transcript at p. 28.

the distinction may be attenuated to the point of rendering it merely semantic. An example, drawn from experience (but without mentioning names due to confidentiality obligations), serves to emphasise this. There have recently been a number of cases in which clubs have sought to charge transfer fees in relation to out-of-contract players, notwithstanding the *Bosman* decision, in relation to transfers between clubs within one member state of the European Union. They have sought to argue that the relevant rules applicable permit such fees to be charged and that the *Bosman* ruling does not apply to intra-state transfers not falling within Article 48 of the Treaty of Rome. The substance of this issue has already been discussed in chapter four. In one such case the transferee club wished to engage a player's services without paying a transfer fee, against the protest of the transferring club. The relevant leagues, under their rules, had to agree to the registration of the transferred player as a player with the transferee club. Without such registration, he would be ineligible to play for his new club.

Assuming, in that example, that the relevant leagues were (as was not in fact **8.54** the position) unwilling so to register the player, the transferee club would have an urgent need for an injunction against those leagues to remove obstacles to receiving the player's services. Or, to put it another way, they would need an injunction to compel the necessary steps by the relevant leagues to register him. Such an injunction, if it had been needed, could be seen as prohibitory, in the same sense as we have argued above in relation to *Jones v. Welsh Rugby Union*, in that the receiving league could be treated as prohibited from attempting to prevent the player from playing. Or, the injunction could be treated as a mandatory one requiring the receiving league to take the positive steps necessary to register him with the transferee club. In that example, the distinction theoretically turns on the point that the registration procedure requires an actual step, probably the signing of a document, to be taken by an official of the league.

The courts are not blind to the fineness of the distinction on particular facts. **8.55** The closer the relief is to being prohibitory in substance, the easier it is to obtain an injunction. In the example above, the "mandatory" injunction, if granted, would not require onerous work on the part of the league, as it would in a case where a plaintiff seeks to compel construction of part of a building.[77] Also in relation to the above example, the important point should be noted that where there is an indication from the European Commission that it views a particular transaction as contrary to Community law, then such an indication, though not binding on a national court, is a factor to be taken into account in the exercise of the court's discretion whether to grant or withhold an injunction.[78] So wide

---

[77] As in *Shepherd Homes v. Sandham* [1971] Ch 340.

[78] See *Lancombe v. Etos* [1980] ECR 2511, ECJ at para 11 (reference under Article 177 of the Treaty of Rome, from the Netherlands); cf. Green and Robertson *Commercial Agreements and Competition Law*, 2nd ed. (Kluwer, 1997) para. 7.112; *Notice on co-operation between national courts and the Commission in applying Articles 85 and 86 of the EEC Treaty*, issued by the EC Commission (OJ 1993 C-39/6).

is the discretion of the judge hearing the application for interim relief, that in practice factors such as an indication from the Commission are likely to be of considerably greater weight than mainly semantic arguments about the distinction between mandatory and prohibitory injunctions which in any event is not a rigid distinction.[79]

8.56   It is necessary at this point to mention the issue of delay. It cannot be stressed too often that delay is usually fatal to an application for an interim injunction in a sporting case. The seasonal nature of most sports make it imperative that the players, clubs and organising bodies concerned know where they stand for the following season. Litigation can only with difficulty be collapsed into the period between two seasons, and only by adopting truncated timetables in a speedy trial case, or deciding the issue taking account of the merits where one is impossible. The maxim that equity aids the vigilant and not the indolent is of respectable antiquity in English law. The court may, and often does, refuse an injunction in a case where the plaintiff has slept on its rights and is guilty of undue delay amounting to laches.[80] The problem of delay is particularly acute in sporting cases which are usually inherently urgent.

8.57   Delay is the banana skin on which plaintiffs are more likely to slip than any other. In *Stevenage Borough FC Limited v. The Football League Limited* Carnwath J refused an injunction more on the ground of delay than on any other ground. It will be recalled that Stevenage had won the Vauxhall Conference and had thus fulfilled the sporting criterion for entry to the Football League. The judge found aspects of the league's other entry criteria open to objection on restraint of trade grounds. Nevertheless, he refused relief because Stevenage had waited until they had won the Conference before launching the proceedings, near the end of the season and only three months or so before the start of the next. The judge said that this might seem fair to Stevenage but it was not fair to all the other clubs and people involved. The criteria it sought to challenge had been in place for over a year and Stevenage had not raised objection at general meetings of the Conference which had been consulted. The commercial risk of launching proceedings at substantial cost with the risk of losing, was not a factor that impressed the judge.

8.58   He attached particular importance to the position of Torquay United, which had come bottom of the League and which would be relegated if Stevenage were promoted. True, that club had benefited adventitiously from Stevenage's failure to comply with the criteria, but that did not alter the point that it had presumably organised its affairs on the assumption that it would not be relegated. The

---

[79] See also *Locabail International Finance v. Agroexport* [1986] 1 WLR 657; *Rover International v. Cannon Film Sales* [1987] 1WLR 670, Hoffmann J; *Nottingham Building Society v. Eurodynamic Systems plc* [1993] FSR 468, citing *Leisure Data v. Bell* [1988] FSR 376, CA.

[80] See Spry, *The Principles of Equitable Remedies*, 5th ed. (1997) *supra.*, n. 71, at pp. 414–16.

judge also took into account certain misleading comments made by Stevenage to Torquay United's management to the effect that Stevenage would not be promoted if they won the Vauxhall Conference. The moral of this difficult case is that clubs must, despite the commercial risk of litigation, proceed at the earliest possible opportunity if they wish to challenge the rules governing entry to competitions. To wait until the club may itself benefit from such a challenge is to wait too long.

The same reasoning would apply to relegation imposed as a disciplinary **8.59** penalty or as a consequence of deduction of points, as occurred in celebrated cases involving Tottenham Hotspur Football Club and Middlesbrough Football Club. A club from whose tally points are deducted as a disciplinary measure in mid-season, must not wait until it knows whether the consequence will be relegation before launching proceedings, if it wishes to do so, to challenge the validity of the deduction of points. That is a quite separate concern from any question as to whether the club has grounds for challenging such a deduction at all. In the case of Middlesbrough, it transpired that deduction of points in the middle of the 1997–98 season did make the difference between relegation and non-relegation (to the benefit of Coventry FC which had a windfall reprieve).[81] Yet in one case an inordinate two year delay by Newport Football Club was, with some hesitation, allowed by Jacob J not to block an injunction against the Welsh Football Association. There was no adequate explanation for the delay, which caused the judge "the greatest concern".[82] The judge commented that it was a wholly exceptional case in that the club's very existence was at risk. No prejudice to the defendant Association or third party clubs was adverted to by the judge, though the Association relied strongly on delay and consequent changes to the status quo during the period of the delay.

Interlocutory injunctions also feature in disputes between sportsmen and **8.60** women, and their employer clubs or managers. In ordinary employment law, an employer may wish to prevent its employee or former employee, from joining another employer or establishing a competing business. This is achieved by two principal methods, the first being a restrictive covenant whereby the employee agrees not to engage in certain competitive activities during employment and for a time thereafter; and the second being a contractual provision, embodied in an express term or otherwise, giving the employer rights to retain a contractual relation with the employee even if the latter is not actively working, provided the employee is paid in full. Arrangements of the latter type are often described as "garden leave" arrangements.

These types of arrangement between employer and employee are fully docu- **8.61** mented in specialist works on employment law, and we do not purpose to

---

[81] See also *Ray v. Professional Golfers Association Limited*, transcript, 15 April 1996 at p. 12B-E (golfer refused injunction to challenge PGA's eligibility criteria, *inter alia*, on ground of delay).

[82] *Newport AFC Limited v. FA of Wales Limited* [1995] 2 All ER 87 at 99b-f.

explain their scope here. They have drawbacks. Restrictive covenants offend against the restraint of trade doctrine if they go further than reasonably necessary to protect the employer's legitimate business interests. Both types of contract term are only enforceable subject to the discretion of the court in an interim injunction application, which may, moreover, take place too late to be of much practical benefit to the employer. As already noted above, normally it is not possible for an employer to obtain specific performance of a contract of employment, for that would be tantamount to personal servitude; nor, conversely, may an employee normally specifically enforce his own employment contract by means of an interim injunction to restrain his dismissal.[83]

8.62   In the sporting field, the position is no different, with the consequence that a manager may not normally restrain his clients from dispensing with his services, even though to do so may be in breach of a valid exclusive services agreement. That was the outcome in *Warren v. Mendy*.[84] The boxing manager and promoter Frank Warren was unable to prevent the well known boxer Nigel Benn from dispensing with Mr Warren's services and working for a new manager, Mr Mendy, during the currency of Benn's contract with Mr Warren, which still had some two and a half years to run. The high degree of mutual trust and confidence between the parties was a factor strongly militating against the grant of an injunction which, in practice, could have the effect of compelling performance of the contract. That did not affect the availability of damages as a remedy.

8.63   In *Colchester United FC Ltd v. Burley and Ipswich Town FC Ltd*,[85] Colchester claimed damages against George Burley, its former player-manager, and against Ipswich Town, alleging that Mr Burley had departed to become manager of Ipswich Town in breach of his contract to play for and manage Colchester. Although Mr Burley had departed during 1995, his contract with Colchester required him to remain until 30 June 1996. An injunction was not sought by Colchester, and could not have been obtained. Damages were also claimed against Ipswich Town for inducing breach of Mr Burley's contract, a cause of action which often goes hand in hand with a claim to enforce a negative covenant. The decision of Sir John Wood in the High Court turned on the effect of an arbitration clause in the rules of the Football Association, but the case draws out the point that an injunction could in principle be obtained to pre-

---

[83] See generally *Harvey on Industrial Relations and Employment Law* (Butterworths, 1995) at A[691] et seq.; *Page One Records Limited v. Britton* [1968] 1 WLR 157; *Warner Brothers Pictures Inc v. Nelson* [1937] 1 KB 209 (the Bette Davis case); cf. *Hill v. Parsons and Co Limited* [1972] Ch 305, CA; *Powell v. London Borough of Brent* [1988] ICR 176, CA. For a useful comparative survey of the English and North American approaches including an account of US and Canadian authority, see McCutcheon, "Negative Enforcement of Contracts in the Sports Industries", *SPTL Journal* Vol. 17 No. 1 (March 1997).

[84] [1989] ICR 525, CA.

[85] Unreported, transcript, 30 October 1995, Sir John Wood.

vent the employee from working for another club (and against that other club to prevent it employing him), even though the court would not by injunction require the employee to work for his old club. The principle is subject to the discretion of the court to leave the first club to its remedy in damages in a case where an injunction would unjustifiably sterilise the talents of a former employee determined not to stay with his old employer.

The same principles can crop up in a case where the contract requires perfor- **8.64** mance of particular sporting obligations, rather than an exclusivity arrangement over a period of time. In *Clansmen Sporting Club Ltd v. Robinson*[86] the plaintiff promoters of the 1993 World Boxing Organisation featherweight championship contracted with the defendant boxer to promote his next three bouts should he win the championship. He duly won, allowed the plaintiff to promote his next two fights, but refused in the case of the third, alleging that his exclusivity obligations were void as a breach of the rules of the World Boxing Organisation. The court held that those rules were not incorporated into the plaintiff's option agreement and accordingly held that the plaintiff had a right to restrain the defendant from fighting a third bout under other auspices. Generally, the court will be more willing to intervene by injunction to restrain a one-off sporting obligation than to restrain general obligations lasting over a period.[87]

To complete our brief account of interlocutory injunctions in the English law **8.65** relating to sport, we should mention finally the important principle, which may help to shorten proceedings and save legal costs, that an appeal will not be entertained from an order which it was within the discretion of the judge to make, unless it can be shown that he exercised his discretion under a mistake of law or in disregard of principle, or that he took into account irrelevant matters or failed to exercise his discretion, or that the conclusion he reached was outside the generous ambit within which a reasonable disagreement is possible.[88]

Interim relief may also be available under other systems of law, and in sports **8.66** law proceedings before international or other arbitral tribunals. The extent to which such relief is available depends on the procedural rules governing the proceedings under consideration. The most important international tribunal dealing with sports law disputes is the CAS. It has the power to order "provisional and conservatory measures", and normally acts on similar principles to those governing interlocutory injunctions in English law, though the threshold of merit which a plaintiff must attain is perhaps rather higher than under *American Cyanamid v. Ethicon Limited*.[89] In Swiss law, which the CAS very often applies,

---

[86] *The Times*, 22 May 1995.

[87] See also Oliver J's decision in *Nichols Advanced Vehicle Systems Inc v. De Angelis*, unreported, transcript 21 December 1979 (Italian Formula 1 racing driver "defected" in mid-contract to Lotus team; injunction to prevent him driving for Lotus refused).

[88] See *Hadmor Productions v. Hamilton* [1983] 1 AC 191, per Lord Diplock at p. 220; *G v. G* [1985] 1 WLR 647, HL, per Lord Fraser at pp. 650-3.

[89] [1975] AC 397; cf. CAS Rules of Procedure, Rule 43.

a "prima facie showing" is sufficient, which means that "reasonable chances of success" must be shown. If that initial hurdle is surmounted, the CAS takes into account three considerations: "first, irreparable harm to the Claimants; second, likelihood of success on the merits; and third, a balance of interests".[90]

8.67   The ad hoc proceedings of the CAS during the Atlanta Olympics in 1996 were by their nature more likely than most proceedings to throw up claims for immediate relief of the utmost urgency. Under the ad hoc rules of procedure, the President of the Ad Hoc Division, or the panel if it had already been set up, was empowered to grant "a stay of execution of the decision being challenged or other provisional relief ex parte". The test applied by the panel was

> "whether the relief is necessary to protect the applicant from irreparable harm, whether the applicant is likely to succeed on the merits, and whether the interests of the applicant outweigh those of the opponent or of other members of the Olympic community."[91]

Multiplicity of proceedings

8.68   Sometimes a question arises in a sporting dispute as to which forum is appropriate for its resolution. In *Enderby Town FC Ltd v. The Football Association Ltd*[92] the FA appointed a commission which found gross negligence in the management of the plaintiff club. The club appealed to the FA on certain points of law "of much complexity and difficulty",[93] which were that the charge was not properly formulated, that it was heard by three men without jurisdiction to hear it, and that the relevant rule on its true construction did not apply to club companies which were not members of the FA. The Court of Appeal, applying a dictum of Romer LJ in *Lee v. The Showmen's Guild of Great Britain*,[94] refused the club an injunction to stop the FA hearing the appeal unless it permitted the club to be legally represented. They reasoned that the rules did not permit representation in every case, and the club had not sought to bring the points of law before the High Court in an action for a declaration.

8.69   The inference is that, had the club brought an action for a declaration, the High Court would have determined the points of law and, presumably, compelled the FA by injunction to refrain from hearing the appeal until the points of law had been determined. However, the current FA rules provide for legally

---

[90] *AEK Athens FC and Slavia Prague FC v. UEFA*, CAS 98/200, Procedural Order on Application for Preliminary Relief, 17 July 1998, paras 29 and 40.

[91] Report of the President of the Ad Hoc Division in Mealey's *International Arbitration Report*, February 1997, p. 20, at 23.

[92] [1971] 1 All ER 215, CA.

[93] Per Lord Denning MR at 217d-e.

[94] [1952] 2 QB 329, CA at 354: "the proper tribunals for the determination of legal disputes in this country are the courts and they are the only tribunals which, by training and experience, and assisted by properly qualified advocates, are fitted for the task".

qualified members to sit on FA appeals, and also an arbitration clause. Now that the rules of many sporting bodies are more sophisticated than in the 1970s, the involvement of the courts in the middle of disciplinary proceedings is less likely, though the possibility cannot be disregarded.

Some five years later, another attempt was made to stop disciplinary pro- **8.70** ceedings by application to the High Court while a disciplinary complaint was pending. The boxer, John Conteh, asked for an injunction to restrain the British Boxing Board of Control from hearing a disciplinary complaint against him. The basis of the claim for an injunction was that an action against him, his former manager and promoter, was pending in the Queen's Bench Division of the High Court.[95] The Court of Appeal held that it has "power to restrain the hearing of a complaint by a domestic tribunal if in special circumstances the interests of justice so demand".[96] The Court allowed the appeal and granted an injunction restraining the Board of Control from hearing the disciplinary case, reasoning that the misconduct charge pending against Mr Conteh raised exactly the same issue as that in the High Court proceedings, namely whether Mr Conteh at the relevant date was bound by the very contracts for breach of which he was sued in those proceedings. The Court was unwilling to countenance duplication of proceedings where the disciplinary case would "amount to a prehearing of the issue pending in the High Court action . . ."[97] and accorded priority to the Court over the domestic body as a preferred forum.

Whether or not an injunction or stay will be granted in cases where there are **8.71** concurrent proceedings is a question of fact in each case. The *Conteh* case was a rare one in which there was (to use a phrase taken from a different context) not merely "virtual total eclipse",[98] but total eclipse of the issues in the respective proceedings. Normally, such a stay will be difficult to obtain, for the

> "power to intervene to prevent injustice where the continuation of one set of proceedings may prejudice the fairness of the trial of other proceedings . . . is a power which has to be exercised with great care and only where there is a real risk of serious prejudice which may lead to injustice."[99]

If the court is satisfied that, absent a stay or injunction, there is a real risk of such prejudice, then the court has to balance that risk against the countervailing considerations, which may include a strong public interest in seeing that the disciplinary process is not impeded.[100] But unless the party seeking a stay can show

---

[95] *Conteh v. Onslow-Fane, The Times* 26 June 1975, transcript 25 June 1975, CA.

[96] Transcript p. 13 G-H.

[97] *Ibid.*, p. 15D-E.

[98] See *R v. ICAEW ex parte Brindle* [1994] BCC 297, CA; *R v. Chance ex parte Smith* [1995] BCC 1095, CA at 1103H.

[99] *R v. Panel on Takeovers and Mergers ex parte Fayed* [1992] BCC 524, per Neill LJ at 531E.

[100] Per Dyson J in *R v. Executive Council of the Joint Disciplinary Scheme ex parte Hipps*, transcript, 12 June 1996, at p. 13B-C.

a real risk of serious prejudice which may lead to injustice, a stay must be refused.[101] Moreover, at least in disciplinary proceedings where a strong public interest is in play, the court will give great weight to the view of the person or body responsible for the decision as to the factors of militating against a stay and the weight to be given to them, though the court is the ultimate arbiter of what is fair.[102]

Damages

8.72   It is well known to lawyers and non-lawyers alike that damages are available as a remedy for breach of contract and other forms of civil wrong such as torts. The principles on which damages are awarded could fill an entire book, and indeed do fill an entire book, much longer than this one.[103] In contract, the fundamental principle is that the measure of damages should be such as to put the innocent party in the financial position he or she would have been in had the breach not occurred. In tort, the principle is that the plaintiff should be put in the position, so far as money can do it, he would have been in had the tort not been committed. Although damages are nearly always claimed in civil proceedings arising in the field of sport, they are rarely awarded at the end of a trial, for the reason already noted above that an injunction or declaration is usually the remedy uppermost in the plaintiff's mind.

8.73   Damages are therefore a less important arrow in the quiver of the sporting plaintiff. Far more important is the threat or spectre of having to honour an undertaking in damages, which is the normal price for an interim injunction as explained above. However, there are cases in which damages have figured prominently as a remedy. In *Modahl v. British Athletic Federation Limited*,[104] Ms Modahl brought an action claiming damages by way of out of pocket expenses of £250,000 and loss of earnings of some £230,000, plus interest. The sole remedy claimed was damages, because Ms Modahl had already been exonerated by an appeal panel of the Federation following a doping charge of which she had previously been found guilty by a disciplinary committee. Media reports of the proceedings stated that she wished to highlight the defects in the Federation's doping procedures.

---

[101] *Ex parte Fayed, supra.*, n. 95 at 531; *ex parte Brindle supra.*, n. 94 at 316G-H.

[102] *Ex parte Smith* at 1101F-G, 1102H–1103F; and *R v. Panel on Takeovers and Mergers ex parte Guinness plc* [1990] 1 QB 146, per Lloyd LJ at 184D-E. But see also Houseman, *Staying Disciplinary Proceedings: Whatever Happened to ex parte Brindle ?* [1999] JR 60, arguing that the "deferential approach" to the views of the inquisitor shown in *ex parte Smith* and *ex parte Hipps* "rests upon a misapplication of Lloyd LJ's dictum in *ex parte Guiness*" (at p. 184B, mentioned above) uttered in the context of supervisory, not original, jurisdiction, and "constitutes an undue restriction upon the court's accepted jurisdiction" to stay domestic proceedings.

[103] See *McGregor on Damages*, 16th ed. (Sweet and Maxwell, 1997).

[104] Transcript, 28 July 1997, CA.

Her claim survived a striking out application, as already noted in the previ- **8.74** ous chapter, but it is unlikely that damages would be available in a case where the internal disciplinary system has operated to correct a defect at first instance through an acquittal on appeal. Ms Modahl was forced to rely on breaches of doping procedures prescribed in the disciplinary code and on an alleged implied term in her contract with the Federation that she would have a fair and impartial hearing at first instance as well as on appeal. It would be surprising if the court were to hold that such a term exists rather than the generally accepted narrower term that a plaintiff must receive fair treatment overall in the operation of a disciplinary process, including its appellate stage.[105]

It would be a different matter if a sportsman or woman had received unfair **8.75** treatment overall and been wrongly convicted through breaches of fair procedure, bad faith or other unlawful conduct. In such a case the right to damages could not seriously be in doubt. However we are not aware of any case in which they have been awarded for wrongful disciplinary action in sport. George Eastham, the footballer, did not succeed in his claim for damages against the directors of Newcastle United Football Club. It was not a disciplinary case, but one in which the club had acted in restraint of trade. That is not a wrong for which damages can be obtained; the only consequence is that the plaintiff can avoid the restraint.[106] Contractual claims also failed in *Newport AFC Ltd v. FA of Wales Ltd*[107], where the judge refused to infer or imply a term in Newport's contract with the FA of Wales whereby the latter undertook not to act in restrain of trade. In any case, the losses had been suffered after Newport's resignation from the Welsh FA, so the losses would not have flowed from any breach in any case.

As to damages for negligence, there is as yet no clear authority to support the **8.76** proposition that a drug tester owes a sportsman or woman a duty of care to conduct the test carefully. However, given the current controversy over testing procedures generally, it may be that such a case will be brought. On ordinary principles of professional negligence it may be held that a duty is owed, though the scope of any duty is another question. It could be argued that the drug tester's duty is primarily owed to his or her employer, the sports body, in the same way as a doctor engaged by an insurance company to examine a person for the purpose of an insurance quote is thought to owe only a limited duty to the person examined, not to damage him physically.[108] If the duty, and a breach of

[105] *Calvin v. Carr* [1980] AC 575, PC; cf. *Lloyd v. McMahon* [1987] 1 AC 625, HL.
[106] *Eastham v. Newcastle United FC Ltd supra.*, n. 44.
[107] Transcript, 12 April 1995, Blackburne J at pp. 55–7.
[108] See the discussion in *X v. Bedfordshire County Council* [1995] 2 AC 633, HL (psychiatrists and social workers); and in *Phelps v. London Borough of Hillingdon*, CA, transcript 4 November 1998 (educational psychologist; pending in HL); cf. *Charlesworth and Percy on Negligence*, 9th ed., (Sweet and Maxwell, 1996) para. 8–18, and *Spring v. Guardian Assurance* [1995] 2 AC 296, HL, per Lord Goff at 318; Lord Lowry at 325; Lord Woolf at 342.

it, could be established in law and on the facts, damages would in principle be available but proof of causation and recoverable loss could be difficult, particularly in amateur sports where no significant financial value can easily be directly ascribed to loss of the opportunity to win a medal.[109]

8.77   In claims founded on economic torts, there is a potential for very large sums to be awarded as damages in proceedings between organisations (through representatives) battling in the commercial arena for the right to enjoy the services of players and clubs and to organise competitions. Litigation of this type is likely to become more frequent as a by-product of the inexorable commercialisation of sport. In competition law claims, of the type discussed in chapters four and six above, the principles on which damages are awarded are not yet fully worked out. But in cases involving simple breach of contract and inducing breach of contract, or interference with the plaintiff's trade or business, loss is assessed on familiar principles. In the substantial litigation arising out of the attempt by a company controlled by Mr Rupert Murdoch to set up a super-league in Australian rugby league football, damages issues have been remitted for determination.[110]

8.78   Perhaps the most significant cases involving awards of damages, and certainly the most colourful, are those in which celebrated libel actions are brought by leading sporting figures. They do not illustrate any particular principles peculiar to sports law, but are really only instances of notorious libel actions in which the protagonists are titans in the world of sport. Unjustified allegations of ball tampering or other unsporting conduct in cricket provide entertainment for the media in the libel courts, as in recent cases involving Allan Lamb, Ian Botham, Imran Khan, and, very recently, Bruce Grobelaar. An entertaining account of earlier libel actions can be found in Professor Grayson's *Sport and the Law*.[111]

Unfair prejudice petitions in company law

8.79 A remedy well known to company lawyers but little used in the sporting field is the statutory one under section 459 of the Companies act 1985 (as amended by the Companies Act 1989), which enables a minority shareholder to petition the High Court for appropriate orders on the basis that the affairs of the company are being conducted in a manner unfairly prejudicial to him. In one Antipodean

---

[109] Cf. *Chaplin v. Hicks* [1911] 2 KB 786, CA; *Kitchen v. RAF Association* [1958] 2 All ER 241, CA; *Mulvaine v. Joseph* (1968) 112 SJ 927.

[110] *News Limited and Others v. Australian Rugby Football League Limited and Others* (1997) 139 ALR 193 (Federal Court of Australia).

[111] 2nd ed. (1994) at pp. 282-3 and 328–9, citing *Russell v. Duke of Norfolk* [1949] 1 All ER 109 and other cases; see also John Welcome's account of *Chapman v. Jockey Club*, an otherwise unreported libel action and appeal in the early 1930s, in New Law Journal, 24 January 1997.

case the Western Suburbs District Rugby League Football Club, with commendable ingenuity but no success, attempted to rely on the New South Wales equivalent of our own section 459.[112] The club was aggrieved at the decision of the defendant League to reduce the number of clubs participating in the premiership competition from 13 to 12 in late 1984, after its entry for the 1985 competition had been refused. Its representative plaintiffs initially obtained an order from Hodgson J restraining the League from implementing the decisions on the ground that they were oppressive in the statutory sense. The League's appeal was successful, and a further appeal by the club was unsuccessful.

The point that emerges from the two very short judgments, and which would **8.80** apply equally in this country, is that the court will not interfere with a decision well within the objects of the company which organises the competition in question, provided there is no bad faith, misdirection in law or taking into account of wrong considerations. The object of the League in the case in question included that of determining which clubs should enter which competitions. The court was astute to distinguish between adverse impact on the club, which the decision challenged undoubtedly had, and unfairness towards the club which was not made out.

Arbitration in sport

We now turn to consider remedies available in sporting disputes outside the **8.81** ordinary courts of law. As noted at the start of this chapter, we assume in the following exposition that internal domestic remedies, that is, before bodies constituted under the relevant domestic rules, have been exhausted. One does not need to dwell very long on the potential advantages of arbitration over court proceedings as an instrument of dispute resolution in sport. As in other fields where the advantages of arbitration are recognised, the benefits appreciated by users of arbitration services are those of specialist expertise, privacy, relative swiftness, and relatively modest cost. It should be said that not all those benefits are delivered to the full in every case that goes to arbitration. But in general they are sufficiently in evidence to have convinced these authors of the virtues of arbitral process over court proceedings, where the choice exists. We say that without the least disrespect to the judiciary, some of whose members are eminent and intellectually gifted sports lawyers who also, on occasion, serve as arbitrators themselves.[113]

---

[112] See Section 320 of the New South Wales Companies Code; and *Wayde v. New South Wales Rugby League Limited* (1985) 61 ALR 225.

[113] On arbitration of international sports disputes see Paulsson, *Arbitration of International Sports Disputes*, Arbitration International, vol.9 no. 4 p. 359. Paulsson argues that international sports federations which seek "maximal control" may find themselves in courts in any event if a party aggrieved by their decision has sufficient funds

8.82   Arbitration in English law is now governed by the Arbitration Act 1996, pro-
gressively superseding the earlier Acts of 1950, 1975 and 1979 and applying to
arbitrations commenced on or after 31 January 1997, and to applications made
on or after that date in respect of arbitrations not yet commenced. The main
purpose of the 1996 Act, as its preamble states, was to "restate and improve the
law relating to arbitration pursuant to an arbitration agreement".[114]

8.83   Arbitration in sport arises in two ways: an arbitration clause may be written
into the rules of a sporting association, requiring that an aggrieved member of the
association must proceed in accordance with the procedure established by the rule,
and not by court proceedings, as a means of resolving the dispute in question
between him and the association. Such a rule is conceptually distinct from a rule
creating a right of internal appeal against a decision of the association's lower
organs, for the latter does not involve recourse to an external body, but the former
does. An arbitration clause in a sporting body's rules presupposes a possible dispute between the member and the association, but a right of appeal merely provides for a second tier ruling emanating from within the association.

8.84   Attempts to resort to the courts without regard to an arbitration clause will normally generate a stay of proceedings by the court at the behest of the defendant.
Thus in *Colchester United FC Ltd v. Burley*[115] the High Court stayed Colchester's
claim because a web of complex rules (respectively of the Football League, the
Premier League and the Football Association) had the effect, on their true construction, that the dispute between Colchester, its former manager, and Ipswich
Town Football Club, fell within the relevant arbitration provisions. Colchester's
attempt to claim damages in court proceedings therefore failed.

8.85   However, the Football League failed to obtain a stay of proceedings brought
by Notts County Football Club against the League and Southend United

and determination. If, however, it wishes to avoid litigation, then agreement to arbitrate
provides the best prospect: "although arbitral awards may under the laws of most countries be challenged collaterally (e.g. if there has been some procedural irregularity) the
designated decision makers will thus have the authority to make definitive rulings on the
merits of the controversy".

[114] The leading text in the commercial sphere, the latest ed. of which however pre-
dates the Arbitration Act 1996, is Mustill and Boyd, *The Law and Practice of
Commercial Arbitration in England*, 2nd ed. (Butterworths, 1989). On the 1996 Act, see
Merkin, *The Arbitration Act 1996; an Annotated Guide* (Lloyds, 1997); Rutherford and
Sims, *The Arbitration Act 1996; a Practical Guide* (Law and Tax, The Financial Times,
1997); see also Cato, *Arbitration Practice and Procedure; Interlocutory and Hearing
Problems*, 2nd ed. (Lloyds, 1998).

[114a] See eg. Manchester United Football Club plc and FA Ltd and FA Premier League
Ltd about FA's power to overrule FA Premier League decision not to extend the 1996–7
football season at the request of Manchester United (Award 24 April 1997: Arbitrator
Michael J. Beloff QC).

[115] Unreported, transcript 30 October 1995. *Quaere* whether the result would have
been the same if the case had been decided under the Arbitration Act 1996, section 9 of
which is more narrowly worded than its predecessors in the Acts of 1950 and 1979.

Football Club[116] in which Notts County sought a determination under Order 14A of the Rules of the Supreme Court that Southend United had no right of appeal under the relevant rules against the League's dismissal of Southend United's complaint that its manager had been approached by Notts County contrary to a League rule. The League commission had declared itself unsatisfied that a breach of the rule had been committed when the manager was approached, but went on to note that Southend United had a right of appeal. Notts County asked the court to make a determination to the contrary effect, and the League asked the court to stay Notts County's action so that the question whether or not Southend really did have a right of appeal could be determined by arbitration under Rule 41(a) of the rules of the Football Association.

8.86 This procedural entanglement was duly unravelled by Neuberger J who held, having heard full argument on the point, that he was, exceptionally, prepared to decide it. He did so on the basis of then current authority to the effect that a point of law not requiring resolution of contested facts, may be resolved on a summary judgment application before a court notwithstanding any arbitration clause.[117] The judge noted that the cost of further arbitration proceedings would be disproportionate, and felt that he might as well decide the point notwithstanding the League's powerful arguments for a stay, which included the point that the international governing body of football, FIFA, requires under Article 58 of its rules all clubs of its member associations to refrain from litigating in court "until all the possibilities of sports jurisdiction within, or under the responsibility of their national association have been exhausted". Moreover, Article 58 also required national member associations, including the Football League, to "ensure, as far as they can competently do so, that their clubs . . . observed this obligation", on pain of "being suspended from all international activity . . . in addition to receiving a ban on all international matches . . .". So the Football League was clearly wise to do what it could to prevent the involvement of the court. The judge, having decided to entertain the matter, then construed the relevant rules as conferring a right of appeal on Southend, so the action failed.

8.87 An arbitration clause is unlikely to displace the right of access to court in a case where the claim is for membership of a body, rather than a claim by an existing member against the body. This is because the non-member will, *ex hypothesi*, not be bound by an arbitration clause in the rules of the body of which it seeks to become a member. However, such a claim may nevertheless proceed by arbitration, either through an ad hoc agreement (of the type further considered below) or through the medium of an arbitration clause in the rules of an umbrella body of which both parties are members such as, in the case of

[116] *Notts Incorporated Football Club Limited v. The Football League Limited and Southend United FC Limited*, unreported, transcript 28 November 1996 (Neuberger J).

[117] *SL Sethia Liners Limited v. State Trading Corporation of India Limited* [1986] 2 All ER 395, per Kerr LJ at 396h–397b (a case decided under the Arbitration Act 1975).

football, the Football Association. Thus in the case of *Stevenage Borough FC Limited v. The Football League Limited*,[118] Stevenage claimed a right of membership of the Football League, but was already a member of the Football Association, which also exercised supervisory powers over various football bodies including the Football League. The Association's rules contained an arbitration clause but it did not, by its terms, cover the dispute. If the rules of the body in question do not contain an arbitration clause at all, or the clause does not apply to the dispute as in the *Stevenage* case, then arbitration may only be used to resolve the dispute if both parties consent. This not infrequently occurs.

8.88   For example, Enfield Town Football Club agreed to submit its dispute with the Vauxhall Conference to arbitration pursuant to an ad hoc agreement, after Enfield Town had come top in the league immediately below the level of the Conference. The Conference had refused to admit Enfield Town, asserting that it did not comply with the Conference's financial criteria. Enfield unsuccessfully argued that those criteria were an unreasonable restraint of trade, but the arbitrators disagreed.[119] Similarly, in the case (discussed above in chapter three) in which Tottenham Hotspur regained admission to the FA Cup and had six Premiership points restored to it, the matter proceeded by way of arbitration pursuant to an ad hoc agreement announced to the media before the arbitration took place.

8.89   A final point to note in cases where disputes are submitted to arbitration by consent, is that the scope of the arbitrators' jurisdiction is strictly limited by the contents of the agreement. In one case in which two of the authors were involved, their opponents sought to argue that their clients were precluded by estoppel from advancing one of their arguments. The arbitrators held that they had no jurisdiction to entertain the estoppel argument which fell outside the purview of the arbitration agreement.

8.90   International arbitration in sport is a fast developing field of legal practice of growing importance and benefit to sport, and a major contributor to the incipient international *lex sportiva* which, we argue in this book, is in the process of taking shape.[120] But we are far from able to say that there is a developed and

[118] [1997] 9 Admin.LR 109, CA.

[119] *Enfield Town v. Vauxhall Conference*, arbitration chaired by Sir Michael Kerr, referred to by Carnwath J in *Stevenage Borough FC Limited v. The Football League Limited supra.*, n. 67 at p. 39 of the transcript.

[120] A recent example of a major sporting arbitration (drawn from our professional experience) is the case subsequently reported in the media which arose under the "Concorde Agreement" of 22 May 1998 between the teams that compete in the Formula One championship, the Fédération Internationale de l'Automobile (FIA) and Formula One Administration Limited, which provides for any dispute arising in connection with the agreement to be submitted to arbitration under the rules of the International Chamber of Commerce (ICC). This provision was the foundation for the unsuccessful challenge by arbitration to the FIA's resolution requiring cars entered by each team to be painted in the same livery (ICC Arbitration Award of 3 February 1999, Case no. 10211/AER).

harmonious system of international legal machinery for dispute resolution in sport. Intractable problems of lack of uniformity and lack of mutual recognition between different bodies persist. The role of national courts varies from one country to another, and the extent to which they intervene in international arbitral process is not uniform. In our view they should intervene as little as possible, since otherwise the development of the international machinery will be hampered.

The principal engine of international sports dispute resolution has been the **8.91** Olympic movement, which lies at the heart of the legal processes driving the development of international sports law. The legal instruments produced by the Olympic movement differ from international treaties in that the movement is non-governmental, its members being national associations, not sovereign states. At present, the Olympic Charter falls well short of being a transnational constitution for sport. No one institution has a monopoly of jurisdiction over sport internationally. Jurisdictional and forum issues therefore abound.

However, what have correctly been termed "normative trends"[121] have been **8.92** identified: national sports bodies resolve disputes within their sports and within their borders; international federations review decisions of national bodies within a particular sport; National Olympic Committees operate across different sports and intervene in disputes at a national level; the organs of the International Olympic Committee or an international federation may review a decision of a National Olympic Committee; independent arbitration panels may deal with ad hoc disputes; and finally the courts of various countries may become involved, and in particular normally recognise and enforce foreign arbitration awards or court judgments to the extent that their national law so provides, in accordance with international agreements and principles of comity, reciprocity and judicial cooperation.

The International Council of Arbitration in Sport (ICAS) exists to promote **8.93** dispute resolution in sport without the need for recourse to national courts. It is composed of twenty members appointed by the international sports federations, the Association of National Olympic Committees and the International Olympic Committee. The ICAS has created the Court of Arbitration for Sport (CAS). An example of the difficulties which remain is provided by cases highlighting discrepancies between the International Olympic Committee Medical Code, applying to doping cases, and the rules of the International Amateur Athletic Federation (IAAF). The IOC Medical Code includes an appeal procedure with a right of final appeal to the CAS. But the IAAF, like certain other international bodies governing particular sports, neither recognises the ICAS nor the CAS. Other international governing bodies, including in football UEFA – but notably not FIFA – and in swimming FINA, do recognise the CAS. Some international bodies, including UEFA, have an exclusive jurisdiction clause in

---

[121] See Nafziger, "International sports law as a process for resolving disputes", [1996] Vol. 45 ICLQ 130 at 133.

their governing statutes giving sole jurisdiction over disputes between it and its members or others with standing to pursue a dispute, to the CAS.[122]

8.94   An example of the difficulties that arise through lack of uniform provision is found in the celebrated case involving the runner Katrine Krabbe. The IAAF has provision in its rules for arbitration before an independent panel of arbitrators. The IAAF had penalised Ms Krabbe for allegedly taking a banned substance, but the independent arbitration panel constituted under IAAF rules held that she could not be guilty of a doping offence because her national federation made no provision (although the IAAF did) for out-of-competition testing. The IAAF arbitration provisions also cover[123] disputes between the IAAF itself and its national member associations, for example in a case where the national association has dealt with a doping case in a manner which the IAAF considers to be flawed by misdirection or an erroneous conclusion in the conduct or conclusion of the hearing. In the *Capobianco* case, already mentioned in chapter seven, that procedure was successfully deployed by the IAAF to overturn a decision of a member association to acquit one of its athletes of a doping offence.

8.95   The same result was reached in the *Decker Slaney*[124] case arising from a positive test revealing the presence of an abnormally high level of testosterone at the Atlanta Olympic trials in June 1996. The domestic member association of the IAAF concerned, USA Track and Field Inc., had purported to exonerate Ms Decker Slaney on the grounds that no prohibited substance was found in the body tissue or fluids of the athlete, and the IAAF's definition relating to testosterone is vague and inconsistent, making it impossible to determine the definitive criteria for determining when a testosterone to epitestosterone ratio ("T/E ratio") positive has occurred. However the arbitrators reversed the decision, declaring on the basis of expert evidence that it was "satisfied beyond reasonable doubt . . . that, if an athlete is found to have a T/E ratio significantly in excess of 6:1, that ratio would not be consistent with normal endogenous production."[125] The panel imposed a mandatory two year ban, not all of which was served in full due to the timing of the hearing.

8.96   In the arbitration in the case of *Bevilacqua* the Italian high jumper of that name was not represented, but her national federation, the Federazione Italiana di Atletica Leggera (FIDAL) appeared to defend the decision of its prosecutor not to bring a disciplinary charge against her following an alleged doping offence just before the Atlanta Olympics in 1996. The arbitration did not take

---

[122] But such a rule may not, depending on its wording, confer a right of appeal on a federation against a decision favourable to the player in a doping case: *Korda v. International Tennis Federation Ltd.*, transcript, 29 January 1999, *The Times* 4 February 1999, Lightman J (ITF could not appeal against a decision by its appeals committee not to impose a ban on the ground of exceptional circumstances).

[123] See IAAF rule 21.3(ii).

[124] *Decker Slaney and USATF v. IAAF*, Arbitration Award, 25 April 1999.

[125] Arbitration Award, 25 April 1999, para. 35, p. 7.

place until after the Olympics. The IAAF argued that the IOC Medical Code had never been ratified by the IAAF and did not form part of its rules. The IAAF's own rules provided for strict liability in doping cases, whereas the IOC Medical Code included a defence of innocent ingestion without negligence. The eventual ruling went in favour of Ms Bevilacqua and FIDAL, but the arguments put by each side again illustrate the point that lack of uniform jurisdiction, and lack of uniform provision, hampers the fight against drugs in sport.

In the case of England and Wales, we have already touched on the role of **8.97** national courts. The rule of the IAAF seeking to make resort to the courts itself a breach of the rules attracting a penalty, is undoubtedly invalid.[126] In *Reel v. Holder*[127] the English Court of Appeal was prepared to hold that the IAAF had misinterpreted its rules permitting only one member association for each country in that it had allowed athletes from China to compete, to the exclusion of Taiwanese athletes. The Court held that a country is not necessarily a recognised state but a term of art. This is consistent with the participation in the Olympic teams of athletes from places such as Hong Kong (before its restoration to China), Gibraltar, Puerto Rico and so on.

However in *Cowley v. Heatley*[128] the then Vice-Chancellor doubted whether **8.98** he had jurisdiction to review, by reference to rules of English law, a decision of the Commonwealth Games Federation concerning the interpretation of the term "domicil" used to determine eligibility to represent a particular country in the Commonwealth Games. The report in *The Times* includes the view of Browne-Wilkinson V-C:

> "that the constitution covered a large number of different nations in the Commonwealth with members upholding many different systems of law. In those circumstances it was the court's view that the articles of the constitution could not be governed by the law of one constituent member country."

In *Gasser v. Stinson*[129] Scott V-C commented:[130]

> "It is not entirely clear under what proper law the Rules of the IAAF fall to be construed and to be given effect. Since, however, the IAAF head offices are and have been since 1946 in London and are required to be there under Rule 2, it has been accepted by counsel that English law should be regarded as the relevant proper law, or, . . . as the law applicable to the issues in the case."

On that basis the judge entertained the attempt by Miss Gasser, a Swiss athlete, to have her ban overturned in a doping case.

---

[126] Cf *Enderby Town FC Limited v. Football Association Limited* [1971] 1Ch 591, 607; *St Johnstone Football Club v. Scottish Football Association Limited* (1965) SLT 171.
[127] [1981] 1 WLR 1226, CA.
[128] *The Times*, 24 July 1986.
[129] Unreported, 16 June 1988, Scott J.
[130] Transcript p. 3A-B.

8.99   In the United States of America, recent case law has been a little confusing. In marathon litigation brought by Harry "Butch" Reynolds, a top class United States four hundred metres runner who had tested positive for the steroid nandrolone during a competition in Monaco, the courts in the United States handed down a bewildering array of decisions going as far as the Supreme Court.[131] Briefly, after initially failing in court and arbitration proceedings to overturn the IAAF's two year ban on him, Mr Reynolds sued the IAAF and the Athletics Congress alleging breach of contract, defamation, denial of due process and tortious interference with business relations. After various procedural battles and negotiations also involving the US Olympic Committee, the IAAF barred him from competing in the 1992 Games. Thereafter, amazingly, he obtained a default judgment for over US $27 million including treble punitive damages, followed by garnishee proceedings against four creditors of the IAAF. The saga ended after nearly four years with the Sixth Circuit Court of Appeals ordering the action to be dismissed for lack of jurisdiction, which the IAAF had never ceased to contest. Clearly, it would have been better if the jurisdictional issue had been decided at the start of the litigation, and not after twelve hearings before various courts and arbitration bodies.

8.100   The US courts did rather better in the litigation arising from an attack on an American figure skater, Nancy Kerrigan, shortly before the 1994 Winter Games. Her rival, Tonya Harding, was accused of complicity in the assault. The US Figure Skating Association (USFA) considered there was reason to suspect a violation of the Olympic code of fair play and in consequence the US Committee proposed to convene a disciplinary hearing in Norway. Ms Harding, however, sought an injunction against the US Olympic Committee to prevent the hearing taking place. She achieved her immediate objective of being able to compete in the Winter Games after which the deferred hearing took place, resulting in her enforced resignation from the USFA, which later stripped her of her 1994 title and banned her for life. The role of the court appears to have been mainly to broker the settlement enabling the disciplinary hearing to be deferred until after the Games.[132]

8.101   By contrast with the IAAF, the CAS has functioned successfully as an international sports dispute resolution body, effectively protected (so far) from undue interference by national courts with its proceedings. It is the only global sporting arbitral body, able to adjudicate in any sport involving any country, where its jurisdiction permits it to do so. Its strength and prestige undoubtedly derives from its pedigree as the official court of arbitration of the Olympic movement, established under the aegis of the ICAS in 1983. The most senior of the authors of this book sits on it as an arbitrator.

---

[131] *Reynolds v. IAAF* 23 F 3d 1110 (1994); 115 S. Ct 423 (1994); 968 F 2d 1216 (1992); 112 S. Ct 2512 (1992); No. C–2–91–003, 1991 WL 179760 (1991); 935 F 2d 270 (1991); and other unreported court and arbitration proceedings.

[132] *Harding v. United States Olympic Committee* No. CCV – 942151 (Clackamas County Cir. Or., 13 February 1994).

The CAS is based at Lausanne in Switzerland, but also sits in Sydney, **8.102**
Australia and Denver, Colorado. It has about one hundred and fifty arbitrators
chosen from some thirty-seven countries. It has determined well over one hundred disputes since 1990. It exercises jurisdiction either by virtue of rules forming part of a sporting body's constitution, or by virtue of an ad hoc arbitration
agreement. It sits in divisions: the Ordinary Arbitration Division, dealing with
disputes of first instance and rendering judgments which are confidential unless
the parties otherwise agree[133]; the Appeal Arbitrations Division, in which decisions are not confidential unless the parties so stipulate[134]; and ad hoc divisions
set up for particular events such as the Atlanta Olympic Games of 1996 and the
Commonwealth Games in Kuala Lumpur in 1998.

Since 1995 the Olympic Charter has provided, by Article 74, for submission **8.103**
to the CAS of "any dispute arising on the occasion of or in connection with the
Olympic Games . . . in accordance with the Code of Sports Related
Arbitration". For the first time in the 1996 Atlanta Olympics, the resulting
Olympic Division (officially named the Ad Hoc Division) was available to
resolve disputes occurring between the opening and closing of the Games. It
operated from a suite of rooms in an Atlanta hotel.[135] For the Atlanta Olympics,
competitors were required to sign an undertaking not to "constitute any claim,
arbitration or litigation, or seek any other form of relief in any other court or
tribunal [than the CAS Olympic Division]" an ouster clause which was never
tested in the local Georgia courts.

However, the *Swiss Equestrian* case[136] established that the CAS was an: **8.104**

"arbitral court whose decisions properly constitute arbitral awards at an
international level. The CAS therefore represents an alternative to state justice while, of course, respecting certain inalienable fundamental rights. This
neutral and independent institution is therefore in a postion to pronounce
final and enforceable awards which have the force of a judgment. Thus,
through recourse to the CAS, sports organisations, athletes and their partners
can avoid refering any disputes they might have to ordinary state courts for
settlement."[137]

Recourse to the Swiss courts would therefore be available only in the narrowest
of circumstances, as in a case where the CAS had fundamentally misdirected
itself in law. No such challenge has yet succeeded. In the case itself, the CAS had
upheld the disqualification of a horse and its rider after a banned substance was

---

[133] See rule R43 of the Code of Sports Related Arbitration.

[134] See *ibid.*, Rule R59.

[135] See Kaufmann-Kohler, *Mealey's International Arbitration Report*, February 1997,
Vol. 12 No. 1, at pp. 20–29; *SLJ*, Vol. 4 issue 3 (1996).

[136] *Gundel v. FEI/CAS*, 1 Civil Court, Swiss Fed. Trib. (15 March 1993).

[137] Citation from the judgment from 18 June 1993 of the Swiss Federal Tribunal, in
Olympic Review, July/August 1993 at p. 305.

found in the urine of the horse. The rider's appeal from the CAS (on his own behalf and *pro equo*) was dismissed with costs – a clear case of horses for courses.

8.105 With such effective judicial protection, the backing of the Olympic movement, and the potential to exercise jurisdiction over any sport in any country, the CAS has justly been described as a particularly promising institution for resolving sports-related disputes whose decisions are helping to articulate the norms of international sports law and strengthen its authority as a governing process.[138] In the absence of a different choice of law by the parties, the CAS applies Swiss law, and can also, with the consent of the parties, decide a case *ex aequo et bono.*[139] In the Atlanta hearings, which were deemed to take place in Switzerland, the CAS was required to decide a dispute "pursuant to the Olympic Charter, the applicable regulations, general principles of law and the rules of law, the application of which it deems appropriate".[140]

8.106 The "applicable regulations" included the IOC Medical Code relating to doping and the rules of international federations regarding the practice of each sport and the organisation of sporting events. The reference to rules deemed "appropriate" for application is familiar in international arbitration.[141] It includes conflict of laws rules relating to proximity or the system of law with which the dispute has the closest connection. The reference to "general principles of law" include those of international contract law mentioned in chapter one, such as *pacta sunt servanda, good faith, legitimate expectation, nulla poena sine lege,* proportionality of sanctions, the proper exercise of regulatory powers and principles of interpretation of regulatory texts.[142]

8.107 It is apparent from the above that presentation of a case before the CAS may require deployment of expertise in more than one legal system. A question that is likely to arise more frequently in future is the applicability of European Community law. EC law is applied by the courts of the member states of the European Union, and by the European Court of Justice at Luxembourg, in which several famous sporting disputes including the celebrated *Bosman* case have been resolved. The resolution of sports law disputes before the Court of Justice in the application of Community law is well documented and we have already discussed in chapters 4 and 6 the substance of Community law relating

---

[138] Nafziger, "International Sports Law as a process for resolving disputes", 1996 *ICLQ* Vol. 45 p. 130 (January 1996).

[139] See Code of Sports Related Arbitration Rule R45.

[140] Kaufmann-Kohler *Mealey's International Arbitration Report, supra.,* n. 135.

[141] Cf. e.g. Article 13.3 of the Arbitration Rules of the International Chamber of Commerce.

[142] As to the latter, see generally the Vienna Convention on the Law of Treaties which entered into force on 27 January 1980 and applies only to treaties concluded after if came into force, but "does no more than codify already existing public international law"(*Fothergill v. Monarch Airlines* [1981] AC 251 per Lord Diplock at p. 282C-D, referring specifically to Articles 31 and 32).

to sport.[143] In the *Beeuwsaert* case[144] the CAS took account of Community law in the context of a dispute between the parties as to the system of law that was applicable. The arbitrators did not expressly need to decide what law was applicable, but commented on the content of Community law as applied to the dispute, without ruling on its status. And in *AEK Athens FC and Slavia Prague FC v. UEFA*,[145] a CAS arbitration governed by Swiss law, it was agreed that the competition law provisions of the Treaty of Rome should be applied, as well as their Swiss law equivalent, even though Switzerland is not a member of the European Union, on the basis that the UEFA decision under challenge (prohibiting two or more commonly owned clubs from playing in the same UEFA run competition) had effects in the territory of both the European Union and Switzerland.

Several CAS decisions have already been discussed in earlier chapters. It represents the best hope for future harmonisation of international sports dispute resolution. But it is not expected ever to replace the referee on the field of play, for purely sporting decisions, such as whether a boxer threw a low punch, are not generally justiciable and will lead to the CAS refraining from interfering with the judgment of the body regulating the sport concerned.[146] The distinction between a purely sporting decision or rules and a rule of law not confined in its effect to the field of play, is not always easy to draw on the facts. Clearly refereeing decisions in the 1998 World Cup in France could not be interfered with, but appeals from them could raise questions of fair procedure and other recognised grounds for interference which might engage the attention of the CAS or other international arbitral bodies. If, as seems likely, "video refereeing" enters the world of football as it has that of cricket (in relation to LBW decisions only, at present)[147] the principle of immunity of a referee from challenge to on the spot decisions could be attenuated. Certain rules regulating eligibility to enter sporting competitions (as described in chaper three above) may also potentially raise questions as to where purely sporting rules end and where rules of law going beyond the field of play begin. **8.108**

---

[143] An unpublished background note of the European Commission dated 15 February 1999 on the application of competition rules to the sports sector provides a fascinating insight into the Commission's current thinking on Community competition law and sport, including observations on some of the issues currently arising in the jurisprudence of the CAS.

[144] CAS 1992/80.

[145] See Procedural Order of 17 July 1998, CAS 98/200.

[146] See *Mendy v. International Amateur Boxing Association*, decided at Atlanta during the 1996 Olympic Games.

[147] See Gardiner, "The Third Eye: Video Adjudication in Sport", in *Sport and the Law Journal*, Vol. 7 issue 1, pp. 26–9 (1999).

Jurisdiction, choice of law and conflict of laws

8.109 We have already demonstrated that sports law is an international phenomenon. In the last section we looked at some of the institutions involved in deciding disputes going beyond national frontiers. Where such disputes are not susceptible of resolution by those international institutions, they have to be decided in national courts but, as shown by the *Harding* and *Reynolds* cases from the USA, the *Swiss Equestrian* case from Switzerland, and *Cowley v. Heatley* in this country, national courts sometimes have to adjudicate on the question of their own jurisdiction and, if they accept jurisdiction, must decide which is the substantive system of applicable law. To do that, the national court must apply its country's rules of private international law. It may have to decide whether the case ought to be disposed of in another country's courts, by applying the doctrine of *forum conveniens*.

8.110 It is not appropriate in a book such as this to attempt a full exposition of English rules of private international law relevant to sport. Still less could we do so in relation to any other jurisdiction. English conflict of laws rules do not, generally, apply to sporting disputes any differently than to other disputes with an international dimension. Private international law is a vast subject and is covered admirably and in depth in specialist works.[148] Our aim here is the more limited one of identifying the main issues that may arise under the rubric of private international law in the context of sport, mentioning by way of example some instances in which the courts have resolved them. We hope thereby to assist the practitioner presented with a dispute involving an international dimension to focus correctly on the private international law issues which may arise in addition to, but are logically prior to, issues as to the merits of the dispute.

8.111 It may be a useful discipline for an English lawyer to consider these issues in the following order:

(1) Can the jurisdiction of the English court be established ?
(2) What is the proper law applicable to each cause of action ? And
(3) Is England the *forum conveniens*?

8.112 The question whether an action should be brought in England or elsewhere depends on a number of factors. A useful initial question to ask oneself is whether the case is one to which the Brussels Convention of 1968 and the Lugano Convention of 1988 applies. Very broadly, those conventions enact, where they apply, an elaborate code of jurisdictional rules common to all contracting states parties to them. The objective is to restrict multiplicity of proceedings in different countries. The Conventions apply in "civil and commercial

---

[148] The best account is in Dicey and Morris, *The Conflict of Laws*, 12th ed. (Sweet and Maxwell, 1993) and 4th Cum. Supp. (1997). See also Kaye, *Civil Jurisdiction and the Enforcement of Foreign Judgments* (Professional Books Ltd., 1987).

matters", in the sense of the term articulated in the case law decided under them. Sporting disputes are well capable of being civil and commercial matters. The Conventions do not apply (inter alia) to matters of administrative or public law, nor to arbitration proceedings. The principal foundation of jurisdiction under the Conventions over persons "domiciled" in a contracting state is the state in which the defendant is domiciled.

The Conventions were made part of English domestic law by the Civil **8.113** Jurisdiction and Judgments Act 1982, as amended by the 1991 Act of the same name. A full account of this area of law lies beyond the scope of this work.[149] The broad scheme of the Conventions is that where they apply, the legal nature of the claim determines which contracting state should be the venue for the action, or whether, in certain circumstances, proceedings may be brought in more than one contracting state. Where the Conventions apply, two practical consequences ensue: first, that the proceedings must be brought in the contracting state identified as the correct forum under its terms; and second, that the permission of the English Court to effect service of process in that jurisdiction is normally not required.[150]

If it is concluded that proceedings in England are appropriate, either on the **8.114** basis that the Conventions do not apply or because their rules dictate that England is the appropriate forum, it is still necessary to establish the jurisdiction of the English court over the case. This involves first considering the question of service of process on the defendants. If the proposed defendant has an established place of business in the United Kingdom, service is effected simply by posting or delivering the writ to that address.[151] Whether or not it has a place of business in this country can be determined, initially, by a search at Companies House, if the body in question is a company. In a dispute involving a national federation and its international counterpart, the former may well have a place of business in this country but the latter may not. In that event, leave to serve the international organisation outside the jurisdiction may be required under Order 11 of the Rules of the Supreme Court, if the organisation is located in a state which is not party to the Conventions.

If the court's permission to serve the defendant abroad is needed, an applica- **8.115** tion to the court must be made, and it must be shown that the case falls within RSC Order 11 rule 1. The most important causes of action in the sporting field to which that rule applies are governed by, respectively, rule 11(1)(b) (where an injunction is sought ordering the defendant to do or refrain from doing anything within the jurisdiction – for example a claim by a sporting body against a foreign player resident outside the jurisdiction to restrain him or her from competing in an English competition); rule 1(1)(c) (where the claim is brought against

---

[149] See the exposition in Dicey and Morris, *supra.*, n. 139, chapter 11, p. 270 ff.

[150] RSC Order 11 rule 1(2)(a), as from 26 April 1999 preserved (with slightly different wording) as part of Schedule 1 and Part 50.1(2) of the Civil Procedure Rules (CPR).

[151] RSC Order 10 rule 1(2)(a); now CPR Part 6.2(1)(b).

a person served within or outside the jurisdiction and the defendant outside the jurisdiction is a necessary or proper party to the proceedings); rule 11(1)(d) (where the claim is brought to enforce, rescind, dissolve, annul or otherwise affect a contract, and the contract was made within the jurisdiction, or through an agent within the jurisdiction on behalf of a foreign based principal, or is governed by English law, or contains a term conferring jurisdiction on the English court); rule 11(1)(e) (where the claim is for breach of a contract committed within the jurisdiction); and rule 1(1)(f) (where the action is founded on a tort and the damage is sustained or results from an act committed within the jurisdiction).

8.116   Thus in *Lennox Lewis v. The World Boxing Council and Frank Bruno*,[152] the boxer Lennox Lewis brought an action against Frank Bruno, who lived in England and could be served in England, and against the World Boxing Council (WBC), whose headquarters are in Mexico. Mr Lewis wished to restrain the defendants from implementing arrangements which would result in Mr Bruno accepting a challenge from Mr Mike Tyson instead of Mr Lewis. The latter was able to obtain leave in an ex parte application to serve the WBC in Mexico or Puerto Rico, where it also had a presence. Leave was obtained pursuant to Order 11 rule 1(1)(c) on the basis that the WBC was arguably a "necessary and proper party" to the action against Mr Bruno in England.[153] In the event, Rattee J subsequently held that suit against Mr Bruno in England was merely a peg on which to hang the action against the WBC,[154] which was the essence of the plaintiff's grievance. It therefore did not assist Mr Lewis that he was an Englishman suing an Englishman in England. Rattee J also held that the action against the WBC ought to proceed in Dallas, Texas, because of an exclusive jurisdiction clause in the rules of the WBC providing for compulsory mediation under its auspices in Dallas. The judge did not accept that such a process would be other than impartial and independent. In the event Mr Bruno may have regretted the result. With no injunction impeding his participation in the title bout, he was knocked out in the fifth round.

8.117   Another context in which questions of jurisdiction may arise is in cases of international transfers of players between clubs located in different states. Where the terms of such a transfer are in dispute, and the states in question are parties to the Conventions mentioned above, then those Conventions will govern the question of jurisdiction. However, transfers may also occur between clubs located within a single state subdivided into more than one jurisdiction. The most obvious example is the United Kingdom itself, in which Scotland and Northern Ireland are treated as different jurisdictions from that of England and Wales. Leave to serve process in Scotland is not needed under English proce-

---

[152] Unreported, transcript 3 November 1995, Rattee J.

[153] See *Seaconsar* [1994] 1 AC 438, esp. at 456F.

[154] See transcript p. 22D-F, applying *Multinational Gas and Petrochemical Co v. Multinational Gas and Petrochemical Services Ltd* [1983] Ch 258, per Dillon LJ at 285C.

dural rules.[155] Intra-UK disputes fall outside the terms of the Brussels and Lugano Conventions but similar allocation of jurisdiction rules are enacted for the United Kingdom by the Civil Jurisdiction and Judgments Act 1982 (as amended).

In one matter involving two of these authors a question arose whether the **8.118** English or Scottish courts would have jurisdiction over a dispute concerning the transfer of a player between clubs, as it were, over Hadrian's wall. Two points emerged from consideration of the position: first, and importantly, the English court has jurisdiction to grant interim relief where proceedings have been or are to be commenced in another part of the United Kingdom.[156] Second, there was a risk, on the particular facts, that both the Scottish and the English courts might hold that they, respectively, each had exclusive jurisdiction.[157] Fortunately, the potential clash of jurisdiction did not materialise as the matter was not litigated.

The above are no more than illustrations of jurisdiction issues that may arise. **8.119** Others will doubtless arise in future cases. The question of forum can arise independently of jurisdiction, and independently of foreign law clauses in relevant contractual documents such as the rules of governing bodies. Even a foreign jurisdiction clause can be overridden by the English court, which can assert jurisdiction itself notwithstanding such a clause; but the onus on a plaintiff to displace the clause and obtain trial in England is a heavy one.[158] In essence the plaintiff would have to show that there could not be a fair trial at the foreign venue corresponding to the jurisdiction clause. Where forum is in issue, the onus is on the plaintiff to show that England is the most just forum.[159] We should also note at this point, briefly, the converse position whereby a party in this country seeks to restrain proceedings abroad. The courts here are cautious in exercising the jurisdiction but will intervene to prevent foreign proceedings where the ends of justice require it, including but not limited to cases where the foreign proceedings are vexatious or oppressive.[160]

Finally the logically separate but in practice closely linked question may arise **8.120** as to the proper law of each actionable wrong relied upon in the proceedings. This again is a substantial topic in its own right. English courts and arbitrators can and do apply foreign law to disputes, or issues forming part of such dis-

---

[155] Rules of the Supreme Court Order 11 rule 1(2)(a).

[156] Dicey and Morris, *supra*, n. 139, 12th ed. Rule 28(22), p. 389.

[157] See Civil Judgments and Jurisdiction Act 1982 Schedule 4, article 1(5) and Dicey and Morris, *supra.*, n. 139, 12th ed. Rule 28(2), pp. 349–361, and 1997 Cum. Supp. At pp. 46–8; *Barclays Bank plc v. Glasgow City Council* [1996] QB 678, CA; cf. *Kleinwort Benson Ltd. v. Glasgow City Council* [1996] QB 57, ECJ; cf. *Strathard Farms Limited v. G.A. Chattaway and Co* [1993] SLT 36.

[158] Dicey and Morris, *supra.*, n. 139, 12th ed. Rule 32(2) Vol. 1 pp. 419–420 and see pp. 433–6.

[159] See *The Spiliada* [1986] AC 460.

[160] See *Société Nationale Industrielle Aérospatiale v. Lee Kui Jak* [1987] AC 871, PC, per Lord Goff at 892–6, helpfully reviewing the authorities.

putes, over which they have jurisdiction and as to which England is the most appropriate forum. The content of foreign substantive law is a question of fact for expert evidence.[161] The questions most likely to concern sports lawyers in litigation before the English courts concern, firstly, the rules for ascertaining the proper law of a contract, or putative contract; and secondly, the rules for ascertaining the proper law applicable to a tort committed abroad, and the condition for it being actionable in this country. As to the first question, in the absence of an express clause stating the governing law of the contract, the test appears to be: what is the system of law with which the transaction has the closest and most real connection ?[162] As to the second question, it is necessary first to identify in which country the tort (or delict) in question has been committed. This is done by looking back over the series of events constituting the tort and asking the question where, in substance, the cause of action arises.[163] The normal rule is that the law applicable to a tort or delict is the law of the state where it was committed, unless it is substantially more appropriate for the applicable law to be that of another state, having regard to factors connecting the tort with, respectively, one country or the other.[164] It is no longer necessary to establish, in English proceedings concerning a tort committed abroad, that the defendant's act would have been tortious if committed in England.[165]

The way forward: towards a unitary system of sports dispute resolution

8.121   Our brief and non-exhaustive account of remedies available in sports law must now be concluded with the observation that those remedies are markedly diffuse and amorphous. There is a notable lack of cohesion and uniformity in the machinery by which redress for wrongs committed in the field of sport may be obtained. Recourse must be had to a bewildering array of principles, doctrines, statutes and procedural rules. We believe the time is now right at least to begin consideration of the concept of unitary sports dispute resolution – that is, the evolution of a code of rules applicable both in the domestic sphere and internationally to the resolution of disputes in the world of sport.

---

[161] Dicey and Morris, *supra.*, n. 139, p. 230 and cases cited at n.41.

[162] *Compagnie Tunisienne de Navigation SA v. Compagnie d'Armement Maritime SA* [1971] QC 572; for a detailed exposition see Dicey and Morris, *supra.*, n. 139, chapter 32.

[163] See generally Dicey and Morris, *supra.*, n. 139, chapter 35, and see now Part III of the Private International Law (Miscellaneous Provisions) Act 1995.

[164] *Ibid.*, section 12(1) and (2).

[165] Private International Law (Miscellaneous Provisions) Act section 10, reversing the effect of the so-called double-actionability rule derived from *Philips v. Eyre* (1870) LR 6 QB 1 (held by the majority of the House of Lords in *Boys v. Chaplin* [1971] AC 356 to be the normal rule; but see also *Red Sea Insurance Co. Ltd. v. Bouygues SA* [1995] AC 190, PC).

The idea of a national unitary sports dispute resolution forum in a particular **8.122** country, coupled with a route in some cases to final tier redress before the CAS, would promote cohesion, uniformity and legal certainty, and would also meet the common criticism that, particularly in doping cases, sporting bodies should not sit in judgment on the efficacy of their own procedures. There is no *a priori* reason why a purely domestic dispute, contained within one country, should generate a right of appeal or review to an international body if a suitable domestic body exists. But sporting competition at the highest level is necessarily international, so disputes whose impact is truly confined to one country will be confined to the lower reaches of sporting endeavour. If no appropriate domestic machinery exists, or the case is one with ramifications beyond the frontiers of the country in which it arises, there is a continuing need for the CAS to be available as a forum of last resort. The CAS is the best model for replication within the purely domestic arena.

In this country, there is now a Sports Dispute Resolution Panel (SDRP) **8.123** founded by the British Olympic Association, the Central Council of Physical Recreation, the Institute of Professional Sport, the Institute of Sports Sponsorship, the Northern Ireland Sports Forum, the Scottish Sports Association, and the Welsh Sports Association. It exists to provide mediation or arbitration in sports disputes offering a "quick, fair, independent and cost effective method of resolving disputes" in sport (SDRP explanatory notes, 15 October 1997). Its advantage over the CAS is that it provides a local service; the CAS operates out of Lausanne, its headquarters, Sydney and Denver only although it may contemplate further expansion. As yet, the SDRP lacks the CAS's experience and pedigree. It remains to be seen how far organisations such as SDRP will attract support within individual countries.

We end this book with the hope that bodies controlling individual sports and **8.124** bodies representing sportsmen and women will recognise their ultimate common interest in establishing uniform systems of dispute resolution cutting across particular sports, and culminating in a right of final appeal or review to a national or international body exercising jurisdiction in sport generally. Support should be given to the establishment of such machinery on a permanent basis. Naturally, that can only happen by consent of the parties appearing as litigants before it. It is increasingly necessary for sporting bodies to recognise the need for their members, and those affected by their actions, to have a right of recourse to a forum separate from, and independent of, the sporting body itself. We hope this book will make a modest contribution to the achievement of that objective, as well as representing an early attempt to establish a theoretical framework for a very practical subject.

Table of Cases

A (A Minor) v Leeds CC (unreported) 2nd March, Leeds Co. Court............119
Adamson v New South Wales Rugby League Ltd (1991)
    103 ALR 319 ....234, **4.52, 4.53**
Adamson v West Perthshire FC (1979) 27 ALR 475 93
AEK Athens FC and Slavia Prague FC v UEFA, CAS 98/200, Procedural
    Order (July 17, 1998) 10, 37, 69, 107, 248, **3.34, 3.67, 3.68, 8.107**
Affutu-Nartoy v Clarke, Times, February 9, 1984 119
Agar v Canning (1965) 54 WWR 302 115
Alcock v Chief Constable of South Yorkshire [1992] 1 AC 310;
    [1991] 3 WLR 1057; [1991] 4 All ER 907 (HL) **5.54, 5.55**
Alnutt v Inglis (1810) 12 East 527 231
American Cyanamid v Ethicon Ltd [1975] AC 397 (HL) 56, 193, 239, **8.66**
Andrade v Cape Verde National Olympic Committee, CAS – Ad Hoc
    Division, No.002 (July 1996) 7, **7.14, 7.15**
Andrade v Cape Verde National Olympic Committee, CAS – Ad Hoc
    Division, No.005 (July 1996) **7.14, 7.15, 7.118**
Angus v British Judo Association, Times, June 15, 1984................................196
Ansac [1993] OJ L152/54 (Commission Decision) 154
Arnolt v Football Association (Unreported, February 2, 1998) (CC) 207
Attorney-General v Hastings Corporation (1950) 94 SJ 225 126
Attorney-General's Reference No.6 of 1980 [1981] QB 715;
    [1981] 3 WLR 125; [1981] 2 All ER 1057; (1981) 73 Cr App R 63 (CA) **5.77**
Attorney-General of Australia v Adelaide Steamship Co [1913] AC 781 54

Baird v Wells (1890) 44 Ch Div 661 42
Baker v Jones [1954] 2 All ER 553 ....**2.13, 2.16**
Balog v Royal Charleroi Sporting Club (Unreported, July 2, 1998)
    (Tribunal de Premiere Instance de Charleroi) **4.43, 4.44**
Barclays Bank Plc v Glasgow City Council *sub nom* Kleinwort Benson Ltd v
    Glasgow City Council (No.2) [1996] QB 678; [1996] 2 WLR 655; [1996]
    2 All ER 257 (CA)..267
Barnard v Jockey Club of South Africa (1984) 2 SALR 35 (W)....................**7.67**
Bayer/BP Chemicals [1988] OJ L150/35; [1989] 4 CMLR 24
    (Commission Decision) 154
Beeuwsaert v Federation Internationale de Basketball, CAS 92/80 ....37, 8.107
Belilos v Switzerland A/132 (1988); (1988) 10 EHRR 466 (ECHR) 205
Blackler v New Zealand Rugby Football League Inc [1968] NZLR 547 93
Blalock v Ladies Professional Golf Association (1973) 359 F Supp 1260
    (Atlanta, US District Court)...178
Bolton v Stone [1951] AC 850 126

Boys v Chaplin [1971] AC 356 268
Breen v Amalgamated Engineering Union [1971] 2 QB 175 (CA)......44, 54, **7.53**
British Actors' Equity Association v Goring [1978] ICR 791 (HL) 31
British Broadcasting Corporation v British Satellite Broadcasting [1992]
    Ch 141; [1991] 3 WLR 174; [1991] 3 All ER 833 (ChD) **6.10**
British Wheelchair Sports v British Paralympic Association (Unreported,
    November 5, 1997) ChD 193
Brown v Lewis (1896) 12 TLR 455 120
Buckley v Tutty (1971) 125 CLR 353 (HC, Australia) 84, 235, 236, 241

Calvin v Carr [1980] AC 574; [1979] 2 WLR 755;
    [1979] 2 All ER 440 (PC)................................193, 200, 251, **7.100**
Capobianco, CAS – Arb. (March 17, 1997)...............................222, **7.48, 8.94**
Casciaroli v Italy A/229—C (1982) (ECHR) 205
Castle v St Augustine's Links (1922) 38 TLR 615 125
Cauliflowers [1978] OJ L21/23; [1978] 1 CMLR D66
    (Commission Decision) 64
Centraal Stikstof Verkoopkantoor [1978] OJ L242/15; [1979] 1 CMLR 11
    (Commission Decision) 154
Central London Property Trust Ltd v High Trees House Ltd [1947]
    KB 130 ....**7.112**
Chagnaud v Federation Internationale de Natation Amateur (FINA),
    CAS 95/141...220, **7.30, 7.31, 7.93, 7.94**
Chaplin v Hicks [1911] 2 KB 786 (CA)............................127, 252, **5.70**
Chapman v Jockey Club, NLJ January 24, 1997 252
Charter v Race Relations Board [1973] AC 885..99
Chicago Professional Sports Ltd Partnership v NBA 961 F 2d 667
    (7th Circuit, 1992) 155
Clansmen Sporting Club Ltd v Robinson, Times, May 22, 1995 (QBD) **8.64**
Cleghorn v Oldham (1927) 43 TLR 465 ....125, **5.31**
Coditel SA v Cine Vog Films SA (No.2) (C262/81) [1982] ECR 3381;
    [1982] 1 CMLR 49; [1983] FSR 148 (ECJ)....................................159
Colchester United FC Ltd v Burley and Ipswich Town FC Ltd
    (Unreported, October 30, 1995) **8.63, 8.84**
Conchita Martinez v Elspa, 30.3.99 (CA) (Unreported) 29
Condon v Basi [1985] 1 WLR 866; [1985] 2 All ER 543 (CA) **5.36, 5.37, 5.40**
Conrad v Inner London Education Authority (1967) 111 SJ 684 119
Constantine v Imperial Hotels [1944] KB 693..**4.81**
Conteh v Onslow-Fane, Times, June 26, 1975 (CA) 55, **8.70, 8.71**
Cook, Cochrane and Hampson v Doncaster BC, Sporting Life,
    July 16, 1993 121
Cooke v Federation Equestre Internationale (FEI), CAS 98/184
    (September 1988) 8, 218

Couch v British Boxing Board of Control, Case No.2304231/97
(IT) 100, 220, **4.87, 4.97**
Cowley v Heatley, Times, July 24, 1986..........................4, 193, **2.40, 3.52, 8.98**
Cullwick v Federation Internationale de Natation Amateur (FINA),
CAS 96/149 (February 1997) 7, 30, 31, 219, 220, **7.32, 7.95, 7.120**
Cunningham v Reading Football Club Ltd [1992] PIQR P141;
(1993) 157 LG Rev 481; Times, March 20, 1991...............................**5.53**
Currie v Barton, Times, February 12, 1988 (CA) **7.74**
Czech Olympic Committee and Swedish Olympic Committee v International
Amateur Athletics Federation (IAAF), OG Nagano (1988), 004–005...........8

D v Ireland 51 DR 117 (1986) 203
Danish Tennis Federation Case, Press Release IP/98/355 (April 15, 1998).....166
Davies v Taylor [1974] AC 207 ....**5.69**
Davis v Carew-Pole [1956] 2 All ER 524..170
Davis v Freasey (CA) 14.5.99 (Unreported) 121
Davis v Rugby Football Union (RFU) (IT) **4.90**
Dawkins v Antrobus (1881) 17 Ch Div 615 (CA) 184, 223
Decker Slaney and USATF v International Amateur Athletics Federation
(IAAF), Arb. (April 25, 1999) **8.95**
Deliege (C51/96) (ECJ) **4.64**
Delimitis v Henninger Brau AG (C234/89) [1991] ECR I—935;
[1992] 5 CMLR 210 (ECJ) 144
Dennis Mitchell, IAAF Tribunal, 3.8.99......................................188
Denver Rockets v All-Pro Management 325 F Supp (CD Ca 1971) 44
Dimes v Grand Junction Canal Co (1852) 3 HL Cas 759 (HL) 205
Distribution of Package Tours During the 1990 World Cup
(Italia 90) [1992] OJ L326/1; [1974] 5 CMLR 253 (Commission
Decision) 165, **4.41, 6.26, 6.81**
Dockers Labour Club v Race Relations Board [1976] AC 285 99
Dona v Mantero (C13/76) [1976] ECR 1333 (ECJ) 69, 71, 74, 107, **4.22,
4.56, 4.57, 4.59**
Donoghue v Stevenson [1932] AC 562 (HL) **5.42, 5.51**
Dundee United Football Club Ltd v Scottish Football Association 1998 SLT
1244 (OH) **7.78**
Dunlop Slazenger International [1992] OJ L131/32 (Commission Decision) **6.88**
Dunlop Slazenger International v Commission (T43/93) [1994] ECR 2441
(CFI) 167

Earl of Ellesmere v Wallace [1929] 2 Ch 1 (CA).............................**2.24**
Eastham v Newcastle United FC Ltd [1964] 1 Ch 413 ....54, 57, 59, 241, **3.51,
4.50, 4.51, 4.52, 8.38, 8.75**
Edwards v British Athletics Federation (BAF) and International Amateur
Athletics Federation (IAAF) [1997] Eu LR 721 (ChD) **4.14, 4.26**

Eccles v Ireland 59 DR 212 (1988) 205
Elliott v Saunders and Liverpool FC (Unreported, June 10, 1994) **5.40**
Enderby Town FC v Football Association [1971] Ch 591;
   [1971] 1 All ER 215 (CA) 54, 198, 259, **8.68**
Engel v Netherlands (No.1) A/22 (1976); (1979—80) 1 EHRR 647
   (ECHR) 205
Esso Petroleum Co Ltd v Harper's Garage (Stourport) Ltd [1968]
   AC 269 (HL) 53
Esterman v NALGO [1974] ICR 635...242
Ettl v Austria A/117 (1987); (1988) 10 EHRR 255 (ECHR)...........................205
European Broadcasting Union (EBU)/Eurovision System [1993] OJ L179/23;
   [1995] 4 CMLR 56 (Commission Decision) 156, **6.67**

Faramus v Film Artistes Association [1964] AC 925 (HL) 42, 84, 184, 223
Fayed v United Kingdom A/194–B (1994); (1994) 18 EHRR 393 (ECHR) 204
Federal Base-ball Club of Baltimore v National League 259 US 200 (1922,
   Sp Ct) 140
Feeney v Lyall 1991 SLT 156 (OH) **5.39, 5.56**
Film Purchases by German television stations OJ L248/36 (Commission
   Decision)..**6.72**
Finnigan v New Zealand Rugby Football Union Inc [1985]
   2 NZLR 159..59, 236
Flood v Kuhn 407 US 248, 282 (1972, Sp Ct)..140
Floral [1980] OJ L39/51; [1980] 2 CMLR 285 (Commission Decision) 154
Football Association v Bennett (Unreported, July 28, 1998) (CA) 100
Foschi v Federation Internationale de Natation Amateur (FINA),
   CAS 95/156 220
Fothergill v Monarch Airlines [1981] AC 251; [1980] 3 WLR 209;
   [1980] 2 All ER 696; [1980] 2 Lloyd's Rep 295 (HL) 262
Fowles v Bedfordshire CC [1996] ELR 51..119
Francis v Cockerell (1820) 5 QB 501 120
Fredin v Sweden (No.2) A/283–A (1994) (ECHR)...205
French v Crosby Links Hotel (Unreported, May 7, 1982) (CC) 100
Frubo v Commission (C71/74) [1975] ECR 563; [1975] 2 CMLR 123 (ECJ)....143

G v G (Minors: Custody Appeal) [1985] 1 WLR 647; [1985] 2 All ER 225;
   [1985] FLR 894 (HL) 247
Gainman v National Association for Mental Health [1971] Ch 317.........**2.41–3**
Gannon v Rotherham MBC (Unreported, February 6, 1991) 119
Gasser v Stinson (Unreported, June 15, 1988) 4, 236, **3.45, 3.50, 7.16,**
   7.19, 7.39, 8.98
Gibbs v Barking Corporation [1936] 1 All ER 115 119
Gibbs Mew v Gemmell [1998] Eu LR 588 (CA) 147
Gillmore v London County Council [1938] 4 All ER 331 125

Gillon (Calson) v Chief Constable of Strathclyde Police, Times,
    November 22, 1996 (OH) 126
Glasgow City Council v Zafar [1998] 2 All ER 953....................................**4.83**
Glenic v Slair and others 1999 (Unreported)..121
Greater London Council v Farrar [1980] 1 WLR 608;
    [1980] ICR 266 (EAT)..**4.94**
Greening v Stockton on Tees BC (Unreported 6.11.98)............................121
Greig v Insole [1978] 1 WLR 302; [1978] 3 All ER 449 (ChD)...........54, 57, 236,
                                                                    3.51, 4.52, 4.73
Griffith v Barbados Cricket Association [1990] LRC (Const) 786 ....**5.84, 5.85**
Grimes v Grand Junction Canal Co Proprietors (1852) 3 HLC 759 195
Grossen (ATF 121 III 350) (Sup Ct, Switzerland) 51
Gundel v FEI/CAS (Swiss Equestrian case) 1 Civil Court, Swiss Fed Trib
    (March 15, 1993) **8.104, 8.109**
Gunter Harz Sports Inc 511 F Supp 1122 44

H v Belgium A/127 (1987); (1988) 10 EHRR 339 (ECHR) **7.83**
Hadmor Productions v Hamilton [1983] 1 AC 191; [1982] 2 WLR 322;
    [1982] 1 All ER 1042; [1982] ICR 114 (HL)..247
Hakansson v Sweden A/171—A (1990); (1991) 13 EHRR 1 (ECHR) 205
Hall v Brooklands Auto-Racing Club [1933] 1 KB 205 (CA)................121, **5.51**
Hall v FINA, CAS 98/218..30, 219
Hall v Victorian Football League [1982] VR 64..93
Hampson v Department of Education and Science [1991] 1 AC 171;
    [1990] 3 WLR 42; [1990] 2 All ER 513; [1990] ICR 511; [1990] IRLR 302
    (HL) *reversing* [1990] 2 All ER 25; [1989] ICR 179; [1989] IRLR 69 (CA)...99
Harding v United States Olympic Committee No.CCV–942151
    (Clackamas County Cir Or, 13 February 1994)............................260, **8.109**
Hargreaves v Football Association, Case No.220651/96 (IT) **4.84**
Haron bin Mundir v Singapore Amateur Athletic Association [1994]
    1 SLR 47 (CA, Singapore) *affirming* [1992] 1 SLR 18 (HC,
    Singapore) **7.4, 7.5**
Harrison v Vincent [1982] RTR 8 (CA) 115, 125
Hassamy v Chester City FC, Case No.2102426/97 (IT)..............................**4.84**
Heatons Transport v TGWU [1973] AC 15 31
Hedley v Cuthbertson (Unreported, June 20, 1997) **5.47**
Hilder v Associated Portland Cement Manufacturing Ltd [1961]
    1 WLR 1434 126
Hill v Archbold [1968] 1 QB 668 (CA) 20
Hill v Parsons & Co Ltd [1972] Ch 305 (CA) 246
Hoffmann-La Roche & Co AG v Commission (C85/76) [1979] ECR 461;
    [1979] 3 CMLR 211; [1980] FSR 13 (ECJ)..149
Hornal v Neuberger Products [1957] 1 QB 247 (CA) **7.45**
Horton v Jackson (Unreported, February 28, 1996) (CA) 125

Hudson's Bay Co/Dansk Pelsdryavlerforening [1988] OJ L316/43
(Commission Decision) 154
Hughes v Western Australian Cricket Association Inc (1987) 69 ALR 660 93

ICI v Commission (C48/69) [1972] ECR 619; [1972] CMLR 557 (ECJ).........143
IRC v McMullen (1981) ACI...15
Ikarian Reefer, The [1993] 2 Lloyds Rep 68; [1993] FSR 563; [1993]
37 EG 158 (QBD) 185
Instone v Shroeder Music Publishing Ltd [1974] 1 WLR 1308 (HL) **4.78, 4.79**
International Cycling Union v Italian National Olympic Committee,
CAS 94/128, advisory opinion (February 1995)................................210, 220
International Equestrian Federation (FEI), CAS 91/53 ....**7.118**
International General Electric Co of New York v Customs and Excise
Commissioners [1962] Ch 784 (CA) **8.40**
International News Service v Associated Press 248 US 215 (Sup Ct, United
States) 135
International Tennis Federation v Korda, CAS 99/223 ....30, 220

James v Eastleigh BC [1990] 2 AC 751; [1990] 3 WLR 55; [1990] 2 All ER 607;
[1990] ICR 554 (HL)..97
James v United Kingdom A/98 (1986); (1986) 8 EHRR 123; [1986] RVR 139
(ECHR) 204
Jockey Club of South Africa v Forbes (1993) (1) SA 648 (Appellate Division,
Witwatersrand) **7.23, 8.22**
Johnson v Appeal Judges, CA 117/86, July 16, 1996 229
Jones v Welsh Rugby Union, Times, January 6, 1998 (CA) *affirming*
(Unreported, 27 February 1997) 198, 204, 211, 217, 226, **7.60, 7.71,
7.72, 7.76, 7.77, 8.46, 8.52, 8.54**
Justice v South Australian Trotting Control Board (1989) 50 SASR 613
(Sup Ct, Australia) **7.59, 7.65, 8.22**

Keck and Mithouard (C267/92, C268/91) [1993] ECR I—6097 (ECJ).............76
Keighley Football Club v Cunningham, Times, May 25, 1960 196
Kemp v New Zealand Rugby Football League [1989] 3 NZLR 463
(HC, New Zealand) 59, **4.74**
Kempf (C139/85) [1986] ECR 1741 (ECJ) 73
Kennaway v Thompson [1981] 1 QB 88; [1980] 3 WLR 361;
[1980] 3 All ER 329 (CA) **5.65**
King v Redlich [1985] 4 WWR 567 (CA, British Columbia) **5.58**
Kitchen v RAF Association [1958] 2 All ER 241 (CA)...........................127, 252
Kleinwort Benson Ltd v Glasgow City Council [1996] QB 57;
[1995] 3 WLR 866; [1995] All ER (EC) 514 267
Korda v International Tennis Federation (ITF), Times, February 4, 1999 221
Korneev, CAS – Atlanta Arb. No.003–4...218

La Roux v New Zealand Rugby Football Union, March 14, 1995 (HC,
    Wellington CP346/94)..229
Lacy v Parker and Boyle, Times, May 15, 1994; (1994) 144 NLJ 485 126
Lamond v Glasgow Corporation 1968 SLT 291...126
Lancombe SA and Cosparfrance Netherland BV v Etos and Albert Heyn
    Supermart BV (C99/79) [1981] ECR 2511; [1981] 2 CMLR 164;
    [1981] FSR 490 (ECJ)...243
Lane v Holloway [1968] 1 QB 379 ....126, **5.57**
Langborger v Sweden A/155 (1989) (ECHR) 205
Laskey, Jaggard and Brown v United Kingdom (1997) 24 EHRR 39 (ECHR)......129
Latchford v Spedeworth International, Times, October 11, 1983 125
Law v National Greyhound Racing Club Ltd [1983] 1 WLR 1302;
    [1983] 3 All ER 300 (CA) 227, **8.20**
Lawrie-Blum (C66/85) [1986] ECR 2121 (ECJ)...73
Le Compte v Belgium A/43 (1981); (1982) 4 EHRR 1 (ECHR) 204, 205
Leatherhead v Edwards (28.11.1998) Unreported 115
Lee v Showmen's Guild of Great Britain [1952] 2 QB 329 (CA)........30, 42, 132,
                                                                        179, 184, 223, **8.68**
Lehtinen v Federation Internationale de Natation Amateur (FINA), CAS
    95/142 (February 1996) 28, 187, **1.18, 7.28, 7.32**
Lehtonen v ASBL (C176/96) (ECJ) **4.38**
Leisure Data v Bell [1988] FSR 367 (CA)......................................195, 242, 244
Lennox Lewis v World Boxing Council and Frank Bruno (Unreported,
    November 3, 1995) (ChD) 236, **2.34, 3.27, 8.116**
Letang v Cooper [1964] 2 All ER 929 126
Levin v NBA 385 F Supp 149 (SDNY, 1974) 64
Levin (C53/81) [1982] ECR 1035 (ECJ) 73
Lewis v Buckpool Golf Club 1993 SLT (Sh Ct) 43 ....**5.39**
Link Organisation v North Derbyshire Tertiary College (Unreported,
    August 14, 1998) (CA) 235, 236
Linseman v World Hockey Association 439 F Supp 1315, 1322
    (D Conn 1977) 44
Lloyd v McMahon [1987] 1 AC 625; [1987] 2 WLR 821;
    [1987] 1 All ER 1118 (HL) 193, 251
Locabail International Finance Ltd v Agroexport and Atlanta (UK) Ltd
    (The Sea Hawk) [1986] 1 WLR 657; [1986] 1 All ER 901;
    [1986] 1 Lloyd's Rep 317 (CA) 244
Loe v New Zealand Rugby Football Union, August 10, 1993
    (HC, Wellington CP209/93) 229
Longley v National Union of Journalists [1987] IRLR 109 (CA) 242
Los Angeles Memorial Coliseum Commission v National Football
    League 726 F 2d 1381, 1397 (9th Circuit 1984) US Court of Appeals 44
Lower Hutt City Association Football Club v New Zealand Football
    Association, March 13, 1993 (HC, Auckland M335/93) 229

Machin v Football Association (Unreported, 1993) (CA) 107
McComiskey v McDermott [1974] IR 75 113
McCord v Swansea City Association Football Club Ltd, Times,
    February 11, 1997 114
MacDonald v FIFA/SFA 1999 (Court of Session) Unreported 121
McInnes v Onslow-Fane [1978] 1 WLR 1520; [1978] 3 ALL ER 211
    (ChD) 4, 35, 191, 234, **3.17, 3.18, 3.43, 3.59**
McKenzie v National Union of Public Employees [1991] ICR 155
    (QBD)...217
Makanjuola v Commissioner of Police for the Metropolis [1992] 3 All ER 617;
    [1989] 2 Admin LR 214 (CA) 128
Mary Decker-Slaney, In re, IAAF Tribunal, 26.4.99 185
Martin v PGA Tours Ltd 1998 US Dist LEXIS 1980 (1998) 99
Meadows Indemnity Co Plc v Insurance Corporation of Ireland Ltd [1989]
    2 Lloyd's Rep 298 (CA) 235, 236
Mendy v International Amateur Boxing Association, CAS – Ad Hoc
    Division, Atlanta Arb. No.006 (1996) 108, 263, **7.117**
Metro SB-Grossmarkte GmbH & Co KG v Commission (C26/76) [1977]
    ECR 1875; [1978] 2 CMLR 1; [1978] FSR 400; [1976] ELR 1353 (ECJ) 158
Metropole Television v Commission (T528/93, T542/93, T543/93, T546/93)
    [1996] 5 CMLR 386; [1996] ECR II–649 (CFI)...........................64, 158
Michelin v Commission (C322/82) [1983] ECR 3461; [1985] 1 CMLR 282
    (ECJ) 149
Mid-South v NFL 720 F 2d 772, 787 n9 (3rd Circuit 1983) 64
Mid-South v NFL 467 US 1215 (1984)..64
Miller v Jackson [1977] QB 966; [1977] 3 WLR 20; [1977] 3 All ER 338
    (CA) 126, **5.65**
Modahl v British Athletic Federation Ltd (Unreported, July 28, 1997)
    (CA) 179, **1.8, 7.54–7, 7.84, 7.112, 8.26, 8.35, 8.73, 8.74**
Morris v Redland Bricks Ltd [1970] AC 655 (HL) 242
Mrs Michelle Smith de Bruin v FINA, CAS, 98/211..........................184, 190
MSG Media Service [1994] OJ L364/1 (Commission Decision) 151
Multinational Gas and Petrochemical Co v Multinational Gas and
    Petrochemical Services Ltd [1983] Ch 258; [1983] 3 WLR 492;
    [1983] 2 All ER 563 (CA) 266
Mulvaine v Joseph (1968) 112 SJ 927 ....252, **5.68**
Murray v Harringay Arena [1951] 2 KB 529................................121
Muyldermans v Belgium A/214–A (1991); (1993) 15 EHRR 204 (ECHR) 205

Nabozay v Barnhill 334 NE 2d 258 (Illinois Appellate Court: 1975) 114
Nagle v Fielden [1966] 2 QB 633 (CA) 45, 236, **2.53, 3.15, 3.43, 4.81, 4.87, 8.50**
National Basketball Association and NBA Properties Inc v Motorola Inc
    and Sports Team Analysis and Tracking Systems Inc 931 F Supp 1124;
    17 USC s102(a) (2nd Circuit) US Court of Appeals.......................**6.5**

National Wheelchair Basketball Association v International Paralympic
  Committee, CAS 95/122 ....30, 220, **7.29, 7.92**
NCAA v Board of Regents 468 US 85 (1984, Sp Ct) 155
Newport Association Football Club v Football Association of Wales Ltd
  (No.1) [1995] 2 All ER 87 (ChD)..........................55, 60, 236, **8.48, 8.49, 8.59**
Newport Association Football Club v Football Association of Wales Ltd
  (No.2) (Unreported, April 12, 1995)..............................50, 55, 60, **3.55, 8.75**
News Ltd v Australian Rugby Football League Ltd (1996) 135 ALR 33 (Fed Ct,
  Australia) 252, **3.30, 3.31**
Nichols Advanced Vehicle Systems Inc v De Angelis (Unreported, December
  21, 1979) 247
Nixon v Australian Cycling Federation Inc, CAS 96/152 ....**3.58**
Nordenfelt v Maxim Nordenfelt Guns and Ammunition Co Ltd [1894]
  AC 535 (HL) **3.39, 3.42**
Nottage, Re (1895) 2 Ch. 649 15
Nottingham Building Society v Eurodynamic Systems Plc [1995] FSR 605
  (CA) *affirming* [1993] FSR 468 (Ch D) 244
Notts Incorporated Football Club Ltd v Football League Ltd and Southend
  United FC Ltd (Unreported, November 28, 1996) **8.85, 8.86**
Nungesser v Commission (C258/78) [1982] ECR 2015; [1983] 1 CMLR 278
  (ECJ) 144

O'Reilly v Mackman [1983] 2 AC 237; [1982] 3 WLR 1096; [1982] 3 All ER
  1124 (HL)...**8.23**
Osman v United Kingdom, Times, November 5, 1998 (ECHR) 204
Otahuhu Rovers RLC v Auckland Rugby League Inc, November 12, 1993
  (HC, Auckland M818/93) 229

Page One Records Ltd v Britton [1968] 1 WLR 157 246
Panayiotou v Sony Music Entertainment (UK) Ltd [1994] EMLR 229;
  (1994) 13 Tr LR 532; Times, June 30, 1994 (ChD) 95
Payne and Payne v Maple Leaf (1949) 1 DLR 369..121
Pearson v Lightning (Unreported, April 1, 1998) (CA) **5.36**
Pett v Greyhound Racing Association Ltd (No.2) (unruly horse case) [1970]
  1 QB 46 (CA) 198, **7.72**
Petty v British Judo Association [1981] ICR 660; [1981] IRLR 484
  (EAT) **4.86, 4.94**
Pharmaceutical Society of Great Britain v Dickson [1970] AC 403
  (HL)...55, 57, 236
Phelps v Hillingdon LBC (Unreported, November 4, 1998) (CA) 251
Philips v Eyre (1870) LR 6 QB 1..268
Piazza v Major League Baseball 831 F Supp 420, 430 (ED Pa 1993)...............64

Piddington v Hastings, Times, March 12, 1932 121
Pinochet, Re, Times, January 18, 1999 (HL) 196, 205
Pittsburgh Athletic Co v KQV Broadcasting Co 24 F Supp 490....................**6.5**
Potter v Carlisle and Cliftonville Golf Club Ltd [1939] NI 114...................**5.64**
Powell v Brent LBC [1988] ICR 176; [1987] IRLR 446 (CA) 246
Powell and Rayner v United Kingdom A/172 (1990); Times,
    February 22, 1990 (ECHR) 204
Priestly v Stork Margarine Social and Recreational Club.........................**4.90**
Pronuptia de Paris GmbH Frankfurt Am Main v Schillgalis (C161/84) [1986]
    ECR 354; [1986] 1 CMLR 414 (ECJ) 155
Puerto Rico Amateur Baseball Federation v USA Baseball, CAS 95/132
    (March 15, 1996)...60

Quigley v Union Internationale de TIR (UIT), CAS 94/129 ....28, 219, **7.27**,
                                                                        7.29, 7.32, 7.74
Quire v Coates [1964] SASR 294..124

R v Barnsley MBC Ex P Hook [1976] 1 WLR 1052; [1976] 3 All ER 452;
    74 LGR 493 (CA) 178, 207
R v Benchers of Lincoln's Inn (1825) 4 B and C 854...................................42
R v Brent LBC Ex p Assegai, Times June 18, 1987; (1987) 151 LG Rev 891
    (QBD)...178
R v Brown (Anthony) [1994] 1 AC 212; [1993] 2 WLR 556; [1993]
    2 All ER 75; (1993) 97 Cr App R 44 (HL) 130, **5.77**
R v Coney (1882) 8 QBD 534..123
R v Disciplinary Committee of the Jockey Club Ex p Aga Khan [1993]
    1 WLR 909, [1993] 2 All ER 853 (CA) 35, 55, **8.15, 8.16, 8.18, 8.50**
R v Disciplinary Committee of the Jockey Club Ex p Massingberd-Mundy
    (No.2) [1993] 2 All ER 207; [1990] COD 260; (1990) 2 Admin
    LR 609..227, 228, **8.20**
R v Dr Askew et al (1768) 4 Burr 2185 42
R v Executive Council of the Joint Disciplinary Committee Scheme
    Ex p Hipps (Unreported, June 12, 1996) (QBD)...............................249, 250
R v Football Association of Wales Ex p Flint Town United Football Club
    [1991] COD 44 (DC) 227
R v Gaming Board of Great Britain Ex p Benaim [1970] 2 QB 417................46
R v General Medical Council Ex p Colman [1990] 1 All ER 489;
    (1990) 9 Tr LR 108; [1990] COD 202; [1989] 1 Admin LR 469 178
R v Gough (Robert) [1993] AC 646; [1993] 2 WLR 883; [1993] 2 All ER 724;
    (1993) 97 Cr App R 188 (HL)..206, **7.64, 7.66**
R v Hampshire CC Ex P Ellerton [1985] 1 WLR 749; [1985] 1 All ER 599;
    83 LGR 395; [1985] ICR 317 (CA) 189
R v HM Treasury and Commissioners of Inland Revenue Ex p Daily Mail
    [1988] ECR 5483 (ECJ)..72

R v Inland Revenue Commissioners Ex p PC Coombs & Co [1991]
2 AC 283 190
R v Inland Revenue Commissioners Ex p Rossminster Ltd [1980] AC 952;
[1980] 2 WLR 1; [1980] 1 All ER 80; [1980] STC 42; (1980) 70
Cr App R 157 (HL)..237
R v Institute of Chartered Accountants in England & Wales Ex p Brindle
[1994] BCC 297 (CA)...249, 250
R v International Olympic Committee (IOC), OG Nagano No.002 (1998) 8
R v Jockey Club Ex p RAM Racecourses Ltd [1993] 2 All ER 225;
[1990] COD 346; (1991) 5 Admin LR 265 (DC) 227, **8.20, 8.39**
R v McHugh (Unreported, February 20, 1998) 131
R v Master and Warden of the Company of Surgeons in London (1759)
2 Burr 893 42
R v Ministry of Defence Ex p Smith [1996] QB 517; [1996] 2 WLR 305;
[1996] 1 All ER 257 (CA)...250
R v Mulvihill [1990] 1 WLR 438; [1990] 1 All ER 436; (1990)
90 Cr App R 372 (CA) 197
R v Oxfordshire CC exp. Sunningwell Parish Council [1999] 2 All ER 385 15
R v Panel on Take-overs & Mergers Ex p Datafin [1987] QB 699;
[1987] 2 WLR 699; [1987] 1 All ER 564; [1987] BCLC 104 (CA) **8.17,
8.18, 8.19**
R v Panel on Take-overs & Mergers Ex p Fayed [1992] BCLC 938;
[1992] BCC 524; (1993) 5 Admin LR 337 (CA) 249, 250
R v Panel on Take-overs & Mergers Ex p Guinness Plc [1990] 1 QB 146;
[1989] 2 WLR 863; [1989] 1 All ER 509; [1989] BCLC 255;
(1988) 4 BCC 714 (CA) 250
R v St Albans Crown Court Ex p Cinnamond [1981] QB 480;
[1981] 2 WLR 681; [1981] 1 All ER 802 (DC)...............................207
R v Secretary of State for Education and Employment Ex p Portsmouth
Football Club [1998] COD 142 ....68, 89, **4.70, 4.71**
R v Secretary of State for the Home Department Ex p Benwell [1985] QB 554;
[1984] 3 WLR 843; [1984] 3 All ER 854 (QBD) 207
R v Secretary of State for Transport Ex p Pegasus Holdings (London) Ltd
[1988] 1 WLR 990; [1989] 2 All ER 481 (QBD) 176, 207
R v Somerset County Council Ex p Fewings [1995] 1 WLR 1037;
[1995] 3 All ER 20 (CA) 106
R v Somerset County Council Ex p Scott [1998] 1 WLR 226 106
R v Tottenham Justices Ex p Dwarkados Joshi [1982] 1 WLR 631;
[1982] 2 All ER 507; (1982) 75 Cr App R 72 (DC) 207
Racz v Home Office [1994] 2 AC 45; [1994] 2 WLR 23; [1994] 1 All ER 97
(HL)...128
Ralph v London County Council (1947) 111 JP 548....................................119
Ray v Professional Golfers Association Ltd (Unreported,
April 15, 1997) 245, **3.22, 3.46**

Red Sea Insurance Co Ltd v Bouygues SA [1995] AC 190;
    [1994] 3 WLR 926; [1994] 3 All ER 749 (PC)............................268
Reel v Holder [1981] 1 WLR 1226; [1981] 3 All ER 321 (CA) 30, **8.97**
Revie v Football Association, Times, December 14, 1979 197
Reynolds v International Amateur Athletics Federation (IAAF) 23 F 3d
    1110 (1994); 115 S Ct 423 (1994); 968 F 2d 1216 (1992); 112 S Ct 2512
    (1992); No.C—2—91—003, 1991 WL 179760 (1991); 935 F 2d 270
    (1991)..**8.99, 8.109**
Ridder v Thaler (Unreported, November 1990)...114
Ringeisen v Austria A/13 (1971) (ECHR) 204
Roebuck v National Union of Mineworkers [1977] ICR 573.......................198
Rootes v Shelton (1967) 41 ALJR 172; [1968] ALR 33 (HC,
    Australia) 124, **5.35, 5.58**
Ross Rebagliati IOC, CAS (OG Nag: No.002) 219
Rover International Ltd v Cannon Film Sales Ltd (No.1) [1987] 1 WLR 670;
    [1986] 3 All ER 772 (Ch D) 244
Russell v Duke of Norfolk [1948] 1 All ER 488 32
Russell v Duke of Norfolk [1949] 1 All ER 109 (CA)...........................44, 252

St George's Healthcare NHS Trust v S [1998] 3 All ER 673 237
St Johnstone FC Ltd v Scottish Football Association Ltd 1965
    SLT 171 ....223, 259
Satanita, The, *sub nom* Clarke v Dunraven [1987] AC 59 (HL) **2.23**
Saunders v Richmond-upon-Thames BC [1978] ICR 75; [1977]
    IRLR 362; (1977) 12 ITR 488 (EAT).......................................**4.83**
Scott v Avery [1956] 5 HLC 81 30
Scottish Football Association v Commission (T46/92) [1994] ECR II–1039
    (CFI)..80, 142
Seaconsar (Far East) Ltd v Bank Markazi Jomhouri Islami Iran [1994] 1 AC
    438; [1993] 3 WLR 756; [1993] 4 All ER 456; [1994] 1 Lloyd's Rep
    1 (HL) 266
Sheler v City of London Electric Lighting (1895) 1 Ch 287 126
Shepherd Homes v Sandham [1971] Ch 340 243
Simms v Leigh Rugby Football Club [1969] 2 All ER 923 ....**5.62**
Simpson v New Zealand Racing Conference, June 24, 1980 (HC,
    Wellington A531–79)..229
Siskina v Distros Compania Naviera SA [1979] AC 210 (HL) **8.50**
SL Sethia Liners Ltd v State Trading Corporation of India Ltd [1985]
    1 WLR 1398; [1986] 2 All ER 395 (CA)...................................255
Smoldon v Whitworth [1997] ELR 249 (CA)...................................**5.45, 5.60**
Societe Nationale Industrielle Aerospatiale v Lee Kui Jak [1987] AC 871;
    [1987] 3 WLR 59; [1987] 3 All ER 510 (PC) 267
Societe Technique Miniere v Maschinenbau Ulm (C56/65) [1966] ECR 235;
    [1966] CMLR 357 (ECJ) 145

Sotgiu v Deutsche Bundespost (C152/73) [1974] ECR 153 (ECJ) 72
Spiliada, The, [1987] AC 460; [1986] 3 WLR 972; [1986] 3 All ER 843;
  [1987] 1 Lloyd's Rep 1 (HL) 267
Sports and General Press Agency Ltd v Our Dogs Publishing Co Ltd [1917]
  2 KB 125 (CA) **6.6**
Spring v Guardian Assurance [1995] 2 AC 296; [1994] 3 WLR 354;
  [1994] 3 All ER 129; [1994] ICR 596; [1994] IRLR 460 (HL)
Staatsfabriek Viking BV v German Speed Skating Association,
  CAS, NAG 3 9
Stevenage Borough FC Ltd v Football League Ltd (1997) 9 Admin LR 109;
  Times, August 1, 1996 (ChD) 4, 35, 43, 60, 191, 226, 229, 236, 256
            3.13, 3.42–4, 3.48, 3.50, 3.66, 6.35, 7.84, 8.51, 8.57
Stewart v Judicial Committee of the Auckland Racing Club Inc [1992] 3
  NZLR 693 (HC, New Zealand) **7.21, 7.76**
Strathaird Farms Ltd v GA Chattaway & Co 1993 SLT Sh Ct 36.................267
Sullivan v NFL 34 F 3d 1091 (Ist Circuit 1994) 64
Surinder Singh (C370/90) [1992] ECR I–4265 (ECJ) 88
Swindon Town FC v Football Association Ltd, Times, June 20, 1990 207

Taylor v National Union of Seamen [1967] 1 WLR 532 198
Thornton v Trustees of School District No. 57 (1976) 57 DLR (3d) 438 119
Tondas v Amateur Hockey Association of the US 438 F Supp 310
  (WDNY 1977) 45
Toolson v New York Yankees Inc 346 US 356 (1953, Sp Ct) 140
Trent Taverns v Sykes [1999] Eu LR 147
Tretorn [1994] OJ L378/45 (Commission Decision)....................................167
Trustees of the Dennis Rye Pension Fund v Sheffield City Council [1998]
  1 WLR 840 ....235, 236
Tsipoulidis v Donald (CA) 11.12.98 (Unreported) 127

UIP [1990] 4 CMLR 749 (Commission Decision)..154
Union Nationale des Entraineurs et Cadres Techniques Professionnels du
  Football (UNECTEF) v Georges Heylens (C222/86) [1987] ECR 4097;
  [1989] 1 CMLR 901 (ECJ) **4.62, 4.63**
Union Royale Belge de Societes de Football (ASBL) v Jean-Marc
  Bosman (C415/93) [1995] ECR I—4921; [1996] All ER (EC) 97;
  (ECJ)...............................68, 71, 74, 75, 84, 85, 107, 108, 155, **4.11, 4.27–32,**
        4.34, 4.35, 4.37, 4.40, 4.43, 4.48, 4.57, 4.59, 4.60, 4.76, 6.35, 8.53, 8.107
United States v NFL 116 F Supp 319 (ED Pa, 1953)....................................156
USA Shooting and Quigley v Union Internationale de TIR (UIT),
  CAS 94/129 ....28, 219, **7.27, 7.29, 7.32, 7.74**
US Swimming v Federation Internationale de Natation Amateur (FINA),
  CAS – Ad Hoc Division – OG Atlanta Arb. No.001
  (July, 21 1996) 8, **3.61, 7.125**

Van Duyn v Home Office [1975] ECR 1337 (ECJ) 73
Van Oppen v Clerk to the Bedford Charity Trustees [1990] 1 WLR 235;
    [1989] 3 All ER 389 (CA) 118, **5.49**
Victoria Park Racing and Recreation Grounds Co Ltd v Taylor (1937)
    58 CLR 479 (HC, Australia) 135
Vlasopoulou (C340/89) [1991] ECR I—2357 (ECJ) 87
Volk v Vervaecke (C5/67) [1969] ECR 295; [1969] CMLR 273 (ECJ) 144
Volkers v Federation Internationale de Natation Amateur (FINA),
    CAS 95/150 (September 1996) 220, **1.17, 7.31**

Walrave and Koch v Union Cycliste Internationale (C36/74) [1974]
    ECR 1405 (ECJ) 69, 71, 73, 107, **4.23, 4.59**
Wang Lu-Nuyeta v Federation Internationale de Natation Amateur (FINA),
    CAS 98/208 (22 December 1998) 189, 190, 220, **7.50, 7.119**
Ward v Bradford Corporation (1972) LGR 27; 115 SJ 606 (CA) 211
Warner Brothers Pictures Inc v Nelson [1937] 1 KB 209 (Bette Davis case) ...246
Warren v Mendy [1989] 1 WLR 853; [1989] 3 All ER 103; [1989] ICR 525;
    [1989] IRLR 210 (CA)...**8.62**
Watson v Bradford, (1999) unreported (HC)...127
Watson v Prager [1991] 1 WLR 726; [1991] 3 All ER 487 (ChD) 58, **4.77,**
    4.78, 8.36
Watt v Australian Cycling Federation Inc, CAS 96/152...............................**3.59**
Watt v Australian Cycling Federation Inc, CAS 96/153 ....219, **3.59, 3.60**
Wayde v New South Wales Rugby League Ltd (1985) 61 ALR 225 .....**3.20, 8.79**
Webb v EMO Air Cargo (UK) Ltd [1994] QB 718; [1993] 1 WLR 102;
    [1992] 4 All ER 929; [1993] ICR 175; [1993] IRLR 27...............................99
Western Australian Turf Club v Federal Commissioner of Taxation (1978)
    19 ALR 167 (HC, Australia) **8.21**
White v Blackmore [1972] 2 QB 651; [1972] 3 WLR 296; [1972]
    3 All ER 158 (CA) 29, 123, **5.63**
White v Chief Constable of South Yorkshire [1998] 3 WLR 1509 ....**5.55**
Widness RFC v Rugby Football League (Unreported, May 26, 1995)
    (ChD) 31, **3.29**
Wilander v Tobin (No. 1) (1998) CA (unreported) 186
Wilander v Tobin (No.2) [1997] 2 Lloyd's Rep 293; [1997] Eu LR 265
    (CA)...230, **4.12, 4.13, 74, 4.25**
Wilkins v Smith (1976) 73 LSG 938 121
Wilks v Cheltenham Homeguard Motor Cycle & Light Car Club
    (CA) [1971] 1 WLR 668; [1971] 3 All ER 369 (CA) 121, 124, **5.44, 5.61**
Williams v Pugh (Unreported, July 23, 1997) 240, **3.47**
Williams v Reason [1988] 1 WLR 96; [1988] 1 All ER 262 (CA) 30
WJ Alan & Co Ltd v El Nasr Export & Import Co [1972] 2 QB 189;
    [1972] 2 All ER 127 (CA)..**7.112**

Woolridge v Sumner [1967] 2 QB 43 (CA) 121, **5.42, 5.61**
Wright v Cheshire CC [1952] 2 All ER 789...119

X (Minors) v Bedfordshire CC [1995] 2 AC 633; [1955] 3 WLR 152;
    [1995] 3 All ER 353; [1995] 2 FLR 276; [1995] 3 FCR 337; 94 LGR 313;
    (1995) 94 LGR 313 (HL) 251

ZTT Ltd v Holly Johnson [1993] EMLR 6 (CA) **4.78**

Table of United Kingdom Legislation

Arbitration Act 1950 ....254, **8.82**
Arbitration Act 1975 ....255, **8.82**
Arbitration Act 1979 ....254, **8.32**
Arbitration Act 1996 ....254, **2.39**, **8.82**
   s. 9 254
Broadcasting Act 1990 ....**6.14**
   Part I 138
   s. 1 ....**6.15**
   s. 6 138
   s. 7 138
   s. 8 138
   s. 9 138
Broadcasting Act 1996 ....**6.14**
   Part IV **6.16**
   s. 97 ....**6.18**
   s. 97(2) 139
   ss. 98—101 ....**6.18**
   s. 101 ....**6.18**
Civil Evidence Act 1968 ....**7.35**
Civil Evidence Act 1995 ....**7.35**
Civil Jurisdiction and Judgments Act 1982 ....**8.113**, **8.117**
   Sched. 4 267
Civil Jurisdiction and Judgments Act 1991 ....**8.113**
Civil Procedure Act 1997
   s. 1 237
   Sched. 1, para. 2 237
Civil Procedure Rules **8.13**
   Part 6.2(1)(b) 265
   Part 25.1(1)(b) 237, **8.40**
   Part 33 184
   Part 50.1(2) 21, 265
      Sched. 1 21
Companies Act 1985
   s. 14 25
   s. 459 ....19, 46, **8.79**
Companies Act 1989 ....46, **8.79**
Competition Act 1998 ....**2.58**, **3.7**, **3.62**, **4.48**, **6.21**, **6.36**, **6.54**
Copyright, Designs and Patents Act 1988 ....**6.85**
   s. 1(1) 136

s. 6(3) 136
s. 9(2)(b) 136
s. 11(1) 136
s. 16—20 136
s. 16(3) 137
s. 30(2) **6.10, 6.11**
Criminal Justice and Public Order Act 1994 ....**5.28**
s. 166 163
s. 166(1) 111
Disability Discrimination Act 1995 ....**98, 4.80**
Part II **4.86**
s. 19 99
Employment Rights Act 1996 ....**2.29**
European Communities Act 1972 ....**2.63, 4.63**
European Economic Area Act 1993 89
Fire Safety and Safety of Places of Sport Act 1987
s. 23(1) 109
ss. 26–30 109
Firearms (Amendment) Act 1997 111
Football (Offences) Act 1991 ....**5.27**
s. 2 111
s. 3 111
s. 4 111
Football Spectators Act 1989 ....**5.25**
ss. 1–9 110
s. 16 111
s. 27(5) 110
Human Rights Act 1998 ....95, 207, **2.61, 2.63, 7.81, 8.29, 8.30**, 8.31
s. 2(1) 233
s. 2(3) 233
s. 4 233
s. 6(1) 233, **8.32**
s. 6(2) 233
s. 6(3) 233, **8.32**
s. 6(3)(a) 205
s. 6(3)(b) 205
s. 6(5) 233, **8.32**
s. 7 ....**8.33**
s. 8 233
Immigration Act 1971 ....**4.66**
Immigration Act 1988 ....**4.66**
Industrial and Provident Societies Act 1965 ....**2.3**
Limitation Act 1980
s. 5 225

Merchant Shipping (Amendment) Act 1862

   s. 54 ....**2.23**

Occupiers Liability Act 1957 ....**5.50, 5.53**

   s. 2(5)..**5.62**

Occupiers Liability Act 1984 ....**5.50**

Offences Against the Person Act 1861

   s. 20 131

   s. 47 ....**5.77**

Private International Law (Miscellaneous Provisions) Act

   s. 10 268

Public Order Act 1986..**5.26, 5.28**

   Part IV **5.25**

   s. 31 ....**5.25**

   s. 44(1) 110

   Sched. 1 Part I 110

Race Relations Act 1976 ....**4.80, 4.83, 4.91**

   Part II 98

   s. 12 98

   s. 20 99

   s. 32 98

Restrictive Trade Practices Act 1976..**3.7**

Rules of the Supreme Court

   Ord. 10 r. 1(2)(a) 265

   Ord. 11..**8.114**

   Ord. 11 r. 1...**8.115**

   Ord. 11 r. 1(1)(c)...**8.115, 8.116**

   Ord. 11 r. 1(1)(f) **8.115**

   Ord. 11 r. 1(2)(a) 265, 267

   Ord. 11 r. 11(1)(b) **8.115**

   Ord. 11 r. 11(1)(d) **8.115**

   Ord. 11 r. 11(1)(e) **8.115**

   Ord. 14A..**8.85**

   Ord. 15 r. 12...**2.15**

   Ord. 15 r. 12(1) 21

   Ord. 38 184

   Ord. 53 r. 4 224

   Ord. 53 r. 4(1) 225

Safety of Places of Sport Regulations 1988 (SI 1988/1807) 109

Safety of Sports Grounds Act 1975

   ss. 1–7 109

   s. 10 ....**5.21**

Sex Discrimination Act 1975..............................95, **4.80, 4.83, 4.91**

   Part II 98

   s. 7(2)(b)(ii) **4.98**

s. 13 ....**4.86**

s. 14 98

s. 29 ....99, 101, **4.90**

s. 34 ....101, **4.98**

s. 35(1)(c) **4.98**

s. 35(2) **4.98**

s. 44 ....**4.91, 4.93–7**

Sporting Events (Control of Alcohol, etc) Act 1985

s. 1 110

s. 1A **5.24**

s. 2A **5.24**

ss. 3—5D 110

s. 6 ....**5.24**

s. 7 ....**5.24**

s. 9(3) 110

Supreme Court Act 1981

s. 31(6) 224

Theft Act 1968 ....**5.6**

Trade Marks Act 1995 ....**6.85**

Table of National Legislation

Australia
  Companies Code (New South Wales)
    s. 320 ....46, **8.79**
Italy
  Penal Code
    Art. 2 210
Switzerland
  Civil Code
    Art. 2 51
  Code of Obligations
    Art. 41 ....**1.18**
    Art. 49 ....**1.18**
  Penal Code
    Art. 2, para. 2 210
    Private International Law Act **7.15**
    Art. 187 ....**1.20**
United States
  Curt Flood Act, 1998 140
  Sherman Act 144, 178, **6.63**
    s. 1 ....44, 66

Table of Treaties and EC Legislation

Brussels Convention on Jurisdiction in Civil and Commercial Matters
(1968) 8.112, 8.117
Council Directive 64/221/EEC 71
Council Directive 68/360/EEC 71
Council Directive 89/552/EEC 6.14
    Art. 3a(1) 6.17
Council Directive 93/16/EEC..87
Council Directive 97/36/EC 6.14, 6.17
Council Regulation EEC/17/62..80, 142, 147
Council Regulation EEC/1612/68 ....71, 88
Council Regulation EEC/1251/70 71
European Convention on Human Rights (1950) 232, 1.10, 8.29, 8.30
    Art. 6 ....204, 7.81–3, 8.31, 8.33
    Art. 6(1) 204, 205, 7.82, 7.84–6
    Art. 7 ....1.23
    Art. 8 129
    Art. 10 205
Lugano Convention (1988) 8.112, 8.117
Treaty of Amsterdam (1997) 140, 5.18
Treaty Establishing the European Community (Rome, 1957) 3.7, 8.107
    Art. 2 ....2.58, 4.10, 4.21
    Art. 6 ....4.19, 6.84
    Art. 12 ....4.19, 6.84
    Art. 30 76
    Art. 39 ....72, 76, 77, 4.9, 4.17–20, 4.21–4, 4.27, 4.30–5, 4.37–41, 4.45,
                                                              4.56, 4.57, 4.59, 4.60
    Art. 43 ....4.9, 4.22, 4.24
    Art. 48 ....72, 76, 77, 2.58, 4.9, 4.17–24, 4.27, 4.30–5, 4.37–41, 4.45,
                                                          4.56, 4.57, 4.59, 4.60, 8.53
    Art. 48(3) 4.20
    Art. 49 ....75, 4.9, 4.13, 4.22, 4.24–6, 4.65, 6.84
    Art. 52 ....2.58, 4.22, 4.24
    Art. 59 ....75, 4.9, 4.13, 4.22, 4.24–6, 4.65, 6.84
    Art. 73b...2.58
    Art. 81 ....80, 81, 142, 4.9, 4.12, 4.15, 4.17, 4.39–46, 4.65, 6.21–3, 6.26,
                    6.27, 6.29, 6.34–6, 6.40, 6.47, 6.48, 6.54, 6.57, 6.71, 6.81, 6.86, 6.88
    Art. 81(1) ....146, 6.23, 6.28—32, 6.37, 6.39, 6.40, 6.61, 6.65–7, 6.71–4,
                                                              6.76, 6.83, 6.84
    Art. 81(2) 6.23
    Art. 81(3) 6.23, 6.37, 6.61, 6.65–8, 6.72

Art. 82 ....80, 81, 142, **4.9, 4.12, 4.17, 4.39, 4.40, 4.45–8, 4.65,**
6.21, 6.27, 6.34, 6.36, 6.40–2, 6.45, 6.54, 6.57, 6.84

Art. 85..........80, 81, 142, 144, 166, **2.58, 3.62, 3.65, 3.67, 4.9, 4.12, 4.15, 4.17,**
4.39–46, 4.65, 6.21–3, 6.26, 6.27, 6.29, 6.34–6,
6.40, 6.47, 6.48, 6.54, 6.57, 6.71, 6.81, 6.86, 6.88

Art. 85(1) 64, 144, 146, 161, **3.67, 4.44, 6.23, 6.28–32, 6.37,**
6.39, 6.40, 6.61, 6.65–7, 6.71–4, 6.76, 6.83, 6.84

Art. 85(2) **3.67, 6.23**

Art. 85(3) 64, **4.44, 6.23, 6.37, 6.61, 6.65–8, 6.72**

Art. 86 ....80, 81, 142, **2.58, 3.62, 3.65, 3.67, 4.9, 4.12, 4.17, 4.39,**
4.40, 4.45–8, 4.65, 6.21, 6.27, 6.34, 6.36,
6.40–2, 6.45, 6.54, 6.57, 6.84, 6.86

Art. 86(2) **6.68**

Art. 90(1) 158

Art. 90(2) 158, **6.68**

Art. 177 ....243, **8.8**

Art. 234 ....**8.8**

Vienna Convention on the Law of Treaties (1980) 262

Index

Actovegin, 7.50, 7.51
Adidas, sponsorship, 2.35
Administrative law *see* Public law
AEK Athens FC, 3.34, 3.67, 3.68, 4.12
Agreements,
　block exemptions, 6.37, 6.38
　competition restricted, 6.30–3
　exclusive purchasing, 6.32
　horizontal, 6.31
　undertakings, 4.41–2, 6.23, 6.28–32
　vertical, 6.31, 6.32
Amateur Swimming Association, 5.47
Anderson, Rachel, 4.89
Andrade, Henry, 7.14, 7.15
Anglia Polytechnic University, 1.1
Appeals,
　earlier defects cured, 7.56, 7.100, 7.112,
　　7.114, 7.115, 8.74
　estoppel, 7.112, 7.113
　fairness, 7.99, 7.100
　fresh evidence, 7.22, 7.66
　Independent Appeal Panel, 7.54, 7.55
　injunctions, 8.65
　reasons, 7.78
　rules, 7.21, 7.22, 7.99, 7.100, 8.2
　waiver, 7.112
Applications,
　licensing *see under* Licensing
　membership *see under* Membership
Arbitration,
　advantages, 8.81
　contracts,
　　contra proferentem, 1.22
　　doubt/obligations, 1.22
　　intention of parties, 1.21, 1.22
　　interpretation, 1.22
　estoppel, 8.89
　Football Association (FA), 8.2, 8.63, 8.84,
　　8.85, 8.87
　international,
　　CAS *see* Court of Arbitration in Sport
　　development, 8.90
　International Amateur Athletic Federation
　　(IAAF), 8.2, 8.94
　jurisdiction, 8.2, 8.7, 8.89
　legitimate expectation, 1.21
　lex mercatoria, 1.21
　membership, applications, 8.87
　remedies, 8.81–108
　rules, 8.2, 8.63, 8.83
　stay of proceedings, 8.84
　summary judgments, 8.86
Arsenal FC, 8.38

Assault,
　see also Torts
　figure skating, 8.100
　football, 5.44
　intention, 5.31, 5.66, 5.72
Associations,
　Swiss law, 3.35
　undertakings, 4.41, 4.42, 6.27, 6.29
　unincorporated *see* Unincorporated
　　associations
Athletics,
　Athletics Australia, 7.48
　BAF *see* British Athletic Federation
　doping *see* Banned substances
　Federazione Italiana di Atletica Leggera
　　(FIDAL), 8.96
　IAAF *see* International Amateur Athletic
　　Federation
　Olympics *see* Olympics
　Singapore Amateur Athletic Association, 7.4
　United States Amateur Athletic Federation,
　　7.43
Australia,
　Athletics Australia, 7.48
　Australian Cricket Association, 4.75
　Australian Rules Football Authority, 4.75
　case law, 1.16
　cricket, restraint of trade, 4.75
　cycling, Olympics, 3.58–60
　judicial review, 8.22
　public law, 7.59
　rugby league,
　　competitions, 3.20, 3.21, 3.30, 3.31, 8.77
　　New South Wales, 4.53, 4.74, 8.36
　　restraint of trade, 4.53, 4.74, 8.36
　trotting horses, 7.59, 7.76
　unfair prejudice petitions, 8.79

Bad faith,
　disciplinary procedures, 7.9, 7.57, 7.58
　public law, 7.57, 7.58
Banned substances,
　see also Disciplinary procedures
　accidental contamination, 7.42, 7.43, 7.49, 7.51
　actovegin, 7.50, 7.51
　anti-technicality, 7.126
　basketball, 7.29, 7.92
　Court of Arbitration in Sport (CAS),
　　principles, 7.8, 7.27, 7.116–27
　Ephedrine, 7.27
　evidence,
　　conclusive, 7.19
　　experts, 7.37

Banned substances (*cont.*):
  Federation Internationale de Natation
    Amateur (FINA), 7.30, 7.31, 7.95, 7.120
  horse racing, 7.23–4
  horse shows, 7.118, 7.122
  innocent ingestion, 7.29, 7.42–3, 7.49–51,
    8.96
  International Amateur Athletic Federation
    (IAAF), 3.45, 4.14, 4.26, 7.16–17,
    7.39–40, 7.48, 8.94–6, 8.99
  IOC Medical Code, 8.93, 8.96
  nandrolone, 8.99
  Naproxen, 7.24
  offences, types, 7.40
  out of season testing, 8.94
  penalties *see* sanctions
  prior notification, 7.28, 7.32, 7.120
  propoxyphene metabolite, 7.31
  restraint of trade, 3.45, 4.26, 7.12, 7.16, 7.17
  rules,
    conclusive evidence, 7.19
    construction, 7.27
    EU law application, 4.13, 4.14
    national law, 4.14, 4.26
    rebuttable presumption of guilt, 7.30,
      7.93, 7.95
    strict liability, 3.45, 7.26, 7.29–32, 7.38–9,
      7.49, 7.92, 7.125, 8.96
    voluntary ingestion presumed, 7.18
  salbutamol, 7.28, 7.32, 7.120
  samples,
    custody, 7.48, 7.49
    degradation, 7.55
    testing procedures, 7.19, 7.37, 7.54, 8.76
  standard of proof, 7.48
  swimming, 7.28, 7.30, 7.31, 7.50, 7.93, 7.94
  tennis, 4.13, 4.25
  testosterone, 7.43, 7.54, 8.95
  triamtarene, 7.50, 7.51
  water polo, 7.32, 7.120
Bar Sports Law Group, 1.1
Barbados, case law, 1.16, 5.81–5
Barcelona, 4.38
Barr-Smith, Adrian, 1.30
Basketball,
  banned substances, 7.29, 7.92
  Harlem Globetrotters, 2.34
  International Basketball Association, 3.56,
    3.57
  National Basketball Association (NBA), 6.5
  National Wheelchair Basketball Association,
    7.29, 7.92
  Puerto Rico, 3.56, 3.57
Benn, Nigel, 8.62
Bertelsmann, 6.66
Blackburn Rovers FC, 7.73
Bosman, Jean-Marc, 4.28
Botham, Ian, 8.5, 8.78

Bowls, non-contact sports, 5.38
Boxing,
  British Boxing Board of Control, 3.10, 3.17,
    4.87, 8.36, 8.70
  contact sport, 5.38, 5.78, 5.79
  contracts, 2.34, 3.27, 3.28, 8.62
  disciplinary procedures, 8.70
  injunctions, 8.64, 8.70
  injury, consent, 5.78, 5.79
  legal disputes, 3.27, 3.28, 8.116
  licensing,
    fairness, 3.17–19
    requirements, 3.5, 3–10
  restraint of trade, 4.77–8, 8.36
  WBC *see* World Boxing Council
  women, 4.94, 4.97
  World Boxing Organisation, 8.64
Brazil, 1998 World Cup, 2.35
British Amateur Weightlifters' Association, 2.13
British Association for Sports and Law, 1.1
British Athletic Federation,
  Independent Appeal Panel, 7.54, 7.55
  Modahl case, 1.8, 7.54–6
British Boxing Board of Control, 3.10, 3.17,
    4.87, 8.36, 8.70
British Broadcasting Corporation (BBC), 6.10,
    6.74
British Judo Association (BJA), 4.86
British Olympic Association, 8.123
British Satellite Broadcasting (BSB), 6.10
Broadcasting contracts,
  anti-competitive practices, 6.77
  Capital Gold Sport, 2.35
  collective selling, 6.8, 6.56–63
  competition law, 2.36, 6.47–77
  exclusive rights, 6.70–6
  joint purchasing, 6.64–9
  markets,
    free to air TV, 6.49–51
    geography, 6.55
    live/recorded, 6.54
    pay-TV, 6.49–51
    relevant, 6.49–55
    types of sport, 6.52, 6.53
  motor racing, 6.62, 6.76
  Netherlands, 6.75
  sponsorship, 2.35
Broadcasting rights,
  commercial value, 6.1–3
  copyright, 6.9–12
  cricket, 6.19
  European law, 6.14–17
  European Parliament, 6.16
  football, 6.2, 6.8, 6.10, 6.19
  golf, 6.19
  horse racing, 6.19
  Independent Television Commission (ITC),
    6.15, 6.18

licensing, 6.6, 6.15
listed events, 6.18, 6.19
Olympics, 6.3, 6.19
regulation, 6.13–19
rugby league, 3.29
sale, league rules, 6.8
scope, 6.4–8
sports grounds, access, 6.6, 6.7
statute law, 6.15–19
tennis, 6.19
unfair competition, 6.5, 6.6
United States, 6.5
World Cup, 6.2, 6.10, 6.19
Bruno, Frank, 3.27, 3.28, 8.116
BSkyB, 6.51, 6.54, 6.66, 6.74
Bungs, football, 2.46
Burden of proof,
    disciplinary procedures, 7.18, 7.38–44
    Federation Internationale de Natation
        Amateur (FINA), 7.51
    general rule, 7.38
    inquisitorial jurisdiction, 7.44
    just cause, 7.41
    restraint of trade, 3.41–4, 3.50
Burley, George, 8.63

Canal Plus, 6.66
Cantona, Eric, 5.44
Cape Verde NOC, 7.14
Capital Gold Sport, 2.35
Capobianco, Dean, 7.48, 8.94
Cardiff RFC, 8.48
Carling, Will, 5.44
Celtic FC, 4.32
Central Council of Physical Recreation, 8.123
Charlton Athletic FC, 6.8
Chelsea FC, 2.4, 2.29, 4.45, 4.60
Children, coaching, 5.47–8
China, participation rights, 8.97
Clausula rebus sic stantibus, meaning, 1.21
Clubs,
    see also Unincorporated associations
    commercial sports clubs, 2.22
    football *see* Football clubs
    indirect members, 3.35
    players' rights *see* Players' rights
Coaching,
    children, 5.47–8
    economic loss, 5.46
    failure to advise, 5.47
    football, sex discrimination, 4.84
Colchester United FC, 8.63, 8.84
Collins, John, 4.32
Comite francais d'Organisation de la Coupe du
        Monde de Football 1998 (CFO), 6.83,
        6.84
Commercial sports clubs, contracts, 2.22
Common law,

contracts of employment, 2.28
damages, 8.34
discrimination, 4.81, 4.82
regulation of play, 5.6
restraint of trade *see* Restraint of trade
right to work, 4.82
Commonwealth, case law, 1.16, 4.53
Commonwealth Games Federation,
    competitions, eligibility, 3.52, 8.98
    constitution, 1.19
Companies,
    see also Unincorporated Associations
    contractual obligations, 2.25, 2.26
    expulsion from membership, 2.41–3
    football clubs, 2.4
    legal background, 2.7–9
    locus standi, 2.15
    shareholders, 2.26
    sporting associations, 2.3, 2.5, 2.6
    unfair prejudice petitions, 8.79, 8.80
Competition law,
    see also Restraint of trade
    broadcasting *see* Broadcasting contracts
    competitions, 2.59, 3.7, 3.30, 3.62–8, 6.33
    direct effect, 6.21
    dominant position, 3.65, 3.67, 6.41–6
    enforcement, 6.39, 6.40
    European Economic Area (EEA), 4.43
    exclusive purchasing agreements, 6.32
    exemptions, 4.44, 6.37, 6.38
    horizontal agreements, 6.31
    inefficient competitors, 3.63, 6.33
    inter-state trade, 4.48, 6.21, 6.23, 6.34–6
    market definition, 6.42, 6.43
    marketing *see* Marketing
    transfer system *see under* Transfer fees
    treaty provisions, 6.22, 6.41
    UK implementation, 6.21
    undertakings,
        agreements, 4.41–2, 6.23, 6.28–32
        associations, 4.41, 4.42, 6.27, 6.29
        concerted practices, 6.23, 6.28
        definition, 4.41, 6.24
        professional clubs, 6.25
    vertical agreements, 6.31, 6.32
Competitions,
    access, 3.1–68
    Australia, rugby league, 3.20, 3.21, 3.30,
        3.31, 8.77
    competition law, 2.59, 3.7, 3.30, 3.62–8, 6.33
    contracts,
        access, 2.23, 2.24, 3.24–36
        economic duress, 3.31
        enforcement, 3.26
        fidelity, 3.30
        international litigation, 3.34, 3.35
        pre-existing rights, 3.25, 3.26
        prior commitment, 3.30–2

Competitions (*cont.*):
  discipline *see* Disciplinary procedures
  doping *see* Banned substances
  eligibility,
    Commonwealth Games, 3.52, 8.98
    cycling, 3.58–60
    domicile, 2.40, 3.52, 8.98
    entry criteria, 3.1–9
    swimming, 3.52, 3.61
  fairness, 3.10–23
  free standing challenges, 3.49–61
  licensing, 3.5, 3.6, 3.10
  nationality, 3.56, 3.57
  non-contractual claims, 3.49–61
  participation rights,
    applications, 3.16
    injunctions, 3.33, 3.36, 8.41
    national teams, 8.97
    rugby league, 3.29
    rugby union, 3.33
  restraint of trade, 3.45–8
  rules, 3.2–6
  selection,
    criteria, 3.58
    domicile, 2.40, 3.52, 8.98
    legitimate expectation, 3.59, 3.60, 7.124
    nationality, 3.56, 3.57
Concerted practices,
  definition, 6.28
  undertakings, 6.23, 6.28
Consent,
  defences,
    criminal law, 5.77–9
    good reason, 5.77, 5.79
  risk *see Volenti non fit injuria*
Contact sports,
  boxing *see* Boxing
  criminal law, 2.45, 5.78, 5.79
  negligence, 5.37, 5.38, 5.48, 5.49
Conteh, John, 8.70
Contra proferentem, meaning, 1.22
Contracts,
  boxing, 2.34, 3.27–8, 8.62
  breach of contract, 4.35, 8.63, 8.72, 9.75
  broadcasting *see* Broadcasting contracts
  chains of obligations, 2.31, 2.32
  commercial sports clubs, 2.22
  competitions *see under* Competitions
  contra proferentem rule, 1.22
  declaratory judgments, 8.36
  disciplinary procedures, 7.4–6, 7.53, 7.61
  doubt/obligations, 1.22
  economic loss, 2.50
  freedom of contract,
    meaning, 1.21
    membership applications, 3.12, 3.13
  functus officio, 7.114
  gaming/wagering, 2.24

  horizontal matrix, 2.21, 2.23, 2.25
  implied terms, 7.53, 7.55, 7.56, 7.75, 7.76
  intention of parties, 1.21, 1.22
  international law,
    applicable law, 8.120
    principles, 1.21, 8.106
  international sporting bodies, 2.31, 2.32
  interpretation, 1.22
  judicial review, 8.16, 8.17
  licensing, 8.16
  mutual obligations, 2.25, 2.26
  penalty clauses, 4.36
  restraint of trade *see* Restraint of trade
  rights/obligations, 2.18–37
  sanctions, 7.87, 7.89, 7.90
  spectators, 2.37
  sponsorship, 2.35
  transfer system *see* Transfer fees
  unincorporated associations, 2.20, 2.21, 2.24
  vertical, 2.26
Contracts of employment,
  common law rights, 2.28
  fairness, 7.75
  garden leave, 8.60
  governing bodies, 2.30
  implied terms, 7.75, 7.76
  injunctions, 8.51, 8.61
  negotiation, 2.27
  restraint of trade, 3.40, 3.51, 4.50, 4.73–9, 8.61
  restrictive covenants, 8.60, 8.61
  specific performance, 8.51, 8.61
  statutory rights, 2.29
  team sports, 2.27
  terms and conditions, 4.73–9
  transfer system *see* Transfer fees
  transparency, 7.25
Contributory negligence, personal injuries, 5.56
Copyright,
  assignment, 6.12
  broadcasting rights, 6.9–12
  fair dealing, 6.10, 6.11
  licensing, 6.12, 6.72
  Sport News Access Code of Practice, 6.11
  substantial part, 6.9, 6.10
Corruption, sport, 2.44, 2.46
Costs, disciplinary procedures, 7.97, 7.98
Court of Arbitration in Sport (CAS),
  Ad Hoc Division, 8.103
  ad hoc rules, 1.19
  Appeal Arbitrations Division, 8.102
  banned substances, principles, 7.8, 7.27, 7.116–27
  Code of Sports Related Arbitration, 8.103
  competitions,
    competition law, 3.68
    late entrants, 3.61

legitimate expectation, 3.59, 3.60, 7.124
  nationality, 3.56, 3.57
  selection criteria, 3.58
decisions, reports, 1.26
effectiveness, 8.101
European law, 2.58, 8.107
forum of last resort, 8.122
ICAS, 8.93
interim relief, 8.66, 8.67
IOC Medical Code, 8.106
judicial restraints, 7.117
jurisdiction, 8.101–8
membership, 1.25
Ordinary Arbitration Division, 8.102
own view substituted, 7.94
purposive construction, 2.40
sanctions, 7.92–5
standard of proof, 7.47
Switzerland, 1.17, 1.18, 1.20, 2.57, 2.58,
  7.116, 8.105
UEFA Cup, 3.33, 3.34, 3.67, 3.68
Coventry City FC, 8.59
Cowley, 3.52
Cricket,
  Australian Cricket Association, 4.75
  Barbados Cricket Association, 5.82, 5.83
  broadcasting rights, 6.19
  International Cricket Council (ICC), 3.51,
    4.52, 4.73
  legal disputes, result of game, 5.81–5
  Marylebone Cricket Club (MCC), 2.17, 4.89
  restraint of trade, 3.51, 4.52, 4.73, 4.75
  Test and County Cricket Board (TCCB),
    3.51, 4.52, 4.73
Criminal law,
  contact sports, 2.45, 5.78, 5.79
  corruption, 2.44, 2.46
  defences, consent, 5.77–9
  general application, 2.44, 5.5
  intoxication, 5.24
  overlapping enforcement, 2.44
  prohibited sports, 2.47, 5.12–14
  public order offences, 5.23–9
  regulation of play, 5.80
  ticket touting, 5.28, 6.79
Cross examination, disciplinary procedures,
  7.60, 7.71, 7.72, 7.113
Cruz, Jose, 3.56, 3.57
Cycling,
  competitions, eligibility, 3.58–60
  Union Cycliste International, 4.23

Damages,
  breach of contract, 8.63, 8.72, 9.75
  common law, 8.34
  economic loss, 8.77
  libel, 8.78
  loss of chance, 5.68–70, 8.76

  negligence, 8.76
  personal injuries, 5.67–70
  public law, 7.56–8
  restraint of trade, 8.75
  significance, 8.35, 8.47, 8.72
  testing procedures, 8.76
  torts, 5.67–70, 8.72
  undertakings in damages, 8.42–5, 8.47, 8.73
  United States, 8.99
Decker-Slaney, Mary, 7.43, 8.95
Declaratory judgments,
  see also Legal disputes
  contracts, 8.36
  declaration simpliciter, 8.37, 8.38, 8.49
  disciplinary procedures, 7.6, 8.10
  discretion, 8.39
  efficacy, 8.36
  final order only, 8.40
  non-contractual cases, 3.50–3, 8.37, 8.38
  procedural exclusivity rule, 8.23
  restraint of trade, 3.49, 3.51–3, 4.74, 8.36
Defamation, torts, 2.51
Defences,
  consent, criminal law, 5.77–9
  innocent ingestion, 7.29, 7.42–3, 7.49–51,
    8.96
  negligence *see under* Negligence
  prior notification, 7.28, 7.32, 7.120
  rebuttable presumption of guilt, 7.30, 7.93,
    7.95
Delay, injunctions, 8.56–9
Denmark,
  merchandising, 6.87
  transfer fees, 4.37
Deutscher Fussball-Bund, 6.62
Direct effect,
  competition law, 6.21
  free movement of workers, 4.23
Disasters, sports grounds, 5.20, 5.54, 5.55
Disciplinary procedures,
  see also Criminal law
  a posteriori application, 5.4
  acquiescence, 7.111, 7.112, 7.113
  adversarial, 7.44, 7.60, 7.61, 7.71
  appeals *see* Appeals
  assault, figure skating, 8.100
  bad faith, 7.9, 7.57, 7.58
  boxing, 8.70
  burden of proof, 7.18, 7.38–44
  check list, 7.106
  contracts, 7.4–6, 7.53, 7.61
  costs, 7.97, 7.98
  declaratory judgments, 7.6, 8.10
  defective charges, 7.9
  discretion, 7.59–61, 7.70, 7.73
  disputed *see* Legal disputes
  doping *see* Banned substances
  equal treatment, 1.23

Disciplinary procedures (*cont.*):
  evidence,
    appeals, 7.22, 7.66
    autonomy of decision, 7.34
    conclusive, 7.19
    disclosure, 7.121
    exculpatory, 7.30, 7.93, 7.95, 7.114
    experts, 7.35–7
    fairness, 7.35, 7.80
    findings unsupported, 7.9
    hearsay, 7.35
    legal disputes, 7.33
    strict rules inapplicable, 7.9, 7.35
    weight of evidence, 7.46, 7.47
  fairness,
    allegations challenged, 7.60
    allegations communicated, 7.62
    appeals *see* Appeals
    as a whole, 7.55, 7.56
    attendance, 7.74, 7.85
    benefit of doubt, 7.122
    bias, 7.54–5, 7.57, 7.64–8, 7.86, 7.112, 7.119
    cross examination, 7.60, 7.71, 7.72, 7.76, 7.113
    discretion, 7.59, 7.70, 7.73
    due process, 7.118
    evidence, 7.35, 7.80
    fair hearing, 7.75
    good faith, 1.23, 7.120
    human rights, 7.81–6
    impartiality, 7.86
    implied terms, 7.53, 7.55, 7.56, 7.75, 7.76, 8.74
    judge in one's own cause, 7.65
    legal representation, 7.69–72
    oral hearings, 7.74, 7.85
    pecuniary/proprietary interest, 7.67
    personal hostility, 7.68
    public law, 7.76
    publicity, 7.65
    reasons, 7.78–80
    representations, 7.60, 7.63
    rules, 7.52
    scope of duty, 7.54–61, 7.84
    third parties, 7.73
    time, 7.86
    unfairness, 7.9, 7.52
    witnesses, 7.71
  findings,
    autonomy of decision, 7.34
    finality, 7.111
    unsupported by evidence, 7.9
  Football Association (FA), 7.25, 7.66
  framework documents, 7.105, 7.106
  general considerations, 7.1–9
  horse racing, 7.21–4, 7.76
  horse trainers, 7.67
  inquisitorial, 7.44, 7.71
  issues,
    agreement, 7.109
    lists, 7.108
    procedural, 7.110
  legal advice *see* Legal advice
  objections, 7.111, 7.112
  omnia rite praesumuntur esse, 7.49
  penalties *see* Sanctions
  practical management, 7.101–15
  presumption of regularity, 7.49
  prior legal relation, 7.3, 7.4, 7.7
  publicity, 7.65
  reservation of position, 7.111
  rugby union, 7.60, 7.71, 7.113, 8.46
  rules,
    appeals, 7.21, 7.22
    burden of proof, 7.18
    doping *see* Banned substances
    drafting, 7.103
    fairness, 7.52
    guidelines, 7.123
    legal disputes, 7.10
    misconstruction/misapplication, 7.9, 7.22–5
    recourse to law prohibited, 7.10
    true construction, 7.20
    unconstitutional, 7.13, 7.14
    validity, 7.11–19
  sanctions *see* Sanctions
  shooting, 7.74
  standard of proof, 7.45–8
  third parties, adverse interest, 7.73
  tribunals,
    bias, 7.54–5, 7.57, 7.64–8, 7.86, 7.112, 7.119
    improperly constituted, 7.13
    independent membership, 7.107
    judge in one's own cause, 7.65
    lawyer membership, 7.104
    pecuniary/proprietary interest, 7.67
  unfairness, 7.9, 7.52
  unlawfully conducted, 7.9
  weight of evidence, 7.46, 7.47
Discretion,
  declaratory judgments, 8.39
  disciplinary procedures, 7.59–61, 7.70–73
  injunctions, 8.65
  sanctions, 7.89, 7.90
Discrimination,
  areas of discrimination, 4.86–90
  common law, 4.81, 4.82
  decency/privacy, 4.98
  direct/indirect, 4.83, 4.91
  exemptions, 4.92–9
  free movement *see under* Free movement of workers
  goods/facilities/services, 4.88, 4.89

justification, 4.91
qualifying bodies, 4.86, 4.87
race, 4.81, 4.84
restraint of trade, 4.82
sex,
    average woman test, 4.93–7
    football coaching, 4.84
    golf, 4.83, 4.99
    horse trainers, 2.53, 3.15, 4.81, 8.38
    judo, 4.86, 4.94
    PFA dinner, 4.89
    RFU Committee, 4.90
    snooker, 4.94
single sex clubs/activities, 4.89, 4.98, 4.99
statute law, 4.80, 4.83
ticket sales, 6.84
vicarious liability, 4.85
Disputes *see* Legal disputes
Domicile, competitions, eligibility, 2.40, 3.52,
    8.98
Dominant position,
    abuse, 6.41–2, 6.45–6
    competition law, 3.65, 3.67, 6.41–6
    dominance, 6.44
    market definition, 6.42, 6.43
Drugs *see* Banned substances
Dundee United FC, 7.78

Eastham, George, 3.51, 8.38, 8.75
Ebbw Vale RFC, 7.113, 8.48
Economic loss,
    coaching, 5.46
    contracts, 2.50
    damages, 8.77
Employment,
    contracts *see* Contracts of employment
    discrimination *see* Discrimination
    employment law, 4.72
    equivalent qualifications, 4.61–3
    free movement *see* Free movement of
        workers
    players' rights *see* Players' rights
    self-employment, 2.27, 4.22
    semi-professional, 4.22
    terms and conditions, 4.73–9
    transfer system *see* Transfer fees
    work permits, 4.5, 4.66–71
    worker, definition, 4.21, 4.22
Enfield Town FC, 3.55, 8.88
Enforcement,
    competition law, 6.39, 6.40
    contracts, 3.26
    criminal law, 2.44
    private action, 6.40
English National Investment Co Plc (ENIC),
    3.34, 3.56
Ephedrine, 7.27
Equal treatment, disciplinary procedures, 1.23

Estoppel,
    appeals, 7.112, 7.113
    arbitration, 8.89
European Broadcasting Union (EBU), 6.3, 6.67,
    6.68
European Commission,
    block exemptions, 6.37, 6.38
    collective selling, 6.56, 6.60–2
    enforcement, 6.40
    exclusive purchasing rights, 6.71, 6.72,
        6.74–6
    joint purchasing, 6.64–9
    merchandising, 6.87, 6.88
    World Cup ticket sales, 6.80–4
European Court of Human Rights, 2.62, 8.29,
    8.30, 8.32
European Court of Justice (ECJ),
    dominant position, abuse, 6.45
    exclusive purchasing rights, 6.71
    rules,
        purpose/effect, 4.10, 4.15, 4.59, 4.60
        sporting interest only, 4.11, 4.16, 4.57,
            4.59–60, 4.65
    vertical agreements, 6.32
European Economic Area (EEA),
    competition law, 4.43
    free movement of workers, 4.23, 4.32, 4.64
European law,
    broadcasting rights, 6.14–17
    competition *see* Competition law
    Court of Arbitration in Sport (CAS), 2.58,
        8.107
    direct effect, 4.23, 6.21
    ECJ *see* European Court of Justice
    economic activities, 4.10
    free movement *see* Free movement of
        workers
    sport, 2.47–60, 4.10–48, 5.18, 6.20–77
European Parliament, broadcasting rights, 6.16
Eurovision, 6.3, 6.67, 6.68
Evans, Janet, 3.61
Evidence,
    affidavits, 8.11, 8.13
    banned substances, 7.19, 7.37
    disciplinary proceedings *see under*
        Disciplinary procedures
    oral, 8.13
    weight of evidence, 7.46, 7.47
Exemptions,
    block exemptions, 6.37, 6.38
    competition law, 4.44, 6.37, 6.38
    discrimination, 4.92–9
    transfer fees, 4.44
Experts, duties, 7.36

Fairness,
    competitions, 3.10–23
    context, 3.23

Fairness (*cont.*):
  contracts of employment, 7.75
  examinations, golf, 3.22
  implied terms, 7.53, 7.55, 7.56
  licensing, boxing, 3.17–19
  procedural *see under* Disciplinary proce-
    dures
  public law, 7.76, 7.77
  rules, United States, 3.16
  sporting associations, 3.10–23
FC Liege, 4.28
Federation Internationale de l'Automobile
    (FIA), 6.76
Federation Internationale de Natation
    Amateur (FINA),
  appeals, 8.2
  banned substances, 7.30, 7.31, 7.51, 7.95,
    7.120
  burden of proof, 7.51
  CAS recognised, 8.93
  dispute resolution, 1.17
  late entrants, 3.61
  strict liability, 7.30, 7.31
Federazione Italia Gioco Calcio (FIGC), 6.81
Federazione Italiana di Atletica Leggera
    (FIDAL), 8.96
Ferguson, Duncan, 5.80
FIFA,
  contracts, 2.31
  free movement of workers, 4.23
  Georgia, 1.4
  ICAS/CAS unrecognised, 8.93
  Switzerland, 2.6, 2.57
  transfer fees, 4.29, 4.37, 4.38
  undertaking, 6.26
  World Cup, 6.2, 6.10, 6.19, 6.26, 6.80–4
Figure skating, assault, 8.100
Football,
  1990 World Cup, 6.10, 6.26, 6.81–83
  1998 World Cup, 2.35, 6.2, 6.83, 6.84
  additional offences, 5.28
  assault, 5.44
  average woman test, 4.95
  broadcasting rights, 6.2, 6.8, 6.10, 6.19
  bungs, 2.46
  coaching, sex discrimination, 4.84
  complex cases, 8.68
  exclusion/restriction orders, 5.25, 5.26
  expert evidence, 7.36
  FIFA *see* FIFA
  fixture cancelled, 7.89
  fouls, 5.36
  Hillsborough disaster, 5.20, 5.54, 5.55
  Membership Authority (proposed), 5.25
  personal injuries,
    fouls, 5.36
    police, 5.53, 5.55
  points deduction, 7.89, 7.90, 8.59, 8.88

  race discrimination, 4.84
  replica kit, 6.43
  stadia,
    disasters, 5.20, 5.54, 5.55
    public order offences, 5.23–9
    safety certificates, 5.21, 5.22
    standards, 3.13, 3.48, 3.66
  ticket touting, 5.28, 6.79
  trainers, qualifications, 4.62
  transfer system *see* Transfer fees
  UEFA *see* Union des Associations
    Europeennes de Football
  Welsh Football Association, 3.54, 3.55, 8.18,
    8.48, 8.59, 8.75
  work permits, 4.68–71
Football Association (FA),
  arbitration, 8.2, 8.63, 8.84, 8.85, 8.87
  disciplinary procedures, 7.25, 7.66
  inquiries, 5.53
  legal status, 2.3, 2.25
  Premier League, 2.25, 6.8, 6.63, 6.74
  qualifying bodies, 4.87
  work permits, 4.68
Football clubs,
  AEK Athens FC, 3.34, 3.67, 3.68, 4.12
  Arsenal FC, 8.38
  Barcelona, 4.38
  Blackburn Rovers FC, 7.73
  Celtic FC, 4.32
  Charlton Athletic FC, 6.8
  Chelsea FC, 2.4, 2.29, 4.45, 4.60
  Colchester United FC, 8.63, 8.84
  companies, 2.4
  Coventry City FC, 8.59
  Dundee United FC, 7.78
  Enfield Town FC, 3.55, 8.88
  FC Liege, 4.28
  Glasgow Rangers FC, 4.45, 5.80
  Inter Milan, 4.38
  Ipswich Town FC, 8.63, 8.84
  Leicester City FC, 4.71
  Lille Olympic FC, 4.62
  Liverpool FC, 1.4, 4.71
  Manchester United FC, 2.29, 6.1, 6.8, 6.43
  Middlesborough FC, 2.4, 7.73, 7.89, 8.59
  Monaco FC, 4.32
  Newcastle United FC, 3.51, 8.38, 8.75
  Newport FC, 3.54, 3.55, 8.49, 8.59, 8.75
  Notts County FC, 8.85
  Portsmouth FC, 4.70
  Raith Rovers FC, 5.80
  Reading FC, 5.53
  SK Slavia Prague, 3.34, 4.12
  Southampton FC, 6.8
  Southend United FC, 8.85
  Stevenage Borough FC, 3.13, 3.55, 3.66, 6.35,
    8.24, 8.57, 8.58, 8.87
  Torquay United FC, 8.58

Tottenham Hotspur FC, 2.4, 7.91, 8.59, 8.88
US Dunkerque, 4.28
Football League,
  entry criteria, 3.13, 3.48, 3.66
  restraint of trade, 3.51
Force majeure, meaning, 1.21
Formula One Administration (FOA), 6.76
Fouls, torts, 5.36, 5.37
France,
  football,
    1998 World Cup, 2.35, 6.83, 6.84
    Comite francais d'Organisation de la
      Coupe du Monde de Football 1998
      (CFO), 6.83, 6.84
    trainers' qualifications, 4.62
    transfer fees, 4.38
  rugby union, 3.33
Free movement of workers,
  see also Nationality
  direct effect, 4.23
  discrimination,
    derogations, 4.20, 4.24
    indirect, 4.19
    prohibition, 4.19, 4.20, 4.30
    reverse, 4.33
    solo players, 4.22, 4.24
  equivalent qualifications, 4.61–3
  European Economic Area (EEA), 4.23, 4.32,
    4.64
  European law, 2.58, 4.9, 4.18–40
  movement hindered, 4.30
  restrictions, 2.58
  semi-professionals, 4.22
  transfer fees, 4.9, 4.30
  treaty provisions, 4.18
  worker, definition, 4.21, 4.22
Freedom of contract,
  see also Contracts
  meaning, 1.21
  membership, applications, 3.12, 3.13
Friedel, Brad, 4.71
Functus officio, contracts, 7.114

Georgia, FIFA, 1.4
Germany, Deutscher Fussball-Bund, 6.62
Glasgow Rangers FC, 4.45, 5.80
Golf,
  broadcasting rights, 6.19
  examinations,
    fairness, 3.22
    restraint of trade, 3.46
  personal injuries,
    participants, 5.36, 5.39, 5.56
    spectators, 5.31
  sex discrimination, 4.83, 4.99
Good faith,
  disciplinary procedures, 1.23, 7.120
  meaning, 1.21

Swiss law of associations, 3.35
Governing bodies,
  see also Sporting associations
  associations of undertakings, 4.41, 4.42, 6.27
  autonomy, 1.7, 1.12, 2.60
  contracts of employment, 2.30
  discipline *see* Disciplinary procedures
  international *see* International sporting
    bodies
  judicial review, 4.63, 8.9, 8.15–20
  legal disputes, 7.58, 7.61
  restraint of trade *see* Restraint of trade
  rules *see* Rules
  UEFA *see* Union des Associations
    Europeennes de Football
Grayson, Edward, 1.30, 5.13
Griffith-Jones, David, 1.30

Harding, Tonya, 8.100
Harlem Globetrotters, 2.34
Hillsborough disaster, 5.20, 5.54, 5.55
Holsten Pils, 2.35
Holyfield, Evander, 5.79
Hooliganism, 5.23, 5.53
Horizontal law, 1.3, 1.6, 1.11, 1.32, 2.18
Horse racing,
  banned substances, 7.23–4
  broadcasting rights, 6.19
  disciplinary procedures, 7.21–4, 7.76
  Jockey Club *see* Jockey Club
  trainers,
    disciplinary procedures, 7.67
    sex discrimination, 2.53, 3.15, 4.81
Horse shows,
  banned substances, 7.118, 7.112
  spectators, personal injuries, 5.42, 5.61
Human rights,
  determination, civil rights/obligations, 7.82,
    7.83
  disciplinary procedures, 7.81–6
  European Court of Human Rights, 2.62,
    8.29, 8.30, 8.32
  legal disputes, 8.29–33
  sport, 2.61–3, 7.81–6, 8.29–33

Ice hockey, personal injuries, 5.58
Iceland, European Economic Area (EEA), 4.32,
  4.64
Immigration, work permits, 4.5, 4.66–71
Implied terms,
  contracts of employment, 7.75, 7.76
  disciplinary procedures, 7.53, 7.55, 7.56,
    7.75, 7.76
Imran Khan, 8.5, 8.78
Independent Television Commission (ITC),
  6.15, 6.18
Injunctions,
  advantages, 8.41

Injunctions (*cont.*):
  appeals, 8.65
  boxing, 8.64, 8.70
  competitions, participation, 3.33, 3.36, 8.41
  concurrent proceedings, 8.70, 8.71
  contracts of employment, 8.51, 8.61
  declaration simpliciter claimed, 8.49, 8.50
  delay, 8.56–9
  discretion, 8.65
  final, 8.42
  interim declarations, 8.40
  interim relief, 8.12, 8.14, 8.66
  interlocutory, 8.14, 8.27, 8.48, 8.60, 8.65
  licensing, applications, 3.14, 3.15
  mandatory, 8.52–5
  membership, applications, 3.12, 3.14, 3.15,
    8.51
  prohibitory, 8.52–5
  relevance, 8.42
  restraint of trade, 3.48, 3.49, 8.48
  South African rugby tour, 3.53
  specific performance, 8.51, 8.61, 8.62
  suspension lifted, 8.46
  transfer fees, 8.54
  undertakings in damages, 8.42–5, 8.47, 8.73
Institute of Professional Sport, 8.123
Institute of Sports Sponsorship, 8.123
Insurance, schools, 5.49
Intention,
  assault, 5.31, 5.66, 5.72
  negligence, 5.31
  parties, contracts, 1.21, 1.22
Inter Milan, 4.38
International Amateur Athletic Federation
  (IAAF),
  arbitration, 8.2, 8.94
  banned substances, 3.45, 4.14, 4.26, 7.16–17,
    7.39–40, 7.48, 8.94–
    6
  broadcasting rights, 6.3
  contracts, 2.31
  discrepancies with IOC Medical Code, 8.93,
    8.96
  ICAS/CAS unrecognised, 8.93
  legal disputes, 8.97–8
  restraint of trade, 3.45, 3.50, 4.26
  rules misinterpreted, 8.97
International Basketball Association, 3.56, 3.57
International Council of Arbitration in Sport
  (ICAS),
  CAS *see* Court of Arbitration in Sport
  dispute resolution, 8.93
International Cricket Council (ICC), 3.51,
  4.52, 4.73
International Equestrian Federation (FEI),
  7.118, 7.122
International law,
  applicable law, 8.120

contracts,
  applicable law, 8.120
  principles, 1.21, 8.106
  conventions, 8.112–14
  forum conveniens, 8.109, 8.111, 8.119
  private, 8.109, 8.110
  service outside jurisdiction, 8.115, 8.116
  torts, 8.120
International Paralympic Committee, 7.29
International Rugby Football Board, 3.36
International sporting bodies,
  contracts, 2.31, 2.32
  discipline *see* Disciplinary proceedings
  disputes, 2.33
  omnia rite praesumuntur esse, 7.49
  Switzerland, 2.3, 2.6, 2.57
International Symposium on Sports law (1997),
  7.40
International Tennis Federation (ITF), 4.13,
  4.25
Intoxication, offences, 5.24
IOC *see under* Olympics
Ipswich Town FC, 8.63, 8.84
Italy,
  Federazione Italiana di Atletica Leggera
    (FIDAL), 8.96
  football,
    1990 World Cup, 6.26, 6.81–3
    Federazione Italia Gioco Calcio (FIGC),
      6.81

Jockey Club,
  judicial review, 8.15, 8.16, 8.18, 8.19, 8.39
  licensing, sex discrimination, 3.15, 4.81
  representative proceedings, 2.24
Judicial review,
  see also Public law
  Australia, 8.22
  availability restricted, 4.63, 8.9, 8.15–20
  certiorari, 8.10
  contracts, 8.16, 8.17
  Jockey Club, 8.15, 8.16, 8.18, 8.19, 8.39
  New Zealand, 8.21
  public rights unaffected, 8.17
  tactics, 8.12
  test for relief, 8.14
  time limits, 8.11
Judo, referees, sex discrimination, 4.86, 4.94
Jurisdiction,
  see also Legal disputes
  adversarial, 7.44, 7.60, 7.61, 7.71
  arbitration, 8.2, 8.7, 8.89
  Court of Arbitration in Sport (CAS), 8.101–8
  inquisitorial, 7.44, 7.71
  international *see* International law
  Olympic Charter, 1.10, 1.19, 1.27, 3.57, 7.15,
    8.91, 8.103, 8.105
  original jurisdiction, 8.4

referees, 5.15–17, 7.117, 8.108
rules, 2.39, 7.10, 8.4, 8.93
sanctions, 7.87–96
supervisory, 8.3
transfer, 8.117–18
voluntary submission, 8.18, 8.19

Kalac, Zelijko, 4.70, 4.71
Keller, Kasey, 4.71
Kennel Club, 4.87
Kerrigan, Nancy, 8.100
King's College, London, 1.1
Kirk, 6.66
Krabbe, Katrine, 8.94

Lamb, Allan, 8.78
Laudrup, Brian, 4.45
Legal advice,
    desirability, 7.101, 7.102
    disciplinary procedures, 7.101–4
    when relevant, 7.103
Legal disputes,
    see also Disciplinary procedures
    appeals *see* Appeals
    arbitration *see* Arbitration
    boxing, 3.27, 3.28, 8.116
    contracts, international litigation, 3.34, 3.35
    courts,
        judicial restraint, 7.117
        original jurisdiction, 8.4
        supervisory jurisdiction, 8.3
    cricket, result of game, 5.81–5
    damages *see* Damages
    declarations *see* Declaratory judgments
    evidence,
        affidavits, 8.13
        challenged, 7.33
        oral, 8.13
    forum, 8.68, 8.109, 8.111, 8.119
    governing bodies, 7.58, 7.61
    human rights, 8.29–33
    interim relief *see* Injunctions
    International Amateur Athletic Federation
        (IAAF), 8.97–8
    judicial review *see* Judicial review
    judiciary, disqualification, 7.67
    jurisdiction *see* Jurisdiction
    legalism, 1.14–16, 7.77
    multiplicity of proceedings, 8.68–71
    procedural exclusivity rule, 8.23–6
    procedural rules, 8.13
    public law, 8.9–28
    remedies, 8.1–124
    representative *see* Representative proceed-
        ings
    rules, 7.10
    sanctions, judicial decision making, 7.91
    time limits, 8.11

unfair prejudice petitions, 8.79, 8.80
unincorporated associations, 2.15, 2.16
unitary system proposed, 8.121–4
United States, 8.99–100
Legal representation, disciplinary procedures,
    7.69–72
Legitimate expectation,
    arbitration, 1.21
    licensing, 3.18
    selection, 3.59, 3.60, 7.124
Leicester City FC, 4.71
Lewis, Lennox, 3.27, 3.28, 8.116
Lex mercatoria, arbitration, 1.21
Lex mitior, sanctions, 7.95, 7.127
Liabilities,
    injuries *see under* Personal injuries
    occupiers *see* Occupiers liability
    strict, banned substances, 3.45, 7.26,
        7.29–32, 7.38–9, 7.49, 7.92, 7.125, 8.96
    vicarious, 4.85, 5.72–5
Libel, damages, 8.78
Licensing,
    see also Membership
    applications,
        application cases, 3.18, 3.19
        compulsion, 3.14
        fairness, 3.17–19
        pre-existing relationship, 3.11
    boxing *see under* Boxing
    broadcasting, 6.6, 6.15
    competitions, 3.5, 3.6, 3.10, 3.18
    contracts, 8.16
    copyright, 6.12, 6.72
    expectation cases, 3.18
    forfeiture cases, 3.18
    greyhound racing, 8.16
    horse trainers, 2.53, 3.15, 4.81, 8.38
    Malaysia, 2.5
    merchandising, 6.85, 6.86
    voluntary activity, 8.19
Liechtenstein, European Economic Area
    (EEA), 4.32, 4.64
Lille Olympic FC, 4.62
Litigation *see* Legal disputes
Liverpool FC, 1.4, 4.71
Locus standi, companies, 2.15
Loss,
    chance, damages, 5.68–70, 8.76
    economic, 2.50, 5.46, 8.77

McStay, John, 5.80
Malaysia, licensing, 2.5
Manchester Metropolitan University, 1.1
Manchester United FC, 2.29, 6.1, 6.8, 6.43
Marketing,
    competition law, 6.78–88
    merchandising, 6.43, 6.78, 6.85–8
    ticket sales, 6.79–84

Markets,
  broadcasting contracts, 6.49–55
  definition, 6.42, 6.43
Marquette University, Milwaukee, 1.1
Marylebone Cricket Club (MCC), 2.17, 4.89
Medical Code (IOC),
  discrepancies with IAAF rules, 8.93, 8.96
  jurisdiction, 8.106
Membership,
  see also Licensing
  applications,
    arbitration, 8.87
    compulsion, 3.12, 3.14, 3.15, 8.51
    entry criteria, 3.10
    freedom of contract, 3.11, 3.12
    pre-existing relationship, 3.11
  expulsion, 2.41–3
  indirect, 3.35
  successor bodies, 2.14
Merchandising,
  licensing, 6.85, 6.86
  marketing, 6.43, 6.78, 6.85–8
  replica strip, 6.43, 6.85, 6.86
  tennis, 6.87
  trade marks, 6.85
Middlesborough FC, 2.4, 7.73, 7.89, 8.59
Misfeasance, public law, 7.57, 7.58
Modahl, Diane, 1.8, 7.54, 7.55, 7.112, 8.35,
    8.73, 8.74
Monaco FC, 4.32
Motor racing,
  broadcasting contracts, 6.62, 6.76
  Federation Internationale de l'Automobile
    (FIA), 6.76
  Formula One Administration (FOA), 6.76
  personal injuries, 5.51, 5.60, 5.63
Motorola, Sportstrax, 6.5
Mountain guides, safety precautions, 5.47
Mundir, Haron bin, 4, 7.5
Murdoch, Rupert, 3.29, 7.102, 8.77
Music industry, restraint of trade, 4.78, 4.79

Nandrolone, 8.99
Naproxen, 7.24
National Greyhound Racing Club, 8.16
National Sports Law Institute, 1.1
National Wheelchair Basketball Association,
    7.29, 7.92
Nationality,
  3+2 rule, 4.56, 4.57
  competitions, 3.56, 3.57
  equivalent qualifications, 4.61–3
  free movement, compatibility, 4.57, 5.59
  league rules, 4.56–65
  national teams, 4.58, 4.59, 8.97
  restrictions, 4.55–71
  sporting interest only, 4.57, 4.59–60, 4.65
  work permits *see* Work permits

Natural justice,
  fairness *see* Fairness
  procedure *see under* Disciplinary procedures
Negligence,
  see also Torts
  care,
    differing standards, 5.40
    duty, 5.32–4, 5.36, 5.41, 5.42, 5.45
    reasonableness, 5.33, 5.35–7, 5.42–3, 5.46
    referees, 5.45
    standard, 5.32, 5.34, 5.40, 5.41, 5.42
  contact sports, 5.37, 5.38, 5.48, 5.49
  damages, 8.76
  defences,
    contributory negligence, 5.56
    volenti non fit injuria, 5.43, 5.57–63
  elements, 5.32
  heat of moment, 5.38
  injuries *see* Personal injuries
  intention, 5.31
  neighbour principle, 5.33, 5.46, 5.61
  participants,
    duty to eachother, 5.34–41
    duty to spectators, 5.42–4, 5.45
  professional, 8.76
  recklessness, 5.43, 5.44
  risk, 5.39, 5.59–63
  rules, action outside, 5.37, 5.38
  schools, 5.47–9
  water skiing, 5.35
Negotiation,
  contracts of employment, 2.27
  weaker parties, 4.79, 6.40
Neighbour principle, negligence, 5.33, 5.46,
    5.61
Netherlands, broadcasting contracts, 6.75
New Zealand,
  case law, 1.16
  judicial review, 8.21
  public law, 7.76
  Rugby Football Union Inc, 3.53
Newcastle United FC, 3.51, 8.38, 8.75
Newport FC, 3.54, 3.55, 8.49, 8.59, 8.75
Nike, sponsorship, 2.35
Nixon, Lynette, 3.58
NOCs *see under* Olympics
Northern Ireland Sports Forum, 8.123
Norway, European Economic Area (EEA),
    4.32, 4.64
Notts County FC, 8.85
Nuisance, enjoyment of land, 5.31, 5.64, 5.65
Nulla poena sine lege, 1.23, 7.40, 7.125

Occupiers liability,
  personal injuries, 5.50, 5.53, 5.62, 5.63
  volenti non fit injuria, 5.62, 5.63
Offences,
  see also Criminal law

intoxication, 5.24
public order, 5.23–9
Office of Fair Trading, BSkyB, 6.51
Olympics,
British Olympic Association, 8.123
broadcasting rights, 6.3, 6.19
Charter, jurisdiction, 1.10, 1.19, 1.27, 3.57,
    7.15, 8.91, 8.103, 8.105
Corinthian ideal, 5.8
cycling, team selection, 3.58–60
International Olympic Committee (IOC),
    consent, 7.15
    contracts, 2.31
    Medical Code, 8.93, 8.96, 8.106
    NOC decisions reviewed, 8.92
    Switzerland, 2.57
International Olympic Executive Board, 7.15
National Olympic Committees (NOCs),
    Cape Verde, 7.14
    contracts, 2.31
    dispute resolution, 8.92
    Europe, 5.18
    United States, 8.100
normative trends, 8.92
Omnia rite praesumuntur esse, 7.49
Onus of proof *see* Burden of proof
Organisers and promoters, liabilities, personal
    injuries, 5.50–5
Overseas Labour Service (OLS), 4.66, 4.68–71

Packer, Kerry, 3.51
Pacta sunt servanda, meaning, 1.21
Penalties *see* Sanctions
Personal injuries,
    see also Negligence
    contributory negligence, 5.56
    damages, 5.67–70
    liabilities,
        defences, 5.56–63
        employers, 5.71–5
        occupiers, 5.50, 5.53, 5.62, 5.63
        organisers and promoters, 5.50–5
        rules broken, 5.52
        vicarious, 5.72–5
    loss of chance, 5.68–70
    participants,
        coaching, 5.47, 5.49
        football, 5.36
        golf, 5.36, 5.39, 5.56
        ice hockey, 5.58
        water skiing, 5.35
    police, football, 5.53, 5.55
    practical issues, 5.71–80
    proof, 2.49
    psychiatric injuries, 5.54, 5.55
    spectators,
        contracts, 2.37
        golf, 5.31

horse shows, 5.42, 5.61
motor racing, 5.51, 5.60, 5.63
motorcycle scrambling, 5.44
risk, 5.51, 5.59, 5.61, 5.63
standard of care, 5.50
successful claims, 5.52, 5.53
volenti non fit injuria, 5.43, 5.57–63
Photographs, property rights, 6.6
Pittsburgh Athletic Co, 6.5
Play, rules *see* Regulation of play
Players' rights,
    discrimination *see* Discrimination
    employment, 4.1–99
    free movement *see* Free movement of
        workers
    player/club relationship, 4.5, 4.72–99
    registration, 4.7
    restraint of trade *see* Restraint of trade
    scope, 4.64
    spouses, 4.65
    transfer system *see* Transfer fees
Police,
    personal injuries, 5.53, 5.55
    regulation of play, 5.80
Portsmouth FC, 4.70
Professional Footballers Association (PFA), sex
    discrimination, 4.89
Proof,
    evidence *see under* Disciplinary procedures
    onus *see* Burden of proof
    standard *see* Standard of proof
Proportionality, sanctions, 1.23, 4.14, 4.25,
    7.17, 7.90
Propoxyphene metabolite, 7.31
Psychiatric injuries, 5.54, 5.55
Public law,
    Australia, 7.59
    bad faith, 7.57, 7.58
    damages, 7.56–8
    fairness, 7.76, 7.77
    human rights *see* Human rights
    judicial review *see* Judicial review
    legal disputes, 8.9–28
    misfeasance, 7.57, 7.58
    New Zealand, 7.76
    restraint of trade, 3.38, 3.42, 3.43, 4.54
    scope, 2.52–4
Public order, offences, 5.23–9
Puerto Rico, basketball, 3.56, 3.57

Qualifications,
    nationality, 4.61–3
    qualifying bodies, discrimination, 4.86, 4.87

Race discrimination, 4.81, 4.84
Raith Rovers FC, 5.80
Reading FC, 5.53
Recklessness, negligence, 5.43, 5.44

Referees,
  duty of care, 5.45
  judo, sex discrimination, 4.86, 4.94
  summary jurisdiction, 5.15–17, 7.117, 8.108
Registration, players' rights, 4.7
Regulation of play,
  common law, 5.6
  criminal law, 5.80
  discipline *see* Disciplinary procedures
  doping *see* Banned substances
  organisation and competition, 5.15–85
  police, 5.80
  prohibited sports, 5.12–14
  rules broken,
    see also Rules
    personal injuries, 5.52
  statute law, 5.18–29
  summary jurisdiction, 5.15–17, 7.117
Remedies,
  appeals *see* Appeals
  arbitration *see* Arbitration
  damages *see* Damages
  declaratory *see* Declaratory judgments
  disputes *see* Legal disputes
Representative proceedings,
  Jockey Club, 2.24
  unincorporated associations, 2.15, 2.16
Restraint of trade,
  see also Competition law
  banned substances, 3.45, 4.26, 7.12, 7.16,
    7.17
  bargaining position, 4.79
  boxing, 4.77–8, 8.36
  burden of proof, 3.41–4, 3.50
  competitions, 3.45–8
  contracts,
    duration, 4.76–8
    employment, 3.40, 3.51, 4.50, 4.73–9, 8.61
    severance, 3.48
    voidable terms, 3.37
  cricket, 3.51, 4.52, 4.73, 4.75
  damages, 8.75
  declaratory judgments, 3.49, 3.51–3, 4.74,
    8.36
  discrimination, 4.82
  evolution of doctrine, 3.38, 3.50
  examinations, golf, 3.46
  injunctions, 3.48, 3.49, 8.48
  music industry, 4.78, 4.79
  non-contractual cases, 3.50–3
  public law, 3.38, 3.42, 3.43, 4.54
  retention systems, 4.51
  rugby league, 4.53, 4.74, 8.36
  salient features, 3.39–48
  sanctions, 3.45, 7.96
  transfer fees, 4.9, 4.35, 4.49–54
Restrictive covenants, contracts of employ-
    ment, 8.60, 8.61

Revie, Don, 7.66
Reynolds, Harry "Butch", 8.99
Riley, Samantha, 7.31
Risk, spectators, 5.51, 5.59, 5.61, 5.63
Ronaldo, 4.38
Rugby league,
  broadcasting, 3.29
  competitions,
    Australia, 3.20, 3.21, 3.30. 3.31, 8.77
    participation rights, 3.29
  New South Wales Rugby League, 4.53, 4.74,
    8.36
  restraint of trade, 4.53, 4.74, 8.36
  Rugby Football League (RFL), 3.29
  sex discrimination, 4.90
Rugby union,
  disciplinary procedures, 7.60, 7.71, 7.113,
    8.46
  Five Nations Championship, 3.33, 3.36, 6.19
  France, 3.33
  International Rugby Football Board, 3.36
  New Zealand Rugby Football Union Inc,
    3.53
  Rugby Football Union (RFU), 3.33, 4.68,
    4.69, 4.90
  Welsh Rugby Union (WRU), 2.3, 3.47, 8.46,
    8.48, 8.52
  work permits, 4.68, 4.69
Rules,
  see also Regulation of play
  appeals, 7.21, 7.22, 7.99, 7.100, 8.2
  arbitration, 8.2, 8.63, 8.83
  broadcasting rights, 6.8
  CAS, ad hoc rules, 1.19
  common ownership, 3.34, 3.67, 3.68, 4.12
  competitions, 3.2–6
  disciplinary *see under* Disciplinary
    procedures
  doping *see* Banned substances
  ECJ interpretation *see under* European
    Court of Justice
  FINA *see* Federation Internationale de
    Natation Amateur
  interpretation, 2.38–43
  jurisdiction, 2.39, 7.10, 8.4, 8.93
  lack of clarity, 2.38
  legal disputes, outcome of game, 5.81–5
  legal rules, 1.2–3, 1.20
  play, 5.1–85
  purpose/effect, 4.10, 4.15, 4.59, 4.60
  purposive construction, 2.40
  sporting exception, 2.60, 3.68, 4.11–13, 4.16,
    4.57, 4.59–60, 4.65, 5.15
  UEFA *see* Union des Associations
    Europeennes de Football
  unincorporated associations, 2.12, 2.13,
    2.20
  United States, fairness, 3.16

Salbutamol, 7.28, 7.32, 7.120
Sanctions,
    automatic disqualification, 3.45, 7.96, 7.127
    contracts, 7.87, 7.89, 7.90
    Court of Arbitration in Sport (CAS), 7.92–5
    discretion, 7.89, 7.90
    excessive, 7.88
    exclusion, 3.9
    judicial decision making, 7.91
    jurisdiction, 7.87–96
    lex mitior, 7.95, 7.127
    nulla poena sine lege, 1.23, 7.40, 7.125
    points deduction, 7.89, 7.90, 8.59, 8.88
    proportionality, 1.23, 4.14, 4.25, 7.17, 7.90
    restraint of trade, 3.45, 7.96
    suspension, 7.54, 7.56, 7.127, 8.46
    unlawful, 7.9
    whole team penalised, 7.92
Schools,
    insurance, 5.49
    negligence, 5.47–9
    swimming, failure to advise, 5.47
Scottish Sports Association, 8.123
Secretary of State, listed events, 6.18, 6.19
Severance, restraint of trade, 3.48
Sex discrimination,
    see also Discrimination
    average woman test, 4.93–7
    football,
        coaching, 4.84
        girls, 4.95
        PFA dinner, 4.89
    golf, 4.83, 4.99
    horse trainers, licensing, 2.53, 3.15, 4.81,
        8.38
    judo, 4.86, 4.94
    MCC, 4.89
    rugby league, 4.90
    snooker, 4.94
Shankly, Bill, 1.4
Shooting, disciplinary procedures, 7.74
Singapore,
    case law, 1.16
    Singapore Amateur Athletic Association, 7.4
SK Slavia Prague, 3.34, 4.12
Smith, Michelle, 3.61
Snooker, sex discrimination, 4.94
South Africa,
    All Blacks tour, injunctions, 3.53
    case law, 1.16
    horse trainers, 7.67
    sporting links, 1.4
    Transavaal and Orange Free State
        Stipendiary Stirrups Board, 7.23
Southampton FC, 6.8
Southend United FC, 8.85
Spain,
    joint purchasing, 6.69

    transfer fees, 4.38
Specific performance, injunctions, 8.51, 8.61,
        8.62
Spectators,
    admission rights, 2.37
    contracts, 2.37
    football stadia *see under* Football
    injuries *see* Personal injuries
    participants, duty of care, 5.42–4, 5.45
    risk, 5.51, 5.59, 5.61, 5.63
    safety, sports grounds, 5.21, 5.22
Sponsorship,
    broadcasting contracts, 2.35
    income generation, 6.1
    public character of sport, 8.28
Sport,
    company law *see* Companies
    competition law *see* Competition law
    competitions *see* Competitions
    contract *see* Contracts
    corruption, 2.44, 2.46
    EC law *see* European law
    human rights *see* Human rights
    injuries *see* Personal injuries
    legalism, 1.14–16, 7.77
    non-competitive, 5.13
    offences *see* Criminal law
    profession, 4.82
    prohibited, 5.12–14
    public character, 8.28
    public law *see* Public law
    range of activities, 5.8, 5.9
    social significance, 1.4, 1.5
    South Africa, 1.4
    statute law, 1.9, 1.10, 2.55, 2.66
    torts *see* Torts
    unincorporated associations *see*
        Unincorporated associations
Sporting associations,
    see also Governing bodies
    companies, 2.3, 2.5, 2.6
    fairness, 3.10–23
    international *see* International sporting
        bodies
    legal nature, 2.2–17
    rules *see* Rules
Sports Dispute Resolution Panel (SDRP), 8.123
Sports grounds,
    access, broadcasting rights, 6.6, 6.7
    disasters, 5.20, 5.54, 5.55
    football stadia *see under* Football
    nuisance, 5.64–5
    public order offences, 5.23–9
    safety certificates, 5.21, 5.22
Sports law,
    case law, 1.16
    definition, 1.12
    development, 1.13–23

Sports law (*cont.*):
  framework, 2.2–63
  international character, 1.10, 1.27
  legal rules, 1.2–3, 1.20
  nature/scope, 1.1–32
  terminology, 1.1
  vertical law, 1.3, 1.6
Squash Rackets Association (SRA), 2.2, 2.3
Standard of proof,
  balance of probabilities, 7.45–8
  beyond reasonable doubt, 7.45, 7.46, 7.48
  comfortable satisfaction, 7.47
  disciplinary procedures, 7.45–8
  weight of evidence compared, 7.46
Statute law,
  broadcasting rights, 6.15–19
  discrimination, 4.80, 4.83
  regulation of play, 5.18–29
  scope, 1.9, 1.10, 2.55, 2.56
Stevenage Borough FC, 3.13, 3.55, 3.66, 6.35,
    8.24, 8.57, 8.58, 8.87
Strict liability, banned substances, 3.45, 7.26,
    7.29–32, 7.38–9, 7.49, 7.92, 7.125,
    8.96
Swimming,
  Amateur Swimming Association, 5.47
  banned substances, 7.28, 7.30, 7.31, 7.50,
    7.93, 7.94
  competitions, eligibility, 3.52, 3.61
  FINA *see* Federation Internationale de
    Natation Amateur
  US Swimming Federation, 3.61
Switzerland,
  associations, good faith, 3.35
  Court of Arbitration in Sport (CAS), 1.17,
    1.18, 1.20, 2.57, 2.58,
    7.116, 8.107
  FIFA, 2.6, 2.57
  international sporting bodies, 2.3, 2.6, 2.57

Taiwan, participation rights, 8.97
Tarasti, Lauri, 7.40
Television,
  contracts *see* Broadcasting contracts
  rights *see* Broadcasting rights
Tennis,
  banned substances, 4.13, 4.25
  broadcasting rights, 6.19
  International Tennis Federation (ITF), 4.13,
    4.25
  merchandising, 6.87
Test and County Cricket Board (TCCB), 3.51,
    4.52, 4.73
Testing procedures,
  banned substances, 7.19, 7.37, 7.54, 8.76
  damages, 8.76
Testosterone/epitestosterone ratio, 7.43, 7.54,
    8.95

Tickets,
  counterfeiting, 6.79
  sales, 6.79–84
  touting, 5.28, 6.79
Time, disciplinary procedures, 7.86
Time limits, legal disputes, 8.11
Torquay United FC, 8.58
Torts,
  assault, 5.31, 5.66, 5.72
  damages, 5.67–70, 8.72
  defamation, 2.51
  economic *see* Economic loss
  fouls, 5.36, 5.37
  international law, 8.120
  negative obligations, 2.48
  negligence *see* Negligence
  nuisance, 5.31, 5.64, 5.65
  personal injuries *see* Personal injuries
  sport, 2.48–51, 5.5, 5.30–75
  standard of behaviour, 5.31
Tottenham Hotspur FC, 2.4, 7.91, 8.59,
    8.88
Trade marks, merchandising, 6.85
Transavaal and Orange Free State Stipendiary
    Stirrups Board, 7.23
Transfer fees,
  competition,
    dominant position, 4.47
    EU law, 4.9, 4.41–8
    exemptions, 4.44
    inter-state trade, 4.48
    restricted/distorted, 4.43
  contracts,
    breach, 4.35
    disproportionate fees, 4.46
    expiry, 4.27–9, 4.34, 4.43, 4.44, 8.53
    indefinite, 4.34, 4.35
    long-term, 4.35
    penalty clauses, 4.36
  financial/competitive balance, 4.31
  free movement of workers, 4.9, 4.30
  injunctions, 8.54
  players' rights, 4.5–9, 4.27–54
  recruitment/training, 4.31
  restraint of trade, 4.9, 4.35, 4.49–54
  transfer,
    abroad, 4.37, 4.38, 8.117
    fixed periods, 4.39
    jurisdiction, 8.117–18
    outside EU, 4.32, 4.43
    within Member State, 4.45
    within UK, 8.117, 8.118
  undertakings,
    agreements, 4.41, 4.42
    associations, 4.41, 4.42
Triamterene, 7.50, 7.51
Trotting horses, Australia, 7.59, 7.76
Tyson, Mike, 3.27, 3.28, 5.79

UEFA *see* Union des Associations Europeennes de Football
Undertakings, competition *see under* Competition law
Unfair competition, broadcasting rights, 6.5, 6.6
Unfair prejudice petitions, companies, 8.79, 8.80
Unincorporated associations,
  see also Companies
  constitutions, 2.12
  contracts, 2.20, 2.21, 2.24
  disputes, 2.13, 2.14
  legal costs, 2.13
  legal disputes, 2.15, 2.16
  representative actions *see* Representative proceedings
  rules, 2.12, 2.13, 2.20
  sport, 2.10–16
Union Cycliste International, 4.23
Union des Associations Europeennes de Football (UEFA),
  3+2 rule, 4.56, 4.57
  CAS recognised, 8.93
  collective selling, 6.62
  common ownership rule, 3.34, 3.67, 3.68, 4.12
  contracts, 2.31
  free movement of workers, 4.23, 4.56
  jurisdiction rules, 8.93
  legal status, 2.3
  transfer fees, 4.29, 4.37, 4.38
  UEFA Cup, 3.34, 3.35, 3.67, 3.68
Union Internationale de Tir (UIT), 7.74
United States,
  Amateur Athletic Federation, 7.43
  broadcasting,
    contracts, 6.63
    rights, 6.5
  damages, 8.99
  legal disputes, 8.99–100
  rules, fairness, 3.16
  US Figure Skating Association (USFA), 8.100
  US Olympic Committee, 8.100

US Swimming Federation, 3.61
USA Track and Field, 8.95
US Dunkerque, 4.28

Vertical law, 1.3, 1.6
Vicarious liability,
  see also Liabilities
  discrimination, 4.85
  personal injuries, 5.72–5
Volenti non fit injuria,
  negligence, 5.43, 5.57–63
  occupiers liability, 5.62, 5.63

Waiver, appeals, 7.112
Warren, Frank, 8.62
Water polo, banned substances, 7.32, 7.120
Water skiing, negligence, 5.35
Watt, Kathryn, 3.59, 3.60
Welsh Football Association, 3.54, 3.55, 8.18, 8.48, 8.59, 8.75
Welsh Rugby Union (WRU), 2.3, 3.47, 8.46, 8.48, 8.52
Welsh Sports Association, 8.123
Widnes, 3.29
Wilson, Bob, 7.36
Women,
  average woman test, 4.93–7
  boxing, 4.94, 4.97
  discrimination *see* Sex discrimination
  testosterone/epitestosterone ratio, 7.43, 7.54, 8.95
Work permits,
  75 per cent test, 4.68–71
  criteria, 4.68
  guidance, 4.67
  Overseas Labour Service (OLS), 4.66, 4.68–71
  restrictions, 4.5, 4.66–71
World Boxing Council (WBC),
  legal disputes, 8.116
  legal status, 2.3
  participation, contracts, 3.27, 3.28
World Boxing Organisation, 8.64